P9-DDW-487 ~~wick~~

Arnulfo L. Oliveira Memorial Library

WITHDRAWN
UNIVERSITY LIBRARY
THE UNIVERSITY OF TEXAS RIO GRANDE VALLEY

LIBRARY
THE UNIVERSITY OF TEXAS
AT BROWNSVILLE
Brownsville, Tx 78520-499

Manitoba Studies in Native History

Manitoba Studies in Native History publishes new scholarly interpretations of the historical experience of Native peoples in the western interior of North America. The series is under the editorial direction of a board representative of the scholarly and Native communities in Manitoba.

Muskekowuck Athinuwick

Original People of the Great Swampy Land

Victor P. Lytwyn

UNIVERSITY OF MANITOBA PRESS

© Victor P. Lytwyn 2002

University of Manitoba Press
Winnipeg, Manitoba R3T 2N2
Canada
www.umanitoba.ca/uofmpress
Printed in Canada.

All rights reserved. No part of this publication may be reproduced or transmitted in any form or by any means, or stored in a database and retrieval system, without the prior written permission of the University of Manitoba Press, or, in the case of photocopying or other reprographic copying, a licence from CANCOPY (Canadian Copyright Licensing Agency), 6 Adelaide Street East, Suite 900, Toronto, Ontario M5C 1H6.

Cover Design: Kirk Warren
Text Design: Karen Armstrong and Sharon Caseburg
Maps: Weldon Hiebert
Cover photograph: *At York Factory,* c. 1880 (Provincial Archives of Manitoba, N227).

Canadian Cataloguing in Publication Data

Lytwyn, Victor P.

  Muskekowuck athinuwick

  Includes bibliographical references and index.

  ISBN 0-88755-651-5

  1. Cree Indians--Hudson Bay Region--History. 2. Cree Indians--Ontario, Northern--History. 3. Cree Indians--Manitoba, Northern--History. 4. Fur trade--Hudson Bay Region--History. 5. Fur trade--Ontario, Northern--History. 6. Fur trade--Manitoba, Northern--History. 7. Hudson's Bay Company--History. I. Title.

E99.C88L97 2002   971.3'1004973   C2001-911727-2

The University of Manitoba Press gratefully acknowledges the financial support for its publication program provided by the Government of Canada through the Book Publishing Industry Development Program (BPIDP); the Canada Council for the Arts; the Manitoba Arts Council; and the Manitoba Department of Culture, Heritage and Tourism.

The Manitoba Studies in Native History series is published with the financial support of the people of Manitoba, through the Department of Culture, Heritage and Tourism, the honourable Ron Lemieux, Minister.

Manitoba Studies in Native History Board of Directors: I. Bear, M. Bennett, J. Burelle, J. Fontaine, G. Friesen, E. LaRocque, P. Kulchyski, W. Moodie, A. Perry, D. Young.

Contents

Maps, Charts, and Illustrations

Acknowledgements

This study of the Lowland Cree was done in archives and libraries. Although I have briefly visited the region on several occasions, my work does not pretend to draw on personal experience with the Lowland Cree. My objective was to challenge many stereotypical views of the Lowland Cree in the previous literature, and to provide a more complete historical picture of their involvement in the fur trade. The setting for my work was Winnipeg, in the Hudson's Bay Company Archives and the University of Manitoba. I arrived in Winnipeg in the late summer of 1979, after completing my undergraduate work at the University of Toronto. I was drawn to Winnipeg by Dr. Wayne Moodie, who was a visiting professor in Toronto during my final year of study. The geography department at the University of Manitoba became the hub of my academic experience and Professor Moodie guided my research. I was fortunate to be able to take the final course on the history of the Hudson's Bay Company taught by the eminent scholar of the fur trade and western Canada, William L. Morton. My research skills were sharpened by work on the *Historical Atlas of Canada,* a project that included scholars from across Canada. The work on the atlas project at the University of Manitoba involved professors Moodie and Barry Kaye in geography, and Douglas Sprague in history. Together, we worked on a number of interesting and innovative maps depicting the history of the fur trade and Aboriginal people in the western interior of Canada. I was also fortunate to collaborate with Arthur (Skip) Ray from the University of British Columbia. His book on Indians in the fur trade of western Canada had been a catalyst for my interest in the Lowland Cree. My involvement grew from research assistant to contributor, and resulted in my authoring one full atlas plate and co-authoring a number of others. During the course of the atlas project, it was a great pleasure to meet and converse with R. Cole Harris, the charismatic and intellectual editor of volume one, while he was in Winnipeg on his tours of the various universities across Canada involved in the atlas project.

The atlas project and university course work directed me into the Hudson's Bay Company Archives, a massive collection of historical documents chronicling the growth of the company since its inception in 1670. Housed in the Provincial Archives building across from the parking lot of the flagship Bay store in Winnipeg, the company records had recently arrived from its London headquarters. Shirlee Smith, Keeper of the archives, encouraged and guided my use of the company's documents. Staff archivists were very helpful in assisting my research, especially Mark Walsh and Maureen Dolyniuk. Jennifer Brown, a recent arrival in the history department at the University of Winnipeg, taught a course at the archives, focussing on the use of the company's documents. That course, as well as Jennifer's continuing interest in my research, helped to shape the methodological aspects of my writing. Professor William Norton's course on historical geography provided some of the philosophical underpinnings for my analyses of historical and geographical data.

One of the first challenges in the *Historical Atlas of Canada* project was the identification and location of hundreds of trading posts that spread inland from Hudson Bay and westward from Lake Superior. A detailed investigation of the company archives and other fur-trade material located dozens of trading posts never before mapped in the available literature. Many of the previously unknown trading posts were within an area east of Lake Winnipeg. That discovery led to the development of my Master's thesis that traced the expansion of fur traders into the region known as the East Winnipeg Country.

The East Winnipeg study kindled my interest in learning more about the Aboriginal people who participated in the fur trade in a region that had been the focus of aggressive competition until the merger of the

Hudson's Bay Company and the Montreal-based North West Company in 1821. I decided to begin my exploration along the western coast of Hudson Bay where the Hudson's Bay Company traders had begun their expansion inland. While engaged in the atlas project, I had been struck with the rich documentary materials that emanated from the bay-side posts and detailed the hinterland trade with the Aboriginal people who lived within the Hudson Bay lowlands. This storehouse of information became the main source for my research concerning the Lowland Cree in the fur-trade period.

This book would not have been possible without the help and encouragement of the people already noted. Many others have assisted, including Jean Friesen, who was a member of the PhD review committee. Gerry Friesen, head of the Manitoba Studies in Native History Board of Directors, was persistent in encouraging the submission of a manuscript. He also provided insightful editorial comments that have helped to transform the academic dissertation into a book. Patricia Sanders and David Carr with the University of Manitoba Press have also helped in the transition from manuscript to book. Professor Weldon Hiebert at the University of Winnipeg prepared the maps for the book.

I would like to thank my wife, Joanne, for her support and patience. Finally, I would like to dedicate this book to Wayne Moodie, advisor, colleague, and friend.

Introduction

Muskekowuck Athinuwick, the original people of the Hudson Bay lowlands, are known by a number of different names, including Swampy Cree,
Homeguard Cree, and Lowland Cree. They were among the first of the
Aboriginal peoples in the northwestern interior of North America to come
into contact with European explorers, missionaries, and fur traders. Their
geographic homeland placed them in a strategic position to become suppliers of furs, food, and other support to the newcomers, and to act as
intermediaries with other Aboriginal people in the interior interested in
the European fur trade. They also acted as buffers against the hostile inten-
tions of other First Nations eager to disrupt or destroy the fur trade in the
Hudson Bay region. The founding of the Hudson's Bay Company in 1670,
and the subsequent building of trading posts at major river-mouth locations in the Hudson Bay lowlands, placed a business enterprise with me-
ticulous, written record-keeping in the midst of Lowland Cree territory.
Daily journals, annual reports, correspondence, and account books were
kept as a storehouse of written information on the history of the Lowland
Cree.

Despite their important position in the fur trade and the availability of the detailed and voluminous records of the Hudson's Bay Company, the Lowland Cree have been shadowy characters in the literature. In fact, until recently, many scholars portrayed the Lowland Cree as relatively new arrivals to the region. The Lowland Cree were depicted as a wretched group of people living in the shadow of the fur-trade establishments, and quickly dependent upon superior Eruopean-manufactured goods.

In 1979, I began a systematic study of the records of the Hudson's Bay Company in Winnipeg, in particular those pertaining to the western coast of Hudson Bay where the company had begun expansion inland. I was surprised to learn that very little had been written specifically about the Hudson Bay Lowland Cree. Part of the explanation was that few scholars had access to the Hudson's Bay Company archives until the 1970s, when the company loosened restrictions on the use of its historical materials. Another reason was the general portrayal of the Lowland Cree as people who became dependant on European trade goods and who loitered around the company's bay-side factories, seeking hand-outs. The term "homeguard" came to symbolize a people quickly dependent on and demoralized by their relationship with the fur traders.

Anthropologists who visited the Lowland Cree in the first half of the twentieth century postulated that the fur trade had rapidly transformed their way of life. Alanson Skinner was the first to conduct ethnological fieldwork among the Lowland Cree, and his 1911 study concluded that they could not have survived in the region without European supplies. Diamond Jenness included a brief description of the Lowland Cree in his 1932 book on the *Indians of Canada*. He believed that the superiority of European goods made them abandon traditional items. Leonard Mason, who worked among the Lowland Cree at Oxford House in 1938 and 1940, agreed with Jenness and he concluded that traditional Cree culture had vanished soon after the arrival of the fur traders. John Honigmann, who conducted fieldwork at Attawapiskat in 1948 and 1949, also noted that culture change had taken place rapidly after the arrival of Europeans.

Historians followed the anthropologists in describing a rapid transformation of Lowland Cree culture based on their dependence on European trade goods. This view was advanced by Harold Innis in his 1930 landmark study of the Canadian fur trade. It was further elaborated upon by A.S. Morton, who wrote in 1939 about the superiority of European fur traders over the Lowland Cree, and "the sway they gained over a fretful race."[1] Edwin E. Rich, historian of the Hudson's Bay Company, penned some of the most enduring images of the Lowland Cree. He wrote that they became dependent upon European goods quickly, and faced starvation if the annual supply ships failed to arrive in Hudson Bay. Rich acknowledged that the Hudson's Bay Company traders also became dependent on the seasonal supply of geese and ptarmigan brought in by Lowland Cree hunters, but explained that this "entailed the obligation to feed them through the winter and keep them both loyal and fit for hunting."[2]

Arthur J. Ray's 1974 book on Indians in the fur trade provided new insights into the relationships between Aboriginal people and Euro-Canadian fur traders. Ray was the first scholar to make extensive use of the Hudson's Bay Company account books, and his work reflected a careful analysis of the quantitative as well as qualitative information produced by the fur traders. He argued that, prior to European contact, Aboriginal people were engaged in sustainable resource-harvesting activities. They were also involved in complex trade and redistribution networks with neighbouring groups, and these factors minimized the risk of severe privation during periodic shortages of subsistence resources. The establishment of Euro-Canadian fur-trade posts changed these traditional patterns so that more time and effort were spent on hunting and trapping small fur-bearing animals or hunting geese and other game for the sustenance of the traders. Ray also explained that the new focus on commercial trade eroded traditional practices of communal resource sharing, thereby further restricting the ability of Aboriginal people to cope with periodic conditions of food scarcity. The impact of this new order was felt most acutely among the Lowland Cree who were located close to the large bay-side trading posts. However, Ray pointed out that the Lowland Cree became more dependent on the Hudson's Bay Company for material goods after the collapse of caribou and beaver populations in the region during the early nineteenth century.

Charles Bishop was the first to engage in a specific study of the Lowland Cree. His first article in 1972 examined the differences between the Lowland Cree and the Northern Ojibway in the early fur-trade period. Bishop concluded that among the Lowland Cree, the impact of European trade goods, especially hunting equipment, was "early and intense." He argued that by the late seventeenth century, the Lowland Cree had come to depend for their survival on the annual supply ships from Europe. In his later work, Bishop built on these arguments and described a radical transformation in the way of life of the Lowland Cree as a result of the fur trade. In particular, he wrote that the coastal trading posts drew the Lowland Cree to live year-round in close proximity. This was a departure from traditional patterns of territorial movement to the coast in spring and summer, and into the upland interior in fall and winter. This change led to over-hunting of animals near the coastal trading posts, and this in turn brought the Cree into a relationship of dependency on the traders who were able to provide year-round supplies of food.

John Foster's 1977 study of the Lowland Cree softened the dependency argument to a degree by depicting the trading posts as safe havens that enabled the Cree to live more comfortably but did not radically transform their culture. He used the term "economic interdependence" to describe the relationship between the Lowland Cree and Hudson's Bay Company traders. He also noted that unions between European men and Cree women added a layer of complexity that also resulted in reciprocal social and cultural adjustments. Toby Morantz's thorough study of the neighbouring Eastern James Bay Cree concluded that they successfully adapted to changes brought on by the Euro-Canadian fur trade. She observed that the Cree of eastern James Bay expanded their range of subsistence and commercial activities during the fur-trade period, and this led to changes in their social organization. However, these changes built upon rather than debilitated traditional culture and Morantz concluded that the fur trade tended to strengthen traditional patterns of social organization.

My study of the Lowland Cree delved into every corner of the Hudson's Bay Company archives, from account books to miscellaneous files. I kept a long scroll of paper recording the names of people, groups, and places from the beginning of record-keeping in the late seventeenth century to the mid-nineteenth century. The "sacred scroll," as I affectionately called it, was often rolled out as a visual reminder of the order of things. Although sophisticated computer database programmes are now used to store the same kind of information, I still prefer rolling out the yellowing scroll to pore over names and dates and make connections that would be impossible to make on a computer screen.

In 1991, I completed my study of the Lowland Cree and this book is a revised edition of that work. I regret that my study at that time did not include an oral history component. My recommendation to engage in an oral history programme for the York Factory area was accepted by Parks Canada and resulted in the publication of oral history narratives in 1996.[3] The relevant oral histories from that book have been incorporated into this book. In addition, I have added oral histories from other recent publications from the western James Bay region.

Muskekowuck Athinuwick

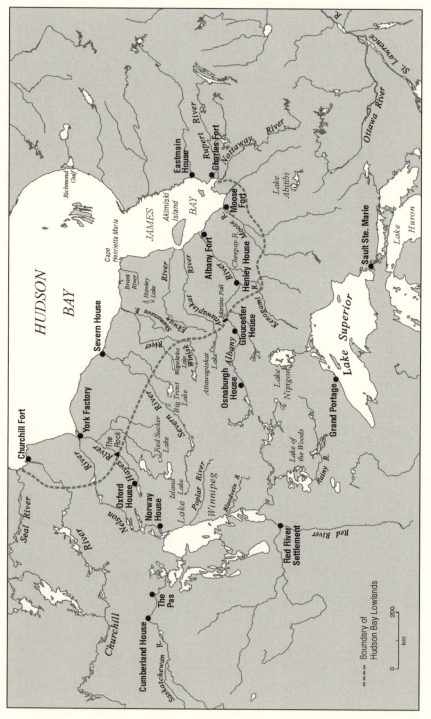

The Hudson Bay Lowlands and Surrounding Area

1.
Who Are the Lowland Cree?

The Homeland of the Lowland Cree

The Hudson Bay lowlands comprise a vast region of predominantly gently sloping, swampy land. The lowlands are underlain by bedrock dating from the Palaeozoic era, about 225 to 570 million years ago; the bedrock of the adjacent uplands is from the older Precambrian era, originating more than 570 million years ago. This geological boundary occurs almost uniformly at about 170 metres above sea level. The lowlands extend inland in a crescent-like shape, reaching a maximum inland extension of about 400 kilometres along the Albany River. The northern boundary of the region tapers toward the Hudson Bay coast north of the Churchill River, and the southern limit of the lowlands reaches the James Bay coast near the Nottaway River.

The line of contact between the lowlands and uplands is most visible across the beds of rivers where waterfalls or rapids emphasize the difference between the harder bedrock of the uplands and the softer sedimentary rock of the lowlands.[1] Along the Hayes River the boundary is crossed at a place called "The Rock." Robert Bell, a nineteenth-century geologist, reported that "the character of the river changes at The Rock; and from that point downward no more rapids occur all the way down to the sea."[2] Along the Albany River the line of contact occurs at Martins Fall, below which "the river changes its character entirely," becoming broader and slower until it discharges into James Bay.[3] Other physical features unique to the lowlands region generally follow and are influenced by this geological boundary line. For example, the general vegetation pattern in the lowlands has been called a "bogs–organic terrain," and the extent of this vegetation regime is roughly coterminus with the geological boundary.

The Hudson Bay lowlands are gradually rising after being submerged by the massive weight of the last great ice sheets about 9000 years ago. In a process called "isostatic rebound," the lowlands are rising at a rate of about 0.7 metres every century.[4] Although barely perceptible, this gradual uplift adds about one to two kilometres of land to the coastline every century. The beach, or strand line, that existed at the time of initial European contact, about 380 years ago, is approximately six kilometres inland today. The Lowland Cree who lived near the coast were well aware of the gradual uplift of the land. In 1878, Robert Bell reported that "the Indians say their old goose hunting grounds along the coast to the northward of the mouth of the Nelson are now deserted by the geese, the water having 'dried up.'"[5]

At first glance, the Hudson Bay lowlands appear as a monotonous, level expanse of muskeg and bog, and over 90 percent of the area is classified as wetland. The dominating feature of the landscape is the flat, swampy terrain. Robert Bell, who surveyed the lower Albany River and surrounding lowlands, reported that "the river is so straight that, sitting in a canoe and looking from one end of them, the sky and water appear to meet on the horizon."[6] W.J. Wilson, another geologist, wrote in 1903 that "the most remarkable feature of the west coast of James bay is its extreme flatness. Looked at from a distance there is no distinct shore line, but the water and land seem to merge into each other."[7]

Although much of the lowlands is characterized as swamp or muskeg, a closer examination reveals subtle yet significant differences in the vegetation. Of special significance is the coastal strip of tundra vegetation that is favoured habitat for caribou and other lowland animals. River valleys and other areas within the lowlands abounded with a rich and diverse ecology, prompting some observers to describe these places as oases within the swampy lowlands. John Pollock and William Noble, who conducted archaeological investigations in the Hudson Bay lowlands, said "the Hawley Lake area stands out as a fertile pocket within an otherwise dismal topography of muskeg bog so typical of the Lowlands. It might even be termed a 'northern oasis.'"[8]

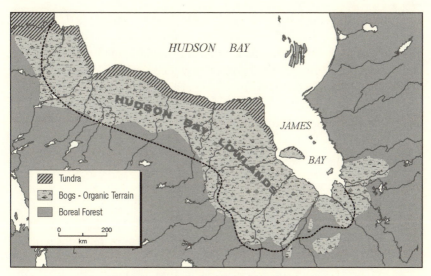

Vegetation Areas in the Hudson Bay Lowlands

Along the coast, marshes provided seasonal habitat and were staging grounds for large numbers of migratory waterfowl. The coastal tundra from north of the Churchill River to Akimiski Island provided favourable habitat for massive herds of caribou that migrated each summer to feed and calve on these grounds. Edible plants, including a variety of berries, were abundant during the brief summer period. Many of the rivers and larger lakes within the lowlands contained numerous fish species such as whitefish, pike, sturgeon, and sucker. In short, the lowlands were not as desolate as some first impressions indicated. According to Jean-Luc Pilon, who conducted archaeological investigations along the lower Severn River in the 1980s, "complexity, diversity and dynamics summarize the environment of the Hudson Bay Lowlands."[9]

When European fur traders settled along the coast of the Hudson Bay lowlands, the Lowland Cree occupied much of the vast lowland tract. Only small portions of the northern and southern extremities of the region appear to have been avoided by the Lowland Cree because of conflicts with enemy groups. The small, northern lobe between the Nelson and Churchill rivers was an uninhabited buffer zone between the Lowland Cree and the Western Hudson Bay Inuit.[10] Because of earlier conflicts with long-distance Iroquois raiding parties, the Lowland Cree also avoided the southern tip of the lowlands near the Nottaway River.[11]

The inland extent of Lowland Cree territory is more difficult to ascertain from the early historical records. Few Europeans ventured inland until long after trading posts had been settled, and details about the geography of the upland territory remained unknown to European fur traders until the late eighteenth century. However, remarks made by some Europeans who interviewed Indian informants point to a wider territorial distribution of the Lowland Cree in the early fur-trade period. The observations of Hudson's Bay Company (HBC) trader Andrew Graham in particular are revealing about the earlier geographic range of the Lowland Cree. In 1775, he reported that the Lowland Cree had been gradually pushed to the north by groups of Northern Ojibway.[12]

A Confusion of Names

The names "Lowland Indians" and "Low Country Natives," used commonly by European fur traders to describe the Lowland Cree, reflected the low-lying nature of the territory they inhabited. These names also distinguished the Lowland Cree from the so-called "Upland Indians" who occupied the upland Shield region. The flatness of the lowlands was reflected in the name "Plains Indian," also commonly used by the European fur traders. Andrew Graham observed in 1762 that "Severn River is situated in the very heart of your Honours Settlements, and am certain in the very middle of the plain, or Misckick Indians."[13] James Isham, who was in charge of the HBC's York Factory in 1757, explained that the name Plains Indian was used to describe the Indian people who lived in the flat land around the factory.[14]

The indigenous people of the Hudson Bay lowlands identified themselves as *A'thin new* or *Athinuwick,* meaning "person" or "people," respectively, in their own language.[15] Names that connoted other identities were conceived of and applied by outsiders. The term "Indian" was a European invention, and misnomer, that was used to describe indigenous peoples throughout North America. The name "Cree" was derived from the French word *Kiristinon*, originally used in the seventeenth century to describe several groups of Aboriginal people who lived in the southern James Bay area. Algonquian linguist David Pentland suggested the French term may have been derived from an Ojibway word.[16] As French fur traders and missionaries moved into the upper country beyond Lake Superior, the term was applied to a widespread nation of Aboriginal people who spoke a similar language.[17] English-speaking observers later shortened the name to "Cree," and it became widely used in the literature to describe Cree speakers who lived throughout much of the subarctic and prairie regions of northern North America.

The Hudson Bay Lowland Cree population was spread over a vast territory, but their group identity was maintained through marriage connections and other social relationships such as feasts, spiritual gatherings, ceremonies, warfare, and trade. The network of social linkages among the Lowland Cree was widespread. Links through marriages were especially important. In 1716, Thomas Macklish, who was in charge of Albany Fort, noted that the "northern Indians," or the Lowland Cree who lived about the lower Severn River, were linked by marriages with the Albany River Lowland Cree, and that "most of their wives is this country Indians."[18] In 1769, Andrew Graham, who was in charge of Severn House, noted the arrival of a family of Lowland Cree from York Factory who were "on a visit to his Relations who are Home Indians here."[19] In 1796, John Ballenden, who was then in charge of Severn House, observed that a Lowland Cree man had died, and his wife and children intended to go to Albany Fort "where she belongs and her friends reside."[20]

Coasters and Inlanders

Within the lowlands are two major physiographical subdivisions: the coastal tundra zone and the interior muskeg zone. These broad sub-regions gave rise to two group identities within the Lowland Cree population: Coasters and Inlanders. Anthropologist Toby Morantz has noted a similar distinction among the people who lived on the east coast of James Bay: "The European fur traders throughout the records of both centuries [eighteenth and nineteenth] always distinguish between coasters and inlanders, a distinction it seems the local people might have made themselves as they do now."[21] However, among the Hudson Bay Lowland Cree, the distinction between Coasters and Inlanders was not as sharp. A major difference between the western and eastern coasts of James Bay is the inland extent of the lowlands region. On the west coast, the lowlands extend inland for more than 400 kilometres. On the east coast, the lowlands are confined to a narrow coastal belt. However, the Coaster/Inlander dichotomy within the Lowland Cree population was a basic subdivision recognized by the European fur traders.

The unique features of the coastal region, such as tundra vegetation, tidal flats, and beach ridges, provided the physiographical basis for the distinct identity of the Indians who lived within this area.[22] The coastal Lowland Cree appear to have made less use of canoes than did the people who lived inland. Since their coastal adaptation was focussed on lateral movement across the coastal plains, pedestrian and dog-assisted transport were more important than riverine transport. They also had less access to canoe-building material. In 1778, Humphrey Marten, who was in charge of York Factory, noted that more than fifty Lowland Cree remained near the factory because they had no canoes.[23] Many other HBC traders noted that the Coasters lacked canoes, and HBC boats were often used to ferry them across rivers. In 1801, John Ballenden, who was in charge of York Factory, gave a small boat to a group of Coasters to enable them to cross the river, because "they have no canoes."[24] The York Factory traders purchased canoes from upland Indians expressly for supplying them to the Homeguard Cree. In 1728, the York Factory accountant noted the purchase of "7 canoes for our home Indians that Hunts Spring and Fall for the Factory."[25]

The Inlanders lived in the low-lying, swampy ground that characterizes much of the lowlands inland from the coast. Bacqueville de la Potherie identified the Inlanders as a group, or "tribe,"[26] called the *Monsaunis* or "people of the marsh." According to La Potherie, the Monsaunis "live in a country which is full of marshes and which is higher than the country of the Ouenebigonhelinis."[27] Graham also used the term *Muchiskewuck Athinuwick,* meaning "people of the swampy ground," to describe the Indians who occupied the interior region of the lowlands.[28] Thus, two regional group identities were recognized within the Lowland Cree population. The Coasters, or Winnepeg Athinuwick, occupied the coastal zone. The Inlanders, or Muchiskewuck Athinuwick, lived in the interior, swampy ground of the lowlands.

River-Basin Groups

Within the Coaster and Inlander populations of the Lowland Cree, specific groups of people were usually named after prominent physiographical features in their home territories.

Andrew Graham noted that "they take their names from the lakes, rivers, or whatever kind of country they inhabit."[29] Group identities were especially associated with river basins. For example, the Lowland Cree who occupied the area within the Albany River basin were known as Albany River Indians, or *Kastechewan* Indians, after the Cree word for the Albany River, meaning "swift current."[30] The Lowland Cree who occupied the Severn River basin were called *Washeo Sepee* Indians, after the Cree word for the Severn River. Rivers cut through inland and coastal zones, and thus river-basin group identities encompassed both Coasters and Inlanders.

Group names also reflected subdivisions of people within larger river-basin groups. According to Andrew Graham's list of Lowland Cree groups, or tribes, who lived in the hinterland of York Factory, the people who lived along the Hayes River valley nearest to the Factory were called *Penesewichewan,* or *Penesewichewan Sepee* Indians, after the name of the lower section of the Hayes River.[31] Upriver from the confluence with the Shamattawa River, the river was known as Steel River, and the people who lived along this section were known as *Apet Sepee,* or Steel River Indians.[32] Farther upriver, the river was known as the Hill River, above the confluence with the Fox River, and the people were called *Chucketenaw Sepee,* or Hill River Indians.[33] The importance of river basins in defining Aboriginal group identities was noted by a number of Europeans involved in the fur trade. An early account written by Thomas Gorst, who was stationed at Charles Fort (at the mouth of the Rupert River) in 1674, outlined the significance of river basins in the political organization of the local people. John Oldmixon, who recorded the Gorst account some forty years later, observed that "the Indians of certain Districhs, which are bounded by such and such Rivers, have each an Okimah, as they call him, or Captain over them, who is an Old Man, consider'd only for his Prudence and Experience."[34]

Other early fur-trade documents confirm that river basins provided significant territorial boundaries for groups of Lowland Cree. For example, early fur traders at York Factory reported that the leader of the Lowland Cree was a man called the "Captain of the [Hayes] River."[35] Another Lowland Cree leader, called the "Captain of Severn River," was also identified in the early York Factory and Albany Fort records. In 1692, the HBC traders at Albany Fort noted that a man named Tickatuckoy was recognized as the "great Leading Indian of this River."[36] He may have been the same man referred to as "the King" by the HBC's Governor Bailey, who met with a group of Indians at the mouth of the Albany River in 1674.[37] By 1695, Tickatuckoy was called "ye old Captain of this River," another indication that he may have been "the King" who, along with one of his sons, met with Bailey twenty-one years earlier.[38] Tickatuckoy had a number of sons who took over the position of captain of Albany River following their father's death.

The significance of river basins in the territorial organization of Lowland Cree was reported by George Sutherland during a trip north of Albany Fort in 1777. He explored the coastal region as far north as the Ekwan River, and noted the location of the hunting grounds of several Lowland Cree leaders who traded at Albany Fort. On March 30, 1777, Sutherland arrived at Thawashe River (Lawash Channel), which was described as "Saquot's river." Farther north, at the Attawapiskat River, he reported that "this is Captain Assup's ground likewise Archekishick." Sutherland also noted that a man named Questach "has a branch in this river [Attawapiskat] that runs to the NW." At the Ekwan River, Sutherland commented that "Pusquothecot is the man that frequents this river."[39] The five men noted in Sutherland's journal—Saquot, Assup, Archekishick, Questach, and Pusquothecot—were prominent leaders of groups of Lowland Cree.

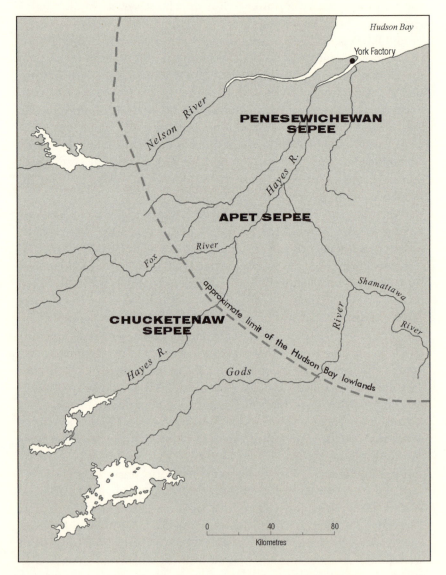

Location of Lowland Cree Groups in the Hayes River Basin

Denominated "captains" by the HBC, they were probably equivalent to the Okimahs described by Gorst.

The river-basin territories were occupied by winter-hunting groups of several related families, led by a respected hunter or elder. While river basins provided natural regions for the traditional territorial ranges of Lowland Cree hunting groups, there was considerable movement of individuals and families throughout the lowlands. HBC traders reported many examples of people moving back and forth between river basins. For example, in 1788, a man named Messescape, who was a brother of a leading Albany River Lowland Cree named Tabethimo, returned to the Albany River area after spending several years in the Moose River basin.[40] In 1787, three Lowland Cree from the Severn River area arrived at York Factory, and HBC trader Joseph Colen noted that "York Factory is their place of birth."[41] Seeseekis, a Lowland Cree man who was usually associated with Albany Fort, was "noted for never staying two years at one place."[42] In 1788, John Ballenden, who was then in charge of Severn House, commented that "many of my Indians is not to be depended on (notwithstanding their many promises) continually running from place to place."[43] In 1790, Ballenden again remarked, "The Chief part of my Homeguards are quite averse to hunting either spring or fall, taking delight in nothing but visiting from place to place."[44]

Many HBC traders commented on the freedom of Lowland Cree people to hunt and travel without restriction. In his report on the York Factory district in 1815, Chief Factor William Hemmings Cook wrote, "There are no Chiefs or men of consequence among them, they assert no claim or prescriptive right to the country they inhabit. The best Hunter is the most independent and respectable man. He is looked up to as the father of the family, is permitted to regulate domestic concerns and determine the route they must take in their Hunting Excursions."[45] In the 1815 Severn House District Report, James Swain made similar observations about the lack of exclusive hunting territories among the Lowland Cree. "The Indians of this Country have not the smallest idea of exclusive right to any particular hunting Grounds," he noted, "but Travel about in these parts where there is the greatest probability of success."[46] In 1814, John Mannall, who was in charge of Moose Factory, noted, "They have a kind of Custom of reckoning their own Ground but as to the propriety or exclusive right I think would not be contended for."[47] This pattern was also observed inland among the Upland Cree and Northern Ojibway. For example, HBC trader George Holdsworth, writing in 1815 about the Berens River district east of Lake Winnipeg, remarked that "the tribes generally live in peace and friendship with each other; and altho the necessity of migration has caused them to encroach on each others territories the circumstances does not appear to have given rise to any jealousies, and several tribes may be seen occupying the same tract of country in the utmost peace and harmony."[48] According to Holdsworth, "As the Indians have little idea of exclusive right to any part of the district, their hunting grounds cannot be defined with exactness."[49] James Sutherland, who was in charge of the Jack River (later named Norway House) district in 1815, wrote, "The Indians roam all over the district in small parties of a family or two. The hunting ground is common to the whole, and any stranger may come and enjoy the same privilege without molestation."[50]

People of the Cree Nation

According to Andrew Graham, the Lowland Cree were members of a larger linguistic family known as the Keishkatchewan Nation.[51] The Keishkatchewan, or Cree Nation, included many groups, or tribes, who lived in a large geographic territory including the lowlands and extending westward into the prairie region. The common factor linking these groups was language.[52] Graham observed that the language spoken by the various tribes of the Cree Nation was "only differing in a few words, and pronounciation."[53] In 1831, when trader John McLean visited York Factory, he remarked, "The Indians of this quarter are denominated Swampies, a tribe of the Cree nation, whose language they speak with but little variation, and in their manners and customs there is a great similarity."[54] Europeans who were familiar with the Lowland Cree were surprised to find that other people who lived as far away as the prairie region spoke the same language. For example, when HBC trader William Falconer met a group of Plains Cree who came to Severn House in the summer of 1769, he observed "some of whom comes six and seven hundred miles from the SW where they chiefly feed on buffalo's flesh, and most of them are cloathed in their skins.... They are robust looking people and talks the same language as our Home-guard Natives."[55] Graham's list of the tribes belonging to the Cree Nation included broad regional group identities such as the *Winnepeg* people who occupied the Hudson Bay coast. The list also included river-basin groups such as the *Washeo-Sepee* people, who occupied the Severn River basin, and subdivisions of groups within the Hayes River basin, such as the *Penesewichewan* people who lived along the lower Hayes River. The distinctiveness of the Lowland Cree in relation to other Upland Cree groups was noted by Europeans such as John West, an Anglican missionary who

Name of Tribe*	Territory**	Trading Location***
Andrew Graham's List of the Keishkatchewan (Cree) Nation		
Winnepeg	Hudson Bay coast	YF, SH, & AF
Muskekowuck	Swampy ground near Hudson Bay	YF, CF, & SH
Washeo-Sepee	Severn River	SH
Kastechewan	Albany River	AF
Moosu-Sepee	Moose River	MF
Penesewichewan	Hayes River (lower Hayes R.)	YF
Apet-Sepee	Steel River (middle Hayes R.)	YF
Chucketenaw	Hill River (upper Hayes R.)	YF
Poethinecaw	Nelson River	YF & CF
Mantua-Sepee	Lower Churchill River	CF
Missinepee	Upper Churchill River	YF & CF
Pimmechikemow	Cross Lake	YF & CF
Pegogamow	Saskatchewan Forks	YF
Muscasicow	Saskatchewan prairies	YF & CF
Amiska-Sepee	Beaver River	YF & CF
Athupescow	Athabasca Lake	YF & CF
Wuskesew-Sepee	Red Deer River	YF & CF
Nemow	Sturgeon River	YF
Ooho-Sepee	Owl River	CF
Wenunnetowuck	not given	YF & CF

Sources: *Graham,1969: 206; **Richardson, 1969, vol.2: 37, ***Graham, 1969: 206, and HBCA, E.2/9, fo. 84. YF= York Factory, AF= Albany Fort, SH= Severn House, CF= Churchill Fort, MF= Moose Fort

visited the York Factory area in 1820. He remarked that "these [Lowland Cree near York Factory] are called Muskeggouck, or Swamp Indians, and are considered a distinct tribe between the Nahathaway or Cree [Upland Cree] and Saulteaux [Northern Ojibway]."[56]

While Graham had extensive, first-hand knowledge about the Aboriginal people who visited Churchill Fort, York Factory, and Severn House, his information about the people who visited Albany Fort, Moose Fort, and Eastmain House came from second-hand sources, and is generally less reliable. A significant omission in his list of tribes belonging to the Cree Nation was the *Moosu-Sepee*, or Moose River Cree. Graham included the Moose River Cree with the *Oupeshepou* who lived on the eastern side of James Bay. However, other HBC records clearly indicated that the Moose River Cree were closely related to the Albany River Lowland Cree, and, therefore, should have been included in Graham's list of the Cree Nation.[57] For example, one of the earliest leaders of the Albany River Lowland Cree, a man named Miskemote, was originally from the Moose River area. Miskemote was regarded as the "Captain" of the Lowland Cree who lived near Albany Fort, but he was also the son of a man named Noah, who was a prominent leader of the Moose River Cree.[58] In 1740, Joseph Isbister, who was in charge of Albany Fort, reported the arrival of three Moose River Cree and commented, "These Indians oregenally were albany Indians."[59]

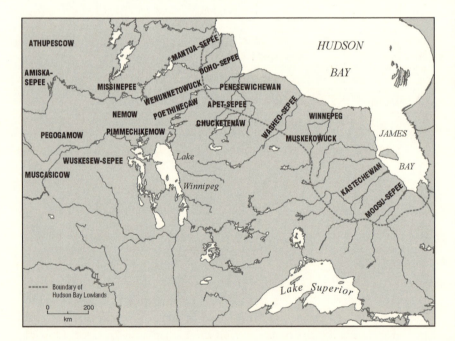

Tribes of the Cree Nation

Homeguard Cree

In the fur-trade records, groups of Lowland Cree came to be identified with the trading post where they regularly conducted their business. Thus, the terms "York," "Churchill," "Severn," "Albany," and "Moose" Indians were usually substituted for traditional names. The fur traders also identified groups among the Lowland Cree according to their type of relationship with the trading post. Those who lived close to the post, and who provided food and other country produce to sustain the European fur traders, were called the Homeguard. That name was first recorded by Andrew Graham: "At the Forts there are Natives which we style home-guards or home-Indians … who are employed as hunters to supply the Forts with provisions."[60] Earlier writers, such as Henry Kelsey in 1690 and Anthony Beale in 1706, used the term "Home Indians."[61]

Historian Arthur S. Morton described three groups of people who were involved in the trade with the HBC coastal factories. These were the Home Indians, Half-Home Indians, and the Uplanders or trading Indians. Morton used a time-distance function to identify the people who belonged to each group. That is, the Home Indians arrived at the post first because of their close proximity to the post, the Half-Home Indians were next, and the Uplanders who lived farthest away were the last to reach the post.[62] Historian John Foster remarked that the Homeguard Cree comprised "small bands of coastal Cree who specialized in supplying the trading posts with goods and services derived from the new world environment."[63]

The Homeguard people were primarily coastal Cree. Inlanders usually spent too much time away from the coastal area to be considered Homeguard. Andrew Graham observed that the name "home-guard Indians" was synonymous with the "sea shore Indians," or coastal Cree.[64] The Homeguard Cree remained near the coast for most of the year except winter, when "they go a little distance inland and traps martins etc."[65] Henry Ellis, agent for Henry Dobbs, who led an expedition into Hudson Bay in 1747, also remarked that "those they call Home Indians [are] always in Parts near the Factory, not going far up into the Country."[66]

Prior to the inland expansion of fur-trade posts in the 1770s, the home territory, or hunting range, of most Homeguard Cree was usually limited to about 160 kilometres from the coastal trading posts. Although oriented toward the coast, the Homeguard Cree periodically ranged over a wider territory for social, commercial, and other reasons. In the hinterland of Albany Fort, the winter hunting grounds of some Homeguard Cree extended as far as the Kenogami River in 1755.[67] In the 1780s, some Severn River Homeguard Cree spent the winter season in areas located over 160 kilometres from the trading post. Near York Factory, the Homeguard Cree also occupied an area that was usually circumscribed by a distance of about 160 kilometres from the post. In the hinterland of Albany Fort, Severn House, and York Factory, the entire range was within the limits of the Hudson Bay lowlands. The situation at Churchill Fort and Moose Factory was significantly different, with a greater overlap of Homeguard Cree territory into the adjacent uplands. Considerable overlap existed in the territories of the York Factory and Churchill Fort Homeguard Cree, and the Albany Fort and Moose Fort Homeguard Cree. In 1750, George Spence, who was in charge of Albany Fort, reported difficulty in distinguishing the Homeguard who traded at Albany and Moose forts. Spence noted "two factories so close that its hard to distinguish to which River the Indians properly belongs."[68] After Moose Fort was re-established in 1730,[69] many of the people who came to be known as Moose River Homeguard Cree were drawn from the Albany River Homeguard population. In addition, movement by individuals and families between the two posts added to the confusion between the identities of the two groups of Homeguard Cree.

A similar overlap was evident between the York Factory and Churchill Fort Homeguard Cree populations. York Factory was the original home territory of the Churchill Fort Homeguard group. When Churchill Fort was established by the HBC in 1717, the traders encouraged some York Factory Homeguard Cree to relocate to the Churchill River area. According to HBC records, "James Knight, when he made his first settlement here [Churchill], for his further advantage took a Indian called Factory with his family along with him and adopted him Captain of this river."[70] The genesis of the Churchill Fort Homeguard Cree population can thus be traced to this HBC-induced relocation of Homeguard Cree from the Hayes River area.

The general seasonal movements of the Homeguard Cree can be reconstructed from HBC documents. In winter, the people usually lived in small groups of several closely related families. These winter-hunting groups were spread throughout about a 160-kilometre radius of the coastal post. Those who lived closer to the post visited several times in the winter to sell furs, provisions, and other country produce. Most remained in their winter camps until the end of winter, when they gravitated toward the coastal area. The movement toward the coastal trading post was motivated by a number of factors. They came to trade extra furs and hides procured in the winter; to renew social relationships with other coastal Cree and the European fur traders; and to give and receive gifts, thereby continuing to renew bonds of friendship and alliance.

The movement of Homeguard Cree toward the coast was also triggered by more ancient influences. The coast abounded with animal and plant resources during the spring, and the Homeguard Cree shifted their annual range to places where caribou, geese, and other resources were available. The gathering of large numbers of people was also necessary for communal caribou hunting. During the summer, the Homeguard Cree moved away from the trading posts to hunt, fish, and gather wild plants along the coastal zone. In the fall, there was a movement back to aggregations near the large rivers and river-mouth marshes to hunt caribou and geese in the migration period. The onset of cold weather dispersed the Homeguard Cree once again to customary winter hunting grounds.

Half-Homeguard Cree

The Muchiskewuck Athinuwick, or "Muskeg people," were Lowland Cree who lived farther inland, especially during the winter months. These people were usually called Half-Home or Half-Homeguard Indians by the coastal fur traders. In addition, some coastal Cree whose hunting grounds were farther removed from the trading posts were also identified as Half-Homeguards, because they spent the winter months farther away from the posts, generally over 160 kilometres away, and usually did not visit the coastal posts until the end of winter. The Half-Homeguard Cree were also occasionally employed by the HBC to hunt geese and bring in other provisions, but their inland or more remote coastal orientation during the winter months made them less reliable than the nearby coastal Cree as provisioners. Henry Ellis explained that "there are others [in addition to the Homeguard Cree] who come at the Time the Geese are going Northward [spring], in order to shoot Geese for the Factories, continue there in the summer, fishing; kill Geese again, when they are going south [fall]; and, the Season being over, return up the Country."[71] During the summer months, Half-Homeguard Cree often hunted in the same area as the Homeguard Cree. In the Severn River watershed, Homeguard and Half-Homeguard Cree hunted caribou together. A popular hunting ground for caribou was Waweaston, or White Seal Falls, on the lower Severn River.

The Half-Homeguard Cree who lived in the hinterland of Albany Fort usually spent the entire year within the lowlands, which was ample territory for both Homeguard and Half-Homeguard Indians to live together in the region. At Severn House, the Half-Homeguard Cree did not hunt geese for the company, but were noted for "bringing in furs in the spring and venison in the summer."[72] William Falconer remarked that

LIBRARY
THE UNIVERSITY OF TEXAS
AT BROWNSVILLE
Brownsville   99

the Half-Homeguard Cree spent the winter in places over 160 kilometres away, thereby making it difficult for them to hunt geese for the company.[73] Some of the Severn River Half-Homeguard Cree wintered in the upland region, more than 200 kilometres inland from the coast. At York Factory, the boundary of the lowlands is about 160 kilometres up the Hayes River and eighty kilometres up the Nelson River, and most Half-Homeguard Cree resided in the upland region during the winter. At both Churchill Fort and Moose Factory, the edge of the lowlands is very close to the coast, and thus both Homeguard and Half-Homeguard Cree lived part of the year outside the Hudson Bay lowlands.

As the inland fur trade developed in the late eighteenth century, trade-related migrations of Homeguard and Half-Homeguard Cree also expanded.

Pensioners, Widows, Orphans, and Domestics

The trading posts served as temporary places of refuge for people in need of emergency aid. In times of scarcity, Lowland Cree men would some-times leave their families at the post until they had obtained sufficient food to provide for them. However, these were usually temporary arrangements, and families rarely remained separated for long periods. Some Lowland Cree used the trading posts to cache preserved foods in case of future need; for example, on October 26, 1723, several families of Homeguard Cree arrived at Albany Fort to retrieve bundles of dried meat they had left at the fort.[74] Among the Homeguard Cree population near each of the coastal trading posts, a few families came to depend on longer term care from the European traders.[75] Among these were elderly people, who were some-times called "pensioners" by the HBC traders because they expected the company to take care of them. These expectations were based on the recip-rocal nature of the relationships that developed between Lowland Cree and Europeans at the trading posts. Hunters who supplied the European traders with food and other goods expected that they and their families would be able to receive similar treatment from the traders. The so-called pensioners included very old and infirm people who were usually without family members to take care of them. At Albany Fort in 1706, Anthony Beale noted: "The Indians are all gone today except those which will be pencheners the hole winter, they are five in number, first a old woman soo decripl'd with age and she is not able to stand, next a lame man, his wife and two children."[76]

Prominent leaders often received special treatment from the fur traders because of their influence over other people. At Albany Fort, a Homeguard

Cree leader named Miskemote became a "pentioner" in the fall of 1712. Miskemote was long considered by the HBC traders to be the "Captain of the Home Indians" near Albany Fort.[77] He had served the company well for many years as leader of the goose hunt, and in his old age he came to expect the company would take care of him and his family. Thomas Macklish noted in 1715 that "here is Miskemote and Wife, and 3 Antient Widows ye I shall be Obliged to keep ye winter, they having no children or relations to keep them."[78] By 1716, Miskemote was unable to travel to his winter hunt-ing grounds because he was "so decripled and antient that he cannot hunt."[79] Despite his old age and disabilities, Miskemote did not depend entirely upon the charity of the HBC. Throughout the rest of his life, he and his family spent much of their time away from Albany Fort to hunt, trap, and fish. Miskemote's health continued to deteriorate, but he was still recog-nized as the leader of the Albany River Homeguard. In 1719, he received gifts from the HBC valued at thirty-one made beaver.[80] No other leader, including upland leaders, received such valuable gifts from the company that year. After a lingering illness, Miskemote died near Albany Fort on September 12, 1721.[81]

Orphans were sometimes left at the trading posts until family members or others came to take care of them. At Fort Albany in 1713, Anthony Beale reported "a lame girl that cant walk was left here, haveing no friends to take care of her."[82] HBC records indicated that orphan children were soon adopted and taken away from the posts. According to William Falconer, "When Parents dies and leaves Children that are not able to provide for themselves; if there are no surviving Relations they are took care of by their neigh-bours, with the strictest affection, and humanity, they could have expected from their Parents."[83]

The European fur traders usually encouraged several Homeguard Cree families to stay near the trading posts year-round. These people, called "domesticks" by the HBC traders, provided food and other country pro-duce for the Europeans. William Falconer, at Severn House, noted in 1775 that "the homeguards all got debt and pitched away except two men with their families who are to stay and make snow shoes etc., these with the infirm and orphan Natives make our domesticks, 16 in number."[84]

Occasionally, large groups of Lowland Cree gathered near the coastal factories in winter. During the winter of 1770-71 at York Factory, large numbers of Lowland Cree arrived for occasional supplies of food, and by December 25, 1770, 106 Lowland Cree were encamped near the factory. However, it appears that unusually severe weather conditions drove many to seek temporary relief at the HBC post.[85] Prior to the smallpox epidemic in 1782-83, most Lowland Cree followed traditional pursuits and lived quite apart from the European traders. The majority spent most of their time away from the trading posts, with occasional visits during the winter and summer, and longer visits in the spring and fall during the caribou- and goose-hunting seasons. Very few Lowland Cree were dependent on the European traders for long-term care or employment.

Leadership Patterns

European observers were impressed by the lack of a rigid, hierarchical political order among the Indians. William Falconer wrote that "they are subject to no foreign power, neither have they any Monarch of their own, every man being sole Governor of his family,"[86] and Andrew Graham remarked, "The father or head of a family owns no superior, obeys no command."[87] Eleanor Leacock was among the first of several scholars who have taken these kinds of statements to mean that the Lowland Cree and neighbouring Indian groups were originally egalitarian, and that individual leaders arose in the context of Indian-European contact.[88] However, a closer examination of the European fur-trade records reveals that leadership was well developed among the Lowland Cree at the time of initial fur-trade contact. The confusion in the literature seems to have derived from the fact that the social and political organization of the Lowland Cree was very much different from European structures of leadership and authority. Zachariah Gillam, the captain in charge of the first trading ventures at Charles Fort on the east coast of James Bay in 1668 and 1670, stated, "As to their government, they have some chief men above ye rest, yet working as ye rest." Toby Morantz observed that Gillam's assessment "seems to have captured well the essence of a leadership operating within an ideology of egalitarianism, a coalescence that seems to have confounded some anthropologists."[89] Lowland Cree leaders were remarkably different from European leaders of the same period. They did not rule with force or dictate the lives of their followers in the same manner as did European monarchs. Rather, the authority of Lowland Cree leaders derived from life skills, experience, and wisdom. Leadership was consultative rather than dictatorial. Group members were able to make independent decisions, but usually followed the advice of their leaders. Thus, it is not surprising that William Falconer remarked that there were no monarchs among the Lowland Cree.

Given the vast territory of the lowlands, it is unlikely that paramount leaders were recognized among the Lowland Cree. However, several leaders were followed by large groups of people, and possessed wide-ranging influence. For example, in the late winter of 1715, a man known as The Swan, or Wapesew, arrived at Albany Fort from the north with his family and a large number of followers.[90] Over 400 people were enumerated in a camp near the fort. Since usually only about 100 Homeguard Cree gathered near Albany Fort for the spring goose hunt, Wapesew's followers must have numbered at least several hundred. Michael Grimmington, who was in charge of Albany Fort, noted this extraordinary assembly of Lowland Cree and remarked that Wapesew was "one of the best Indian to the English upon all this Cost [coast]."[91]

Another incident recorded in the early fur-trade records provides evidence of wide-ranging leadership by an individual. In the summer of 1683, a group of fourteen or fifteen people, including a man who was known as the "captain of the Indians of the river New Severn," arrived at the French trading post located at the mouth of the Hayes River.[92] The Severn River leader demanded gifts from the French fur traders because they had not paid for the privilege of building their trading post in Lowland Cree territory. According to Jean Baptiste Chouart, the Severn River leader stated that "I [Chouart] had not paid by presents for the country I inhabited to him who was chief of all the nations."[93] Although this claim was later refuted by others who came to the French trading post, the actions of the Severn River leader indicated his claim to wide-ranging authority within the Lowland Cree territory.

Lowland Cree leaders were usually associated with river-basin groups. The leadership of so-called Captains of Rivers was recognized by Europeans during the early fur-trade period. For example, Tickatuckoy, the leader of the Albany River Lowland Cree when the HBC re-established a trading post in 1692, was described as "ye great Leading Indian of this River,"[94] and when the HBC re-established Moose Fort in 1730, the Lowland Cree leader named Sacaconapit was said to have "Great Sway over the Indians."[95] The European traders were impressed by the power of these leaders and showed their respect by giving them valuable presents, including decorative clothing.

Many European traders noted that heredity was an important factor in determining leaders among the Lowland Cree. Although Andrew Graham wrote that "merit alone gives the title to distinction,"[96] other HBC traders observed that leadership patterns usually followed paternal lineage among the Lowland Cree. For example, the Albany River Lowland Cree leader named Tickatuckoy, who died in 1700, was succeeded by one of his sons named Neepeennawtai. However, as early as 1695, Neepeennawtai was considered to be the leader in waiting, and was referred to as "the young Captain of this River."[97] Many other Lowland Cree leaders were hereditary chiefs. In 1725, the son of a leader from Moose River named Sococomekee, also known as the White Flag Merchant, took over the role of leader when his father became too old to visit the post.[98] In 1769, a leader at Albany Fort named Tobateekeeshick died and his son Winnenaywaycappo was recognized as the new leader of a group of Half-Homeguard Lowland Cree. Thomas Hopkins, who was in charge of Albany Fort, remarked that "Lieutenant To-ba-tee-kee-shick's son brought 2 canoes to trade, his father being dead, gave him his coat as usual, the same as his father used to have."[99] In 1785, a leader named Lieutenant Wauchusk was succeeded by his eldest son, Tabethimo.[100] After the death of an Albany River Lowland Cree leader named Wapiswacatho in 1787, his son Cookenap was recognized by the HBC as the new leader. Edward Jarvis explained that "as he is the only surviving son of Lt. Wapiswacatho, gave him his father's coat."[101]

The HBC also "created" leaders in order to stimulate greater efforts in the fur and provision trade. For example, after the death of Captain Questach in the spring of 1785, a man named Moosumas was recognized by the HBC traders at Albany Fort as the new leader of the Albany River Lowland Cree. Moosumas was not related to the recently deceased Captain Questach, but Edward Jarvis explained that he was made a captain "on account of his numerous connexions by his daughters marriages."[102] However, Moosumas died eleven days after becoming captain, and he was replaced by Pusquothecot, who was the brother-in-law of the former captain. Family size also played a role in elevating a man named Monk to the rank of captain in 1796 at Albany Fort. Trader John McNab explained that Monk was made a captain because he had "a promising family, and being the oldest Indian here."[103] Many Lowland Cree leaders were elderly men who were past their prime hunting years. One of the oldest on record was a man named "Uncle Thomas," who died near York Factory in 1751. According to James Isham, "its computed he was near a 100 years old, had been a leading Indian upwards of 40 years."[104]

When Churchill Fort was built in 1717, a Lowland Cree man from York Factory, called Factory, was "adopted" by the HBC as the captain of Churchill River. Factory had been encouraged by the HBC to move with his family from the York Factory area to the newly established post at the mouth of the Churchill River. However, this HBC appointment was not well received by the traditional leader of the Hayes River Lowland Cree, a man named the Old Captain, who claimed authority over the Churchill River area. In the summer of 1718, the Old Captain and some of his followers arrived at Churchill and confronted Factory. The Old Captain refused to recognize the authority of Factory as leader of the Churchill River area, and he also made it clear to the traders at Churchill Fort that his leadership extended to the Churchill River. The HBC trader at Churchill said that "if I dont use him according to his expectation that I shall find he will interpose his authority in his Nation to make a general warr with the Northern [Chipewyan] Indians."[105] Although the HBC traders privately disdained the Old Captain's attitude, it is clear they respected his authority among the other Lowland Cree. He spent the winter of 1718 in the area around Churchill Fort and received gifts from the HBC commensurate with his position as leader. In the spring of 1719, he sent some of his followers to the fort for "provisions and a silk handkerchief." The HBC trader complied with this request, "it being a usuall custome to give him one every spring."[106] The Churchill Fort account also records that gifts were given to the Old Captain of Hayes River, his wives, and his brother.

While the HBC respected the authority of the Old Captain of Hayes River, the company continued to nurture the leadership of Factory as their choice for captain of Churchill River. The HBC system of creating leaders or captains was motivated by a desire to stimulate extra efforts by these company captains to bring furs and other country produce. While the upland leaders who were recognized as HBC captains were encouraged to bring down more furs, the Lowland Cree captains were usually asked to bring in more provisions. For example, the man named Factory, Captain of Churchill River, was often rewarded for his ability to lead other Indians in the spring and fall goose hunts.

The difference between traditional leaders and company-appointed leaders was noted by Henry Ellis, who, in his description of company leaders, noted that "the other Indians will join him, obey his Directions during the Voyage [to the HBC post], while at the Factory, and upon their Return; but no longer does the obligation continue." In contrast, the traditional leaders, called Captains of Rivers by Ellis, were men of "distinguished Merit," who were leaders because of "the Esteem which the People have for him." A Captain of a River was "the leading Indian of the Indians about that River, or a Person whom the others consult in such Affairs as they think his Advice necessary in; and they will attend to what he at any Time may propose, as to going in Parties to Hunt, to War, or to Trade."[107]

Population

The population of the Lowland Cree was small for the vast area they inhabited. William Falconer noted that "the Indians are not numerous, especially near the sea coast,"[108] and Andrew Graham remarked, "I know for truth that from Nelson River to Moose River, and from the sea inland to the Great Lake, the country is thinly inhabited."[109] In 1771, Graham estimated that the Homeguard Cree population at York Factory and Albany Fort was about 150 to 200 people in the hinterland of each establishment.[110] The Homeguard Cree populations were less at Churchill Fort, Severn House, and Moose Factory, averaging about seventy-five to 100 people at each post.[111] Using these rough figures, the total Homeguard Cree population in the Hudson Bay lowlands was about 500 to 700, prior to the smallpox epidemic in 1782-83.[112]

The population of the Half-Homeguard Lowland Cree is more difficult to estimate because they did not usually participate en masse in the goose hunts near the trading posts. However, large groups of Half-Homeguards came to the posts in the summer with furs or provisions. The wide area between Albany Fort and Severn House was home to a large number of Half-Homeguard Lowland Cree who occasionally traded at both posts. Based on the size of their hunting grounds, it would appear their population was at least twice that of the Homeguard Cree. Thus, the Half-Homeguard Cree population in the hinterland of Albany Fort and York Factory may have been about 300 to 400. At Churchill Fort, Severn House, and Moose Fort, there were about 150 to 200 Half-Homeguard Cree who visited each post. Using these figures, the total population of the Half-Homeguard Cree would have been about 1000 to 1400.

Combining the Homeguard and Half-Homeguard populations, the total Lowland Cree population was about 1500 to 2100. This rough estimate supports Andrew Graham's statement that "I am certain the total of Indians along the whole coast of Hudson's Bay, would not exceed two thousand."[113] The smallpox epidemic in 1782-83 reduced the population by about half. However, by the 1820s, the Lowland Cree population appears to have rebounded to near the pre-smallpox numbers. For example, at Albany Fort in 1829, an enumeration counted seventy-one men, fifty-one women, sixty-eight boys, fifty-three girls, and sixteen widows, giving a total population of 259, which included Homeguard and Half-Homeguard Cree.[114] A few Half-Homeguard Cree were probably among the 167 people enumerated in the Martins Fall district in 1829.[115] At York Factory in 1815, there were 180 adults in the population of Lowland Cree.[116] If the population structure of the Lowland Cree near York Factory was similar to that of the people living near Albany Fort, the total population would have been about 380. By 1820, the HBC reported that only eight Lowland Cree hunters lived in the vicinity of the Churchill Fort.[117] At Severn House in

1823, there were 151 adults in the population of Lowland Cree, or about 320 people, including children.[118] At Moose Fort, thirty-five hunters were enumerated in 1816, which indicated a total population of about 130.[119] These data suggest that, by the 1820s, the total population of the Lowland Cree had recovered to approximately the same level as in the pre-smallpox period.

2.
The Lowland Cree before European Contact: Images and Reality

The Image of an Unoccupied Land

According to oral traditions, the Lowland Cree occupied the Hudson Bay lowlands long before the arrival of the Europeans. In 1985, James Wesley, a Lowland Cree elder from Moose Factory, told historian John Long about the way of life in the lowlands "before the coming of the white man." Wesley explained, "My grandfather said it was just Indian people living in this particular area, on the west shores of James and Hudson Bays."[1] Jesuit missionary records also state that the Lowland Cree were there at the time of the arrival of Europeans. In 1667, Jesuit missionaries interviewed an elderly Lowland Cree man who told them "he had also seen a House which the Europeans had built on the mainland, out of boards and pieces of wood; and that they held Books in their hands, like the one he saw me holding when he told me this."[2]

Unfortunately, Lowland Cree oral traditions have not been extensively published and, until recently, little weight has been assigned to their validity as historical information. The Lowland Cree did not possess a literate tradition, and the physical conditions in the lowlands quickly eroded many of the visible signs of past occupancy. Seasonal encampments in river valleys were washed away annually by the scouring action of ice and water during spring breakup. Camps built on higher ground were exposed to the erosive action of wind, rain, and snow. The accounts of the early European exploring expeditions are also inconclusive about the nature of the Aboriginal occupation of the lowlands. Only in the past few decades have archaeological investigations uncovered artifacts confirming that Aboriginal people lived in the lowlands for over 1000 years before European settlement in the region. Prior to these findings, historians depicted the Hudson Bay lowlands as a region devoid of humans before European fur-trade settlement.

The theory of the Hudson Bay lowlands as a *terra nullius* was first advanced by Arthur S. Morton in 1939. According to Morton, the Aboriginal people who came to live in the lowlands near the mouth of the Nelson and Hayes rivers were "Maskegon or Swamp Crees" whose aboriginal homeland was the upland forest of the Canadian Shield near Lake Winnipeg. Thus, Morton concluded, when Thomas Button and his crew wintered at the mouth of the Nelson River in 1612-13, they met no people because "they would be inland in the forest." Morton also thought Jens Munk's failure to meet with Aboriginal people at the mouth of the Churchill River was because "the Indians must have been in the interior in their winter home in the forest."[3] Morton's views on the pre-European-contact territory of the Lowland Cree were strongly influenced by his interpretation of the role of the environment in determining where and how Aboriginal people lived: "The climate, then, and in particular the moisture of these three North-Wests [forest, prairie, and barren grounds], determines the plant life in the respective areas. The plant life in turn limits the animal life, and all of these together define the possibilities of human existence."[4] The Hudson Bay lowlands were equated with the barren grounds, and Morton ruled out human settlement in the region because of harsh environmental conditions.

The image of the lowlands as an uninhabited region was further developed by another historian, William L. Morton. In 1957, W.L. Morton reviewed the accounts of the early European explorers who visited the lowlands, and he concluded that, "as the explorers had noted, the Indians did not inhabit the coast, but frequented it only in summer." According to him, Indian occupation of the lowlands on a year-round basis was made possible only after the establishment of fur-trade posts. He also inferred that the people who came to inhabit the lowlands were formerly part of the "tribes of the farther interior." These tribes were among the Cree Nation who inhabited the forests of the Canadian Shield prior to the arrival of the European fur traders. After the establishment of trading posts, Morton concluded, some of the Upland Cree came to live in "the seaward forest belt," and were described as "the later 'Home Indians' of Company [HBC] parlance." According to this view, the Lowland Cree became geographically separated from the majority of the Cree Nation, who continued to occupy their original upland territory, and who were described by W.L. Morton as "the merry-hearted Crees of the inland forest." [5]

Archaeologist Walter Hlady was a proponent of the myth of an uninhabited Hudson Bay lowlands before European contact. In 1961, he presented a paper to the Historical and Scientific Society of Manitoba that supported the view that Aboriginal people did not live year-round in the lowlands before the arrival of the Europeans. Although trained as an archaeologist, Hlady did not present archaeological evidence to support his conclusions. Instead, he relied upon interpretations formulated by A.S. Morton and W.L. Morton. He was especially influenced by W.L. Morton's views about the effect of the European fur trade in attracting Indian people from the upland forest to live in the coastal lowlands. Following Morton, Hlady commented that:

> The setting up of fur trade posts on Hudson Bay begins to provide many check points on the location and movements of tribes. The Cree were first contacted by a party [of French fur traders] from the mouth of the Nelson and Hayes Rivers in 1682. The party must have travelled about one hundred miles inland before establishing contact. It was obvious that the Cree had preferred being inland, spending some time on the coast. [6]

Puzzling Pottery:
Early Archaeological Investigations in the Lowlands

In 1878 and 1879, Robert Bell conducted geological surveys in the Hudson Bay lowlands along the lower Hayes and Nelson rivers, and recorded a wide range of information about the natural history of the area. At the mouth of the Nelson River, he found fragments of pottery that appeared to predate the arrival of Europeans. These artifacts were catalogued along with many other geological specimens and transported to Ottawa, where they were stored in the National Museum. Although Bell had uncovered important evidence of Aboriginal life in the lowlands, he did not appreciate the significance of these ancient artifacts. The pottery fragments remained literally buried in storage for almost 100 years. [7] Bell's fieldwork took place during a period when there was little academic interest in archaeology. In Canada, interest in Aboriginal artifacts such as pottery and arrowheads was generated initially by people who collected these items for their value as curiosities and objects of antiquity. The establishment of museums in the late nineteenth century increased the interest in collecting Aboriginal artifacts for public display. (The first Canadian museum was established in Halifax, Nova Scotia, in 1868. Museums in Ontario and British Columbia were built in 1886.) The growth in museum collections led to the development of scholarly interest in the field of archaeology. Museums sponsored archaeological fieldwork in order to add to their collections, and to provide valuable contextual information for their displays. The work of archaeologists thus enabled the museums to fulfil educational goals in addition to attracting the public to places of curiosity and entertainment. In 1926, the University of Toronto established a department of anthropology and became the first university in Canada to offer courses in the field of archaeology. By 1946, archaeology was well established as a professional and scholarly discipline in Canada. Field investigations, although concentrated in southern Ontario, spread throughout much of Canada.

Despite the post-war expansion in the field of archaeology, the Hudson Bay lowlands remained unexplored for decades. Initially, archaeologists were uninterested in the lowlands because of the prevailing view in the literature that the region was uninhabited until Europeans established fur-trade settlements in the late seventeenth century. The image of the Hudson Bay lowlands as barren land offered little incentive for archaeologists to undertake costly and difficult investigations. The first archaeological excavation in the lowlands was motivated by interest in discovering the remains of early European fur-trade settlements. In 1960, Walter Kenyon investigated the site of the first HBC trading post near the mouth of the Albany River. Between 1960 and 1970, he returned to the site seven times and uncovered numerous artifacts that belonged to the European traders. Although he found several Aboriginal artifacts such as flint arrow-points, bone awls, and bone lances, he believed these items had been deposited at the site after the Europeans had built Albany Fort. According to Kenyon, the arrow-points made of flint "were either collected by the fur traders (possibly as souvenirs) or left in the fort by native visitors."[8] He did not expand his investigation beyond the boundaries of the trading post, and therefore his contextual analysis was limited to the post-European settlement period.

Kenneth Dawson was the first professional archaeologist to conduct fieldwork specifically focussed on Aboriginal sites within the Hudson Bay lowlands. In 1962 and 1966, Dawson made "cursory" investigations along the lower Albany and lower Hayes rivers. He was unimpressed with the potential of these areas for Aboriginal settlements; like Walter Hlady and the others before him, Dawson considered the environmental conditions of the lowlands to be "generally unsuitable for human habitation."[9] His brief visits were relatively unproductive, but he did find several pottery fragments near the mouth of the Hayes River that were from the pre-European settlement period. However, he believed that the pottery was left by Aboriginal people who lived in the uplands and who visited the lowlands occasionally before Europeans established fur-trade settlements. Therefore, Dawson concluded there was "no evidence of prehistoric settlement in the lower reaches [of the Albany and Hayes rivers]."[10]

During the summers from 1967 to 1969, Dawson returned to the Albany River, but concentrated his efforts higher upriver between the confluence with the Kenogami River and Miminiska Lake. This stretch of the Albany River included about 160 kilometres located within the lowlands downstream from Martins Fall. Dawson was unable to locate any archaeological sites in the lowlands section. However, he did find ample evidence of pre-contact Aboriginal settlements along the Albany River in the upland Shield. Ten sites upriver from Martins Fall produced stone, bone, and pottery artifacts. He believed that the failure to find artifacts in the lowlands section was related to the lack of permanent occupancy of the region.

> Given the very short seasonal abundance of exploitable littoral resources on this dismal post-glacial uplifted coast, it seems reasonable to speculate that the pattern of occasional visits only has been a long standing pattern. In other words, prehistoric populations were living inland on the Shield where resources, while scarce, could be exploited year round and in the course of this subsistence pattern they would make an occasional visit to the shores of Hudson Bay.[11]

Dawson's failure to find artifacts in his river-valley surveys within the lowlands may have been due to natural factors. The river valleys were annually scoured by water and ice, especially during spring breakup. According to Henry Ellis, the Lowland Cree preferred to camp in places that were subject to flooding and erosion, and "tents are seldom pitched in the Middle of the Woods, or upon Heights, but upon Creek or River-sides, in Bottoms; which may be done for the Convenience of getting water or Ice."[12] Any remains of encampments in these places would have been easily washed away by the spring floods.

By 1970, the information about the pottery found by Bell and Dawson near the mouth of the Nelson and Hayes rivers was available to other archaeologists, but the idea of permanent human occupation of the lowlands was still discounted. In 1970, Walter Hlady incorporated these findings to slightly readjust his earlier views. He observed that "initial attempts to contact the Cree from York Fort were well inland. It is obvious that the shores of Hudson Bay were not as attractive as the inland areas to the Cree except possibly in the autumn when geese congregated in tremendous numbers."[13] According to him, the lowlands became attractive to Aboriginal people on a year-round basis only after Europeans built trading posts along the coast.

William Mayer-Oakes, an archaeologist who had done fieldwork at Grand Rapids on the Saskatchewan River, puzzled over the source and antiquity of the pottery found near the mouth of the Nelson River. Mayer-Oakes believed it was probably left by upland people who came to trade with the Europeans during the early fur-trade period.[14] He argued that pottery continued to be used, despite the availability of more durable replacement European wares, and that the pottery found at the mouth of the Nelson River postdated European settlement in the area. Thus, Mayer-Oakes contributed to the image of an unoccupied Hudson Bay lowlands by advancing the view that post-European-contact, fur-trade influences were responsible for bringing upland people to the coast for trade purposes.

Accidental Discoveries:
Archaeological Research in the 1970s

The minimal results of Dawson's brief investigations discouraged follow-up archaeological fieldwork in the lowlands until the accidental discovery of artifacts near Cape Henrietta Maria in 1972. During the course of wildlife surveys in the area of Polar Bear Provincial Park, park officials came across bones and other artifacts along the Brant River and notified other government authorities. In September of 1972, John Tomenchuk and William Irving spent three days investigating two sites on the Brant River, located about twenty kilometres south of the Hudson Bay coast and forty kilometres from Cape Henrietta Maria. One of the sites, known as BRS-2, or Brant River Site Number Two, yielded a number of artifacts that appeared to predate European contact. These included a number of bone and stone fragments, a small chert projectile point, and some pottery shards. The projectile point was similar in appearance to other stone points found in sites attributed to "late prehistoric northern Algonquian" peoples.[15] The pottery fragments resembled pottery found in sites in southwestern Manitoba and at Michipicoten on the northern shore of Lake Superior. Other archaeologists had interpreted the Manitoba sites to be ancestral to modern Cree, while the Michipicoten site had been associated with ancestral Ojibway occupancy. Tomenchuk and Irving interpreted the pottery as being brought to the Brant River site by Upland Cree or Ojibway peoples who lived to the south or southwest. They pointed to twentieth-century ethnographic studies done by Skinner (1911) and Honigmann (1956) that indicated the local Aboriginal people of the lowlands did not have a knowledge or a tradition of pottery manufacture. Tomenchuk's and Irving's fortuitous investigation of the Brant River sites produced the first systematically described archaeological evidence for occupation of the Hudson Bay lowlands. Their report also stimulated the second systematic archaeological study within the lowlands. What intrigued archaeologists the most was a footnote in the report that described finding fire-cracked rocks and a cervid bone at Hawley Lake during a brief stopover on a trip to Brant River. This information became available to other archaeologists before the publication of the Brant River report, and in the summer of 1974, John Pollock and William Noble travelled to Hawley Lake to investigate the site further.

Pollock and Noble spent two weeks surveying archaeological sites along beach ridges near Cape Henrietta Maria and along the shoreline of Hawley Lake, located about ninety kilometres southwest. They found only one site during their brief survey of the beach ridges. This site, known as GeHo-3, comprised six noticeable depressions on the crest of a prominent beach ridge. When one of the pits was excavated, it proved to be a subterranean cache that contained caribou remains. No scientific dating of the cache was attempted, but the investigators assigned an approximate date as "late prehistoric or historic" on the basis of descriptions of similar subterranean caches by John Honigmann, an anthropologist who had conducted ethnographic fieldwork in the area around Attawapiskat in 1947-48. The survey work around the shore of Hawley Lake was also brief, but Pollock and Noble located sixteen sites (two sites were found along the Sutton River about eight kilometres downstream from the lake) that contained archaeological artifacts. Of these, two sites yielded important new data about the pre-contact Aboriginal history of the area. One site, known as GdId-1, or the Hawley Lake Site, was located on the west side of the lake about three kilometres from its outlet. It contained evidence of a number of hearths, and the artifacts included a projectile point made from greyish-white chert and a number of fragments and flakes from stone tools. Most importantly, charcoal extracted from the hearths yielded a date of 915 AD +/- 100 years. This finding represented the first indisputable evidence of human occupation of the lowlands prior to European contact. Another site, known as GdId-7, or the Cowell Site, was located on the eastern shore of Hawley

Lake. The excavations uncovered "hearth materials, decorated pottery, bones, cores, and numerous flakes, all at a substantial depth beneath a heavy layer of peat."[16] Dating of this site was estimated at 1410 AD +/- 95 years. The faunal material revealed a heavy focus on caribou, and analysis of the remains suggested that the caribou had been killed and butchered elsewhere and the meat carried back to the site. The pottery shards found apparently came from a single, medium-sized pot, "manufactured by a paddle method, decorated near the rim by corded impressions, and on the body by babiche. The interior was smoothed over by a comb-like instrument."[17] Typologically, the investigators had some trouble assigning this pot to pottery traditions known from other subarctic sites. They concluded it probably belonged within the pottery tradition known as Selkirk, which was common in sites apparently ancestral to modern Cree. However, they did not rule out a connection with the Black Duck tradition, which was commonly attributed to ancestral Ojibway. Pollock and Noble observed that this incongruity could be explained if "exchange systems were operating between these two different groups [i.e., Cree and Ojibway]."[18]

Kenneth Dawson incorporated Pollock's and Noble's findings in his updated overview of the "prehistory" of northern Ontario, published in 1983. Dawson noted that the archaeological investigations around Hawley Lake had confirmed the presence of Aboriginal people in the area before European contact. However, he was not convinced that these findings could be applied to other areas within the lowlands. As a result, he portrayed the Hawley Lake area as an island of human occupation within the vast, unoccupied lowlands, saying "the Hudson Bay Lowland ... except for the Hawley Lake area appears to have been virtually unoccupied in prehistoric times."[19]

An unpublished archaeological investigation in the lowlands conducted in 1977 and 1978 by Christopher Trott escaped the notice of other archaeologists. In the summer of 1977, Trott investigated the area along the Albany River near the confluence with the Cheepay (Ghost) River, and located a small site on a high, level terrace that was protected from the annual ice-scouring erosion along the beaches and slopes of the river valley. EiHu-2, or the Cheepay River Site, produced artifacts that included burned bone fragments, fire-cracked rocks, and ten fire-treated chert flakes, which, Trott concluded, was "the only clear evidence of prehistoric occupation found during the survey."[20] He also recorded some oral history of the people at the nearby Constance Lake Indian Reserve that corroborated the antiquity of these findings. The people at Constance Lake talked "of finding bones and 'arrowheads' eroding out of the banks at Mammattawa indicating a similar [pre-European contact] type of occupation."[21]

In the summer of 1978, Norman Williamson conducted additional archaeological investigations at the Cheepay River site and found more pre-contact artifacts, including two pottery rim shards. These fragments were difficult to compare to other pottery found elsewhere, but Williamson noted that "similar specimens are known from south-eastern and northern Manitoba and north-western Ontario."[22] Based upon this rough comparison, the pottery at the Cheepay River site was dated about AD 800-1000.

In areas adjacent to the Hudson Bay lowlands, other archaeological field-work in the 1970s and 1980s yielded additional data about the pre-contact Aboriginal peoples who lived in the bordering upland Shield region. During the summers of 1978 and 1979, David Riddle investigated ninety-four sites along the Albany River from its headwaters downstream to Washi Lake, about eighty kilometres above the edge of the lowlands. The artifacts found in these sites confirmed that the Albany River had been "a well-used area in both prehistoric and historic times," and Riddle calculated that some of the material was 5000 years old. The sites diminished in number as he moved downstream, and he postulated that "less use was made of the periphery of the Shield near the edge of the Hudson Bay Lowland/Canadian Shield." Although Riddle had not investigated the Albany River within the lowlands region, he presumed that "the differences in the environment between the Shield and Lowlands may have caused the population to view the Lowlands with disfavour."[23]

In the summer of 1980, Riddle investigated fifty-three sites around Attawapiskat Lake, and reported abundant evidence of pre-European-contact Aboriginal occupancy around the lake. Six sites yielded artifacts that were attributed to the Archaic period. Although scientific dating was not done on these sites, James V. Wright, who had originally surveyed the sites in 1968, estimated that the Archaic period in the Shield region began about 3000 BC.[24] A number of sites contained pottery fragments. FbJa-7, or the Sandy West Narrows Site, produced a pottery rim shard considered to be of Iroquoian or mixed Iroquoian-Algonkian origin. Riddle thought the presence of Iroquoian-style pottery as far north as Attawapiskat Lake posed problems for interpreting pre-European distributions and movements of Aboriginal peoples. However, he observed, "the rim from FbJa-7 while adding little to this as yet poorly understood problem adds a northerly extension to the spatial distribution of such material." He believed the artifacts represented the farthest downstream, pre-European habitation of Aboriginal people within the Attawapiskat River basin. As in his earlier Albany River survey, he based this opinion on the assumption that Aboriginal people did not occupy the lowlands prior to European settlement in the region. He concluded, "If Laurel peoples had no predilection to travel onto the Lowlands, Attawapiskat Lake may be the eastern terminus of this movement."[25]

In 1989 and 1990, Scott Hamilton investigated a burial site at Wapekeka, located on the shore of Angling Lake in the upland Shield, near the edge of the Hudson Bay lowlands. Radiocarbon dating indicated the burial had occurred about 7000 years ago. The site was near the edge of the Tyrrell Sea, the precursor of modern Hudson Bay; the people who were connected with the burial were thus geographically akin to the coastal Lowland Cree. Hamilton suggested that the Wapekeka burial confirmed that Aboriginal people quickly occupied the land in the wake of the receding Tyrrell Sea.[26]

While archaeological investigations increasingly pointed to a long period of human occupation of the Hudson Bay lowlands and adjacent uplands, the image of an unoccupied land continued in the literature. For example, in 1975, Dale Russell suggested the lowlands was a "no-man's land" before Europeans built trading posts, and that the migration of Indian people into the lowlands after European settlement "necessitated a displacement of Indian people to the coast, originating the Home Guard Indians. Because of adverse aspects of the coastal environment, the Home Guard Indians became dependent on the Hudson's Bay Company."[27] Charles Bishop provided a different view of the pre-European-contact population dynamics among the Lowland Cree who lived in the Albany River basin. Bishop argued that, prior to European fur-trade settlement in the region, the Albany River Lowland Cree hunted geese along the coastal lowlands in spring and early summer. However, the arrival of European fur traders caused some of the Lowland Cree to remain year-round in the lowlands to hunt geese in the fall for the traders, and then they were unable to reach their traditional upland winter territories.[28]

The Reality of an Occupied Land: Archaeology in the 1980s

In the early 1980s, two archaeological investigations in different parts of the lowlands began to put the pieces of the puzzle together, and the picture of the pre-European-contact occupancy of the area began to emerge. Patrick Julig investigated the area along the lower Albany River within the lowlands in the summer of 1981 and located twenty pre-contact sites, but only a few were excavated because of time and other constraints. Despite these limitations, Julig found several significant features in these sites that yielded new information about the pre-contact Aboriginal people who lived in the area. For example, some of the sites were located on high terraces, which suggested winter occupation. Julig observed:

> Many of these were, on the basis of site location, cold weather encampments. They were often situated well back in the bush from summer beaches, on high terraces above maximum spring flood levels. Such general site locations were anticipated prior to the field surveys, on the basis of ethnographic information. Native bands wintering in the interior would return to the locations where their canoes were cached before spring breakup and soft snow conditions. This suggested camp locations on high terraces near major tributaries during late winter/early spring, when travel was difficult.[29]

His interpretation that Aboriginal people lived in the lowlands during cold weather was a major departure from the established archaeological and historical literature. He searched for sites near the Albany River estuary, but severe erosion had washed out into the bay all evidence of past human occupation. He noted "tremendous annual flooding of the lower terraces, which would likely have destroyed many, if not all sites over the past three centuries."[30] Despite this lack of information, Julig concluded that the pre-contact Aboriginal people occupied sites near the Albany River estuary in the summer months, and moved to interior sites during the cold-weather months. In 1988, however, he concluded that some bands occupied the lowlands on a year-round basis; some people occupied the region only seasonally but others did not "rush back" to the Shield in winter.[31]

Julig may have been influenced by the conclusions drawn by another archaeologist, Jean-Luc Pilon, who began fieldwork in the vicinity of Fort Severn in the summer of 1981. Pilon spent four seasons excavating and studying over thirty archaeological sites along the lower Severn and Sachigo rivers. His work represents the most detailed archaeological investigation within the lowlands to date. After extensive fieldwork and laboratory analysis of artifacts found in pre-contact sites, Pilon concluded that Aboriginal people had lived within the lowlands near the Severn River for 1500 to 2000 years. He thought that "the failure, until now, to find evidence for regular prehistoric seasonal or year-round occupation of the Hudson Bay Lowlands cannot be attributed to the unsuitability of the region for human habitation. It had game, fish, fuel, and raw materials necessary for the manufacture of shelters and tools, all in relative abundance."[32]

Pilon's study provided a detailed outline of Aboriginal occupancy in the Severn River lowlands. The fact that Aboriginal people inhabited the lowlands before European contact was significant in terms of challenging prevailing theoretical assumptions about Aboriginal history. As Pilon noted, "The existence of a prehistoric indigenous population affects both our larger understanding of subarctic subsistence systems, and our interpretation of relations between Native people and Europeans in the Lowlands."[33]

Many of the numerous sites excavated by Pilon and his crew provided significant new information. One site, known as Ile de l'Ourson (Bear Island), or G1Iw-5, was located on a large island in the Severn River about twenty kilometres from the coast and just upstream from the confluence with the Amiskou Sebe (Beaver River). Although radiocarbon testing was not done on this site, stratigraphic analysis indicated it was occupied in the "prehistoric" (pre-European contact) period. A large quantity of caribou bones were recovered, and Pilon noted that the caribou were probably killed by "the use of some mass capture technique, such as a fence or snares, on the island, which is a natural crossing point in the river for migrating caribou."[34] An examination of antler fragments suggested that the caribou were killed during the late spring or early summer migration period.

The Mahikoune (Wolf) site, or G1Ix-1, was located about thirty kilometres upstream on the east shore of the Severn River. Radiocarbon testing produced a date of 730 +/- 90 years BP (before present), or about AD 1165-1395. The Severn River narrows at this point, and it offered another strategic location for hunting caribou as they crossed the river. Most of the artifact remains at the site were caribou bones, suggesting that it too was a caribou-hunting camp. Pilon also recovered moose bones, which was unexpected since biologists had assumed that moose had only recently extended their range north of Lake Superior. Pilon's discovery clearly refuted that assumption: "Without a doubt then, the pre-contact range of Alces alces can be described as within a few kilometres of the shores of Hudson Bay."[35]

About forty kilometres up the Severn River from the coast is a waterfall known as Ouaouiastine, or Whiteseal Falls. A site called Ouabouche (Hare), or GkJa-3, was located near the foot of the falls. A large number of artifacts was found at this site, indicating that it was a well-used camp location both before and after European contact (although no radiocarbon dates were obtained). The faunal remains included a significant number of caribou bones, and also numerous fur-bearer, fish, and bird remains, suggesting a diversified subsistence and fur-trade occupancy. These artifacts also suggested a multi-season occupancy at the site, including the winter months, based, in part, on the number of small fur bearers that were present. Pilon also suggested that fishing could have taken place year-round with hooks, nets, and weirs; and, in 1988, Kenneth R. Lister provided evidence of year-round use of fish weirs both before and after European contact. Lister's radiocarbon date of 3920 +/- 180 years BP for a site on the Shamattawa River, which flows into the Winisk River, is the earliest recorded date for human occupation in the lowlands.[36] Fish weirs were known to have been used after the river was frozen, and gill nets were also used under the ice. Pilon concluded that the Ouabouche site was "used at different times of the year within a well-co-ordinated round of resource exploitation."[37]

Pilon was able to show that Aboriginal people have occupied the Severn River lowlands for 1500 to 2000 years.[38] This occupancy was based upon exploiting a number of seasonally available animal species, of which caribou was a primary resource. Pilon concluded that this pattern of resource use remained relatively unchanged until the nineteenth century, when the caribou resource was seriously reduced. He thought the material culture of the Severn River Lowland people closely reflected their adaptation to the seasonal movements of the caribou, which "stands in marked contrast to their neighbours, who today share the same ethnic label."[39] Pilon argued that the identification of the Severn River Lowland people as "Cree" did not recognize the distinct difference between regional groups, and that "instead, it may perhaps prove more fruitful to examine changes in the adaptive strategies through time in particular areas and in larger regions in order to understand the nature of the adaptations to different environmental settings within the Subarctic."[40]

3.

Upland Neighbours: The Northern Ojibway, Upland Cree, and Eastmain Cree

The Northern Ojibway

By the time European fur traders ventured into the area north of Lake Huron and Lake Superior in the 1770s, much of the region bordering the Hudson Bay lowlands was occupied by groups of people known as Ojibway or, more specifically, Northern Ojibway.[1] Their northern territorial range extended along the edge of the lowlands from the Moose River to the Hayes River. According to several accounts by European fur traders, the Northern Ojibway had migrated into the upland territory adjacent to the lowlands some time before 1770. Andrew Graham remarked in 1775, "It is my opinion that this people [Northern Ojibway] have drawn up to the Northward gradually as the Keiskatchewans [Lowland Cree] receded from it toward the southwest," and, in 1839, George Barnston observed that the Northern Ojibway had pushed northward from Lake Superior to the edge of the lowlands near Martins Fall.[2]

The European accounts of migration conform in general to Ojibway oral traditions. According to an oral tradition recorded by Ojibway historian William Warren, the Northern Ojibway migrated into the area north of Lake Superior from the Lake Huron area beginning about 1530.[3] The migration was two-pronged, with one division moving north and west of Lake Superior, and the other moving south and west of the lake. At the time of this migration, "they were living in a primitive state, when they possessed nothing but the bow and arrow, sharpened stones, and bones of animals,"[4] which corroborates that the migration began before European contact. Some Ojibway remained in the vicinity of Sault Ste. Marie, and were subsequently called *Saulteaux* by the French traders. The Ojibway who migrated into the area north of Lake Superior divided into a number of regional groups. Those who settled along the north shore of Lake Superior were known generally as *Sug-wau-dug-ah-win-in-e-wug*, or "men of the thick fir woods." The French traders usually called these people *Bois Forts* or *Gens des Terres*. Another group settled at the lakehead near Grand Portage, and was known as the *Ke-nouzhay* or "Pike." A large group who migrated westward to Rainy Lake was called *Ko-je-je-win-e-wug*, a name describing the "numerous straits, bends and turnings of the lakes and rivers which they occupy."[5] The Rainy Lake Ojibway became allies with the *Ke-nis-te-no* (Upland Cree) and *Assineboins* (Assiniboine). At that time, a large group of Upland Cree lived in a village at Ne-bo-se-be, or Dead River (Netley Creek), near the mouth of the Red River, and the Assiniboine were their neighbours.[6]

Scholars have different opinions about Ojibway migration, but these may be reconciled if greater reliance is placed on the Ojibway oral tradition, which asserts that the Northern Ojibway migrated into the area about 1530. Thus, they would have been well established north of Lake Superior before Europeans arrived. The migration was gradual and continued beyond 1770. They probably displaced Upland Cree groups in many areas north of Lake Superior, and also caused the Lowland Cree to gradually shift their territorial range farther north. According to Warren, the group who moved farthest north was called *Omushke-goes*, or "Swamp People." However, he also identified the *Omush-ke-goag* (*Musk-e-goes*), "Swamp People," or Lowland Cree, as a different tribe. The confusion may have arisen because of the close proximity of the Northern Ojibway and the Lowland Cree. Other eighteenth- and nineteenth-century observers made similar remarks about the identity of the Northern Ojibway who lived adjacent to the Lowland Cree. For example, in 1795, an unnamed North West Company fur trader wrote, "The Indians to the North of Lac Winnipic are a mixture of Saulteux [Ojibway] and Christineaux [Cree], speaking a mixt language and are called Masquegons they extend to Nipigon and Hudson Bay."[7] John Lee Lewes, who was in charge of Oxford House in 1833, remarked that the Indians who lived near the post "may be classed under two Heads, Muskago or Swampy Souteaus [Northern Ojibway], and the Swampy Crees [Lowland Cree]."[8]

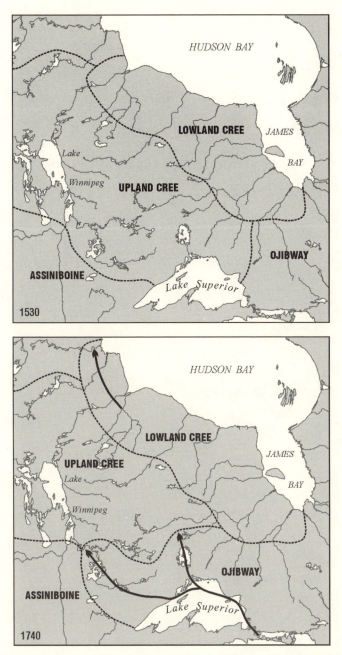

Approximate Territorial Distribution of the Lowland Cree and Their Neighbours, 1530 and 1740 (arrows indicate direction of population movements)

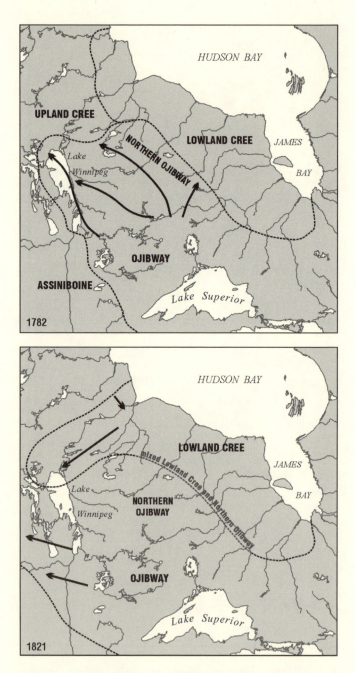

Approximate Territorial Distribution of the Lowland Cree and Their Neighbours,
1782 and 1821 (arrows indicate direction of population movements)

The HBC fur traders commonly used the name *Nakawawuck* to describe the Northern Ojibway. According to one translation, the name meant "those who speak differently."[9] From the perspective of Europeans who were familiar with the language spoken by the Lowland Cree, it would have been a useful descriptive term for the Northern Ojibway. Andrew Graham observed, "Their [Northern Ojibway] speech differs greatly from the Keskachewan Indians [Cree]; they having so many words to represent one thing makes it difficult to converse with them."[10] George Sutherland, who was the first HBC trader to winter among the Northern Ojibway at Sturgeon Lake (west of Lake Nipigon), noted that "these Indians ... differe far in their language from our Indians at hudsons bay."[11] Another name for the Northern Ojibway was *Bungee* or *Pungee*. According to HBC trader George Barnston, the term Bungee was "a name, I imagine, given to them from their use of the Sauteux word Pungee—a little."[12] Charles Bishop suggested that Bungee was used by the HBC traders because of "their practice of begging" when they visited the trading posts.[13] Peter Fidler, the HBC trader in charge of Fort Dauphin in 1820, explained that the "Soteaux," or Northern Ojibway, "obtained the name of <u>Bungees</u> by us [HBC traders] from the word Bungee in their language signifying small or little which they so frequently repeated when their supplies was not adequate to their wants, that they have thus obtained the word as a fixed term to the whole Tribe."[14] The HBC traders at York Factory and Severn House also used the name "Lake Indians" to describe the Northern Ojibway. The origin of the name may have been related to their former homeland around the Great Lakes. By the mid-eighteenth century, the term Lake Indians could also have been descriptive of the geographic location of the Northern Ojibway in the upland Shield area along the margins of the Hudson Bay lowlands. The Shield is literally dotted with lakes and stands out in marked contrast to the lowlands, which is characterized by vast expanses of swamp and bog. The difference between the two regions can be easily seen in maps depicting drainage patterns.

The names Lake Indians, Nakawawuck, and Bungee were used commonly in the area around York Factory and Severn House, but not farther south near Albany Fort. George Barnston, who was in charge of Martins Fall House in 1839, noted that the name "Suckers" was used in that locale instead of Bungee. He said the majority of Indians in the vicinity "belong to that tribe of Sauteux, denominated the Suckers—a Band of the Great Chippewa Divisions which appears to have pushed farthest to the northward, at least in this quarter [near Martins Fall]," and the "purer Chippewas" lived to the south of the Albany River.[15] The name Suckers

represented an animal-named group, or division, among the Northern
Ojibway. This is consistent with the oral history of the Ojibway people.
According to Ojibway historian William Warren, the general population
was subdivided into a number of animal-named clans, or totems.[16] In addi-
tion to the Sucker totem, Warren included the Goose, Beaver, Sturgeon,
Gull, Hawk, Cormorant, and Whitefish totems among the Northern
Ojibway. Significantly, Warren also remarked that the Suckers and other
Northern Ojibway clan groups migrated north and settled near the "Musk-
keegoes," or "Swamp People." The Suckers were reported to be the north-
ernmost group of the Northern Ojibway. However, European fur traders
also identified other animal-named groups. Duncan Cameron, a North
West Company trader who operated in the area near the headwaters of the
Severn River in the early nineteenth century, enumerated eleven other
"totems or tribes," who lived north of Lake Nipigon: Moose, Reindeer
[Caribou], Bear, Pelican, Loon, Kingfisher, Eagle, Sturgeon, Pike, Sucker,
Barbue [Catfish], and Rattlesnake.[17]

Company inland traders also noted the significance of animal-named
groups among the Northern Ojibway. According to David Sanderson, an
experienced HBC inland fur trader, the "Succars tribe of Indians" lived in
the area around the upper Berens and Poplar rivers in 1797.[18] In 1815,
George Holdsworth, who was in charge of the HBC's post on the Berens
River, observed that the Indian population was divided into four bands, or
tribes. The Pelican, Moose, and Sucker tribes occupied the area east of Lake
Winnipeg and north of the Bloodvein River. The Kingfisher tribe lived in
the area around the Bloodvein River. In 1814, William Thomas, who was
in charge of Osnaburgh House, identified "several different Tribes (as they
are called) of Indians inhabiting the District viz: Cranes, Suckers, Loons,
Moose, Sturgeons, Kingfishers and Pelicans."[19] According to Thomas, the
Suckers and Cranes were the northernmost groups, occupying the territory between Osnaburgh House and Trout Lake. The Loons hunted between Osnaburgh and Lake Nipigon, the Moose and Sturgeon groups lived
to the southwest of the post, and the Kingfishers and Pelicans lived toward
Lake Winnipeg. Farther west, other HBC traders reported the identification
of animal-named groups among the Northern Ojibway. For example, in
1823, Joseph McGillivray, who was in charge of the Norway House District, enumerated four "tribes" who lived in the district, and identified the
heads of families and the locations of their hunting grounds. The Lowland
Cree were called "Maskegons or Swampies" by McGillivray, while the
Northern Ojibway were divided into three animal-named groups, called
Pelican, Moose, and King Fishers.

Lowland Cree and Northern Ojibway Groups in the Jack River District, 1823

"Tribe"	Hunting Grounds	Heads of Families
Maskegon (or Swampies) [Lowland Cree]	Northside Lake Limestone Lake Cross Lake Jack Lake Jack River Little Winnipeg	Mistunnisk Uchegan Ku ku wa thinish Pah pethukes
Pelican [Northern Ojibway]	Cross Lake Jack Lake Jack River Deers Lake Thunder Lake Winipeg Jack Head	Pakekan Namuch Keg Memechis Indian Legs Squirrel Bear Peritess Hepass Sloterry Little Swan
Moose [Northern Ojibway]	Sandy Point Lake	White Coats Sturgeon
King Fishers [Northern Ojibway]	Bad Lake	Sharp Eyes Arrow Legs

Source: HBCA, B.154/e/2, fos. 12d–14

European fur traders rarely recorded animal-named groups among the Lowland Cree, as they did with the Northern Ojibway. However, Alanson Skinner reported in 1911 that

> the clans once found among the Albany Cree, may have been derived from the Northern Saulteaux. The Albany natives remember the following totems, but there were many others which they could not recall: moose, caribou, fish, sucker, sturgeon, loon, and Hell-diver [cormorant]. The whale and seal were never known. Some of the old men are of opinion that in former times young men occasionally dreamed the clan to which they were to belong, as well as their personal guardians. Descent was in the father's line and there were no marriage restrictions.[20]

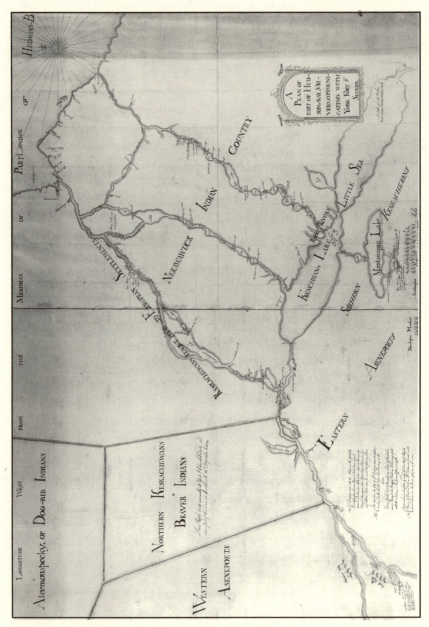

"A Plan of Part of Hudson Bay and Rivers, Communicating with York Fort and Severn," 1774, map drawn by Andrew Graham

The only reference in the fur-trade records to an animal-named group among the Lowland Cree was a group called the "Jack [northern pike] Indians." However, the name Jack Indians fell into disuse, and the group was commonly known as the Severn or Seaside Indians after 1733.[21]

While the initial migration of Northern Ojibway began before European fur-trade settlements were established in the Hudson Bay lowlands, it is clear that some Northern Ojibway continued to move north and west throughout the eighteenth century. They were first reported in the HBC records at York Factory in 1741, when James Isham recorded the name "Bungee Indians" as one of the upland groups who traded at York Factory that summer.[22] Although Isham had carefully recorded the group names of Uplanders since 1737, this was the first specific mention of Northern Ojibway at York Factory. Earlier HBC traders at York Factory who also recorded upland group names did not mention Bungee, Nakawawuck, Lake Indians, or any other name that can be linked specifically to the Northern Ojibway.[23] After 1741, the Northern Ojibway were regularly reported at York Factory during the summer trading season. Given these facts, it is probable that the year 1741 marked the beginning of Northern Ojibway trade at York Factory, and it may have also indicated their recent arrival in the York Factory hinterland. By 1749, James Isham had become more acquainted with the Northern Ojibway, and he observed that they lived in the area that "borders with the french at the Little sea [Lake Winnipeg]."[24]

Between 1749 and 1782, some Northern Ojibway shifted their territorial range farther northward, becoming increasingly involved in the provision trade at York Factory and Severn House. For example, on June 6, 1773, eight canoes of Northern Ojibway visited York Factory and traded thirty-six sturgeon.[25] On May 26, 1774, seven canoes of Northern Ojibway traded eleven caribou, four caribou hearts, and one sturgeon at York Factory,[26] and in 1781, a group of Northern Ojibway in ten canoes traded over 300 caribou skins at York Factory.[27] In 1769, Andrew Graham observed that "we get provisions from the Nekawawuck or lake Indians, who are every now and then, summer and winter, coming in to trade furs."[28] In 1771, he observed that "this game [caribou hunting] formerly was the business of the poor home-guard natives, but at present is the employment of above sixty families of lake Indians.... Since the year 1762 the lake Indians have forsaken their rich hunting grounds and harboured about York Factory killing deer for brandy, which prevents them from getting up to the lakes before the frost sets in."[29] The northward shift of some Northern Ojibway in 1762 may have been in response to declining fur-trade opportunities in the south as a result of the fall of New France to British forces in the early 1760s.

By 1775, some Northern Ojibway who traded at York Factory had moved close enough to the coast to be considered residents of the lowlands. Ferdinand Jacobs reported on June 17, 1775, that "7400 Beaver [made beaver] have been traded from the Bungees [Northern Ojibway], Port Nelson [Nelson River Cree] and home Indians [Lowland Cree], we having neither seen nor heard from any upland Indians."[30] Earlier, in 1771, Andrew Graham had also observed the northward movement of the Northern Ojibway in the vicinity of York Factory. He said they "command all the lakes from York Fort rivers [Nelson and Hayes] down towards Canada; leaving the poor degenerated home-guards [Lowland Cree] scarcely room between them and the sea."[31] By 1775, he was more specific about their location: "These [Northern Ojibway] inhabit the Country from about an hundred miles from the sea-coast of Hudson's Bay south and easterly unto the great Lakes of Christinaux.... It is my opinion that this people have drawn up to the Northward gradually as the Keiskatchewans [Cree] receded from it towards the south-west."[32] In 1775, Graham identified eight "tribes" or subgroups within the Northern Ojibway population who traded at the HBC coastal posts. Graham was familiar with the upland country only through Indian reports and a few HBC inland travellers.

Andrew Graham's List of the Nakawawuck (Northern Ojibway) Nation

Name of Tribe*	Territory**	Trading Location***
Shumataway	Henley House River+	AF, SH, & YF
Mithquagomow	Red or Bloody River	AF
Ougibowy	Winnipeg River	AF
Uinescaw-Sepee	Winisk River	SH & AF
Wapus	Hare River	SH & AF
Nameu-Sepee	Trout River	SH
Christianaux	Lake Winnipeg [Nipigon]	AF, MF, & SH
Mistehay Sakahegan	Great Lake Winnipeg	YF, SH, & AF

Sources: *Graham, 1969: 206; **Richardson, 1969, vol. 2: 37; ***Graham, 1969: 206, and HBCA, E.2/9, fo.84. YF= York Factory, SH= Severn House, AF= Albany Fort, MF= Moose Fort + Shumataway may also refer to the Shamattawa River near York Factory

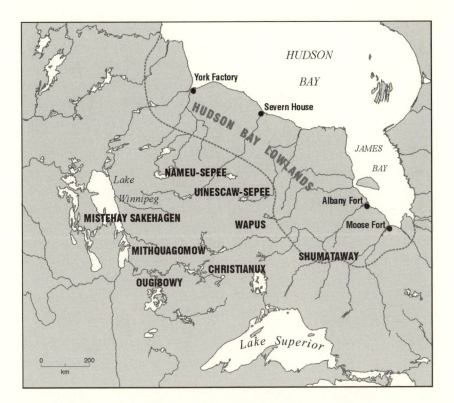

Tribes of the Northern Ojibway Nation

By the time HBC fur traders established inland trading posts in the 1770s, the boundary between the Lowland Cree and Northern Ojibway followed roughly the boundary between the Hudson Bay lowlands and the upland Shield region. In 1839, George Barnston described the boundary line between the Lowland Cree and the Northern Ojibway near Martins Fall as crossing the "Atawapiscut and Capusco Rivers somewhat obliquely, and runs through swamps and forests."[33] The boundary was sharply defined in the area between the Hayes River and Gods River. The HBC report for the Island Lake District in 1827 noted the differences between the Lowland Cree who lived near Oxford House and the Northern Ojibway who lived near Gods Lake. In a reply to a company directive that one of the trading posts should be closed, and the two groups made to visit one post, the trader stated:

I am afraid not—they are not only distinct Tribes, but the Damn Algonquons [Northern Ojibway] have but an indifferent opinion of the

Swampy Crees [Lowland Cree] of Oxford—while the latter proffess an unutterable aversion to the hostile disposition of the former, which in my opinion is a pretty strong proof against an immediate union of these two tribes.[34]

In 1824, Alexander Stewart, who was in charge of the HBC's Island Lake trading post, also noted the difference between the Lowland Cree who lived near Oxford House and the Northern Ojibway who lived in the vicinity of Island Lake and Red Sucker Lake. Stewart remarked that the Northern Ojibway were "good hunters, superstitious and very ignorant and some of them, particularly at the latter place [Red Sucker Lake], very quarrelsome not only with the traders but amongst themselves." In contrast, he depicted the Lowland Cree as "industrious and much more civilized than the above [Northern Ojibway]."[35] The characterization of the Lowland Cree as cooperative, even timid in the face of armed challenges, and the Northern Ojibway as aggressive, was common in the nineteenth-century HBC records. Stewart attributed the milder disposition of the Lowland Cree to their long association with HBC traders.

In many other areas, the interface between the Lowland Cree and Northern Ojibway resulted in considerable overlap in the territory occupied by the two groups. By the early 1800s, many European fur traders noted a mixed Cree-Ojibway dialect spoken by Indians who lived in territories shared by Lowland Cree and Northern Ojibway. In 1804, Duncan Cameron observed that the Indians who lived in the Severn River basin near the edge of the lowlands spoke a language that was "a mixture of the Ojiboiay, or Chippeway as some call it, spoken at Lake Superior and the Cree or Masquigon spoken at Hudson's Bay." Cameron believed that the unique language was a result of several generations of intermarriage and mixing between the Ojibway and Cree people: "Every old man with whom I conversed, and from whom I made some enquiry on this subject, told me that his father or grand father was from either of these two places [Lake Superior or Hudson Bay]."[36] In 1833, a report from the HBC post at Long Lake near Lake Superior noted a mixed Cree-Ojibway language spoken there by "a mixed race of Solteauxs and Masquegongue Tribes. Their language is a mixture of both the latter tongues, but in many instances varies much, for a pure Solteaux speaker requires to be for some time with the Indians of this post before he can understand them perfectly."[37] In 1839, George Barnston commented that the mixing of Lowland Cree and Northern Ojibway near Martins Fall had "produced a Half Cree, Half Sauteux Breed, affecting the Language and Character in no slight degree."[38] The HBC traders referred to some people as "half-Bungee," further suggesting that marriages occurred between Lowland Cree and Northern Ojibway. The half-Bungee population in the hinterland of York Factory appears to have grown after the 1782-83 smallpox epidemic. Joseph Colen was the first to use the term, in August 1786 at York Factory. In the summer of 1792, he noted the arrival of several large groups of "half-Bungees." One group came to the factory in ten canoes and two other groups arrived in six canoes each.[39] As late as 1929, the term Bungee was used to describe people of mixed Lowland Cree and Northern Ojibway ancestry who lived near Big Trout Lake on the margins of the Hudson Bay lowlands. Sydney Keighley, who worked for the HBC at the Big Trout Lake post, remarked, "The native people were a mixture of groups. There were some Cree, some Ojibway and some were called Bungee. I believe this last group should properly be called Saulteaux. They were a mixture of Cree and Ojibway, and had developed a language using both parts of the parent languages."[40] In 1852, Peter Jacobs, an Ojibway-speaking travelling missionary, visited the Rossville Mission near Norway House and commented, "I am not a competent judge of this mixed language of Ojibway, Cree, and Swampy. The Cree and Swampy are nearer kin to each other than either to the noble and majestic Ojibway."[41] In 1831, John McLean noted that the Indians who lived near Norway House "speak a jargon of Cree and Sauteux, which sounds very harshly."[42] The mixing of Lowland Cree and Northern Ojibway extended to the area north of Lake Superior near Michipicoten where George Keith, who was in charge of the HBC post there, remarked in 1830 that "there does not exist a doubt that the majority [of the Indian population] derive their origin from the Ojhibeway or Saulteau Tribe, altho' a number of them are descended from the Maskegon or Swampy Cree Tribe."[43]

The mixing of Lowland Cree and Northern Ojibway also occurred among other groups of Indians who lived near the edge of the lowlands. In 1886, at Trout Lake, A.P. Low noted that "these Indians speak a language made up chiefly of Cree words, with a mixture of the Saulteaux dialects,"[44] and W. McInnes, who conducted a geological survey in the area around the headwaters of the Winisk and Attawapiskat rivers, reported: "They are of the Ojibway tribe, though mixed to a certain extent with the Cree of Hudson Bay basin, the purest Ojibway stock being found among the bands about the heads of the rivers. They seem to be men of larger frame than the Crees of the coast."[45] J.C. Boileau Grant, at Island Lake in 1929, reported that "Father Du Beau of the Roman Catholic mission at Island Lake, a very good linguist, tells me that the language spoken around the part of Island Lake at which he is stationed is a mixture of Saulteaux and Cree; some words being Saulteaux, others being Cree; compound words being in many cases hybrids of the two."[46]

The mixed Lowland Cree and Northern Ojibway speech has been the subject of several recent linguistic studies. Evelyn Todd, who conducted linguistic studies among Indian communities in the upper Severn River basin in the 1960s, explained that "Native speakers, who do not differentiate between language and dialect, refer to their language as anihsinapemowin, 'language of the Indians', and describe it as a mixture of Cree and Saulteaux."[47] Todd concluded the language was "definitely Ojibwa," and called it the Severn Ojibwa dialect. Although a number of Lowland Cree lived among the Severn Ojibwa communities, she thought "few of the dialect features of Severn Ojibwa can be directly attributed to the influence of Cree."[48] H.C. Wolfart came to the same general conclusions in his study, with S.M. Shrofel, of the Severn dialect among the people who lived in the area around Island Lake.[49] Shrofel and Wolfart concluded that it is "a dialect of Ojibwa with an admixture of Cree," and that "the interference of Cree is not very prominent in the verbal morphology."[50] They also agreed that the Severn Ojibwa dialect was distinct from the Ojibway dialect spoken at Berens River and points farther south. Wolfart believed the differences could be attributed to the migration routes followed by the two groups, and suggested that the dialect of the Ojibway living at Berens River and south along the east coast of Lake Winnipeg was more closely connected to that spoken by the Ojibway in the Lake of the Woods and Rainy River region.

In the 1930s, Irving Hallowell traced the genealogies of the Ojibway who lived at the mouth of the Berens River and found that migration to the area had occurred from all directions except the north.[51] The Island Lake Ojibway traced their immediate origins to the upper Severn River area. This northern migration route was noted as early as 1815 by James Sutherland, the HBC trader in charge of Norway House.[52] The two-pronged migration of the Northern Ojibway can also be deduced from cultural traits that distinguish the people who occupied the upper Severn River area from those who lived along the Berens River. Edward Rogers noted, "Cultural traits generally graded imperceptibly into one another [Northern Ojibway groups] throughout the region. One partial exception is between the Indians of the Deer Lake area [upper Severn River] and those of Pikangikum [upper Berens River]. Between the two runs a southeast-northwest line above which are the Northern Ojibwa who lack clan names, Midewiwin, and the sucking tube, traits found among the Indians below the line."[53] The migration of the Northern Ojibway north of Lake

Superior probably followed the transportation routes later used by European fur traders who settled in that region known as Le Petit Nord (Little North). Some Ojibway probably followed the most direct route connecting Lake Superior and Lake Winnipeg. Other groups of Ojibway entered the region from the Lake Nipigon basin. Some ventured westward toward Lake Winnipeg, while others moved northward to the edge of the Hudson Bay lowlands.

The Upland Cree

By the time HBC traders established inland trading posts in the 1770s, the Upland Cree occupied the territory upriver in the valleys of the Hayes, Nelson, and Churchill rivers. According to Andrew Graham, the Upland Cree were known as the *Pimmechikemow, Poethinecaw, Missinepee,* and *Wenunnetowuck.* The Upland Cree probably occupied a larger territory, including an area east of Lake Winnipeg, prior to the northwestward migration of the Northern Ojibway. This is consistent with Upland Cree oral traditions. For example, in the winter of 1787-88, David Thompson interviewed an Upland Cree elder named Saukamappee, who related accounts of the westward migration of his people. The ninety-year-old Saukamappee, who was born near the confluence of the Saskatchewan and Pasquia rivers (near The Pas, Manitoba), recalled that his people moved up the Saskatchewan River and settled beyond the Eagle Hills because they were pushed away from their homelands by people who came from east of Lake Winnipeg.[54]

Later fur-trade accounts indicate that the westward migration of Indian people continued in the early nineteenth century. George Holdsworth, who was stationed at Berens River in 1815, thought it "probable that these tribes were formerly confined to the East side of Lake Winipic, but from the difficulty of procuring subsistence occasioned by the diminution of animals, there appears to have been a general migration to the westward, one tribe displacing or rather driving back other tribes till at length a greater part are now found to the westward of it whilst the original inhabitants of the westward are driven still farther into the interior."[55]

Relations between the Lowland Cree and their adjacent Upland Cree neighbours were generally amicable. However, the fur traders noted that the Upland Cree who lived farther away often extorted food and other goods from the Lowland Cree when they met near the trading posts. The far-away Upland Cree and other upland nations, such as the Assiniboine, usually travelled into the lowlands to trade at the coastal posts in large

flotillas of canoes. These large groups were able to intimidate the Lowland
Cree, and the Lowland Cree stayed away from the posts during the summer trading season to avoid contacts with the upland people. In the summer of 1716, parties of Upland Cree who had arrived at York Factory to
find that the annual supply ship from England had failed to arrive robbed
Lowland Cree of goods and food. Even the captain of the Lowland Cree
was victimized by these marauders. James Knight reported that "the Captain of this River and his Gang arrived to Day but they mett with about 40
of the Upland Indians that Plundered him and took away all there Victualls."[56]
Later that month, the captain warned Knight that the failure of the HBC
supply ship had caused extraordinary suffering, and that there might be an
attack on the factory by the upland Indians. Knight described how

> came in the Captain of this River in very bad humour and told me that
> all the Indians were very much exasperated against us for their Disap-
> pointment of a Supply of Goods after such a fatigue in coming so farr for
> it and not having any and withall he told me he would be gon from the
> factory for he desires not stay any longer for he believes the Indians
> would come and attempt to do us a Mischief that cuts us of[f] that they
> shall never be no more disappointed in their coming down as they have
> been Both by the french and us and withall cautioned me not to send any
> Man abroad.[57]

In the summer of 1717, a group of Upland Cree led by "Old Caesar"
terrorized the Lowland Cree who were near York Factory. James Knight
commented that "they are very rude amongst our Indians here takeing
away their wives and daughters by force and lyes with them and these poor
fellows [Lowland Indians] are so fearfull as they darst not offer to hinder
them."[58] The Lowland Cree usually kept clear of York Factory for fear of
being molested by the upland people. The Lowland Cree were knowledgeable about the usual travel times of the upland traders, and stayed clear of
the Hayes and Nelson rivers during the peak trading period. John Newton,
who was in charge of York Factory in the summer of 1749, observed: "Sent
ye Longboat over to the French Creek, brought 3 familys of Indians who
intend for the N. [Nelson] River, but they as well as those who came
before, are afraid to goe till ye great gang of trading Indians that comes
down that River have been here and gone again."[59]

In 1786, Humphrey Marten noted that the Upland Cree who lived in
the upper Nelson River area were still accustomed to robbing the Lowland Cree of their goods. He observed that "the North [Nelson] river
Indians did not chuse to trade, while they stayed; consequently, they were

disappointed in the rich harvest, they hoped to obtain, by plundering (in their usual unmerciful manner) the home Indians, who dare not refuse them, what goods they take a fancy to."[60]

At Severn House, the HBC traders noted that the Lowland Cree also feared the Uplanders, and avoided contact as much as possible. In 1783, William Falconer remarked that "they [Lowland Cree] being afraid of the Uplanders, as I have seen during my stay here, when only one canoe of Uplanders come down, the very sight of them drove every one of these Homeguards away."[61] The traders there sometimes helped the Lowland Cree move away from the post before the upland traders arrived. The upland people who traded at Severn House sometimes acted in a belligerent way to the HBC men as well as to the Lowland Cree, and, in 1760, Humphrey Marten was forced to arm his men in order to get some "saucy" Uplanders out of the house.[62]

The Albany River Lowland Cree appear to have been more at ease with their upland neighbours. In some cases, the Lowland Cree extorted goods from the upland traders who visited Albany Fort. In the summer of 1725, company trader Richard Staunton complained that the Lowland Cree were very troublesome because they waited near the fort to drink brandy that they received from upland traders.[63] Some Albany River Lowland Cree acted very aggressively against the upland people who came to trade at Albany Fort. An Albany River Lowland Cree leader named Wappisiss or Woudbe was noted for intimidating the upland traders and extorting furs and other goods. Because of his behaviour, Woudbe was also called the "Land Pirate" by the HBC men.[64]

The Eastmain Cree

The eastern neighbours of the Lowland Cree were called *Oupeshepou*, or "Eastmain Cree."[65] The Nottaway River marked the approximate boundary between the Lowland Cree and the Eastmain Cree. Although the dialect spoken by the Eastmain Cree was derived from the same basic language (Algonquian), it was noticeably different from the speech of the Lowland Cree. Richard Preston observed that the Lowland Cree "cannot follow a conversation in the East Main language at all."[66] Truman Michelson, who conducted linguistic studies among the communities on the west and east coasts of James Bay, stated that "Rupert's House Cree and East Main Cree are really not Cree at all, but Montagnais-Nascapi dialects."[67]

The Eastmain Cree did not interact much with the Lowland Cree. The Moose River Lowland Cree occasionally visited East Main House to trade with the HBC, but they did not have close ties with the Eastmain Cree. Toby Morantz noted that the Moose River Lowland Cree often bullied the local people whom they met near East Main House. One Moose River Cree extorted payment from the Eastmain Cree for protection. Morantz quoted an HBC trader at East Main House who stated in 1792 that the Eastmain Cree were "naturally timid [therefore] they are soon imposed upon."[68]

Albany and Moose River Lowland Cree often passed through the territory of the Eastmain Cree during the summer, en route to war against the Inuit who lived on the eastern coast of Hudson Bay. During these forays, the Albany and Moose River Lowland Cree were unopposed by the Eastmain Cree. Not only did the Eastmain Cree not get involved in these raids against the Inuit, they were occasionally the targets of frustrated warriors. In the summer of 1738, a war party of Lowland Cree warriors killed three or four families of Eastmain Cree after failing to find their intended Inuit victims.[69] The killing of Eastmain Cree instead of Inuit was a common occurrence, according to the testimony of Eastmain Cree who told HBC traders in 1755 that it was "Common for ye Albany and Moose River Indians when they cannot find the Eusquamays they kill Our Indians, for their Scalps and Makes their country Men Believe there Scalps is Eusquamays. Robinson Crouseo [an Eastmain Indian] tells me that his Brother and 3 More was kill'd by the Albany and Moose River Indians about 12 years ago and scalp'd."[70]

The Eastmain Cree did not attempt to rebuff the aggressive behaviour of the Lowland Cree. On the other hand, the Lowland Cree were not interested in territorial expansion or gaining access to resources in the East Main territory. Although they were relatively close neighbours, relations between the Lowland Cree and the Eastmain Cree remained distant during the fur-trade period. The Aboriginal fur trade that focussed on James Bay from rivers draining into the bay from west and east probably promoted closer ties between the Lowland Cree and Eastmain Cree in the pre-European fur-trade period. After European fur-trade posts were built in the region, the fur-trade orientation was focussed away from the bay, and thus weakened earlier linkages that may have supported a closer relationship between the two groups. The Europeans split the bay-side trade into two, largely autonomous, administrative units. As a result, there was little interaction between the Lowland Cree and Eastmain Cree during the European fur-trade period.

4.
Distant Enemies:
The Inuit, Chipewyan, and Iroquois

The Inuit

Collectively, the Lowland Cree occupied a territory spanning about 2000 kilometres along the Hudson Bay coast, stretching from the Churchill River on the north to the Nottaway River on the south. During the sixteenth to eighteenth centuries, the Lowland Cree engaged in warfare against enemies whose home territories were situated a thousand or more kilometres inland and in all directions. Such well-defined "external relations" suggest how they viewed their territories and their relations with their more distant neighbours.

When European fur-trade posts were established on the coast of Hudson Bay and James Bay, the Lowland Cree were actively engaged in warfare with the Inuit who lived in the northern areas, on both the western and eastern coasts of Hudson Bay. Warfare patterns described by early European observers suggest that hostility between the Inuit and the Lowland Cree predated European contact, and involved reciprocal revenge-raiding into each other's territory. However, Inuit raids into Lowland Cree territory ceased soon after the fur-trade posts were established. On the other hand, the Lowland Cree continued to raid into Inuit territory long after the posts were built.

Many European observers attributed the success of the Lowland Cree in their warfare against the Inuit to their early acquisition of firearms and other European weapons such as knives and bayonets. Recently, several scholars have disputed the view that European arms were superior to Aboriginal weapons. Joan Townsend's comparative study of the effect of European and Aboriginal weapons in Alaska concluded that European firearms provided neither technical nor tactical advantages in early warfare.[1] In order to accept Townsend's theory, one must assume that the Europeans who visited the Hudson Bay trading posts must have consistently exaggerated the impact of European firearms in the warfare between the Lowland Cree and the Inuit. In fact, the evidence clearly shows a correlation between the acquisition of European weapons by the Lowland Cree and their success in war against the Inuit. Shortly after the establishment of fur-trade posts within the Lowland Cree territory, the Inuit on both coasts of Hudson Bay responded by shifting their territorial range farther northward.

Lowland Cree raiding parties travelled hundreds of kilometres to reach the Inuit. Generally, men were involved in the warfare, but some accounts indicate that women and entire families occasionally accompanied the warriors. They travelled in small canoes, ranging in number from several to several dozen. War parties were mobilized in early summer, usually after the spring goose hunt, and returned in late summer, generally in time for the fall goose hunt. The warfare was characterized by surprise attacks on small Inuit camps. The objective was to kill adult males and the elderly, and to take young women and children captives.

The cause of the warfare between the Lowland Cree and the Inuit has perplexed scholars. Territorial expansion for economic or other reasons can be ruled out because the Lowland Cree did not occupy Inuit territory, nor did they use these areas for hunting or other purposes. Andrew Graham commented that "revenge, jealousy, animosities, death of one of the family, or even the indulgence of an inhuman levity, are sufficient for a hostile expedition."[2] Daniel Francis's study of Lowland Cree-Inuit warfare on the eastern coast of Hudson Bay concluded that warfare was "motivated by a complex of psychological and cultural needs."[3] He pointed to a number of explanations offered by contemporary European observers. These included the Lowland Cree belief that the Inuit possessed magical powers that caused shortage of game, sickness, and death among their ranks.[4] Another factor was prestige for Lowland Cree men, who gained warrior status by participating in these raids. The taking of Inuit captives, especially children and young women, suggests that the warfare satisfied other needs. Some Europeans noted that gifts of Inuit captives to southern Indian groups such as

the Ottawa cemented alliances and prevented outbreaks of warfare be-
tween the Lowland Cree and their southern neighbours.[5] Sales or gifts of
Inuit captives to the HBC, although portrayed by the latter as motivated by
Indian economic gains and company compassion for the Inuit "slaves,"
may have also been linked to alliances between the Lowland Cree and the
HBC. Another factor suggested by Francis, and supported by historical accounts, was revenge for former Inuit attacks against the Lowland Cree.
Although no Inuit raids into Lowland Cree territory were recorded by
European observers, there is sufficient evidence from Indian accounts that
point to aggressive Inuit warfare against the Lowland Cree prior to European contact. It is possible that revenge continued to be a factor that motivated hostility against the Inuit even after generations had passed since the
last Inuit attacks. The memory of those raids may have been kept alive
through the transmission of stories that recorded the oral history of the
Lowland Cree.

The Western Hudson Bay Inuit, also known as the Caribou Eskimo,
periodically ranged as far south as the Churchill River at the time of European contact.[6] The Lowland Cree formerly called the Churchill River
Manoteou-sibi or *Manato-e-sepe*. Jeremie, who recorded the former name,
translated it as meaning "strangers' river,"[7] and Coats offered the latter version, which he translated as "a sea-like river."[8] In 1716, James Knight, who
was in charge of York Factory, learned from some Lowland Cree that great
numbers of Inuit visited Churchill every four or five years to hunt white
whales and build boats.[9] Earlier, Nicolas Jeremie had written that Inuit
sometimes came by boat to the mouth of the Churchill River to scavenge
for iron left behind by Jens Munk, who wintered there in 1619-20.[10] James
Isham recalled that "the Ehuskemay's, who before the English Setled here
us'd frequently to come to Churchill River or Ehuskemay point so Call'd,
from their g'raves and mark's of their Dwellings, some of which are still
Remaining."[11] Joseph Robson provided another account of pre-European
Inuit occupation of the Churchill River area.

> Churchill was much frequented by the Eskimaux before we settled there,
> the point on which the fort is built, being called Eskimaux-point. Upon
> digging for the fort many traces were discovered of their abode here,
> such as the pit in which they secured their provisions, pieces of stone-
> pots, spears, arrows, &c. This point they kept for some time after they
> were driven from the adjacent country, because it lies far in the open sea,
> they could discover the distant approaches of their enemies, and repair in
> time to their canoes, in the management of which they are peculiarly

dextrous: but they were at length forced to go farther northward to Cape
Eskimaux and Whale Cove: and are now totally dispossessed of this retreat.[12]

Andrew Graham added that "many of them [Inuit] formerly resided
upon Churchill River, but on the Company's building a Fort there, in the
beginning of this present century, and the Indians resorting thither to trade,
the Esquimaux retired farther to the north."[13]

The Lowland Cree depiction of the Inuit as "bloodthirsty people"[14]
suggests that the Inuit had been aggressors in the warfare against the Lowland Cree in the period prior to European contact. Nicolas Jeremie provided a rather fantastic story of Inuit barbarism: "They make war on all
their neighbours, and when they kill or capture any of their enemies, they
eat them raw and drink their blood. They even make infants at the breast
drink it, so as to instil in them the barbarism and ardour of war from the
tenderest of years."[15] There is also intriguing evidence that formerly the
Inuit had raided deep into Lowland Cree territory. For example, James
Knight was informed in 1716 that "they [Lowland Cree] see one of them
[an Inuit umiak] off Severn once which they took it by the bigness of it to
be one of our Ships under Sail twill they see them putt into Shore and take
in a great number of there Men as was along Shore hunting Deer and
Geese."[16] This was a hostile raid, and the phrase "take in a great number of
there Men" probably referred to Lowland Cree who were casualties of the
skirmish, or possibly captives. The event appears to have taken place after
European contact, because the Inuit vessel had been mistaken for a European ship. The reference to "one of our ships" suggests the attack took
place some time after the HBC settled at York Factory.

Although no Inuit raids in the area around the Severn River were recorded by the HBC after 1717, animosity between the Severn River Lowland Cree and the Inuit endured until at least the mid–eighteenth century.
In the spring of 1747, James Isham, Chief Factor at York Factory, recorded
that a "Severn Indian or more properly an Albany Indian [perhaps because
he usually traded at Albany Fort] came here with his family to trade. But
with a Design for to go to war against the Esquimau's to ye Northward of
here. But [I] argued the case with him and persuaded him from it."[17]

It is also evident that the Lowland Cree who traded at York Factory had
raided deep into the Inuit territory north of the Churchill River prior to
the arrival of the Europeans.[18] James Knight interviewed several Lowland
Cree at York Factory in the summer of 1716, one of whom remarked that
"he has been many times in their [Inuit] country to Warr against them but
they never had the luck to kill any Iskemays."[19] Other Lowland Cree described to Knight geographical details of the Hudson Bay coast far to the

north of the Churchill River, where "the Shore is very flatt all along a foul broken ground out a great way towards the Sea and the water ebbs so farr out that they cannot see the Land in there Canoos at Low water but when they are gotten pretty ways to the Norward the Land rises very high again and the water begins to grow deep to the very Shore and that there is abundance of islands and many Iskemays."[20] Knight estimated that these people had been as far north as 64 degrees, in the vicinity of Chesterfield Inlet. This agrees with statements made to Jeremie by Lowland Cree who had travelled along the coast of the bay north of the Churchill River to "a strait where one can readily see across from one side to the other."[21]

During the early European fur-trade period, the region between the Nelson and Churchill rivers was an unoccupied buffer zone between the warring parties.[22] For a long period after the establishment of Churchill Fort in 1717, the Inuit kept far to the north. Contemporary HBC observers believed the Lowland Cree were able to drive the Inuit northward because of their acquisition of superior European firearms.[23] The HBC traders at Churchill were unsuccessful in discouraging Lowland Cree war parties from going north to war against the Inuit. When Henry Ellis visited York Factory in 1746-47, he described Lowland Cree raids against the Inuit that persisted at least into the mid-eighteenth century. He believed the Lowland Cree blamed the Inuit for any misfortunes that befell the Lowland Indians.

> The Indians are inclinable to War; if there is a bad season of hunting in the Winter, or if anyone of their People is missing, or that they have a Sickness amongst them, they must prepare in Spring to go and seek out the Eskemaux, and make a Carnage of them; for they attribute to them the Cause of their Misfortunes: It is the Eskemaux that have killed their Friend; it is the Eskemaux have kept the Deer away; and the Sickness is occasion'd by a Charm or Witchery of the Eskemaux.[24]

According to Ellis, the Lowland Cree prepared for war in the spring. War parties were made up of men and a few women, and specially built canoes facilitated quick travel to the Inuit territory and flight in the aftermath of the raid. Dried meat was taken to provision the war parties because time was not available to hunt on the war trail. The Indians endeavoured to kill all the Inuit men, but captured women and children. Male children were sold to the HBC as "slaves" in exchange for brandy. The York Factory account book for 1719-20 included expenditures for "ye Esquemoes and Company's Slave Boys."[25] Ellis also noted that Inuit scalps were taken and displayed prominently in festive dances when the warriors returned to York Factory.

The Lowland Cree warfare against the Western Hudson Bay Inuit gradually diminished after the building of Churchill Fort in 1717. The HBC traders at Churchill actively discouraged the Lowland Cree from raiding the Inuit in the hope that Inuit would be drawn in to trade. However, the Lowland Cree, assisted by European firearms, had already driven the Inuit far to the north by the time Churchill Fort was established. Churchill Fort soon attracted other Aboriginal people, including Chipewyan from the upper Churchill River region, and this further minimized contacts between the Inuit and Lowland Cree.

The Eastern Hudson Bay Inuit, also known as the Inuit of Quebec, occupied the territory north of Richmond Gulf during the early fur-trade period. According to the fur traders, the territorial range of the Eastern Hudson Bay Inuit extended farther south prior to European contact. Joseph Robson observed that the Inuit "used to inhabit the country on the eastmain between the straits and the bottom of the Bay: but they are since driven away to the northward by the Indians, who are rendered much superior to them, on account of the supply of arms and ammunition which they receive from the English."[26] Other early fur-trade accounts indicated that the Inuit had formerly conducted raids into Eastmain Indian territory. John Oldmixon reported that the Inuit "sometimes in slight Parties make Incursions on the other Indians, and, having knock'd 8 or 10 on the Head, return in triumph."[27] William Coats remarked that the Indians who lived on the eastern coast of James Bay "have been cruelly ravaged by the Usquemows, with whom at present [they are] at peace." Elsewhere, Coats commented that the Eastmain Indians "live in a sort of servile frindship with them."[28]

Like the Lowland Cree-Inuit warfare on the western Hudson Bay coast, the pre-European-contact wars on the Eastmain were characterized by revenge-raiding into each other's territory. Lowland Cree raids into Inuit territory there were noted as early as 1686, when Chevalier de Troyes, who met four Indians near the mouth of the Rupert River, commented that "ils venoient de faire la guerre aux Eskimos."[29] Although it is impossible to determine who these people were, the presence of Inuit slaves living among the Lowland Cree indicates that the Lowland Cree were involved in warfare against the Inuit at the time of initial European fur-trade contact. For example, the 1693-94 Albany Fort account book noted that James Knight purchased "an As'scomore slave boy for the use of ye factory." The price paid was a gun, blanket, kettle, one pound of tobacco, and a woman's shroud.[30]

Lowland Cree warfare against the Eastern Hudson Bay Inuit was recorded in other early Albany Fort journals. On April 27, 1707, Anthony

Beale noted that six Lowland Cree warriors left Albany Fort and headed toward the Eastmain. That party was followed on May 19, 1707, by a canoe of "Home Indians" who went to the "Wars against the Eskemaise."[31] The first detailed account of Lowland Cree warfare against the Eastmain Inuit was recorded in the journal on May 25, 1728. Joseph Myatt, who was in charge of Albany Fort, noted "eight Curnoes of our home Indians fitted out from hence in order to goe to Warrs with the Esquomays." The war party was headed for the Eastmain, north of the Slude (Eastmain) River. Although HBC policy directed its officers to discourage warfare, Myatt was unable to prevent these Lowland Cree from going to war because "severall of the Home Indians being Disordered the last Winter they attribute all those things to the Mallice of their Enimies."[32] Several of the warriors returned to Albany Fort on August 7, 1728, without having found any Inuit. On May 29, 1730, a war party consisting of several Albany Lowland Cree travelled to Moose River "in order to joyne the Indians of that place to goe to Warrs against the Esquomeas."[33] Once again, Joseph Myatt tried but was unable to stop them from going to war. In the summer of 1735, a war party of Albany and Moose River Lowland Cree raided into Inuit territory on the Eastmain coast. On May 29, 1735, five canoes of Albany River Lowland Cree warriors arrived at Moose Fort, and on June 2, seven canoes departed "to the Eastmain to wars with the Usqueemay." The warriors returned to Moose Fort about two months later with fourteen Inuit scalps and one girl prisoner.[34] On June 8, 1736, a large war party was assembled at Albany Fort, led by "ye Old Captin of this River [Indian Doctor]." The Albany Fort records indicate that this was an all-male war party, who left their families at home. On July 24, Joseph Adams noted that "several of our home Indian familys came here today whose husbands are at ye warrs."[35] Seventeen canoes of Albany River Lowland Cree, or "Westmain Indians," were joined by eight canoes of Moose River Lowland Cree on this war expedition. On July 30, 1736, some of the warriors returned to Moose Fort and reported they had killed five Inuit men and fifteen women, and they had taken ten Inuit children prisoners.[36] Six Inuit children were taken by the Albany River Lowland Cree, while four remained with the Moose River Lowland Cree.[37]

One of the Inuit captives brought back by the Albany River Lowland Cree that year was purchased by the HBC. The Albany Fort account book noted that one pound of tobacco, one gallon of brandy, and one and one-half yards of blue cloth were paid for "a young Eskemoe boy."[38] Several Inuit boys were raised at Albany Fort, and became productive employees of the company. Jack Eskemay, who began serving the company in 1742, may have been the boy who was purchased by the HBC in 1736. Other Inuit children had difficulty in adapting to life in the company's service. For example, Joseph Isbister, who was in charge of Albany Fort on August 30, 1746, wrote that he "confined ye Eskemay Boy for stealing Goods out of ye Wharehouse and shirts from ye men, he is such a wicked Boy, that he never will prove a good servant to the Company, therefore am resolved to turn him away among the Northern Indians on ye East Main coast."[39]

Inuit slaves continued to be purchased by the HBC throughout much of the eighteenth century. On June 10, 1780, Thomas Hutchins noted that "Tolio the Esquimaux" drowned at Moose Fort,[40] and on April 19, 1783, Edward Jarvis reported that he had "traded an Esquimaux boy" from the Albany River Lowland Cree. The Inuit boy was about seven years old, and Jarvis gave him the name Easter. Jarvis paid thirty made beaver for Easter, but he justified the expenditure because the Lowland Cree had planned to kill the boy.[41]

In most cases, the HBC reported that the war parties consisted of Albany River and Moose River Lowland Cree, although on September 10, 1738, Thomas Bird at Albany Fort noted that "five Uplanders came here today that has been att ye Warrs with ye Eskemoes."[42] The identity of these upland people is uncertain, but since they travelled up the Albany River it is likely they were Northern Ojibway. Lowland Cree raids against the Eastmain Inuit continued to be reported by the HBC in the 1740s and 1750s. On June 6, 1755, a group of people in twelve canoes arrived at Albany Fort from the north. Joseph Isbister described them as mostly "home Indians" who intended to go to war against the Eastmain Inuit, and tried unsuccessfully to dissuade them from their intended plan: "I taulkt with the leading Indian about it and forbid him to go and used my utmost indeavours to perswade them from going upon so idle an enterprise, but all to no purpose, they said that they must go because they are displeased with the Eskemays for the loss of their friends and some children that died this last winter (as if they were ye cause thereof) so idle are the notions of these people."[43]

On June 7, 1757, Robert Temple, who was in charge of Albany Fort, reported that "a great many of our Indian hunters are gone a Usquemeaux hunting." Some of them returned on August 22, 1757, in time for the fall goose hunt.[44] On June 9, 1766, a large group of Lowland Cree assembled at Albany Fort and prepared for war against the Eastmain Inuit. Humphrey Marten, who was in charge of the fort, observed that "25 men came dressed and painted to the Fort, they said they were determined to go to war with the Esquemaes, on which they sang the war song, after which about 60 more men, women and children, all home guard, came to joyne with them in the Begging dance, they said it was usual for the Chief to give them great Presents on such occasions." Marten complied with their request because "they expected I would do as my Predecessors had done before."[45] The war party set off from Albany Fort the next day, but most of the warriors returned ten days later because of sickness that had spread through their ranks shortly after leaving Moose Fort.

On May 28, 1770, Humphrey Marten again noted that "eleven canoes of home Indians set off for the Uskemay hunt, as they phrase it."[46] On July 1, 1770, one man, four women, and three children belonging to the warriors arrived at Albany Fort for food. On April 7, 1774, four Albany River Lowland Cree went to Moose Fort to join with the Lowland Cree there in an "Esquimaux hunt."[47] The warriors were unusually late in returning. By September 2, 1774, Marten remarked that "almost all the other hunting Indians in despair, at not hearing from their friends that went to war with the Esquimaus."[48] The warriors were also missed by the company men at Albany Fort because they were usually employed as goose hunters. Thomas Hutchins, who was in charge of the fort in 1775, complained in a letter to William Falconer at Severn House that "our Goose season turned out but poorly, having ten of the best hunters about at war with the Esquimaux."[49] Finally, almost six months after they had left Albany Fort, the warriors returned with a prominent leader of the Lowland Cree goose hunters, Lieutenant Wauchusk, among them. No information relating to their success or failure was reported in the HBC records.

On May 14, 1777, Thomas Hutchins again noted, "I find the hunting Indians are bent upon another Expedition against the Esquemaux."[50] However, he did not elaborate on this planned raid so it is difficult to assess whether a war party was actually mustered. And again, on May 23, 1781, he reported that "several of our Hunters set off for the Esquimaux War."[51] Apparently, they had been invited to participate in this war, because several days earlier Hutchins had noted the arrival of some Moose River Lowland Cree who had "come to see their friends." Some of the Albany River warriors returned to the fort on July 1, 1781, but Hutchins did not report on the success or failure of the war party. Some HBC reports of Lowland Cree war parties indicated that entire families took part in these expeditions. For example, on June 5, 1782, Hutchins noted "3 families of Indians going on the Esquemay hunt."[52]

The HBC records from Severn House (beginning in 1759) did not contain specific information concerning the participation of Severn River Lowland Cree in warfare against the Inuit. However, indirect evidence clearly indicates that the local Lowland Cree were involved. For example, on August 14, 1793, John Ballenden, who was in charge of Severn House, noted, "Invalid Natives repairing the seine net, a Blind Esquimaux woman superintends."[53] On March 3, 1796, he recorded the death of the same blind Inuit woman and that "she has resided many years at Severn, and was taken when a child from the Eastmain Esquimaux by the Albany and Moose River Indians who annually wars with them."[54]

On June 10, 1791, Edward Jarvis, who was in charge of Albany Fort, reported that a prominent Lowland Cree hunter named Saquot had led a war party against the "Esquimaux."[55] This war party included Half-Homeguard Cree who lived near Henley House. A leader of the Henley House Cree, Captain Wausakeeshick, was among these warriors. A year later, at Henley House, Captain Wausakeeshick and his followers celebrated their victory over the Inuit the previous summer. John Hodgson, who was in charge of Henley House, reported on May 15 that Captain Wausakeeshick and his "gang" were "drinking and exulting over the scalps of the Esquimaux some of these Indians having had a hand in the murders of 4 last summer."[56] On May 27 the next year, 1793, Saquot and his "gang" left Albany Fort for an expedition against the Inuit. Once again, they were joined by Captain Wausakeeshick and some of his followers. This was the last Lowland Cree raid against the Inuit recorded in the HBC documents.

The warfare between the Lowland Cree and the Eastmain Inuit appears to have been motivated by a desire for revenge. Andrew Graham remarked that "all the men and old women are slain; and if the spirit of revenge is very raging none escape."[57] However, it is difficult to believe that revenge motivation could be an overriding factor when there is little evidence in the written records of Inuit incursions into Indian territory (an exception was the report of the Inuit raid against the Lowland Cree near the mouth of the Severn River that was recorded by James Knight at York Factory in 1716). Perhaps the period of aggressive Inuit warfare against the Lowland Cree predated the arrival of Europeans, which could explain why Andrew Graham called the Lowland Cree and the Inuit "inveterate and hereditary foes."[58] For their part, the Inuit appear to have also harboured long-standing and deep feelings of anger and revenge against their enemies. Speaking of relations between the Inuit and the HBC, Graham said that "revenge, often under the mask of friendship, lies brooding in his heart for months and years; and only waits for its effect until the unhappy object is found in an unguarded moment."[59] Edward Chappell, who visited the eastern Hudson Bay region in 1814, observed that it is a curious fact, that the inland or hunting tribes of Indians in Hud-son's Bay believe the Esquimaux to be a nation of sorcerers. Should the season prove a bad one in procuring their furs, they say that the Esquimaux have enchanted the game; and they then set off to the northward, to punish them accordingly. Whenever they discover the tents of the sup-posed magicians, they remain lurking about the place until a favourable opportunity offers; when, raising the dreadful war-whoop, they rush on to the attack with inconceivable fury. Every individual of the vanquished is instantly massacred, whether they make resistance, or implore for mercy. The animosity between them is hereditary, bloody, and implacable.[60]

Victorious Lowland Cree war parties often returned with captives and trophies such as scalps of their Inuit victims. Their return was attended with much feasting and dancing. Graham said that "those who have killed an enemy are painted all over with black; and when they meet their fami-lies they have a grand dance."[61] A grand ceremony was also held in which every warrior ate a piece of raw flesh from a slain Inuit. This practice was remembered in the oral history of the Moose River Lowland Cree in the early twentieth century. Alanson Skinner, a field anthropologist who con-ducted surveys in that area, noted in 1911 that "scalping was carried on, and in the old wars against the Eskimo, it was customary for the victor to eat a piece of fat cut from the thigh of the slain enemy."[62] Earlier, Bacqueville de la Potherie, writing in the seventeenth century, observed similar festivi-ties near the mouth of the Hayes River: "When their enemies fall into their hands they scalp them. They tear off the skin which covers the skull and they put as many marks on themselves as they have taken scalps. I saw three Ouenebigouchelinis [Coastal Cree] who had wild goose feathers attached to their caps above their ears as trophies of their victories over their en-emies."[63] Henry Ellis described how "an Indian who kills an Eskemaux scalps him; then takes and rounds a Bit of Willow, sowing the Scalp to it, and hangs one or two, or more of them, if he hath them, on a Stick at the End of his Canoe, when he returns; when at Home carries it to all Feasts, there dancing with it in his Hands."[64]

The HBC records after 1793 do not mention warfare between the Low-land Cree and the Inuit. Daniel Francis attributed the cessation of Lowland Cree raiding activities to developments in the HBC fur trade. The establish-ment of inland trading posts in the 1780s and 1790s required Lowland Cree labour, especially during the summer transport season, which was the traditional time for raids against the Inuit.[65]

The Chipewyan

At the time of European fur-trade contact, the Lowland Cree who lived in the vicinity of the Hayes and Nelson rivers were also engaged in warfare against the "Northern Indians," or Chipewyan, who occupied a large area north of the upper reaches of the Churchill River. The most easterly groups of Chipewyan lived in the region north of Lake Wollaston, Reindeer Lake, and Seal River, hundreds of kilometres away from the lowlands. Like their warfare with the Inuit, the Lowland Cree carried on long-distance raids against the Chipewyan. Andrew Graham observed that the Chipewyan "hold no intercourse with any of the southern Indians; and are looked on by them in the same despicable light as the Esquimaux."[66] According to the earliest European accounts, this warfare predated their arrival and appears to have involved reciprocal revenge-raiding. Jeremie commented that a "nation called Dogribs," who lived in the direction of the upper Seal River, "make war on our Maskegons [Lowland Cree]."[67] However, he observed, the Lowland Cree also raided successfully into Chipewyan territory. The Chipewyan had "no experience with fire arms," and the sound of gunshots was sufficient to cause the Chipewyan men to retreat, leaving women and children behind, who were captured by the Lowland Cree. By the time the HBC re-established York Factory in 1714, the Lowland Cree held a definite advantage in the wars against the Chipewyan. James Knight estimated in 1716 that 5000 to 6000 Chipewyan Indians had been killed in war since the first European trading post was built at the mouth of the Hayes River.[68]

When the HBC re-settled York Factory in 1714, it was anxious to facilitate a peace between the Lowland Cree and the Chipewyan. The company had economic motivations for encouraging such a peace initiative; it planned to establish a trading post at the mouth of the Churchill River to collect furs from the Chipewyan. There were also rumours of precious metals in the Chipewyan territory, and the company wanted to develop a friendly relationship to exploit these mineral resources. The motivation for peace on the part of the Lowland Cree is more difficult to ascertain. There were no obvious economic advantages to be gained by making peace with their traditional enemies. However, the peace initiative does make sense if it is viewed from the perspective of the alliance between the Lowland Cree and the HBC. As allies of the company, the Lowland Cree may have participated in peacemaking with the Chipewyan in order to solidify their relationship with the English traders. A careful examination of the peace mission in 1715-16 clarifies the role of the Lowland Cree in this initiative. This peace mission has been previously analyzed by scholars who have been interested

in the role of the HBC or the Chipewyan slave woman who acted as interpreter. However, the role of the Lowland Cree who actually made the
peace with the Chipewyan Indians has been downplayed or ignored.[69]

The leader of the Lowland Cree who lived in the area of the lower
Hayes River was called the Captain of the River. He was also known as the
"Frenchifyd Captain," a reference to his former allegiance to the French
traders who occupied a post at the mouth of the Hayes River before 1714.[70]
James Knight, who re-established York Factory for the HBC, was careful to
pay due respect to the Captain of the River. In the fall of 1714, Knight
presented the captain with a coat in recognition of his position as leader of
his people. The coat was made of two and a half yards of cloth, six yards of
baize lining, thirty-six fancy buttons, and twenty-two and a quarter yards
of lace gartering. In the spring of 1715, the captain's son also received a
coat from the HBC, and the captain's wife received gifts in exchange for a
"Slave Boy."[71] That summer, James Knight made several feasts and promised many presents to convince the Lowland Cree captain to make peace
with the Chipewyan. The gifts included 100 lbs of shot, 50 lbs of powder,
18 lbs of Brazil tobacco, 8 lbs of roll tobacco, 16 oz of vermilion, 1 gun, 28
hatchets, 72 knives, 20 ice chisels, 20 scrapers, 16 bayonets, 18 mocotogans
(crooked knives), 3 skeins of twine, 24 fire steels, 60 hawks bells, 15 blankets, 18 ivory combs, and 27 yards of cloth. The total value of these gifts
amounted to 469 made beaver.[72] The captain agreed to undertake the peace
mission, and he was followed by seventeen men and their families, numbering about 150 people in total. Accompanying this large group of Lowland Cree was a young company employee named William Stewart (Stuart)
and a Chipewyan woman named Thanadelthur, who had been captured by
the Lowland Cree.

The Lowland Cree captain and his party left York Factory on June 27,
1715, and headed north along the Hudson Bay coast toward the Churchill
River. Nothing was heard of the peacemakers until April 13, 1716, when
three Lowland Cree who had accompanied the captain arrived at York
Factory with news that the party had suffered from a shortage of food and
was forced to break into four or five smaller groups. According to their
report, the Lowland Cree captain had taken four men, along with Stewart
and Thanadelthur, in the direction of the Chipewyan winter hunting
grounds. Another group of eight Lowland Cree men also continued along
a different route toward Chipewyan winter hunting grounds, while the rest
returned to their home territory. This story was confirmed by other Lowland Cree who arrived at York Factory in the following days and weeks,
including three men who had been among the party of eight who went

toward the Chipewyan territory. These men reported that they had met a group of Chipewyan and killed nine people in self-defence. After the skirmish, they took four women and five children hostages, and allowed one woman and a boy to return to their countrymen as a gesture of peace.

On May 7, 1716, the Lowland Cree captain returned to York Factory with Stewart, Thanadelthur, and four Chipewyan men. The latter had joined the captain as evidence of the peace that had been made between the two groups of Indians. According to Stewart's report, their party came across the bodies of the Chipewyan who had been slain by the other Lowland Cree. Thanadelthur agreed to go out and bring her countrymen to the camp in order to explain the situation and reach a peace. Within ten days, Thanadelthur returned with 400 Chipewyan, including 160 men. Using Thanadelthur as an interpreter, the Lowland Cree captain explained that they had come in peace and offered his pipe to smoke in friendship. The Chipewyan leaders accepted and, after two days of meetings and gift exchanges, they parted company in peace. The Lowland Cree captain took four Chipewyan boys who were "adopted" as a sign of this peace. One of these boys remained with the captain, and he was thereafter treated as his own son.[73]

The Lowland Cree captain had accomplished his mission, and Knight rewarded him with "very large presents."[74] Despite the success of the peacemakers, Knight was cautious about the future relations between the Lowland Cree and the Chipewyan because, he thought, the Lowland Cree were the "[most] saucy fellows in the world when any number are gott together, they have been so flushed in blood."[75] On April 17, 1717, he said "the [Lowland] Indians are in a Curs'd Ill humour by reason so many Indians dying all this winter and doo think that the makeing of the Peace with the Northern Indians has been the Occasion of it, for they are of the Opinion the Devill must have so many every year if they can but kill their Enemys they may spare themselves."[76] Several days later, the captain arrived at York Factory with an expressed intention of going to war against the Chipewyan. Knight reported that "his Mind was to go to warr to Revenge himself upon the Norward People to sacrifice the Ghost of some of those Indians for those as are Dead that he might kill so many of his Enemys to pacifye the Devill." The Lowland Cree captain had other motivations for expressing his desire to go to war against the Inuit. Knight said that "the Captain of this River and some other Indians came and brought their friendly pipe to smoke it and gave me some presents and told me that he obey'd me in going to make peace with ye Northern Indians, and he did expect I shall fall the price of Guns." Although Knight refused to lower the price of guns, which remained at thirteen made beaver, he did give presents to the captain and made feasts for him and his followers to discourage them from going to war. These gifts included one gun, two knives, one coat, one pair of stockings, one white shirt, one yard of cloth for his two wives, and one coat for his brother. In his journal, Knight noted, "I Gave them a feast of Oatmeall, Plumbs and Tobacco and a present of a Coat and Capp to ye Captain and I promised him another feast when 5 or 6 Tents more of the Indians was come in."[77] The York Factory account book explained that these expenditures were "presented to the Frenchifyed discontented Captain of this River to keep him in tempor from Going to warr with the Northern Indians, he often threatning it and never thinking himself gratified for his going and making Peace with them, but is often Rehearsing up the French's Benevolence to him and complaining of our unkindness."[78]

The HBC continued to provide gifts annually to the Lowland Cree captain for his peace initiative. The 1719-20 York Factory account book noted that goods valued at ninety-three and a half made beaver were given to the captain as "the Old Capt. yearly sallery for making ye Peace."[79] However, the captain became ill soon after, and he died near York Factory on January 29, 1722. The Lowland Cree leaders who succeeded him made few attempts to rekindle the warfare against the Chipewyan.

Although Chipewyan captives were called slaves, some were adopted by the Lowland Cree. For example, the Lowland Cree named Factory, who assisted the HBC in establishing Churchill Fort, had a Chipewyan wife. The captain of the Lowland Cree near York Factory had a Chipewyan boy who was adopted as a son. According to James Knight, he was about eighteen years of age. Knight tried unsuccessfully to buy the Chipewyan boy from the captain, but "he [the Captain] is so jealous of him [the boy] that he doth not care for him to come near the factory and part with him I believe he would not for half the Goods in the Country."[80] Other Lowland Cree were less attached to their Chipewyan captives, and sold them to the HBC. However, the price was high, according to Knight, who paid sixty made beaver in goods for a Chipewyan woman. Captain Swan, the leader of the Missinepee (Upper Churchill River) Cree, also adopted a Chipewyan boy after he made peace with them in 1716. Captain Swan told James Knight that the two nations agreed to hold a special meeting in which boys and girls would be exchanged and adopted as a symbol of the peace.[81]

The establishment of Churchill Fort in 1717 promoted peaceful relations between the Lowland Cree and the Chipewyan by drawing the latter to trade with the HBC. In the winter of 1723-24, the HBC sent a young employee named Richard Norton to winter among the Lowland Cree. His purpose was to "divert 'em [Lowland Cree] from going to warr and to desire 'em to go to trade at York Fort and not come here for they should not have any Encouragement."[82] Anthropologist James G.E. Smith credited Norton with preserving the peace between the Lowland Cree and the Chipewyan,[83] but other accounts point to the importance of Lowland Cree peacemakers. William Coats interviewed a man named "Mack-qua-ta, or Long Day's son" who stated that he and two other Lowland Cree had been sent by Norton into the territory of the Chipewyan and arranged the peace, which "by this means effected and established such a peace as has not been broke since, and now are so united by marriages and kindnessis as give a hopeful prospect for the time to come."[84] Coats's comments indicate that the Lowland Cree could not afford to jeopardize their alliance with the company by continuing their hostility against the Chipewyan. Andrew Graham observed later that "before their [Chipewyan] intercourse with the English they were pursued by Enemies by the Keiskatchewan Indians [Lowland Cree], as they themselves pursu'd the Esquemaux, who border on the North and East coasts of the Bay, but by the interposition of the Chief at Churchill, their animosities are almost subsided and they are brought to smoak a pipe together, or at least to avoid destroying each other as formerly."[85]

The Iroquois

At the time of initial European contact in the Hudson Bay lowlands, a powerful confederacy of five nations known as the *Haudonoshone*, or "Longhouse People," occupied villages located south of Lake Ontario. These people spoke the Iroquoian language and their five nations were known as the Mohawk, Onondaga, Oneida, Cayuga, and Seneca. Beginning in 1650, the Five Nations conducted raids into the north, penetrating as far as the lowlands and causing widespread fear among the Lowland Cree. The Albany and Moose River Lowland Cree called the Iroquois *Nataway* Indians, *Nattawees, Nattaways,* or *Nottaway* Indians, after the Cree word for "enemy." The Nottaway River was so named because it was used by Iroquois war parties to reach the lowlands and attack the Lowland Cree. Iroquois raids in the direction of the Hudson Bay lowlands were first documented in the summer of 1650, when Jesuit missionaries in New France reported that Iroquois war parties travelled up the St. Maurice River and attacked the Attikamegue (Whitefish) Nation. It is uncertain whether the Iroquois extended their raids into the lowlands in 1650, but the Lowland Cree were undoubtedly aware of the raid because of their trading connections with

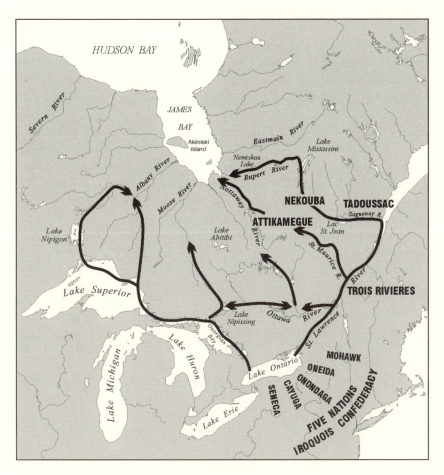

Iroquois War Routes

the Attikamegue. In 1657, Iroquois warriors launched another raid into the north, and attacked the people living between Lake Abitibi and Lac St. Jean.[86] By 1660, the Iroquois raids had prompted the northward migration of a number of Aboriginal nations to the James Bay region. In the summer of 1661, the Iroquois launched a major northern war campaign. Three hundred Mohawk warriors raided in different directions north of the St. Lawrence River from Trois-Rivières to Tadoussac. Two Jesuit missionaries, Claude Dablon and Gabriel Druillettes, were caught in the middle of the conflict. They had accompanied a party of eighty Montagnais and Algonkian middlemen on a journey up the Saguenay River to trade with the "Kiristinons" on the coast of James Bay. The party was forced to return at a place called Nekouba near the headwaters of the Saguenay River because of nearby Iroquois war parties. Dablon noted that "the panic is said to have spread to the Sea-coast whither we were going, and whither these barbarians fully intend this year to extend their cruelty, in order to push their conquests as far toward the North as they have done, of late years, toward the South."[87] The Jesuits were informed that the Iroquois spent the winter of 1661–62 near Nekouba and killed many people in the vicinity. "All the lands of the North, which had never before seen any Iroquois, have become so infested with them that there is no cavern in those vast regions of rocks dark enough to serve as a place of concealment.... We were told that the plan of the Iroquois was, not to pause there, but to push on as far as the North sea, to carry all before them, like a torrent, then to descend by way of Lake St. John and Tadoussac."[88]

In 1665, Iroquois war parties returned to the headwaters of the Saguenay River and terrorized the people in the surrounding territory. In 1672, Father Albanel visited Lake Nemiskau and described the ruins of various settlements and an Iroquois fortification.

> Five large rivers empty into this lake [Nemiskau], making it so rich in fish that the latter formed the main subsistence of a populous savage nation dwelling here eight or ten years ago. The sad monuments of their place of residence are still to be seen; and also, on a rocky islet, the remains of a large fort constructed of stout trees by the Iroquois, whence he guarded all the approaches and made frequent sallies. Seven years ago [1665] he killed on this spot, or led away captive, eighty persons; this caused the entire abandonment of the place, its original inhabitants departing thence.[87]

The last of the recorded Iroquois attacks in the north took place in 1673 and 1674. In 1673, Iroquois warriors were reported to have made raids in the Moose River area. A group of Aboriginal traders who came from "Quebec" to the HBC post at the mouth of the Rupert River on October 23, 1673, reported that "as they past Moose River, about 10 Days journey from Rupert's, they saw some dead bodies of Indians, which they suppos'd to be Onachanoes, most of that Nation being destroyed by the Nodwayes, who were then about Moose River."[88] In 1674, the Jesuits reported that Iroquois warriors were in the vicinity of Lake Mistassini, and "fear reigned everywhere."[89] In addition to recorded attacks, the oral history of the Lowland Cree at Albany Fort tells of an Iroquois raid down the Albany River. Christopher Trott, who conducted an archaeological survey of the Albany River in 1978, reported that "the people at Constance Lake tell a story that a 'battle' between the local Cree and the Iroquois took place in this area."[90] The same oral tradition was told in 1985 by James Wesley, an elder from

Albany Fort (Kashechewan).Wesley explained that Ghost River was originally called Sturgeon River, but the name changed after the battle with the
Iroquois. His story told of the Iroquois, or *Natoowaywuk*, coming down the
Albany River in ten large canoes, each carrying ten men.They were ambushed by a small party of Lowland Cree at the confluence of Ghost River,
and all were killed. Wesley said, "From that time on the name Sturgeon
River was changed to Ghost River, because of the ambush and the common sight of human bones, usually after spring break-up."[91] John Wynne,
also from Albany Fort, told a similar tradition in the 1950s.The Iroquois
had gained access to the Albany River from the English River, located
hundreds of kilometres southwest.This route would have taken the Iroquois
warriors far into Lake Superior and probably through Lake Nipigon, thereby
escaping the notice of Jesuit missionaries and French fur traders.Wynne's
account explained that the Lowland Cree knew of the Iroquois war party
by consulting a conjurer.They ambushed the Iroquois and killed many, but
also took some captive and held them as slaves.[92]

The reasons why Iroquois warriors raided so far north were probably
complex, but an important factor was the control of the fur trade.After the
fall of Huronia in 1650, the French fur trade depended on getting pelts
through Aboriginal middlemen who were able to bypass the dangerous
Ottawa River trade route.Alternative routes took furs from the area north
and west of Lake Superior to James Bay and then southeast to Tadoussac.
The northern raids by the Iroquois were aimed primarily at disrupting
the flow of furs to the French.The Iroquois were also in need of new
sources of fur, especially beaver, which was the mainstay of the trade.
Daniel Richter noted that "by about 1640 the Five Nations perhaps had
exhausted the beaver stock of their home hunting territories; more important, they could not find in relatively temperate Iroquoia the thick northern pelts prized by Euro-American traders."[93] The Five Nations raided in
all directions, covering a vast territory, the geographical extent of which
may never be known with certainty. However, this warfare also stretched
the logistical limits of the Five Nations and, by the 1680s, they were no
longer in a position to sustain their long-distance raiding activities.Their
position was weakened by war casualties, and by epidemic diseases that
swept through the St. Lawrence valley and Great Lakes region during the
seventeenth century. Instead of war, the Five Nations began to seek a general peace with the nations who lived north of the Great Lakes and St.
Lawrence valley.These peace initiatives eventually included the Cree nation, and ended in a peace treaty at Montreal in 1701.

The 1701 Montreal Treaty, sometimes called the Grand Settlement, was the largest recorded gathering of Aboriginal nations. More than 1000 people representing over thirty nations converged at Montreal that summer to make peace. The nations included the Cristinaux, or Cree, who were listed along with the Temiskamingues and Gens des Terres.[94] The treaty council meetings lasted nearly two weeks, and on August 4, the treaty was ratified. The French text of the treaty indicated that a primary aspect of the agreement was to allow each nation to share in each other's hunting grounds. That agreement, also known as "a dish with one spoon," had been the subject of many speeches and recorded in the treaty as that "whenever you shall meet each other [agree] to act as brothers and to agree as regards hunting, that no disturbances may occur, and this peace may not be troubled."[95]

The Cree involvement in this treaty may have been stimulated by the arrival of a group of Mohawks at the mouth of the Nelson River in 1694, who had come with a French naval force that took over the HBC trading post.[96] These were Mohawks who had recently settled in villages near Montreal and were known as "mission" or "praying" Indians. Although converted to Catholicism, they maintained close political and social ties to the Mohawk nation. The HBC, backed by the English navy, re-took Port Nelson in 1695. Four Mohawks, including two chiefs, were taken to London as prisoners but later released after it was learned that the Mohawk nation was an English ally. The other Mohawks remained at Port Nelson. Some were still there in the winter of 1696-97, when the HBC account book noted gifts given to "Mohawke Indians."[97] The ultimate fate of these Hudson Bay Mohawks can not be determined from the written records, which are missing after 1697. However, it may be connected to the arrival of Cree delegates at the Montreal peace treaty in 1701.

After the Montreal Treaty, the period of Iroquois warfare ended, but the alliance that developed between the French fur traders and the Iroquois on the one hand, and the Lowland Cree and the English fur traders on the other, continued to pose a threat to the security of the Lowland Cree. While threats of Iroquois attacks were usually more imagined than real, periodic raids into Lowland Cree territory were reported. For example, on May 27, 1706, a rumour circulated around Albany Fort that the French and their allies planned to attack the fort. Anthony Beale reported that "the french and Indians that where coming against our factory are hindered by those Indians that lies between them and us who will not suffer them to pass through their countrey, notwithstanding they have offered them presents to that end but they have been utterly refused."[98]

By 1713, French fur traders had established trading posts at the headwaters of the Moose and Albany rivers, and rumours of French attacks against Albany Fort were common.[99] One upland trader who visited Albany Fort in the spring of 1713 told Anthony Beale that he had been among the "ba bi tim my [Abitibi] Indians," and he was told that the French planned to attack Albany Fort.[100] This story caused most of the Albany River Lowland Cree who usually hunted geese for the HBC to move northward away from the fort to be out of the way of the intended attack. Other upland traders who visited Albany Fort that summer reported that the French raid failed because the leaders of the upland people who lived near the headwaters of the Moose River refused to join them. Beale noted that "the french had designed to come against [Albany Fort] this summer, that they were gott up into the Lakes [at the head of Moose River] for that end, and had called together severall leading Indians, giving them presents of tobacco and other things to gett them to joyne them in their expedition, butt ye Indians disdainfully refused in taking their present that lay on ye ground before them broke with their fitt [feet]."[101] On May 14, 1716, one canoe of "French Indians" arrived at Albany Fort with news that the French traders had promised to pay the value of thirty beaver skins to any person who brought them the scalp of a HBC trader.[102] In the fall of 1723, sightings of strange people near Albany Fort caused the goose hunt to come to an abrupt end, and the Lowland Cree goose hunters told Richard Staunton that the "Cannadie Indians are come to kill them."[103] In the spring of 1729, some upland traders informed the HBC that the French fur traders had mobilized a force that included "Morohawkes (who are in their interest)" to attack Albany Fort.[104] On June 7, 1729, the HBC sentries shot and wounded an Iroquois who had been sent to scout the area around the fort, and on June 18 that year, HBC men opened fire on a war party of ten or twelve men who were in sight of the fort.[105]

The fear of the Iroquois among the Albany and Moose River Lowland Cree continued throughout much of the eighteenth century. The Lowland Cree showed great fear of the Iroquois. Joseph Isbister wrote that rumours that the Mohawk intended to attack Albany Fort in the summer of 1744 "works on the superstitious Indians and frightens them out of their wits."[106] In 1787, many Albany River Lowland Cree stayed clear of Albany Fort because of a fear that "a tribe of Indians called the Notaways which they expected were coming to invade their country."[107] The fear of the Iroquois that derived from seventeenth-century, and possibly earlier, attacks was kept alive in oral traditions that have continued to the present.

5.
The Lowland Cree and the Land:
Seasonal Adaptations to Regional Resources

The Seasonal Cycle

Residents of the Hudson Bay lowlands adapted to and depended upon the ebb and flow of the seasonal cycle, which shaped the locale and numbers of different animals and other natural resources within the vast lowland region. The Lowland Cree understood the seasonal rhythm of the natural world around them, and patterned their activities according to the changing abundance and decline in resources. For the Lowland Cree, the quest for food and shelter was a circular journey, leading them to traditional places of seasonal resource availability that had sustained their ancestors for countless generations. The significance of the patterns of resources was reflected in the Lowland Cree concept of time. Their yearly calendar described the changing moons in terms of important natural events such as animal migrations. Andrew Graham recorded the Lowland Cree names and meanings of the months.

Lowland Cree Calendar

Month	Indian Name	Translation (Graham)
March	Mekisseu–Apeshem	Eagle Moon – when the eagles make their appearance
April	Niscock–Apeshem	Goose Moon – when the grey geese [Canada geese] make their appearance
May	Atheak–Apeshem	Frog Moon – when the frogs begin to croak
June	Oupinnihou–Apeshem	Incubation Moon – when the geese lay their eggs
July	Oupusakou–Apeshem	Moulting Moon – when the geese are moulting
August	Uppahau–Apeshem	Flying Moon – when the young geese fly
September	Wuskaohow–Apeshem	Shedding Moon – when the deer [caribou] shed their horns
October	Wesack–Apeshem	Rutting Moon – when the deer are rutting
November	Askuttateswa–Apeshem	Frost Moon – when the rivers freeze over
December	Powatchinchanisish–Apeshem	Short Day Moon – when the days are short and nights are long
January	Shepowartiscinum–Apeshem	Cold Moon – when the severe cold sets in
February	Shea–Apeshem	Old Moon – when the winter is old and the day is lengthening

Spring

The Lowland Cree calendar year began with the month of March, which, Graham noted, "seems to be the most remarkable by them."[1] The bald eagle, known as *Mickesew* (Graham) or *Me ke su* (Isham) in the Lowland Cree language, was the first migratory bird to arrive in the lowlands. Thus, the arrival of the bald eagle to the coastal lowlands was the first sign of spring and, for the Lowland Cree, a spiritual signal of the rebirth of a new year.

As the Moon of the Eagle (March) waned, caribou began to arrive in the coastal lowlands near the Nelson and Hayes rivers. Great herds of migrating caribou, or *Attick* (Graham),[2] travelled each spring from the upland forest, following well-worn paths that crossed over the frozen Nelson, Hayes, and Severn rivers.[3] The caribou herds moved southeast, parallel to the Hudson Bay coastline, before dispersing in summer breeding grounds on the coastal tundra as far away as Cape Henrietta Maria and Akimiski Island. After calving and feeding on the tundra vegetation, the caribou aggregated into large herds for the return migration in late summer. Retracing ancient pathways, and crossing ice-free rivers, the caribou returned to the upland forest where they dispersed into smaller herds for the winter. The spring migration of caribou across the Hayes River usually began in late March or early April. Joseph Colen, who was in charge of York Factory in 1788, noted that the "usual season" for caribou to begin crossing the Hayes River was the "Change of this Moon [March]."[4] Nicolas Jeremie, who was stationed at the French post at the mouth of the Hayes River, observed that the caribou "pass twice a year. The first time is in the months of April and May, on which occasion they come from the north and go south."[5] The Lowland Cree called the spring migration the season when "Deer walk."

Many European observers were impressed with the large numbers of caribou that migrated into the lowlands during the early fur-trade period. Jeremie remarked that "the number of them is almost countless,"[6] but Gabriel Marest was more specific, noting that individual herds numbered more than 300 to 400 caribou, and more than 10,000 caribou crossed the Hayes River in two days.[7] Bacqueville de la Potherie estimated that each herd contained 700 to 800 caribou.[8] In 1747, T.S. Drage, who visited York Factory, wrote, "The latter part of this Month [March] the Deer began to cross the Hay's River, twenty miles above the Factory; where Indians were waiting for to kill them. One year they passed in four Columns or in four different Tracks, all within three miles space, one of the Columns passing near the Factory, and the whole four Columns did not contain less in Number than eight or ten thousand Deer. This happen'd in the Month of April."[9]

In the spring of 1792, David Thompson recorded a graphic description and enumeration of several caribou herds that crossed the Hayes River. Thompson encountered the caribou about thirty kilometres upriver from York Factory. His sighting of the caribou was preceded by a noise that sounded like "distant thunder."[10] The caribou travelled in a long column, about 100 metres wide. Beside the main column, there were small, outlying groups of caribou, numbering ten to twenty each. It took an entire day for the main column to ford the river. The following day, a second great herd and several smaller herds crossed the river. Thompson, who was trained in mathematics and surveying, estimated that three million caribou crossed the river in two days. Although this extraordinary figure more likely reflected flaws in his memory (his memoirs were written more than fifty years after the event) than his experience as a scientific observer, Thompson undoubtedly witnessed a spectacular caribou migration across the Hayes River that spring.

The caribou herds usually followed the same routes each year, and crossed rivers at well-worn places. These habits made them relatively easy prey for Lowland Cree hunters,[11] who set up hunting camps in late winter near migration routes in anticipation of the arrival of the caribou.[12] The herds usually crossed the Hayes River about thirty to 100 kilometres above York Factory.[13] Caribou crossings on the Nelson River were located about the same distance inland from the coast. On August 25, 1775, Samuel Hearne was about eighty kilometres up the Nelson River when he "arrived at the Place where several Home Natives are waiting to kill Deer, several crossing the River Here at times." The next day, he observed "many Deer crossing the River in Places."[14] Smaller herds sometimes crossed the rivers closer to the coast, and occasionally large herds came within sight of York Factory.

After crossing the Nelson and Hayes rivers, most of the caribou continued southeast, parallel to the Hudson Bay coast, crossing the Severn River about thirty to sixty kilometres inland from the coast. Many of the Severn River Lowland Cree established hunting camps about thirty kilometres upriver at a place known as Ouaouiastine or White Seal Falls. On March 26, 1775, at Severn House, William Falconer reported that "the Indians that came yesterday went away to Waweaston about 22 miles up the river; from whence came two more who inform us the most of our Homeguards are there waiting for Deer."[15] Sometimes, scouting parties were sent from Severn toward York Factory to detect the movement of the caribou herds. On April 11, 1769, two hunters arrived at Severn with news that "the Deer were plenty within 3 days journey to the Northwest."[16] The caribou did not migrate as far south as the Albany River during the fur-trade period. The most southerly destination was Akimiski Island, where large numbers spent the summer on the tundra of the island's northern shore. According to William Coats, the name *Akimiski,* or *Agomisco,* meant "where deer [caribou] herds."[17] Coats also stated there were "herds of deer all the summer, where our home Indians go to kill and dry quantities of it for their and ours uses at Albany."[18]

During the spring migration, caribou usually crossed over frozen rivers, and the best method of hunting then was to build fences or hedges with snares set in them to trap the animals. During the return migration in late summer, the caribou swam across the open rivers, and the most productive hunting method was to spear them from canoes. The two techniques did not require European technology, which suggests that caribou could be harvested easily during both the spring and fall in the period before European contact. Archaeologist Jean-Luc Pilon identified the remains of many caribou at Ile de l'Ourson, a site located about twenty kilometres above Severn House. It was a pre-European campsite, with a heavy focus on caribou as a food resource. Pilon concluded that, "Given the relatively large number of animals represented at the site, it can reasonably be assumed that they died during either of the two annual migrations. The recovery of antler fragments lacking cortex suggests occupation of the site during the spring migration or early in the summer."[19]

Deer Snare, by James Isham, pen and ink drawing, 1743, in James Isham's *Observations on Hudson's Bay, 1743,* vol.2 (HBCA, PAM, E.2/2, fo. 43).

The caribou fence, or hedge, was an Aboriginal invention, and European fur traders built copies patterned after the Indian model. James Isham described the construction of the Lowland Cree caribou hedge.

> Their snares are made of Deer, or other skins Cutt in strips, platting several things togeather,—they also make snares of the Sinnew's of beast after the same manner, they then make a hedge for one or two mile in Length. Leaving Vacant places,—they then fall trees and Sprig them as big as they can gett, setting one up an End at the side of the Vacant place, fastning the snare to one of these trees, then setting the snare round they Slightly studdy the snare on Each side, the bottom of the snare being about 2 1/2 foot from the ground, Driving stakes under'ne that they may not creep under, they then Leave them when the Deer being pursued by the Natives other way's they strive to go thro these Vacant places, by which they are Entangld. and Striving to gett away the tree falls Downe, sometimes upon them and Kills them if not they frequently hawl these trees for some miles tell a growing tree or stump brings them up,—when the Indians going to the snares the next Day, trak's them and Knock's them on the head.[20]

Caribou hedges were noted in the early European records from the York Factory area. The locations of the hedges near York Factory varied over time, but generally ranged from five to twenty-five kilometres upriver. Caribou hedges were also built near Severn House and Churchill Fort. These, too, were constructed within walking distance of the post, and were patterned after Lowland Cree hedges. Unfortunately, there are very few descriptions in the HBC records of caribou hedges built and operated exclusively by the Lowland Cree. It is apparent that hedges built by Lowland Cree hunters were located farther upriver, away from the hinterland of the factory. Upriver hedges were also more effective, since most of the caribou herds passed over the river at least thirty kilometres from the factory, beyond the reach of the uppermost HBC hedges. In the spring of 1718, Lowland Cree who lived close to York Factory built a hedge that, Henry Kelsey reported, was located "almost from this River to Port Nelson a cross a neck of land that is about five mile through. It's but eighteen mile up this River and will be far more advantageous than that which is twenty four miles up [another caribou hedge]."[21]

Caribou hedges required large numbers of people to build, maintain, and operate. The caribou-hunting camps near York Factory attracted large gatherings of Lowland Cree. On July 19, 1780, Humphrey Marten noted that "about 180 young and old home Indians came to the Fort with a little dryed meat and upwards of 100 deer skins."[22] Lowland Cree ceremonies associated with the caribou hunt were rarely recorded by the European traders, perhaps because the hunting camps were usually located at a distance from the trading posts. However, there are a few comments about caribou-hunting ceremonies in the HBC records. For example, Joseph Colen, who was in charge of York Factory in 1787, reported that the Lowland Indian caribou hunters "had their Grand Hunting Feast and Dance."[23]

Other methods of caribou hunting, such as spears and bow and arrows, were employed, but the caribou hedge was evidently the best technique to capture large numbers of caribou in the spring. After the acquisition of European firearms, guns may have replaced Aboriginal technology such as spears and arrows, but the hedge persisted as a preferred method. Night hunting was not mentioned in the records before 1821, and apparently was not a traditional hunting technique. The reason for this is not clear, but the lack of suitable birchbark or other incendiary materials may have been a contributing factor. John Neepin, who was born in 1916 at Wanatawahak (Crooked Bank) near York Factory, explained, "We were taught certain ways of hunting. People weren't allowed to build a fire at night. We weren't allowed to hunt after dark or when it was calm."[24]

Caribou were least desirable as a food and commercial resource in the spring. Caribou skins were of little value then because many were infested with warble fly larvae that began to eat holes in the skin in late winter and early spring. Ernest Burch noted that "as winter wanes and the molt approaches, warble fly larvae, developing from eggs deposited under the skin the previous summer, begin to eat holes in the hide. From this point [February] on, the skins are worthless for any purpose."[25] During the spring migration, caribou depleted fat reserves, and little fat was available for commercial sales to the European fur traders. Caribou meat was also usually lean during the spring period, and therefore of little value as a trade item at that time of the year.

Shortly after the spring caribou migration, geese and other migratory birds arrived in the coastal marshes. The Cree word for the spring arrival of geese is *mâtâw-ispanihowak*, meaning "flying through in great flocks." The northward spring migration of geese and other birds was closely associated with the spring breakup of ice in the lakes and rivers. Coastal ponds and sloughs, which comprised the main feeding areas for most migratory waterfowl, became clear of ice before lakes and rivers broke up. Waterfowl generally made their first appearance on the coast several weeks before the spring ice breakup. The beginning of the spring thaw was a critical event in the seasonal movement patterns of the Lowland Cree for a number of reasons. Thawing conditions hampered overland travel as hard-packed snow gave way to slush and mud. Movement across rivers and lakes was also restricted once the thaw melted ice to the point that it could not sustain the weight of human travellers. The breakup of lake and river ice made these water bodies extremely dangerous. Broken ice, driven by the current, scoured riverbanks and ice jams caused flooding that spilled over onto adjacent valley lands.

The spring breakup of ice in rivers flowing into James Bay and Hudson Bay occurred at different times, and was generally influenced by the latitudinal location of each coastal estuary. Thus, the more southerly Albany River broke clear of ice before the Severn River, which, in turn, was ice-free before the Hayes River. Because both the arrival of the first geese and the spring breakup were very significant events in the yearly cycle at the HBC coastal posts, they were often carefully recorded in the HBC journals. At Albany Fort, the first geese arrived about April 20 and the river-ice broke around the first of May. Farther north, at York Factory, the timing of these events was about two weeks later. Unusual wind conditions often caused deviations from the usual timing of the spring migration.[26] For example, William Falconer, who was in charge of Severn House in the spring of 1784, attributed a delayed arrival of geese to the lack of westerly winds,[27] and, in the spring of 1788, John Ballenden also noted the importance of westerly winds near Severn House when he wrote that "the wind harbouring so much in the eastern quarter will make but a poor goose hunt this spring."[28] On May 13, 1717, at York Factory, James Knight remarked that strong southerly winds had caused the geese to move north, and he wrote, "I am afraid this hard Wind has Carry'd away most of the Geese too ye Northward and I believe wee shall have butt a very indifferent Season without a Northerly Wind comes and brings them back again."[29] Air temperature also influenced geese migrations. For example, the spring of 1797 near Severn House was unusually cold and geese were late in coming to the coast. By May 16, 1797, the temperature began to warm, although, as HBC trader Thomas Thomas noted, "the Weather rather milder tho' not sufficiently so to admit of the Geese coming to the Coast."[30] That year, the Severn River did not break up until May 28, and the first goose was killed on May 23. In the spring of 1735, warm weather and southerly winds were blamed for a poor goose hunt near York Factory. HBC trader Thomas White observed that although he had employed "20 extraordinary goose hunters ... the only cause of our Disappointment has been ye weather here having been nothing but hot weather with Southerly winds for these 6 Days past, which Drove ye Geese to ye Northward, and so far out to Sea, out of Reach of all our hunters."[31] Snow conditions also played a role in influencing the migration patterns of geese. For example, the goose hunt in the spring of 1790 was extremely poor at York Factory, with only 401 geese killed in total. Joseph Colen commented that "the old Natives say they never knew such a scarcity of Geese.... The few Geese seen is imputed to the small quantity of snow falling in the Winter, and which disolved early in the Spring, that most of the Lakes and Ponds were open in the plains, where the Geese resort and feed during the cold weather, and took their flight Northerly without visiting the Coast as was usual at this time of the Year."[32] Thomas White recorded a similar explanation at York Factory on May 14, 1743, when "ye winds hanging so much easterly, and ye snow being so soon consumed of ye ground has drove all ye geese inland."[33]

European visitors to the Hudson Bay and James Bay coasts were impressed with the number of migratory birds that visited the coastal lowlands. Gabriel Marest reported from the mouth of the Nelson River in 1694 that "in spring and autumn, there are also found a prodigious number of wavys [lesser snow geese], Canada geese, ducks, brants, and other river birds."[34] Bacqueville de la Potherie, writing about the same time, commented that "the wild geese and ducks are so plentiful in spring and autumn that the banks of the river Ste. Therese [Hayes River] are all covered with them."[35] Among the various species of migratory waterfowl, ducks and plover (a term used to describe shore birds in general) were usually the first to arrive on the coast. The snow bunting, which was called *Wapathecusish* (Graham) or *Wap pa tha ko sish* (Isham) by the Lowland Cree, arrived in early April and stayed along the coast for five to six weeks before continuing northward to their breeding grounds. Andrew Graham noted that numbers of these birds were caught with nets, and that they were "very fat and reckoned a delicacy."[36] The mallard duck, also known by the HBC men as the Indian Duck, and called *Etheenieship* (Graham) or *E'thi thu ship* (Isham) by the Lowland Cree, was described by Graham as a "beautiful duck [which] is of great service, being good food both to Indians and Europeans."[37]

Canada geese were usually the first species of geese to arrive in the coastal marshes, although flocks of lesser snow geese sometimes arrived at the same time. For example, near Severn House in the spring of 1790, the first Canada goose was sighted on May 5, while the first lesser snow goose was reported on May 23. In the spring of 1792, Canada geese appeared near Severn House on April 27, and lesser snow geese were first sighted on May 17. Occasionally, lesser snow geese arrived before Canada geese, and this was seen as a bad omen for the goose hunt. On April 14, 1707, Anthony Beale, Chief Factor at Albany Fort, was informed by some Lowland Cree hunters that "Whay waies begun to be very plentiful about and the Gray

Geese scarce, which make much fear a Bad Goose Season."[38] Called grey geese by the HBC, and *Niscock* (Graham) or *Neishcoock* (Isham) by the Lowland Cree, Canada geese were especially numerous in the James Bay area, where they arrived in flocks of ten to thirty, and stayed near the company's posts for about three weeks, feeding in the coastal marshes. Thereafter, the geese separated into pairs and moved into the coastal plains to breed.

A closely related species of goose, the Richardson's goose, known as the Canada goose by Graham, and *Apistiskish* (Graham) or *Appiskeske* (Isham) in the Lowland Cree language, usually arrived in large flocks several weeks after the Canada geese. The Richardson's goose resembles a small Canada goose, but they seldom mixed. Their feeding habits were also different, and Graham explained that Richardson's geese were "always found about the high-water mark feeding on salt grass and sea-slime, which food causes their flesh to taste disagreeable." Despite this negative assessment of its taste, "many hundreds are killed by the natives for the service of the factories." [39]

The most numerous geese to migrate past the Severn and Hayes rivers was the lesser snow goose (white phase). It was also known as white geese by the HBC traders, and wavy after the Lowland Cree name, *Wehwe* (Graham) or *Wappawewewuck* (Isham). Lesser snow geese usually arrived several weeks after the Canada geese and often travelled in huge flocks that numbered in the thousands. Although flocks of lesser snow geese flew over the Albany River area, they were generally too high to be killed by the hunters. In the Severn River area and northward along the Hudson Bay coast, these geese usually stayed in the marshes for about three weeks before moving northward to their summer breeding grounds. Andrew Graham remarked that "at the height of the season the shores are quite covered with them, they rise like clouds and make a great noise."[40] James Isham wrote, "They are Extrordinary good Eating fresh or Salt, and a Great help to the mentanence of the English who Setles these parts, the Natives Killing for them some thousands of a Season, and is the chief of our Diet."[41] While lesser snow geese (white phase) generally overpassed the coastal area around Albany Fort for more northerly regions, the blue phase known as the blue goose, and *Cathactew Whewe* (Graham) or *Kurskatawawawuck* (Isham), came to feed in the Albany River marshes in the thousands during the same migration period.

Another species of goose that frequented the coastal lowlands was the brant goose, which was known as *Withawapapew* (Graham) or *Wirthawappawawuck* (Isham) by the Lowland Cree. The brant goose is small, resembling a large duck in size rather than a goose. It remained along the coast all summer, feeding, breeding, and rearing its young. Despite their availability, brant geese were not an important food or commercial re-source for the Lowland Cree because, as Andrew Graham explained, they were "so fishy tasted that they are quite disregarded both by Europeans and Indians."[42] HBC trader George Barnston agreed: "The Brant goose the Calliwappemaw of the coast Crees, is but little looked after or cared for in Hudson's Bay, being a small species, keeping out to sea on the shoals, and towards lowest watermark, and affording a dish not high in estimation."[43]

Swans, including the trumpeter swan and whistling or tundra swan, were also migratory visitors to the lowlands. Known generically as *Wapesew* by the Lowland Cree, swans arrived together with the various species of geese, sometimes slightly in advance of the Canada geese. Although much less numerous than geese, and a minor commercial resource, swans were highly regarded by the Lowland Cree. Isham stated that he had seen hundreds of swans together, but Graham remarked that he never saw more than twelve in a flock, [44] and George Barnston also said that "the swan, except in a few particular localities, is a scarce, rather than a plentiful bird, on the shores of Hudson's Bay."[45] Graham noted that "their flesh is coarse, and therefore not regarded by Europeans, but the natives are very fond of them."[46]

Generally, Canada geese and blue geese were the main species taken at Albany Fort during the spring goose hunt. Lesser snow geese dominated the Severn House and York Factory areas, with additional numbers of Richardson's geese taken at the latter post each spring. Thomas Macklish, who became Chief Factor at York Factory in 1722, had been previously in charge of Albany Fort, and he noted that "here [York Factory] being but few Gray Geese at the Sea Side, where is plenty at the Bottome of the Bay [Albany Fort]."[47]

Some scholars have downplayed the importance of waterfowl as a sub-sistence resource for the Lowland Cree prior to the acquisition of Euro-pean firearms. Charles Bishop commented that

> it is unlikely that Indians exploited geese either early in the spring or late in the fall: goose-hunting during the late April and early May break-up would have been hazardous; and after late August, full feathered birds unencumbered by flightless offspring would have been difficult quarry. Furthermore, and probably more important, Indians who remained near the coast after mid-September would have been exposed to an unpre-dictable existence in an area where travel was difficult.[48]

Dale Russell made a direct correlation between the arrival of European fur traders and the advent of goose hunting by the Lowland Cree. Russell, as noted earlier, believed that the coastal region was a "no-man's land" prior to the establishment of European fur-trade posts, and he concluded that European fur-trade settlement "necessitated a displacement of Indian people to the coast, originating the Home Guard Indians."[49] Other scholars have advanced different views on this subject, indicating that migratory waterfowl may have been an important resource to the Lowland Cree prior to European contact, despite the apparent limitation imposed by the lack of firearms. John Honigmann, who conducted ethnographic studies among the Lowland Cree near Attawapiskat in the 1940s and 1950s, stated, "While waterfowl may not have played the outstanding role in diet aboriginally that they do today (the assumption being that shotguns are better suited for their killing than bow and arrows), they must have been fairly significant nevertheless."[50]

The significance of migratory waterfowl as a subsistence resource for the Lowland Cree before European contact is difficult to assess from the available archaeological data. Jean-Luc Pilon did not find significant amounts of migratory waterfowl bones in the remains of pre-contact sites along the lower Severn River. However, he pointed out that avian remains may have been absent because the killing and butchering may have taken place elsewhere. Pilon also noted that "although guns were not available, evidence from the Brant River suggests that waterfowl could be taken in significant numbers, especially during the moult, with technologically simpler means. Snares and blunt-tipped arrows and perhaps bolas were important hunting devices."[51] This conclusion is supported by comments made by HBC traders. For example, Andrew Graham reported that "a great many" Canada geese were taken by the Lowland Cree during the summer moult in the coastal plains, by simply knocking them on the head.[52] Lowland Cree also used dogs to hunt moulting geese and ducks. Joseph Colen, who was in charge of York Factory in 1798, commented: "Our whole dependence at present for fresh victuals is on young ducks and moulting water fowl killed by Indians with dogs."[53] James Isham noted that snow bunting were caught with nets.[54]

Several early European observers also suggested that the Lowland Cree hunted migratory waterfowl successfully prior to obtaining European firearms. For example, in the summer of 1631, Luke Fox described an abandoned Indian camp near the mouth of the Nelson River, which contained the "bones of fowle."[55] Pierre Esprit Radisson, who claimed to have visited the James Bay area in the summer of 1660, stated, "We went from isle to isle all that summer. We plucked abundance of ducks, as of all other sorts of fowle. We wanted not fish nor fresh meat." Radisson's use of the word "pluck" suggests that the birds were taken by hand, possibly with a club as noted by Graham above. Radisson also explained that a bow and arrow were used to kill waterfowl, and he noted that "I have seen wildmen [Indians] killing three ducks at once with one arrow."[56]

Like caribou and geese, fish were seasonally abundant in the lowlands, especially during spawning periods. The spring spawners included sucker, lake sturgeon, and northern pike. Edward Umfreville observed that the fishery resource in the lowlands was superior to that found in the upland regions: "On the whole, fish are not so numerous in the inland parts, as in those waters which join to the sea."[57] The Lowland Cree used a number of techniques to catch fish, including nets, spears, hooks, and weirs or traps.[58] Weirs, also called traps or baskets, were reported by Andrew Graham as a method used by Lowland Cree to catch hundreds of whitefish.[59] Kenneth Lister described the construction and operation of fish weirs in the lowlands as follows:

> Such weirs were built in fast water and were comprised of a combination of fence and trap. In both the ice-free and ice-covered seasons a fence of poles spanned the river blocking the movement of fish downstream. This fence of poles is referred to as a weir. The trap element of the structures, however, differed between the two seasons. In the ice-free season the trap consisted of a ramp and an open-top box-like enclosure made from poles lashed together. The ramp and box were placed on the downstream side of the weir. Through an opening in the weir the ramp angled obtusely from the river bottom. The top of the ramp remained slightly below the surface of the water with a thirty centimetre overhang into the box enclosure. The sides of the box, with the exception of the ramp side, were raised above the water level. The weir channelled the fish into the ramp opening where the fish were forced up the ramp and into the box. The fast moving water combined with the ramp overhang impeded the fish from escaping back down the ramp. The fish were then scooped out of the box with a dip net.[60]

Fish weirs were built in a number of rivers flowing through the lowlands. James Swain, who was in charge of Severn House in 1815, reported "almost innumerable places convenient for weirs, in the interior, most of which produce vast quantities in the proper seasons."[61] In the Winisk River basin, weirs were located on the Shamattawa and North Washagami rivers. Lowland Cree operated several fish weirs in the Nelson River; the "lower fishing weir" was located downstream from the last fall in the river. The Albany River Lowland Cree operated weirs at a number of locations along the Albany River and its tributaries. An important fish weir was located at the Fishing Creek, a tributary of the Albany River, located about ninety

kilometres above Albany Fort. Other weirs were located at the mouth of
Chemohoggan Creek and the Little Fishing Creek. John Martin made a
trip from Albany Fort to Henley House in 1774, and he recorded some
other fishing stations. One, called *Pue kee tee wan* or the "Fishing Place," was
located near the confluence of Sandy Creek, about fifty kilometres above
the fort. Another, called *Mechiscanashish* or the "Little Fishing Place," was
located near the mouth of the Fishing Creek, about fifty-five kilometres
farther upstream. Martin observed that the Little Fishing Place was "a noted
place for Trout, Jack, Tickomeg, Methy and Perch."[62]

The Lowland Cree used a number of different types of fishing nets.
Scoop nets were employed mainly in connection with fish weirs. Gill nets
were set in many locations and could be operated at all times of the year,
including winter, when they were set under the ice. Seine nets, also called
drag nets, were used in ice-free conditions.[63] In the Albany River, seine
nets were considered to be "the only sure means of success."[64] At Moose
Fort, seine nets were productive, especially in the fall. On October 16,
1739, Richard Staunton noted he "sent all hands to gitt a hawl with ye
Saine and when they came home they brought near 2000 fish small and
great, for our Saine is like Death, it spares neither small nor great."[65]

The sucker was usually the first fish to make spawning runs in the
lowlands. Two species were common in the region: the white sucker,
known as *Namepith* (Graham) or *Ne ma pett* (Isham) in the Lowland Cree
language, and the longnose sucker, or *Mithnamepith* (Graham). Both species preferred spawning in shallow streams with gravelly bottoms, shortly
after the spring ice breakup. The longnose sucker usually spawned several
days before the white sucker. According to information obtained from
the people living in the area around Sandy Lake near the headwaters of
the Severn River, the spawning behaviour of the sucker denoted special
significance. Thomas Fiddler, a Chief of the Sandy Lake people, and who
belonged to the Sucker Clan, stated that "when suckers spawn, even when
there is little water—a trickle—a sucker can still climb to the top of the
falls. With strong fins it will even go over the tops of steep falls. It's like it
flies to the top of rivers. So a sucker can go places other fish can't go."[66]
Suckers were plentiful throughout the lowlands. During the spring spawning period, they could be caught easily because they congregated in large
numbers and weirs captured thousands of suckers each day in certain
locations. The Lowland Cree preferred other species of fish for food, but
the sucker afforded a large and dependable subsistence resource when
other fish were not easily available. Suckers were also an important source
of dog food.

After the sucker, other species of fish made spring spawning runs in the lowlands. Notable among these fish was the lake sturgeon, which was called *Nemew* (Graham) or *Ne ma u* (Isham) in the Lowland Cree language. Sturgeon were not commonly found near the coast, but they were abundant in the upper portions of the waterways in the lowlands. Edward Umfreville, who was stationed at Severn House and York Factory from 1771 to 1782, observed that "in the spring of the year, the river [possibly the Severn or Hayes River] is known to abound with exquisite Sturgeon."[67] Andrew Graham said they "are found in great plenty in the Lakes one hundred miles up the country, and sometimes (though rarely) a strayed one is found in the creeks near the Fort."[68] Sturgeon spawned several weeks after the sucker, near river rapids or at the foot of waterfalls. A sturgeon fishing station was located near the mouth of the Cheepay River, about 150 kilometres upriver from Albany Fort. In 1743, when he established Henley House, Joseph Isbister reported that the people who had been hired to assist the HBC abandoned their duty when they arrived at the sturgeon fishery. He noted that "our Indians are loth to leave this place, having caught some sturgeon," and on his return journey he found them still engaged in sturgeon fishing.[69] The slow-growing and late-maturing sturgeon could attain an enormous size. The average sturgeon caught in the lowlands appears to have been rather modest in comparison with sturgeon caught elsewhere. Andrew Graham observed that the average weight of sturgeon ranged between nine to fourteen kilograms,[70] and James Isham, on May 21, 1748, traded seventeen sturgeon that weighed 150 kilograms, or about nine kilograms each.[71] Much larger sturgeon were occasionally encountered by the HBC traders. For example, James Isham remarked that one sturgeon measured two and a half metres in length.[72]

Lowland Cree fishermen commonly used spears to capture these large fish, but nets and weirs were also used effectively in certain locations. Sturgeon weirs were noted on the Albany River above the location of Henley House, near the confluence with the Kenogami River.[73] In 1833, George Barnston described a sturgeon weir on the Winisk River as "a fishing station of the Crane tribe, where they bar up the River, tho' it be full 150 yards across, and have a Basket on one side, in which they take in some seasons an immense number of sturgeon."[74]

In addition to fresh sturgeon, the Lowland Cree consumed and traded other types of sturgeon flesh. A common method of preparing sturgeon flesh for later consumption was sun-drying or smoke-drying over a low fire. Quantities of dried sturgeon could be prepared and cached for future needs. Lowland Cree also processed some of the sturgeon flesh into a dry,

powdery mixture called *ruaheggan* (Graham) or *ruhiggan* (Isham), a nutri-
tious, portable food supply that could be kept in sturgeon-skin containers
for long periods of time before spoiling. Ruhiggan was flesh that had been
dried and pounded. Ruhiggan made from caribou flesh was tied into bundles for easy transportation, and could be kept for years without spoiling.
Isham distinguished pimmegan, or pemmican, as a mixture of ruhiggan, fat,
and cranberries.[75] Sturgeon pemmican was produced by adding fat and
berries to the ruhiggan.[76]

Northern pike, called *Keneshue* (Graham) or *Ke no shue* (Isham), was
another important spring spawner. Although most easily caught in spring,
the pike was an important food resource year-round. Andrew Graham remarked, "They are very numerous and are much valued by the Lake Indians [Northern Ojibway], as they are a supply for them at all seasons, when
their gun and ammunition fails, or other food fails. Great numbers are
caught at the forts and are reckoned excellent food by us."[77] The Lowland
Cree employed several methods for catching pike, including nets, hooks,
and spears. The lake whitefish, known as *Tickomeg* (Graham) or *Tickomegg*
(Isham), spawned in the fall but quantities were caught in the spring. According to Graham, "in summer they frequent the rivers, but are then very poor.
In autumn they are in good condition and then is the time we catch them."[78]
Henry Ellis, who visited York Factory in 1746-47, remarked that the spring
fishery was "extremely successful," and catches of up to 500 fish, mostly whitefish, were common with a single haul of a seine net. Ellis noted that "Salmon
Trout" (probably the brook trout, also a fall spawner, was caught in the spring
with "set nets" (gill nets) in the creeks near York Factory.[79]

Summer

The warm winds of summer ushered a quick departure of most geese from
the coastal marshes to breeding grounds farther afield,[80] but the caribou
hunt continued as Lowland Cree pursued the caribou to their summer
calving grounds along the coastal tundra. James Knight, who was in charge
of York Factory in 1717, noted "ye Deer is comeing down out of the
Country to calf their young ones upon the Sandy Banks [coastal beach
ridges] which they doo once in 2 years."[81] The Hayes and Severn River
Lowland Cree moved eastward with the migrating herds. The Albany River
Lowland Cree began their caribou hunt in summer, travelling north to
meet the migrating herds.

Many of the Lowland Cree who had been employed in the goose hunt
turned their attention to caribou after receiving payment for their geese. If

the goose hunt failed early, the attraction of the caribou hunt was strong, and many goose hunters gave up their positions in the marshes in order to search for caribou in the coastal calving grounds. Often, HBC boats at York Factory carried hunters and their families across the Hayes River. The Lowland Cree travelled on foot, following the beach ridges in pursuit of the caribou. Most Lowland Cree spent the entire summer along the coastal lowlands, returning only to set up camps upriver to wait for the crossing of caribou in the fall migration. The main caribou calving grounds were reported to be east of the Severn River in the vicinity of Cape Henrietta Maria, but some caribou spent the summer between York Factory and Severn House. For example, Thomas Macklish, Chief Factor at York Factory, observed on June 10, 1732, that "severall of our home Indians kill'd some breeding Deer about 80 miles to ye Southward."[82]

The Severn River Lowland Cree who hunted caribou in the summer divided into regional hunting groups. Those who hunted along the coast east of Severn House were known as the "eastward Homeguards," while other Severn caribou hunters remained at upriver locations during the summer and were known as "southern Homeguards."[83] Another group hunted caribou in the region northwest of Severn House, and were known as the "northern Homeguards." On April 29, 1777, William Falconer noted that the southern and northern Homeguards remained to hunt geese near Severn House while the eastern Homeguards and the upriver Half-Homeguards returned to their caribou hunting camps.[84]

As with the spring hunt, large groups of Lowland Cree hunted caribou in the summer. In the summer of 1779, York Factory boats were sent across the river to French Creek to transport sixty-five Lowland Cree who brought 170 caribou skins and dried venison to trade.[85] In the summer of 1780, a group of 180 Lowland Cree traded dried meat and over 100 caribou skins at York Factory.[86]

Many Albany River Lowland Cree spent the summer on Akimiski Island, hunting caribou. In most years the hunt must have been successful, because the Indians brought venison, tongues, and fat to trade at Albany Fort. In some years the caribou did not migrate as far as Akimiski Island and the Lowland Cree were forced to return early to the vicinity of the Albany Fort to wait for the arrival of the geese. For example, on July 27, 1726, Richard Staunton, Chief Factor, reported that "11 canows of our home Indians came here they being all starved upon Ogomiska, ye deere having failed them this summer."[87]

Preserving caribou meat was an important industry for the Lowland Cree during the summer months. Food preservation was generally done by women. William Falconer observed, "The women['s] work is to do all the domestick duty of the tent, make and mend the tent, make shoes, make their birch rind victualling vessels (called by them thogans) dress skins and sew them together for cloathing, unpitch and pitch the tent, and in winter they draw all their goods on sleds as also the children that are not able to walk, and nimakeg (to ornament the cloathing with glass beads or quills etc.) their cloathing etc. etc. and indeed their task is never finished."[88] The meat was cut into thin strips and dried in the sun or smoke-dried to prevent it from spoiling. Another method of preparing caribou meat, similar to that described for sturgeon above, was to beat the dried meat into ruhiggan powder. James Isham described the method of preparing caribou ruhiggan:

> The Leg's and thigh's they cure otherways, they cutting all the flesh of the bones, and Cutt itt in slices, which is to be Dryd. in the same manner as aforemention'd [meat hung on poles over a fire until dried], this meet when Dry'd they take and pound, or beat between two Stones, till some of itt is as small as Dust, which they styl (Ruhiggan) being Dryd. so much that their is Little moisture in itt;—when pounded they putt itt into a bag and will Keep for Several Years.[89]

Caribou ruhiggan was prepared for consumption by mixing caribou fat, fish oil, or bear fat with the powdered meat. Polar bear fat mixed with cranberries and caribou ruhiggan was "one of their [Lowland Cree's] greatest dainties."[90] Moose fat was also mixed with the ruhiggan, as was bison fat, suggesting a trade in this product between the Indians of the uplands and prairie parklands and the Lowland Cree. Other food stuffs such as lichen and dried fish were added to ruhiggan for flavour and substance. Caribou pemmican (also spelled pimmegan), was also sometimes called finished venison.

Preserved caribou meat was stored for later use in underground caches and above-ground stages. The importance of caches was noted by HBC fur traders. On December 19, 1736, Thomas White reported the arrival at York Factory of three families of Lowland Cree, and that

> the said Indians have been to the Northwd. about halfe way to Churchill, expecting to Sight of beaver and deer, but were much disappointed, not having kill'd one deer, nor but very few furs, but just what would pay their fall Debt, and had itt not been for a stage of meat they had Laid up the Latter part of the Summer, they would have been near Starving, they are Designh'd to go to the South'd to Look for beaver, in a short time, as soon as they have made Sleds.[91]

Although caches were designed to keep the meat safe from animals, they sometimes failed and the consequences could be severe for the Lowland Cree. At York Factory on December 16, 1744, Thomas White reported that "three families of home Indians came from ye north [Nelson] river, for relief, 18 in number, the cause of their coming in so soon is they have met with no deer, and another misfortune is they had laid up 3 stages of dry'd meat in ye fall but the vermin got foul of itt and destroyed itt all."[92] John Work, who explored the Winisk River for the HBC in the summer of 1819, noted that the people who accompanied the expedition buried fifteen to twenty "bits of pemmican" near the mouth of the Winisk River for provisions on their return journey.[93] Some Lowland Cree found it more convenient to store their dried provisions at the trading posts. For example, on October 3, 1737, four women came to York Factory from their camp located several days' journey up the Nelson River with "bundles of dry'd meat to Lye up against they comes in, in ye Spring."[94] On October 10, 1742, two "home Indians," who had spent the fall in the south hunting caribou, returned to York Factory unsuccessful and took "some bundles of dry'd meate they left here when they went away."[95]

In addition to caribou hunting, the Lowland Cree were able to hunt some wildfowl along the coast. Canada geese and brant geese remained in the lowlands to breed during the summer, and were available as a food and commercial resource. Canada geese preferred breeding grounds in the coastal plains. Although dispersed over a large area, the geese were hunted successfully by the Lowland Cree, especially during the summer moult. Brant geese were also available during the summer near the coast and, despite their "fishy taste," were hunted by the Lowland Cree and occasionally traded to the HBC posts. Ducks were also plentiful in the lowlands during the summer. The whistling duck, or *Mimmenick* (Graham), bred in the marshes and plains near the coast. According to Graham, the most valuable species was the mallard duck, which he described as a "beautiful duck of great service, being good food both to Indians and Europeans."[96] The Lowland Cree usually traded numbers of ducks, mature and newborn, every summer at the coastal trading posts. Most often, ducks were brought in together with caribou meat after the caribou hunt.

Passenger pigeons visited the southern James Bay region in great flocks during the summer. On July 2, Richard Staunton, Chief Factor at Albany Fort, remarked that his men had killed twenty-six "pidgeons."[97] Andrew Graham received one at Severn House in 1771, but considered it rare in that area. He observed, "They are numerous inland and often visit our southern settlements in summer. They are about Moose Fort and inland, where they breed choosing an arboreous situation." Graham recalled that passenger pigeons had migrated as far north as York Factory in the summer of 1750, and many were killed by the Lowland Cree and HBC men. Passenger pigeons were considered to be "among the many delicacies [of] Hudson's Bay."[98]

Fishing during the summer months was generally not as productive as during other seasons. After the spring spawning runs, sturgeon and suckers moved to deeper waters and were less active. Other fish, such as whitefish and trout (brook trout and lake trout), spawned in the fall, and were also more difficult to catch in the summer. Some fish, such as northern pike, continued to be caught throughout the summer and quantities were regularly traded by the Lowland Cree at the coastal posts.[99] Summer encampments at fishing stations, as they were sometimes called by HBC traders, attracted large numbers of Lowland Cree before the fall caribou and goose hunts. Samuel Skrimsher, who was in charge of York Factory on July 3, 1750, noted that "three of our home Indians with their familyes went for the North River in order to Lay wate for Deer and catch fish."[100] He also reported that fishing stations were located on the Hayes River, upstream from York Factory, and that "one family of home Indians went up the [Hayes] River to catch fish to support on and to Lay wate for the Deer." Two days later, four more families of Indians set off upriver to set up a camp to catch fish while waiting for the caribou herds to cross the river.[101] Like the York Factory Lowland Cree, those at Severn combined fishing and gathering activities at their caribou hunt camps. The summer whitefish fishery was especially productive at Ouaouiastine.

White whales, also known as beluga whales, and *Wapameg* (Graham) or *Wap po meg* (Isham) by the Lowland Cree, visited the estuaries of large coastal rivers each summer.[102] Andrew Graham said they were "very numerous in the rivers immediately after the breaking up of the ice, and many are killed annually which supply the Factories with oil, and furnish several tons to be imported into England."[103] The Lowland Cree did not usually eat the flesh or fat of white whales, but it was commonly used for dog food and for sale to the European traders.[104] The Lowland Cree employed several techniques to capture white whales. Harpoons were used effectively at times, despite the fact that the Lowland Cree had only small canoes to go after the whales. A good description of the Indian harpooning technique was made by Samuel Skrimsher at York Factory on July 22, 1750:

An Indian man had killed [white whales] with an Enstrument of his one makeing fasend to a stafe and a Leather thong with a small Boye at the End of it which he heaves over Board as Sune as he Strikes the fish and follows it till such time as the fish Dyes, he commonly goes in two or three Cannoes Lashed to Gather for fear of over Seting. Should have incouraged him on the Same head but [he] was gone to look for Deer.[105]

The HBC whale fishery that developed later was similar to the Lowland Cree method described by Skrimsher. Andrew Graham noted that

they [white whales] are caught in the following manner, having boats for that purpose built after the form of the Greenland whale fishing boats, only larger. They are manned with four men and a harpooner who rows out on the river where the fish is, then lay in their oars and drives with the tide amongst the fish, and when one comes up to blow alongside it is struck with a harpoon; and a large fish will run out one hundred fathoms of line, and haul the boat after it above a quarter of an hour before they can shorten in any line, always minding to play with the fish, hauling in and veering out line according as the fish swims to or fro from the boat; for if it were to be brought up all at once the harpoon would lose its hold, which is often the case. When its strength fails he gathers in the line with judgement, until he gets it within reach, then gives it another harpoon and lances it to death.[106]

White whales were sometimes captured by driving them into shallow water and beaching them on the tidal flats. This method was employed by the Indians at the mouth of the Severn River. White whales were very abundant in the Nelson, Hayes, and Severn rivers during the summer, and often damaged fish nets, as at York Factory on May 26, 1725, when Thomas Macklish observed that his men "took the net up, being much broak with the White Whales."[107] Near Severn House, the white whales came into the Severn River in great numbers shortly after the ice broke in the estuary. Humphrey Marten remarked on June 17, 1760, "the Whales are so thick, Obliged to take up the Netts."[108] Marten also noted many white whales on July 3, 1760, but his fascination with the whales turned to anger on July 9, when he wrote, "We cant get a Single Fishe for the Dam'd Whales, they break the Netts and have carryed one entirely away."[109] The HBC traders at Albany Fort also occasionally purchased whales or whale blubber from the Lowland Cree.

The relatively short growing season in the lowlands produced an extraordinary profusion of plant life. William Falconer remarked, "In this short liv'd summer, grass grows in and about the plains and swamps to a surprizing length, having observed it to grow 16 inches in 6 weeks, and goose-berries, cran-berries, straw-berries, rasp-berries and corron berries with many other berries grows in plenty in the woods, and to full perfection."[110]

Lowland Cree used many different types of plants for food, medicinal, and other purposes, and sold small quantities to the European fur traders. A large variety of edible berries was available in the lowlands, including: cranberries, *Wusiskumenuck* (Graham) or *we sa ke ma nuck* (Isham); strawberries, *Skesheckamenuck* (Graham) or *U ske she co me nuc* (Isham); raspberries or yellowberries, *brackatuminack* (Falconer) or *Bo ro ca to me nuck* (Isham); gooseberries, *Shapomenuck* (Graham) or *Shap po me nuck* (Isham); crowberries or mawsberries, *Askemenuck* (Graham) or *as ke ma nah* (Isham); willowberries, *Neneekamenuck* (Graham); partridge berries, *Pethaymenuck* (Graham); dewberries, *Outamenuck* (Graham); huckleberries, *Mis ke ma na* (Isham); juniperberries, *Kawkawimenuck* (Graham) or *wur sus qua tu uc* (Isham); blackcurrants, *Mantoomenuck* (Graham); redcurrants, *Atheekimenuck* (Graham) or *A tha kim mi nuck* (Isham); and whitecurrants, *Wapeckumenuck* (Graham). Berries were often dried and stored for later consumption, and added to flavour dried meat and fish.[111] The Lowland Cree also subsisted on berries during times when other resources were scarce. For example, in the summer of 1750, few caribou were killed by the Lowland Cree who lived near York Factory, and James Skrimsher remarked that "two cannoes of our home Indians with their familys came in, in order to hunt geese, being no Deer to be got, haveing liv'd on Beryes and fish, the Latter of which having been scarcest this Summer I ever knew."[112]

The Lowland Cree lived north of the range of maple trees, but they likely had access to maple sugar through trade contacts with their southern neighbours. During the fur-trade period, maple sugar was carried north by Aboriginal fur traders who visited the coastal trading posts. On July 5, 1720, Thomas Macklish, Chief Factor at Albany Fort, observed:

> One of the [upland] Indians that came last night presented me with 12 pounds of very good sugar of their own making, which is as follows. In the spring of the year they go to a Lake where grows a plenty of large birch [probably maple] trees. In those trees they cut a hole and put a tap and out of one they get 7 or 8 gallons of sweet liquor which they boil 12 hours after which, when cold, turns to sugar, then they dry it in the sun or over the fire in their tents.[113]

Wild rice, known as *Nicoshemin* (Graham) by the Lowland Cree, was not indigenous to the Hudson Bay lowlands, but a trade in this product had developed between the Lowland Cree and upland people. Andrew Graham hinted at an Aboriginal trade in wild rice: "I have seen several samples of Indian corn [probably wild rice] brought to the Factories by some of the distant trading Indians. They report that it does not grow in their country, but farther to the southward, where they barter it from other nations."[114]

Fall

By early fall, caribou were in prime physical condition after feeding all summer on coastal grasses and other vegetation.[115] Mature male caribou were particularly good food in early fall, prior to the rut. They had built up reserves of fat for the strenuous rutting season, including a layer of back fat up to ten centimetres thick and over thirty centimetres in length.[116] On August 11, 1717, Thomas Macklish, Chief Factor at Albany Fort, noted that "an Indian brought me a Rump of a Buck Deer, weighed 40 pounds and cut 3 inches deep of fat."[117] Macklish was later Chief Factor at York Factory, where he also noted the quality of male caribou meat in the fall. He reported on September 24, 1723, that "four Cannoes of home Indians came down the River, brought twelve Noble, fatt Buck Deer."[118]

HBC traders tried to encourage Lowland Cree hunters to kill caribou in late fall or winter when the skins were in prime condition. However, the early fall caribou hunt was more important as a source of food for both Lowland Cree and Europeans, and large numbers were killed when the skins were not acceptable for trade purposes. Humphrey Marten, Chief Factor at York Factory, noted that the fall was "one of the deers grand crossing seasons, consequently be they fatt or lean, are killed in great numbers, now as the weather is very fine and warm consequently the skins are not in season, and yet this inconveniency cannot be helped, for should we slip this opportunity or oppose the Indians hunting them, we should get no venison and the Indians be disgusted."[119] During the fall hunt, many caribou were killed while crossing rivers. Andrew Graham observed:

> When the deer are pretty far advanced into the river, the canoes are all manned, and paddle after them, one party surrounding them and preventing their landing on the opposite shore; whilst the women, children and dogs by making a noise and throwing stones, hinder them from returning. The men in the other canoes immediately approach the unhappy victims, and stab them with spears, bayonets, knives, arrows, or even a stick sharpened at the point and hardened in the fire.[120]

The Lowland Cree purchased metal spear-tips specially made for caribou hunting. The HBC blacksmiths at York Factory furnished extra spear-tips by reworking other metal goods.

Caribou killed in the rivers were easy to transport to the trading posts. Large quantities of caribou flesh, tongues, fat, and skins could be easily floated downriver on wooden rafts.[121] At York Factory, James Isham reported on August 10, 1753, that "one cannoe came Down the River with a float of 19 Deer."[122] These rafts or floats were made by "falling severall trees, and tying them togeather with the bark of willow, interwoven with the Branches of the tree, which Carry's them safe over such Rivers &c, or will go downe River's on such floats some miles."[123]

Andrew Graham observed, "When the Indians are travelling and have no canoe, yet have occasion to cross a river, they make a float of wood three tier deep, securing the ground-floor of this curious conveyance with the fibrous roots of trees, shrubs etc. Upon this they place themselves and baggage, and with a long pole push themselves over."[124]

The caribou herds usually crossed the Severn and Hayes rivers several weeks before the onset of the fall goose hunt. The Lowland Cree hunters set up camps in advance of the caribou herds at crossing places, and subsisted on fish until the arrival of the caribou. Similar caribou-hunt camps were also set up along the Hayes River. For example, Skrimsher noted on July 15, 1750, that "one family of home Indians went up the [Hayes] River to catch fish to support on and to Lay wate for the Deer," and two days later, four more families went upriver to set up a camp and catch fish while waiting for the caribou herds to cross the river.[125]

Like the spring hunt, the fall caribou hunt was conducted about thirty to 100 kilometres inland from the coast, near traditional crossing places. In 1716, a "great herd" was reported crossing the Nelson River at a location about two days' paddling upriver. The Lowland Cree who were camped nearby killed sixty caribou.[126] Small herds sometimes passed within view of York Factory. For example, on August 15, 1720, Henry Kelsey counted thirty-two caribou in a herd that crossed the Hayes River in sight of the factory.[127] If the caribou failed to pass nearby, the hunters removed to alternative places, sometimes at great distances from the factory. Speed was essential at these times in order to intercept the caribou at other passes along the rivers. Old and disabled people were left at the original camps to subsist mainly on fish while the others went in search of caribou. The locations of fall caribou-hunting camps on the Severn River were similar to the spring camps. A favourite site was Ouaouiastine, or White Seal Falls. In June 1773, Andrew Graham at Severn House reported "the Deer crossing in many thousands twenty miles up this river, going northwards."[128] The next summer, he noted the arrival of "the deer hunters from the great fall 22 miles up the river, [they] brought upwards of 300 dryed deers tongues and some fatt."[129]

Some of the Lowland Cree shifted their focus to geese soon after the caribou finished crossing the rivers. Near York Factory, the caribou sometimes migrated west before the fall goose hunt, which prompted many Lowland Cree to repair to the factory to wait for the geese to arrive. For example, Thomas White recorded on August 2, 1745, that "severall familys of home Indians who had been a deer hunting came to waite ye flying of ye geese, ye Deer being all gone."[130] The fall goose hunt was preceded by duck hunting that often produced large quantities of food and trade resources for the Lowland Cree. In the coastal marshes around the mouth of the Albany River, duck hunting usually began in early August. By the end of August or early September, geese arrived in the marshes around Albany Fort. The Cree word for the return of the geese in fall is *akwânâwak*, meaning "driven by the wind," because they fly with the wind and are driven to the shore.[131] Goose hunting continued for three or four weeks, and by early October, the geese had usually left the Albany Fort area. The timing of the fall geese migrations in the Severn House and York Factory areas was similar, except that the geese arrived and departed several weeks earlier. During certain years, the fall migration of geese failed to produce the usual numbers of geese. These occasions were often blamed on unusual weather patterns, such as cold, wet, and windy weather. Sometimes, unusual weather during the summer was blamed for reducing the number of young geese. For example, the summer of 1770 had been unusually wet near Albany Fort, and Humphrey Marten noted that "no young geese [are] to be seen, their eggs being spoiled by the wetness of the hatching season."[132]

The fall fishery was also important to the Lowland Cree and European fur traders. The Lowland Cree who lived near Severn House operated a weir to catch whitefish during the fall. The weir was located about thirty kilometres upriver from the post, probably near Ouaouiastine. Andrew Graham, who was in charge of Severn House in 1766, reported on October 3 that Indians had traded "230 fine fish called tikomeg from a Lock, or Wear, made by the Indians 20 miles up the River."[133] The weir produced hundreds of fish that were traded to the HBC, in addition to the fish that were consumed and stored for use by the Lowland Cree.

Winter

Caribou were not plentiful near the coast during the winter, but Lowland Cree hunted caribou successfully in the upper regions of the Hudson Bay lowlands. The winter caribou hunt focussed on woodland caribou that frequented the wooded river valleys. Occasionally, Lowland Cree brought large quantities of caribou meat to trade at Albany Fort near the end of winter as hunting groups moved closer to the coast to prepare for the goose-hunting season. For example, on March 14, 1707, three families of Lowland Cree arrived at Albany Fort and presented Chief Factor Anthony Beale with a gift of thirty-six caribou tongues.[134]

Occasionally, the Albany Fort records noted that Lowland Cree hunted caribou on Akimiski Island in winter. For example, on February 16, 1747, Joseph Isbister, Chief Factor at Albany Fort, reported that three Lowland Cree had been hunting on Akimiski Island, and they had killed more than thirty caribou but did not bring any to trade with the HBC. Isbister was insulted, and commented: "what devouring Creatures they must be."[135] The next winter, George Spence, the next Chief Factor, observed that many Lowland Cree had camped on the island because there was "plenty of Deer on that Island." Nine hunters came from Akimiski Island to Albany Fort and traded 108 caribou tongues and thirty-one rumps.[136] It is difficult to ascertain whether these accounts refer to migratory barren ground caribou that had remained on the island, or to an indigenous woodland caribou population. Since winter hunting on the island was not reported in most years, the former is more likely.

Snow conditions were significant in determining the success of winter caribou hunting. For example, on December 24, 1728, Joseph Myatt, Chief Factor at Albany Fort, remarked that "there is so little snow on the ground they [Lowland Cree] cannot possibly come up with any Beast."[137] Very little caribou meat was traded by the Lowland Cree during the winter months. On occasion, when hunting groups were near the trading posts, they would bring in caribou flesh. However, winter caribou hunting was usually at a considerable distance from the posts, and this precluded much trade in caribou meat during the winter.

Moose, known as elk to the early European fur traders,[138] were prized for their meat but they were rare in the lowlands. The upland Indians sometimes brought moose meat down in the summer to trade at the coastal factories,[139] and there may also have been some traffic with the Lowland Cree. There is some evidence that moose populations in the adjacent uplands declined during the fur-trade period, and they had entirely disappeared by the beginning of the nineteenth century.[140] Moose populations have increased over the past 150 years, and their range has expanded greatly. Today, moose are found near the coast of Hudson Bay and throughout much of the lowlands.

Fur-bearing animals were harvested during the winter for their pelts, but hunting and trapping these animals for food took place year-round.

Beaver, or *Au misk* (Isham) in the Lowland Cree language, were valuable as commercial and subsistence resources. Beaver pelts worn as clothing by the Lowland Indians could be sold to the fur traders in the spring. This kind of beaver pelt, called coat beaver, was generally preferred to unused skins, called parchment beaver, because the long guard hairs were worn away in the coats. The removal of the longer hair was desirable because the soft underhair, called beaver wool, was used in manufacturing felt for the hat industry in Europe.[141] Beaver also produced a substance called castoreum, or castor, which the Lowland Cree called *weshenow* (Isham). Castoreum was valued by Europeans for its musky scent and it was used in making perfumes. The Lowland Cree valued castoreum as a bait for trapping lynx, wolverine, marten, and other small fur bearers. Andrew Graham noted that the Lowland Cree made traps for lynx that were baited with sticks rubbed over with castoreum,[142] and James Isham commented that "the Natives usses [castoreum] in trapping Rubbing the baits with itt, being Extrodinary good for martins and other Vermin, Espetially Quequahatches [wolverine], itt having a Very strong cent."[143]

According to Andrew Graham, beaver hunting was a group effort, with several families, including women, children, and the elderly, usually participating together. However, while the flesh was distributed among the group, the beaver skins were "the sole property of the person who first discovered the house."[144] Any small, or so-called "half beaver," skins belonged to the women. According to Graham, the same rules applied to upland women: "The cub beaver, musquashes and the like are esteemed the women's property, who barter them for beads, vermilion, bracelets and other trinkets."[145]

Winter hunting and trapping of beaver was a difficult and laborious task.[146] During winter, the common method involved a complex system of traps and barriers placed around the beaver lodge. Central to the task was breaking into the lodge, which was difficult because the walls of the lodge, built of branches, twigs, and mud, were usually almost a metre thick. Andrew Graham accompanied a group of Lowland Cree on a beaver hunt.

> There were eight of us in company including women. We set out early in the morning and in a few hours arrived at the place of action, which had previously been narrowly examined by an old and experienced Indian. Our first care was to stake the creek across both above and below the house to prevent the beaver from escaping. Afterwards we endeavoured to discover all the holes or cells about the creek, by thrusting a long hoop-stick under the ice; all these retreats were likewise barricaded by driving down stakes. Our next business was to cut a large hole in the ice near the mouth of the house, and set a net made of leather-thong, which

is constantly watched by one of the oldest and most experienced men, who knows when the beaver approaches by the undulation of the water, whilst others make a noise, and beat upon the house, when out jumps the beaver, and it is caught in the net, which is immediately replaced. The women then break up the house with their hatchets and if any beavers are in the house they knock them on the head, and carefully watch the return of others. They are extremely shy, and seldom hampered a second time in a net, and will almost drown themselves before they will return to their house when they have once been disturbed. We caught all that were

Hunting Beaver, by James Isham, watercolour and ink, 1743 (PAM, HBCA, E.2/2, fo.12).

in that house, which amounted to only two....The flesh of the beaver is equally distributed, but the skins are the sole property of the person who first discovered the house. We [HBC] divide the beaver into three sizes. Firstly the whole or full-grown beaver, which is the standard. Secondly the three-quarter. Thirdly the half or young beaver, which last size generally belongs to the women.[147]

Beaver were hunted for food as well as for their fur and castoreum. Mature beaver weighed about twenty kilograms, and the amount of meat and fat obtained from each animal comprised a significant food resource. Both Europeans and Aboriginal people relished the taste of beaver. James Isham said "they are Extrodinary good Eating if young and the tail which is of a Different taste from the other part of the body, I think is the finest eating in the Country, Cutting firm, itts all fat Except a bone in the midle and Very Lucious food."[148] Beaver flesh was also preserved by drying, and occasionally dried beaver meat was traded by the Lowland Cree.

The flesh of most fur-bearing animals was consumed by the Lowland Cree. These included the otter, called *Neekeek* (Graham) or *Ne Kick* (Isham) by the Lowland Cree;[149] marten, *Wappestan* (Graham) or *Wap pa stan* (Isham); mink, *Jakash, Shakweshue* (Graham) or *Au cha Karsh* (Isham); wolverine, *Quiquahack* (Graham) or *Qui qua ha ku* (Isham); lynx, *Pisshu* (Graham) or *Pir shuee* (Isham); red fox, *Makesheu* (Graham) or *Me ke shue* (Isham); Arctic fox, *Wappekeseu* (Graham) or *wap pa ke shue* (Isham); skunk, *Shicauk* (Graham) or *She cow wuck* (Isham); porcupine, *Caqua* (Graham) or *Caw qua* (Isham); black bear, *Musqua* (Graham) or *Mus qua* (Isham); polar bear, *Wapusk* (Graham) or *Wap pusk* (Isham); and snowshoe hare, *Wapuss* (Graham). Very few species of fur bearers were not esteemed as food resources by the Lowland Cree. However, even these were eaten when other subsistence resources were unavailable. These included the fisher, *Wejack* (Graham) or *Shar qua she wuck* (Isham); badger, *Nanaspacheneskeskesewick* (Graham); marmot, *Wenusk* (Graham); and wolf, *Mahigan* (Graham) or *Me hi gan* (Isham).

Small fur bearers were usually caught in deadfall traps or snare mechanisms. These traps worked best under certain types of snow and weather conditions. Joseph Myatt, Chief Factor of Albany Fort in 1721, explained:

I have oftentimes observed whenever the winter sets in so extraordinary early, and attended with such great flights of snow it generally proves a year of great scarcity among the Natives, but on the contrary when the fall proves long with hard frosty weather, and but little snow upon the ground, they [Lowland Indians] seldom fail of catching good quantities of small furrs.[150]

Marten were the most valuable among the small fur bearers in the fur trade, even more than the beaver trade, most of which was brought in by upland traders. George Spence, who was in charge of Albany Fort in 1745, noted the significance of the marten trade: "Our settlement at Kitchimatawan [Henley House] answers our intention, which prevents the French Pedlars drawing the Sea Side Indians from us, who catch that valuable commodity, vz. Martins."[151]

Among the animals traded for their fur, the black bear and polar bear were significant food resources because of their large size. Polar bears were unique to the coastal environment, and valued by the Lowland Cree for their flesh and fat. Andrew Graham observed, "The Indians likewise eat the flesh of all [polar bears] they kill, and mix the fat with cranberries, pounded venison [ruhiggan] etc. which constitutes one of their greatest dainties."[152] Around the coastal factories, bears were seasonally abundant. Near York Factory, polar bears were hunted during the fall before they migrated farther north. In the fall of 1747, James Isham noted "more [polar] Bears about this fort this fall than ever was knowne."[153] Polar bears were also abundant near Severn House in the fall. On October 10, 1783, William Falconer at Severn House complained he had great difficulty in persuading several York Factory Lowland Cree who had delivered a packet of correspondence to return to York, because "they hung about [Severn House] ever since eating Bears flesh, which it seems our Natives have plenty of."[154]

Among the smaller fur bearers, the snowshoe hare was generally the most important subsistence resource available to the Lowland Cree. Although usually very abundant and easily caught throughout the lowlands, they were subject to extreme cyclical fluctuations. Every nine or ten years the population reached a peak and then suddenly crashed.[155] The snowshoe hare furnished the Lowland Cree with food and clothing; the "rabbit-skin" blanket was a common article of winter clothing. They were caught with snares set across runways that were easy to find in the winter snow cover. The introduction of European wire probably increased the efficiency of the snare traps.

Several species of birds indigenous to the Hudson Bay lowlands provided important subsistence and commercial resources for the Lowland Cree during the winter. Foremost among these was the willow ptarmigan, known commonly by the HBC men as partridges, and *Wapethew* (Graham) in the Lowland Cree language. Large flocks of willow ptarmigan gathered during the winter months, and the Lowland Cree used a number of techniques to capture and kill these birds easily. Nets were employed effectively to capture thousands near the coastal trading posts. Andrew Graham noted that more than 10,000 ptarmigan were captured annually by nets in the vicinity of Severn House.[156] In 1776, Humphrey Marten, who was in charge of York Factory, noted, "I pay the Indians four beaver for every hundred birds [ptarmigan] they bring to the fort."[157] During the winter of 1743-44, a total of 2086 ptarmigan were caught with nets for the HBC at Albany Fort.[158]

In most seasons, ptarmigan were available in large flocks near the coastal posts, but periodically they failed to appear in their accustomed winter grounds; for example, in the winter of 1777-78, near York Factory, "the North Side of the North River, that used to be swarming with partridges every year, is now destitute of a single bird and indeed our eastern shore, except at Stoney River, is in the same condition nearly."[159] When conditions were unfavourable for netting ptarmigan, hunting was done with guns. Such was the case in the winter of 1758-59 around Albany Fort, when 3666 ptarmigan were shot and only 1612 were netted for the HBC.[160] HBC records also noted the use of bows and arrows to kill ptarmigan in winter. In 1769, at Severn House, Lowland Cree boys killed over 100 ptarmigan with bows and arrows.[161] It appears that the gun had replaced the bow and arrow in the hunting equipment of men who could afford to purchase them, but boys continued to use traditional technology quite effectively. The HBC records indicated that the Lowland Cree did not hunt ptarmigan during the breeding season in late winter. According to Joseph Colen, at York Factory in 1790, "The Indian hunters returned from the Northward, much tired with sleds loaded with partridges, say it is useless to go out more as the Birds are pairing, and by killing of one, many are destroyed."[162]

Sharp-tailed grouse or *Aukuskow* (Graham), spruce grouse or *Mistic Apethou* (Graham), and ruffed grouse or *Uscathachish* (Graham) were known commonly as pheasants by the HBC men. These birds contributed to the winter subsistence and commercial needs of the Lowland Cree, although to a lesser degree than ptarmigan. Large numbers were easily caught with simple technology. For example, the spruce grouse could be caught by hand, and Andrew Graham explained, "The Indians frequently fasten a noose to the end of a stick, and slipping it over the head of the bird haul it down at once."[163]

Fishing during winter was an activity that involved specialized technology and skills. The HBC traders learned from the Indians how to set nets under the ice in winter. Winter fishing was sometimes critical for the support of the men employed at the coastal posts, especially if the fall fishery failed to produce the required quantity of fish. Such was the case in 1705 at

Albany Fort. Anthony Beale remarked, "I wish with all my hart it may frese hard that we may set our Netts under the ice for I have but 14500 fish in the Factory as yet."[164] Northern pike were caught in winter by angling with lines and hooks through holes in the ice, or caught in gill nets set under the ice. One species of fish that was caught especially in the winter was the burbot, which was called *Mathy* (Graham) or *Mur thy* (Isham) by the Lowland Cree. Burbot spawned in winter, usually between January and March. The bottom-feeding burbot could be caught easiest with a baited hook and line. Pieces of caribou meat were often used as bait. The HBC men disliked the flesh of the burbot, but they traded quantities from the Lowland Cree in times of need. The liver and roe of the burbot were considered to be a delicacy.[165]

Coaster and Inlander Lowland Cree Seasonal Cycles

The Lowland Cree who lived near the coast followed a seasonal cycle focussed upon resources usually available within about 160 kilometres from the coast. Compared to the inland people, the Coasters spent more time hunting geese and other migratory waterfowl that preferred coastal marshes for feeding and staging grounds. Coastal sloughs and offshore islands were also favoured breeding habitat for several species of ducks and geese. The best time for hunting migratory waterfowl was in the spring and fall, when huge flocks congregated along the major flyways that transected the Hudson Bay lowlands. The Lowland Cree who lived inland were usually unable to travel to the coastal marshes in time for the spring hunt. The fall hunt was also a difficult event for them because they had to travel to their winter hunting grounds before the onset of freezing weather. Both Coaster and Inlander Lowland Cree were able to hunt migratory birds that spent the summer along the coast. The summer moult left the birds vulnerable to hunters who used nets, clubs, and other Aboriginal technology.

Until the beginning of the nineteenth century, hunting migratory birds was secondary to the caribou hunt. The Coasters preferred hunting caribou when they were available, and goose camps were usually quickly abandoned when caribou herds were sighted nearby. Since the caribou generally crossed the major rivers at traditional crossing places, the spring and fall caribou hunts brought both Coaster and Inlander groups to these well-known places. During the eighteenth century, Northern Ojibway caribou hunters also arrived at the crossing places in the lowlands to join in the hunt. The location and timing of the spring and fall caribou migrations were usually predictable, and the hunting took place during a relatively short period. An important activity was preserving excess meat and fat for later consumption. The work of women at this time was critical to the future success of the hunting groups. Preserved caribou products were cached at strategic places for use during the winter season, when the supply of other food was sometimes less predictable. The availability of caribou meat and fat at other times of the year also added variety to the Lowland Cree diet.

Fisheries were also seasonally and spatially variable. The best fishing was usually conducted during the spring and fall, when most species of fish congregated at spawning grounds. The Coaster Lowland Cree depended more upon the riverine fisheries near the coastal estuaries. The fall fishery was the most important for the Coasters because fall-spawning whitefish were the most valuable fish in the rivers near the coast. Fishing was relatively more important to the Inlander Lowland Cree. Sturgeon were more abundant in the rivers at inland locations, especially near rapids and waterfalls that were favoured sturgeon spawning grounds. Lake whitefish were also more abundant in the larger lakes in the inland sections of the lowlands.

Fur-bearing animals were more plentiful inland, especially beaver, which was highly valued by the European fur traders. The Coaster Lowland Cree were relatively less productive fur hunters and trappers, but small fur bearers such as marten were generally available near the coast. The decline in beaver populations around 1800 was, therefore, a more significant setback for the Inlander Lowland Cree. The loss in food value was probably as critical as the loss in commercial value.

Birchbark was more easily obtained by the Inlander Lowland Cree, who made greater use of canoes than did the Coasters. The more complex drainage patterns inland also made the use of canoes more essential to the Inlanders for travel. The Coaster Lowland Cree depended more upon pedestrian travel along the coastal beach ridges. Rafts built of branches cut from locally available trees also facilitated river transport in the summer ice-free period. The HBC records indicate that company-owned vessels often shuttled the Coasters across the major rivers. The company also purchased birchbark canoes from upland Indians to supply the Coasters with additional watercraft. Although the Coaster Lowland Cree were more adapted to the resources available along the coastal strip, they were not especially focussed on marine mammals, such as the white whale and seals that frequented river estuaries. Whales and seals were occasionally harvested for dog food or for sale to the European traders, but the numbers were usually low and an industry in sea-mammal products did not develop among the Coaster Lowland Cree.

In summary, the Coaster and Inlander groups of Lowland Cree developed distinctive strategies for living in their different ecological zones. The Coasters were more adapted to migratory bird hunting, riverine fisheries, and, to a lesser extent, marine mammal hunting. The Inlanders focussed more of their activities on larger fur bearers such as beaver, and fish such as sturgeon that preferred upriver habitat. However, Coasters and Inlanders came together during the seasonal caribou hunts. Caribou was a focal resource for most Lowland Cree until the decline in caribou populations that took place around 1800.

6.
The Lowland Cree in the Fur Trade before 1713

Middlemen Traders from the St. Lawrence River Valley

Prior to the arrival of European fur traders, the Lowland Cree were probably involved in an extensive Aboriginal trade with their upland neighbours. The commerce between the Lowland Cree and upland nations may have involved products such as copper, silica, obsidian, and pottery, in return for furs, food, and other country produce. The Lowland Cree acquired European goods through these Aboriginal trading connections shortly after the beginning of the European fur trade along the St. Lawrence valley in the late sixteenth century. By the early seventeenth century, Aboriginal middlemen based in the valley were supplying European goods to the Lowland Cree in exchange for furs.

French fur traders and missionaries learned about the trading routes between the St. Lawrence River and James Bay from Aboriginal people. Samuel de Champlain was the first to record information about the James Bay trading connection in 1603, seven years prior to the "discovery" of the bay by Henry Hudson. Champlain visited Tadoussac, a trading post at the mouth of the Saguenay River, and met with local Montagnais who told him they traded with other people who lived near a northern saltwater sea.

The Montagnais, so-called because of the hilly terrain near Tadoussac, acted as middlemen in this exchange, bringing French merchandise to trade for furs procured by other Aboriginal people. The Montagnais travelled to a trading rendezvous located near the headwaters of the Saguenay River, and met with people who came from the James Bay region. Champlain reported that "on the banks of the said rivers [headwaters of the Saguenay River] are many lodges, where other tribes come from the north, to barter beaver and marten skins with the Montagnais for other merchandise, which the French ships bring to the said Montagnais. These said savages from the north say they are in sight of a sea which is salt."[1]

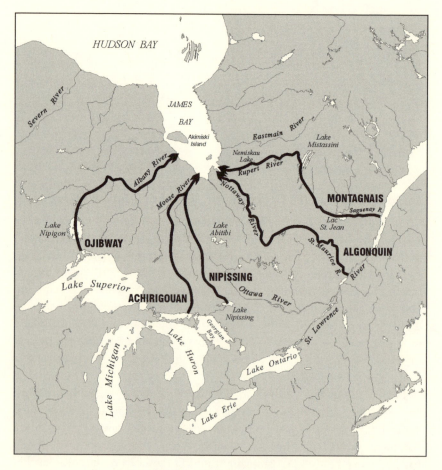

Indian Middlemen Trade Routes to James Bay

In 1608, when Champlain visited Tadoussac again, the Montagnais reported they made trading trips to the "northern sea," which took forty to fifty days. Champlain was eager to accompany the Montagnais on their northern trading trips, but they refused to take him or any other Frenchman. Their reluctance to take the French to James Bay was motivated by a desire to protect their position as middlemen in the fur trade with the Lowland Cree. Champlain learned later that other groups of people who lived along the St. Lawrence River also traded with the Lowland Cree. In 1609, he visited the area near the mouth of the St. Maurice River known as Trois-Rivières, and the local people, known as Algonquin, reported that their trading trips to James Bay took forty days.[2] Other Aboriginal groups who lived along the Ottawa River and the upper Great Lakes also traded with the Lowland Cree. In 1615, Champlain visited the Nipissing who lived around Lake Nipissing, and they also reported that their trading journeys to James Bay took forty days.[3]

European Explorations into Hudson Bay, 1610–1632

Five European exploring expeditions seeking a northwestern sea passage to the Pacific Ocean ventured into Hudson Bay and James Bay between 1610 and 1632. Only one face-to-face encounter with an Aboriginal person was recorded by the European explorers, but other evidence, such as abandoned campsites and sightings of distant campfires, clearly indicated that the people who lived in the region purposely avoided contact with these strange sea-faring newcomers. Henry Hudson was the first European to command an exploring party into Hudson Bay in 1610. Hudson piloted his ship *Discovery* from London across the Atlantic Ocean and into the bay, exploring its eastern and southern coastlines. When winter began to set in, he and his crew hauled their ship ashore in the southern part of James Bay, probably in the vicinity of Point Comfort.[4] The winter was long and difficult, and dissent among the crew turned to mutiny shortly after the ship set sail again the following summer. On June 23, 1611, Hudson and eight of his men were cast adrift in a boat near Charlton Island, and the others returned to England in *Discovery*. The only written account of Hudson's ill-fated voyage came from the testimony of Abacuck Pricket, one of the mutineers who was interrogated by English officials shortly after his return. Pricket's brief account mentioned only one encounter with an Aboriginal person, which occurred in the spring of 1611, "about the time the Ice began to breake out of the bayes."[5] Pricket observed that "there came a Salvage to their Ship, as it were to see and to be seen, and was the first, that they had seen all that time." Hudson communicated with this lone person in sign language, and gave him a knife, looking glass, and buttons. He must have been camped nearby because he returned the next day with two beaver skins and two "deere skins" (probably caribou). His actions indicated a familiarity with trading animal skins for European goods. In sign language, he communicated that other Indians lived to the north and south, and that he would return, presumably with others, to trade more furs. Hudson soon tired of waiting for their arrival, and he sent some of his men to search for them in the neighbouring woods. Pricket reported that other people were nearby and "set the woods on fire before him, yet they would not come to him."[6] According to Pricket's account, no other Aboriginal people were encountered by Hudson or his men during the remainder of their stay in the James Bay region.

Although Hudson's voyage ended in failure and mishap, a follow-up expedition was quickly organized. In the spring of 1612, Thomas Button set sail with two ships to venture into Hudson Bay. Button wintered near the mouth of the Port Nelson River, which was named after Robert Nelson, one of the ship's masters, who died there. Button lost many men through sickness during the winter, but there appears to have been an abundance of game and fish nearby. Button's men killed over 20,000 "Partridges [ptarmigan] and other Fowle," as well as a number of "Deare [caribou]" and plenty of "Fish, as bigge as Mackrils [probably whitefish]."[7] Fox's brief account of Button's stay at Port Nelson mentioned no encounters with Aboriginal people. However, the written account of Button's expedition is so sketchy that it is not possible to assess whether any Lowland Cree were encountered by Button or his men during their stay at the mouth of the Nelson River in 1612-13.

In 1619, Jens Munk led a Danish exploring party in two vessels into Hudson Bay, and they wintered near the mouth of the Churchill River. On October 7, 1619, they made a short exploration upriver. Although they did not meet with Aboriginal people, they "saw traces of their summer camps in a number of different spots.[8] These traces included piles of stones that Munk believed to be religious sites, and a pictograph drawn with charcoal that Munk likened to the shape of a devil. Munk and his men were ill-prepared for the winter at the mouth of the Churchill River, and sixty-two of his sixty-four crew members died at their winter camp. No people came to the camp, and Munk's men were too weak to venture far afield to search for the people who had made the curious stone structures and pictograph. Munk and two other survivors managed to sail one of the ships out of Hudson Bay and returned to Denmark in the fall of 1620.

The oral tradition of the Kashechewan (Albany River) Lowland Cree has preserved an account of the first encounter with Europeans at Church- ill River. The tradition, as told by James Wesley in 1985, and recorded by John Long, was an account of two people who discovered a ship at the mouth of the river. They described the ship with sails, and a boat being lowered with strangers who came to shore. Initially afraid of these stran- gers, the Cree approached them and were taken aboard the ship. They were treated well, and received gifts of tobacco, matches, and a gun. They had never seen such a weapon, which was described as a flintlock that fired after being loaded with a primer, but since no ammunition was given, it must have remained a curiosity to the Lowland Cree. The Cree oral tradi- tion is markedly different from the Munk written account, which did not record a meeting with Aboriginal people during the 1619-20 visit to Churchill River. These differences are not easily reconcilable, but it is pos- sible the Munk account is incomplete or the Cree tradition relates to a later visit by Europeans.[9]

In 1631, two English explorers, Thomas James and Luke Fox, set off on separate expeditions into Hudson Bay. Fox set his course toward the west- ern shore of Hudson Bay and then worked south toward the Nelson River. He and several crew members made a quick exploration of the river mouth area and found the remains of Button's encampment. They also saw signs of a recently abandoned camp. Fox's journal entry on August 17, 1631, noted that "upon the shore we found, the broad footing of Deere, and hard by them, the frame of a Tent standing, which had lately been made, with the studdle of the fire, the haire of Deere, and bones of fowle, left here."[10] Fox continued his voyage southeastward along the coast of the bay and met Thomas James near the mouth of the Winisk River. After a brief exchange of information about their respective journeys, the two explorers parted ways. Fox continued to sail eastward along the coast to the cape, which James had named Henrietta Maria after his ship. With winter fast approaching, and with the spectre of an ominous season ahead of him, Fox headed north and then home to England.

Thomas James had also explored the western coastline of Hudson Bay before meeting with Fox. Unlike Fox, James decided to spend the winter in the bay. He headed south into James Bay and searched for a safe harbour and wintering site. On October 4, 1631, James and several crew members went ashore on Danby Island. A cursory exploration revealed signs that people had recently been on the island. James finally settled on nearby Charlton Island and spent the long winter months struggling to keep his men healthy and alive. No signs of Aboriginal people were evident on the island during the winter. In the summer, before setting sail for England, James made a second brief exploration of Danby Island and he noted again that people had been on the island. On July 2, 1632, "when we came ashore, whilst some gather'd Wood, I went to the Place; where I found two Stakes, drove into the Ground a Foot and half, and Firebrands, where a Fire had been made by them. I pull'd up the Stakes, which were about the Bigness of my Arm; and they had been cut sharp at the Ends, with a Hatchet, or some other good Iron Tool, and driven in as it were with the Head of it."[11]

The wooden stakes may have been sharpened by a hatchet or other tool made of iron that had been lost or stolen from Hudson's party more than twenty years earlier. However, it is more likely that European iron goods were available to the local people through trade with Aboriginal middlemen who had had access to these items from European trade in the St. Lawrence valley for at least fifty years. James returned to England, stopping only briefly at Cape Henrietta Maria on July 22, 1632, where he erected a cross in honour of the king. He saw no Aboriginal people, but he noted that caribou and geese were numerous in the vicinity.[12]

James's departure from Hudson Bay in 1632 ended the initial brief flurry of European exploration in the region, and thirty-six years passed before the next European visit to the bay. However, events to the south, in the St. Lawrence valley and Great Lakes basin, continued to shed significant light on the region and the Lowland Cree. In particular, the written accounts of French fur traders and missionaries incorporated evidence from Aboriginal oral accounts of the Lowland Cree in the fur trade through southern upland middlemen.

The James Bay Trading Connection

Beginning in the 1630s, Jesuit missionaries visited various Indian groups who lived in the St. Lawrence valley and Great Lakes basin, and learned more about the James Bay trading connection. In 1637, the Jesuit missionary Paul Le Jeune reported that the Nipissing carried "divers wares from New France" to James Bay to trade with the "nations of the North."[13] In 1640, Le Jeune was the first person to record the name of the Indians who lived in the James Bay region, calling them the "Kiristinon who live on the North Sea whither the Nipisiriniens go to trade."[14] The name *Kiristinon*, first recorded by Le Jeune in 1640, became the common term used by the French to describe the Lowland Cree who lived in the James Bay area. However, it is quite evident that the French also applied the name more generally to include the Upland Cree and perhaps other Aboriginal people who visited the James Bay region to trade each summer. A Jesuit report for 1660-61 noted: "We have long known that we have the North Sea behind [to the north of] us, its shores occupied by hosts of Savages entirely unacquainted with Europeans.... Upon this bay are found, at certain seasons of the year, many surrounding Nations embraced under the general name of Killistinons [Cree]."[15]

In 1641, the Jesuit missionary Claude Pijart reported that "our Nipisiriniens, returning not long since from the Kyristinons [Cree], who trade on the Northern sea,"[16] had told him the trip to James Bay took thirty days, and ten more days of travel along the coast of the bay was needed to reach the place where the Cree had gathered for trade. According to the Nipissing, 400 Cree men were gathered at the trading place and they spoke the same language as the Montagnais who lived near Tadoussac.

By the 1640s, the annual summer trade on James Bay had attracted a number of Indian groups. The Attikamegue, who occupied the area around the headwaters of the St. Maurice River, had developed close trading connections with the Kiristinon on James Bay. The Achirigouan, who occupied the region near the mouth of the French River, also made trading trips to James Bay. In 1658, Jesuit missionaries visited them and noted that some were prepared to "go in a few days to trade with the Ataouabouskatouk Kilistinons."[17] A number of other nations who lived near the Achirigouan also made trading trips to James Bay. In 1648, a Jesuit report noted "there are various Algonquin Tribes to the north of the Huron who roam as far as the North Sea."[18] These nations likely included the Ouasouarini, Outchougai, Amikouai, and Oumisagi, who lived along the north shore of Lake Huron, and the Saulteur Nation, who lived near Baouitchigouian or Sault Ste. Marie. Later Jesuit accounts indicated that the Huron also visited James Bay to trade.[19]

In his report of Jesuit missionary work in 1657-58, Gabriel Druillettes described five routes to the "Bay of the Kilistinons," or James Bay. Druillettes had obtained his information "partly from two Frenchmen who have made their way far inland [probably Groseilliers and Radisson], and partly from several Savages who are eye-witnesses."[20] From east to west, these routes included the Montagnais trade route from Tadoussac up the Saguenay River. The second route was used by the Algonquin at Trois-Rivières, who ascended the St. Maurice River and passed through the territory of the Attikamegue. The third route was used by the Nipissing, who departed from Lake Nipissing and ascended the Sturgeon River. According to Gabriel Druillettes's account of 1659-60, the Huron traders also used this route to reach James Bay.[21] The fourth route, used by the Achirigouan, probably followed the Spanish River. Finally, the fifth route, which was used by the "Upper Algonquins," or Ojibway, began at "Lake Alimibeg [Lake Nipigon]." Druillettes's account of the trading routes to James Bay also provided information about the Aboriginal nations who were encountered along the shores of the bay by the Indian traders from the south. All these people were embraced under the name Kilistinon, but four specific "Nations" were recorded. These included the Alimibigouek Kilistinons, Kilistinons of Ataouabouscatouek Bay, Kilistinons of the Nipisiriniens, and Nisibourounik Kilistinons.[22] Druillettes remarked that these four nations comprised about 600 men who were "not very stationary." The names of these nations appear to be derived from their association with southern-based trading partners. For example, the Kilistinons of the Nipisiriniens referred to the people who traded with the Nipissing, probably near the mouth of the Moose River. The Kilistinons of Ataouabouscatouek Bay traded with the Achirigouans. Their trading rendezvous may have also been near the mouth of the Moose River. The Alimibigouek Kilistinons traded with the Upper Algonquins of the Lake Superior region, who travelled to James Bay by way of Lake Nipigon (Alimibig). These trading activities probably took place near the mouth of the Albany River. The Nisibourounik Kilistinons traded with the Montagnais, and their summer meeting place appears to have been near the mouth of the Rupert River.

In the summer of 1660, Druillettes obtained important new information about the James Bay trading connection from a Nipissing chief named Awatanik. The Nipissing had been temporarily driven away from their homelands around Lake Nipissing by Iroquois attacks in the early 1650s. Some Nipissing sought refuge in the area around Lake Nipigon, but they continued their trading contacts with people on James Bay through new routes. Druillettes met Awatanik about 160 kilometres up the Saguenay River. Awatanik was among a group of eighty people in canoes who were bringing furs from James Bay to trade at Tadoussac. Awatanik told Druillettes his trip had begun when he moved with his family from Green Bay on Lake Michigan to Chequamegon on the south shore of Lake Superior. From Chequamegon, they eventually journeyed on a river flowing north of Lake Superior to James Bay. It is likely that the river flowing to the bay was the Albany River, which can be reached from a number of points to the north and west of Lake Superior. Awatanik described a large island in the middle of the bay that "takes its name from the white Bears inhabiting it," which accurately describes Akimiski Island, located about forty-five kilometres north of the mouth of the Albany River.[23] On his route to James Bay, Awatanik met various nations, but he "noticed especially the

Kilistinons, who are divided among nine different residences, some of a thousand, others of fifteen hundred men; they are settled in large villages where they leave their wives and children while they chase the Moose and hunt the Beaver." The locations of these large villages is unclear, but it is unlikely that they refer to places near James Bay. Awatanik's description of moose and beaver hunting probably refers to places farther south and west, closer to Lake Superior where beaver and moose were more plentiful. The villages probably referred to Upland Cree settlements, a view supported by later European accounts of large gatherings of Upland Cree. The only nation on James Bay specifically mentioned by Awatanik was called the *Pitchibourenik*. These may have been the same people Druillettes called the Nisibourounik Kilistinons. Awatanik reported that the Pitchibourenik were "dwelling at the entrance to the Bay, whither the Hurons and Nipisiriniens formerly were wont to go for trade."[24] This "entrance to the Bay" may have referred to the mouth of the Rupert River, since Awatanik travelled to the mouth of the Rupert and then ascended the river on his route to the Saguenay River. In 1673, the Jesuit missionary Charles Albanel visited the mouth of the Rupert River and reported that a nation called *Pitchiboutounibuek* lived to the northeast.[25]

Awatanik visited "all the Nations surrounding the Bay" and obtained furs, which he was transporting to Tadoussac when he met Druillettes. Awatanik's account of his trip from the western end of Lake Superior to Tadoussac confirmed a vast Aboriginal trading network focussed on James Bay, radiating in many directions. During the 1650s and 1660s, the period of intensified Iroquois warfare in the Great Lakes region, these northern trading corridors focussing on James Bay became essential for moving furs and European goods. Awatanik's account of his journey from Lake Superior to Tadoussac through the northern routes sparked interest among missionaries as well as fur traders. The Jesuits were anxious to visit James Bay to spread the Christian faith to the many nations who congregated there each summer. In the spring of 1661, Druillettes and Claude Dablon accompanied a group of Aboriginal traders from Quebec and Tadoussac who intended to travel north to trade at a "general fair" on James Bay. At the same time, a group of French fur traders set off from Trois-Rivières with another party of Aboriginal traders, who were also headed north toward James Bay. The Jesuits proceeded up the Saguenay to Lake St. Jean, where they met eight "stranger Savages, natives of the country whither we were going—some of them having wintered at Kebec, and others having wandered among the Lakes of these regions during the past winter, with no fixed abode."[26] On July 2, 1661, they reached Nekouba near the height of land that separated St. Lawrence River drainage from waters flowing north into James Bay. Nekouba was "a place noted for a Market that is held there every year, to which all the Savages from the surrounding country resort for the purpose of conducting their petty traffic."[27] At Nekouba, they also received news that the French and middleman traders who had left Trois-Rivières had been ambushed by an Iroquois war party. Other reports indicated that Iroquois warriors had "destroyed the Squirrel nation" who were located "several days' journey hence."[28] These reports caused panic among the Aboriginal people who travelled with the Jesuits, and since other reports indicated the Iroquois intended to attack the people who gathered at James Bay, the mission was cut short and the party returned to Quebec without reaching the bay.

Iroquois warriors continued their attacks in the northern regions throughout the winter of 1661-62, causing a significant disruption in the fur trade of the French colony. A Jesuit observed that "the fountainhead of Beaver-Skins is dried up with the ruin of those who bring them to our settlers."[29] The Iroquois attacks in the north were short-lived, but they continued to plague the region between the upper Great Lakes and the St. Lawrence valley. The Iroquois wars motivated the French to search for alternative ways to secure furs. The routes to James Bay had previously been well guarded by Indian middlemen, but the disruptions caused by Iroquois attacks forced new strategies of cooperation between Aboriginal and French fur traders.

In 1659, two French traders, Médard Chouart, Sieur des Groseilliers, and Pierre Esprit Radisson, who had been successful in bringing furs from the Lake Superior region down to the French settlements in the St. Lawrence valley, attempted to break into the northern trading network. Like Champlain and the Jesuits, Radisson noted that the route from Tadoussac to James Bay was well known to the French, but access was prevented because the Montagnais and other Indian middlemen traders "would have hindered them because they make a livelihood of that trade." Radisson explained that the furs brought from James Bay to the French at Tadoussac passed through the hands of three nations: from north to south, the nation of the Squirrel, the nation of the Porcupine, and the Montagnais nation.[30] However, Groseilliers and Radisson thought they could succeed by gaining access to the western source of furs and bringing them to the St. Lawrence by the route to James Bay and down the Saguenay River. They travelled to Lake Superior by way of the Ottawa River and Lake Huron route. Along the southern shore of Lake Superior near Chequamegon Bay, they met a camp of "Christinos" (probably Upland Cree) whom the French traders had seen in their previous trips. They spent the winter at Chequamegon, and in the spring travelled to the country of the "Nadoueceronons," or Sioux. The Sioux were at war with the Upland Cree, and Groseilliers and Radisson were anxious to facilitate a peace treaty between them. A grand council was held, which attracted 500 people from eighteen different nations. Groseilliers and Radisson spoke on behalf of the Upland Cree, describing them as "brethren, and [we] have frequented them many winters; and we adopted them for our children and took them under our protection."[31]

Following the peace treaty, Radisson went with fifty people to visit a large, fortified, Upland Cree village. The trip took only three days, and Radisson reported more than 600 Cree warriors in the village. This appears to have been similar to the large Upland Cree villages described by Awatanik. The Upland Cree were obviously well established in the fur trade in the western Lake Superior region—they had a large quantity of beaver skins and gave Radisson a present of 500 pelts. According to Radisson, the two French traders crossed Lake Superior during the summer at a place about seventy-five kilometres across. The most likely place for this crossing was from the vicinity of the Apostle Islands to the north shore of Lake Superior near Silver Bay. Near a deep bay, they were met by a large party of Upland Cree, who guided them to their camp. From that point, Radisson's route is difficult to follow.[32] His narrative explained, "We went away with all haste possible to arrive the sooner at the great river. We came to the seaside, where we find an old house all demolished and battered with bullets."[33] Perhaps this was a reference to the house built by Henry Hudson in 1610-11, or by Thomas James in 1631-32. A more remote possibility is that it was the remains of a structure built by Thomas Button in 1612-13 at the mouth of the Nelson River. Radisson claimed that his party coasted along the shore of the bay and visited a number of islands before coming to the mouth of a river (probably the Rupert River) that led to Tadoussac. By this time, winter was setting in, and the French traders decided to head back toward Lake Superior

Radisson's report, whether obtained through first-hand experience or reconstructed from oral reports of Aboriginal people, confirmed what other people had told the Jesuits about the fur trade in the James Bay region. The rivers draining into James Bay from all directions drew in Aboriginal traders who met and exchanged goods. It is also evident that the Cree visited French traders in the St. Lawrence valley. For example, in 1670, the Jesuit missionaries noted that a Cree, or "Kilistinon," man had visited Montreal and became ill with a disease that had become infectious there.[34] Thus, the

Lowland Cree who lived in the James Bay region were exposed to a large number of visitors, and had access to European goods long before European traders established posts in the area.

Lowland Cree Relations with European Traders, 1668–1713

In 1668, Médard Chouart, Sieur des Groseilliers, led a company of English fur traders by ship into Hudson Bay and established the first European fur-trade post on the eastern coast of James Bay at the mouth of the Rupert River. Two ships had sailed from England in 1668. Pierre Esprit Radisson travelled in *Eaglet*, but the ship was damaged in the voyage and returned to England. Groseilliers sailed on *Nonsuch*, which succeeded in reaching James Bay. The trading post was built at the mouth of the Rupert River, so-named in honour of their English patron, Prince Rupert. The post itself was named Charles Fort, after the English king, and re-named Rupert Fort in 1776 in honour of Prince Rupert. The decision to locate the post at the mouth of the Rupert River may have been guided by Groseilliers's familiarity with the Aboriginal trade route between Tadoussac and James Bay. In its first year of operation, about 300 people traded at the post. The Aboriginal people were not specifically identified, but it is likely that some were Lowland Cree.[35]

By 1670, the English fur-trade company, thereafter called the Hudson's Bay Company, was sending men to the mouth of the Moose River to trade directly with the Lowland Cree. In the summer of 1674, a party of HBC traders at the mouth of the Moose River met a group of "Shechittawams," or Albany River Lowland Cree, who traded about 1500 skins.[36] That meeting was followed up by a visit to the mouth of the Albany River by Charles Bailey, the governor of the HBC. Bailey met with a group of Albany River Lowland Cree, including their leader, who was called the "King," and his son. Guided by a "Washahoe Indian," or Severn River Lowland Cree, Bailey sailed north to "Viner's [Akimiski] Island," and met a small group of people who guided them to the mouth of the "Equon [Ekwan] River." Upon surveying the area, Bailey commented that "there had been a great Mortality among them, and several were starv'd to Death for want of Food; this Country being such a miserable Wilderness, that it affords not sufficient Sustenance for the wretched Inhabitants…. The Indians on New Severn River are as poor as the Eiskimoes; and indeed all the Northward Indians are more beggardly and brutal than the Southward."[37] Although Bailey attributed the impoverished condition of these Lowland Cree to the lack of food resources in the area, other factors were undoubtedly involved. Death by starvation in the summer season seems unlikely, given the availability of fish, waterfowl, caribou, and other resources in the lowlands at that time of year. It was more likely that the deaths were caused by an infectious disease transmitted to the Ekwan River area from the outside. Since there was no record of disease at Moose Fort, it seems unlikely that the Hudson's Bay Company employees had brought the disease from Europe. A more likely source for the disease was the St. Lawrence River valley, with the sickness being carried into the lowlands by Aboriginal middlemen traders.[38]

Bailey's expedition in 1674 signalled the beginning of expansion of the HBC's settlements in the western James Bay area. A trading post was built at the mouth of the Moose River shortly after Bailey's visit there in that summer. The company's next trading post was built at the mouth of the Albany River some time between 1675 and 1679. Thus, by 1679, the European fur trade was well established in the James Bay region. The building of trading posts at the mouths of the Moose and Albany rivers marked the beginning of continuous interaction between Europeans and the Lowland Cree who lived along the west coast of James Bay. European fur-trade contacts in the northern parts of the Hudson Bay lowlands developed shortly after the James Bay posts were settled. In the 1670s, the HBC traders made several trips to the mouth of the Nelson River, but these produced few results. For example, in the fall of 1670, Radisson led a party of HBC traders on a brief visit to the mouth of the river. No Indians were seen, but there was "a very fine Marsh land, and great plenty of wood about a mile beyond the Marshes, yet not very large. There were ye remaines of some of ye Natives Wigwams and Sweating houses and some peeces of dressd Beaver skins, and they supposed the Indians had not long been gone from that place further Southward or higher into the Country."[39]

In August 1673, the HBC sent Groseilliers on a brief exploration of the area near the mouth of the Nelson River. His report contained a similar description of "several Wigwams, where they had lately been, and suppos'd them to be gone up the Country."[40] In 1682, three trading posts were built near the mouth of the Nelson and Hayes rivers by different European traders. Groseilliers and Radisson, who had temporarily left the employ of the HBC, returned to Hudson Bay in 1682 with a French ship and crew. They landed at the mouth of the Hayes River about the same time as a ship from New England, under the command of Benjamin Gillam, landed at the mouth of the Nelson River. Shortly after, John Bridgar arrived in a HBC ship to build a third trading post in the vicinity.

Radisson's account of the events in 1682–83 provided the first eyewitness account of the Lowland Cree in the vicinity of the Hayes and Nelson rivers. Radisson arrived at the mouth of the Hayes River on September 27, 1682. According to him, the Lowland Cree called this river *Ka Kirva-Kiouay*, which he translated as "who goes, who comes." The nearby Nelson River, called the "Grand River" by Radisson, was called *Karoringaw* by the Lowland Cree, which apparently meant "the wicked."[41] The next day Radisson and two men embarked in a canoe and explored about 160 to 200 kilometres upriver. At the end of their journey, on October 5, they encountered a man who had been hunting caribou. Radisson called out to him, and he responded in a language that Radisson, who was familiar with several Aboriginal languages, including Ojibway and Upland Cree, "understood very well." The next day the hunter returned with twenty-six men in nine canoes. They were well prepared to trade furs with Radisson and his men, for they traded their beaver robes and "all the peltry" they had in their canoes for tobacco, pipes, and knives. These men were knowledgeable about iron goods, and one used a small piece of iron to cut his tobacco. Radisson later learned that they had previously traded at Albany Fort. Radisson also gave a musket, gunpowder, shot, and a blanket to their leader, who adopted Radisson as his son. The leader, an elderly man, was "the chief of the nation who inhabited the place where the fort was building [the mouth of the Hayes River]." Radisson repeated this point later in his narrative, and explained that the chief had allowed Radisson to build a trading post in his country.[42]

Radisson's nephew, Jean Baptiste Chouart, and another French trader spent the winter of 1682–83 with the Lowland Cree. At the beginning of April, before the breakup of river ice, Chouart and his companion returned with several Lowland Cree, who brought provisions and furs. Radisson confirmed that these Lowland Cree had had previous dealings with the English traders in James Bay. They showed a keen familiarity with European goods, and complained about the poor quality of the French goods. Later in the spring, Radisson noted the arrival of "the captain of the Indians of the river New Severn."[43] The leader of the Severn River Lowland Cree, known as "the Bearded Chief," who was related to the Hayes River chief, was also familiar with the English traders at Albany Fort, and appears to have come to the mouth of the Hayes River to trade specifically with the HBC. The leader of the Hayes River Lowland Cree (Radisson's adopted father) arrived shortly after the Severn River group. A ceremony preceded the business of trading, and began with a display of gifts that included "beavers' tails, smoked Caribou tongues, and bladders of the fat of bears, elk and deer." Radisson reciprocated with a feast and presents, and then the Lowland Cree traded furs for other European goods. Radisson observed that the Lowland Cree expected the French "to trade with them on the same footing as the English did at the head of the bay [James Bay]." When Radisson refused to lower the price of his goods, one of the Indians (possibly the Bearded Chief) remarked, "You know what beaver is worth and the trouble we have to take it, you call yourselves our brothers and you will not give us what those give who are not so [HBC traders]. Accept our presents, or we will come no more to pay you a visit and will go to the others [HBC]." Radisson's adopted father, the old Hayes River chief, remained near the coast until the departure of the ships. Radisson learned that the chief had killed a man who belonged to another nation led by a chief known as the Marten. After hearing that the Marten planned to exact revenge by killing the old chief and his family, Radisson attempted to reach a peaceful settlement by sending gifts inland to the Marten. The significance of this affair was evident in the package of gifts, which included a musket, two large kettles, three coats, four sword blades, four chisels, six garters, six dozen knives, ten axes, ten fathoms of tobacco, two blankets, three caps, gunpowder, and shot. Radisson further pledged military support to the Lowland Cree if the Marten did not accept the gifts and make peace. Unfortunately, Radisson left the region before hearing about the outcome of this peace initiative.

Shortly after Radisson's departure on July 27, 1683, the Bearded Chief and fourteen or fifteen followers from Severn River visited the French post with a load of furs. They had traded earlier with the HBC, probably at Albany Fort, but seemed prepared to trade the rest with the French. However, during the pre-trade ceremony, the Bearded Chief demanded that the French traders pay him for allowing them to build their post on his land. Chouart reported that the chief stated that "I [Chouart] was worthless because I did not love the English and that I had not paid by presents for the country I inhabited to him who was chief of all the nations and the friend of the English." Despite a warning from one of the Hayes River Lowland Cree that the French would "be avenged by the upper nations on all our families," insults turned into a brief scuffle in which Chouart was slightly wounded by the Bearded Chief. Although the Severn River Lowland Cree left the French post without further incident, the event caused general alarm among the Hayes River Lowland Cree. They sent messengers after the Severn River people and convinced them to return to the post for a feast and council to resolve the matter. During the council, the Bearded Chief repeated his disdain and contempt for the French. This enraged one of the Hayes River Lowland Cree (Chouart's adopted brother-in-law), who attacked the Bearded Chief and killed him. The other Severn River Lowland Cree departed after hearing that "if they intended to avenge the death of their chief they had only to say so and that war would be declared on them."[44] According to Chouart's report, the killing of the Bearded Chief also incited the Hayes River Lowland Cree to attack the English traders at their nearby post. Several English traders were killed, and the French, although reluctant to condone further acts of aggression, gave a feast in honour of their Hayes River allies. Following these killings, the French traders feared attacks from both the English and Lowland Cree. As a measure of security, they persuaded some of their Lowland Cree allies to "spend the winter with us on condition of feeding them." The winter passed uneventfully, except that "the Indians performed several acts of jugglery, to learn from their Manitou, who is a familiar spirit among them, if my father and uncle [Groseilliers and Radisson] would come in spring."[45] This may have been an early reference to the "shaking tent" ceremony, which was used frequently by Lowland Cree and Ojibway people to divine future events.

At the beginning of April 1684, a group of Lowland Cree "from the south coast," or James Bay, arrived at the mouth of the Hayes River. They traded with the English and obtained gifts of muskets. According to Chouart, the English provoked these Lowland Cree to attack the French. In a brief skirmish, one of the French traders was wounded by a gunshot. Significantly, this incident occurred at a place where the Hayes River Lowland Cree were preparing and smoking caribou meat. The James Bay Lowland Cree fled after this incident, but the local Lowland Cree were determined to avenge the attack and couriers were "sent to solicit all the nations who had sworn friendship to my father and uncle [Groseilliers and Radisson] to come down and make war on the English and on the Indians of the south coast."[46] One of the first to arrive was the Hayes River chief who had adopted Radisson the previous year. Chouart remarked that this elderly man was "one of their most considerable chiefs," and "one of the best friends of the French." The elderly chief played the role of peacemaker by convening a feast of friendship between the French and English. After the breakup of ice in the river, other groups of "friendly nations" arrived at the French post. Chouart noted particularly the "Assinipoets" who were described as "descendants of the great Cristionaux, old acquaintances of my uncle [Radisson]." The Assinipoets, or Assiniboine, included more than 400 men and an unidentified number of women. After learning about the events of the past winter, the chief of the Assiniboine declared war against the

English and their southern Lowland Cree allies. Despite the Assiniboine chief's call to arms, the upland traders soon dispersed and eventually all of them left without facing their enemies.

Before the arrival of the annual supply ships, Radisson had formulated a plan to desert to the English Hudson's Bay Company. One of his final acts before sailing to England was a meeting and feast with the Lowland Cree. Radisson explained that he was invited to their cabins and met with a group including men, women, elders, and children. A "venerable old man" spoke first and thanked him for making peace between the French and English. A young man then spoke and thanked Radisson for supplying weapons and other European goods. After the speeches, gifts of white beaver robes were presented to Radisson and his nephew, and a great feast was held. The food included "beavers' tails, bladders of the marrow of deer [caribou], several tongues of the same animal smoked, which is among them the most exquisite food ...[and] two large boilers full of smoked and boiled meat."[47] Radisson left Hudson Bay with a tentative peace established in the Nelson and Hayes River area and a cargo full of rich furs.[48] In 1685, he would return for two more years of trading for the Hudson's Bay Company at York Factory.

The fur-trade rivalry between the French and English brought Aboriginal nations into the fray as allies of one or both of the European powers. The Lowland Cree were affected by the so-called "beaver wars" during the 1650s to the 1670s, when the pro-English Iroquois warriors raided into the north to disrupt the fur trade with the French. These attacks were aimed at preventing furs from the west reaching the French in the St. Lawrence River by way of James Bay. The English trading posts on the bay proved to be an additional threat to the French fur trade. In 1685, a French military force from Montreal captured the southern posts in James Bay. Jacques René de Brisay, Marquis de Denonville, the French governor in Montreal, recommended to the king that the northern post at the mouth of the Hayes River be taken to complete the French control of Hudson Bay. Denonville explained that if the English continued to occupy that post, "we must expect to see all the best of the Beaver trade, both as to quality and quantity, in the hands of the English."[49] However, diplomatic initiatives between England and France resulted in an uneasy peace along the bay until 1690, when renewed European wars spilled into Hudson Bay. French naval forces captured the English post at the mouth of the Severn River in the summer of 1690, and the English retaliated in 1693 by retaking Albany Fort. In 1694, the French captured York Factory, but a year later an English naval force seized it.

Until then, the military campaigns had been relatively quiet affairs, with the French and English exchanging few volleys before the trading posts capitulated. However, in 1697, York Factory was the scene of a serious engagement between French naval forces against the fortified English post. Cannon fire boomed and smoke filled the air as the two sides battled.[50] The French succeeded in landing some of their cannons on shore and encircled the English, who were forced to surrender. That victory secured York Factory to the French, while the English held the posts in James Bay until the Treaty of Utrecht in 1713, which awarded all of Hudson Bay to the English.

A year before the French were forced to hand over Fort Bourbon at the mouth of the Hayes River, seven French traders were killed by a group of Lowland Cree near the fort. According to E.E. Rich, the killings were motivated by starvation among the Lowland Cree because the French traders ran out of gunpowder and shot. The French traders reported "their Indians dying round them for lack of powder and shot." A re-examination of this particular incident reveals that the murders were not motivated by a short-age of gunpowder and shot. In fact, the killings were caused by the refusal of the French traders to share food with the Lowland Cree. According to Nicolas Jeremie, "These natives, considering themselves dared by the reck-less way my men were shooting every kind of game, and feasting before their eyes without sharing anything made a plot to kill them, and seize what they had."[51] Jeremie stated that the Indians had lost their skill with the bow and arrow and many died of hunger when French powder was unavailable, but other statements contradict this explanation. For example, Jeremie described caribou hunting with Aboriginal technology such as snare-fences and by spearing. Jeremie also remarked that geese, ducks, ptar-migan, hare, and fish were plentiful near Fort Bourbon and could be easily obtained with Aboriginal hunting equipment. James Knight, an HBC trader at York Factory, who learned about the incident later, possibly from both the French and the Lowland Cree, provided additional details that cast serious doubt on Rich's assessment that the killings were motivated by the need to obtain French goods. Knight reported that "after they killd them they broke open their warehouse and to show them they did not value their Goods for they broke and tore what they found and throwd and Scattered 7 Barrells of Powder in the Water so that their design by that was to show that they could Live without their Goods and discourage them from comeing here any more."[52]

The written accounts from the period of French and English fur-trade rivalry on the bay-side indicate that the Lowland Cree were involved in a complex web of relationships with upland and European traders. The competition between French and English traders also promoted rivalry between regional groups of Lowland Cree. Those who lived in the southern lowlands, near James Bay, were closely allied to the English HBC traders. The northern groups of Lowland Cree, who lived in the vicinity of the Nelson and Hayes rivers, were more closely allied with the French traders. The fur trade within the lowlands operated within a framework of delicate political alliances in which ceremonies, feasts, and gift-giving were important factors. The French traders withdrew from the Hudson Bay lowland region in 1713, but the customs of gift-giving and other rituals valued by the Lowland Cree continued to be important elements in the HBC's fur trade.

7.
The Lowland Cree in the Fur Trade, 1713-1782

Lowland Cree Fur-Trade Patterns, 1713-1782

Following the withdrawal of the French traders from the bay-side in 1713, the HBC maintained a monopoly in the Hudson Bay lowlands fur trade. Although the HBC kept detailed records of the furs purchased from and the goods sold to Aboriginal people, it is difficult to assess the involvement of the Lowland Cree in the trade before 1782 because the accounts included the trade with upland people. Large numbers of upland traders travelled each summer to the coastal HBC posts and, according to HBC reports, brought in most of the furs. The composition of the fur returns in the pre-1782 period also reflected the inland origin of many furs. For example, the presence of moose, fisher, badger, and raccoon in the fur returns indicated an upland origin, since these animals were rare in the Hudson Bay lowlands. Upland traders also brought in the great majority of wolf and lynx skins. Other animals that were absent from the lowlands, but which appeared in the HBC fur returns, included elk, bison, swift fox, and grizzly bear. The HBC daily post journals usually enumerated the numbers of upland traders by recording the number of canoes that arrived at each post. The records from Albany Fort and York Factory illustrate that the numbers of upland people who visited the coastal trading posts closely reflected the volume of furs traded each year. Since most trading canoes carried at least two individuals, and sometimes three or four, a reasonable estimate of the numbers of upland people can be obtained by multiplying the canoes by a factor of three. The numbers of upland traders at Albany Fort declined gradually over this period, except for a brief increase in the late 1750s and early 1760s, when the St. Lawrence-based fur-trade competition was suspended because of war. By 1782, the HBC traders had begun to establish inland trading posts and the numbers of upland traders visiting Albany Fort dwindled to a few canoes. At York Factory, the inland trade was not immediately affected by competition from St. Lawrence-based fur traders. However, the trend was similar, and by 1782, the numbers of upland traders visiting York Factory had decreased significantly. The establishment of inland trading posts from York Factory, beginning in 1774, precluded the necessity for upland people to make long, annual, trading trips to the bay.

While the exact numbers of furs brought in by the Lowland Cree can not be deduced from the HBC records, it is evident that relatively few furs were obtained from the Lowland Cree, compared to the volume brought in by the upland traders. Andrew Graham noted that "there are Indians always coming to the settlements, but the main body which make up the bulk of the trade arrives in the months of June and July."[1] According to Graham, each canoe of upland traders usually brought eighty to 100 made beaver in various furs.[2] Each Lowland Cree hunter received an advance, or debt, in the fall that amounted to twenty or thirty made beaver.[3] While more furs may have been traded after the debt was repaid, it is apparent that the contribution of the Lowland Cree to the total HBC fur returns was relatively insignificant in the pre-1782 period.

The Lowland Cree in the Provision Trade

In addition to furs, the Lowland Cree provided food to the European traders in exchange for European goods. The role of the Lowland Cree as provisioners was slow to develop, but by the mid-eighteenth century, a significant population of Homeguard Cree was involved in supplying geese, caribou, fish, and other country foods to the European traders. Geese and caribou were the most important food resources, and the spring and fall migration seasons were the busiest periods for the Lowland Cree who became involved in the provision trade. Many European fur traders commented on the important role of the Lowland Cree, and especially the Homeguard Cree, as provisioners. Local food resources were necessary to supplement the limited supplies of imported European foodstuffs. In addition, local foods were more healthful and apparently more palatable than pickled and salted European provisions. Andrew Graham commented, "The Company's servants lives like Princes. Seldom a week passes but they have fresh provisions of different kinds, and the Factors and officers lives in so grand a manner beyond description."[4] Joseph Isbister, who was in charge of Albany Fort in 1755, pointed out the dependence of the HBC on the Homeguard Cree goose hunters: "Here is nothing but trouble and plague with these home Indians on account of their hunting, that is shooting geese for the factory and yet we cannot help ourselves in present condition, but do think, had we a good breed of cattle and hogs, might soon shake off our dependence on ye Indians for Country provision."[5]

Despite many attempts by the HBC to promote animal husbandry and agriculture at the coastal trading posts, dependence on country provisions remained high. In his study of the social history at York Factory from 1788 to 1870, Michael Payne commented that "overall neither gardening nor stock-rearing produced more than a tiny fraction of the food consumed at York."[6]

Among the regional food resources, geese, ducks, and other migratory birds comprised a significant portion of the provision trade at the coastal trading posts. The potential value of migratory waterfowl as a source of food was appreciated very early by the European fur traders. Gabriel Marest noted that "in spring and autumn, there are also found a prodigious number of wavys [lesser snow geese], Canada geese, ducks, brants, and other river birds,"[7] and Bacqueville de la Potherie wrote, "The wild geese and ducks are so plentiful in spring and autumn that the banks of the river Ste. Therese [Hayes River] are all covered with them."[8] Despite the large numbers of waterfowl that were available near the coastal trading posts, the involvement of the Lowland Cree in hunting migratory waterfowl for the European traders was slow to develop. The earliest HBC records indicated that very few Lowland Cree were employed as "goose hunters" for the company. For example, at Albany Fort in 1693-94, only two men hunted geese for the company. During the 1698-99 season at Albany Fort, the total expenditure on geese amounted to only three pounds of gunpowder and nine pounds of shot. In 1699-1700, only one man was employed as a goose hunter at Albany Fort, and the total expenditure on the goose hunt amounted to only four pounds of Brazil tobacco and a pair of yarn gloves.[9] At Moose Fort, the close proximity of French traders made it difficult for the HBC to attract Homeguard Cree to hunt geese. William Bevan, who was in charge of Moose Fort in 1734, remarked that "we have not above four Indians that will hunt for us they are so much linkt in with the french and we have no dependence on them."[10] In part, the reluctance of the Lowland Cree to hunt geese for the HBC can be attributed to the dangers of hunting in the coastal marshes during the spring season. The annual spring floods during the breakup of river ice often inundated the coastal marshes, and made the spring goose hunt an uncomfortable and sometimes dangerous activity. For example, in the spring of 1725, during a large flood of the Albany River, the water rose to five feet above the ground around the fort.[11] The Homeguard Cree goose hunters regularly built stages above ground level as places of refuge from the spring torrents. At York Factory, the spring breakup of the Hayes and Nelson rivers occasionally caused dangerous flooding that threatened the safety of the goose hunters and disrupted the hunt. During the spring breakup in 1797, Joseph Colen reported that "the high water yesterday filled the Marsh with heavy ice, drove the Geese from their feeding ground, and that it was with difficulty the Hunters saved themselves, the water rose so suddenly on them."[12]

The numbers of Homeguard Cree employed in the goose hunts gradually increased during the eighteenth century. Encouraged by gifts and other rewards, the Homeguard Cree populations around the trading posts coalesced into relatively large seasonal concentrations each spring and fall. The numbers of Homeguard Cree who participated in the spring goose hunts were occasionally enumerated by the HBC traders. At Albany Fort, the total population ranged from a few families to about 130 men, women, and children by the end of the period. At York Factory, the numbers of goose hunters and their families appears to have been more variable, with very few in some years and as many as 149 people in the spring of 1753. Very few Lowland Cree participated in the goose hunt at Severn House in the pre–1782 period.

The goose hunters and their families usually arrived at the coastal posts in the spring and fall in small groups of several families. They encamped on the plantation near the trading post until the geese arrived in the marshes. The plantation was a clearing near each trading post that was used as a camping place for Indians who came to visit and trade. If the usual arrival of geese was delayed, the HBC traders were forced to support the Homeguard Cree with food from the company's storehouse. Richard Staunton, who was in charge of Albany Fort in the spring of 1725, reported that some of the goose hunters and their families were forced to evacuate the marshes during an unusually high flood and came to the fort for relief: "Here is 30 Indians, men, women and children which lay in ye Factory last night, and must remain until we see further, they being come over on our account to hunt us provisions, soe I am double duty bound to take care of them in case the factory should meet with ye like misfortune of a ships company wintering in ye country, the natives should be the more ready to assist our necessity, in case it should happen more than we are at present not."[13]

In addition to providing emergency·food supplies to the Homeguard Cree, the company attracted Indian goose hunters by offering feasts and gifts. The spring goose-hunting feast was especially important, and it was attended with considerable ceremony. This feast was held prior to the departure of the Indian goose hunters to the marshes. James Isham provided an account of a goose feast that took place away from the HBC post.

> There was abou't 30 Indians very merry Dispos'd with two old men, one Drumming on a piece of parchment tied on an op'n Kettle,—the other with a ste'k Like a Ratle, with a parchmt. on both sides, and shott or stones on the inside to make itt Ratle, asking the Reason of all this seeming mirth,—one made answer itt was a goose feas't as they styl' itt, when I was immediately ask'd by the Chief of the tent to take part,— accordingly being willing to Satisfie my Curiosity, I sitts downe upon a Bundle of Ruhiggan which was handed to me; when looking round me I see them all sett to work, some a picking, and some a trussing of Geese, downe they went to the fire,—some Roasted, some Boyl'd &c. when in two or three hour's, singing, Dancing, and talking, Every one took their seat, round the inside of the tent, when the feast was serv'd up,—Each had his goose to Devou'r. [14]

The feast was usually held on the plantation, and the European foods usually included oatmeal, peas, and salted fish. Tobacco and liquor were also distributed by the HBC, and English brandy became indispensable in the annual feasts. In 1742, Joseph Isbister, Chief Factor at Albany Fort, attempted to implement a change in the tradition by withholding brandy and substituting extra oatmeal, because it was "better for their health."[15] However, the Homeguard Cree resisted this change in tradition, and the following spring the company was forced to reinstate the custom of giving brandy "as an encouragement to hunt." Another ritual that developed in regard to the goose hunt was the presentation of a gift, or prize, of a bottle of brandy for the first goose killed. Although first recorded in the HBC journals in 1728, Joseph Myatt observed that it was, by then, already a customary practice.[16] In the spring of 1732, Richard White described the gift of brandy for the first goose as an "Old Custome."[17] Other goose-hunting customs developed at· the HBC posts. For example, liquor was given to the Lowland Cree goose hunters as well as to company employees to celebrate St. George's Day (April 23). Joseph Isbister commented that

Population of Homeguard Cree Goose Hunters at Albany Fort, York Factory, and Severn House, pre-1782

(* denotes families)

Year	Albany Fort hunters/population		York Factory hunters/population		Severn House hunters/population	
1706		50				
1717		90				
1718			40			
1719		95				
1723			8	40		
1728			5*			
1731				122		
1733				80		
1735			20			
1737			12*			
1738			19*	92		
1739			30	112		
1741	6	36	26*	130		
1744			20*			
1746		70				
1747			25*			
1751			21*	130		
1752			35*			
1753				149		
1754				126		
1755			34*			
1756			30*			
1757				157		
1758		93	24*			
1759			37*			
1761	30	118			10*	

Population of Homeguard Cree Goose Hunters at Albany Fort, York Factory, and Severn House, pre–1782

(★ denotes families)

Year	Albany Fort hunters/population		York Factory hunters/population		Severn House hunters/population	
1762		100		97		
1763		139				
1764		138	30			
1765		94		98		
1766		109				
1767		116				
1768			24			
1772			19★	78		
1773		135	24	108		
1774		117				
1775				106		
1776				92	7	48
1777				90		
1778				98		
1779				110		
1780				113		
1781				122		

he gave "a little strong beer as an Encouragement for them to hunt being an old Custom."[18] The use of liquor as an inducement to hunt geese was not confined to the spring season. Thomas Bird, Chief Factor of Albany Fort in 1739, gave brandy and tobacco for that purpose to a man who visited the post on January 29. Bird noted that he was "one of our Chief goose hunters," and that these gifts were intended to "encourage him to come in to kill geese for us in ye spring."[19]

The Lowland Cree also held their own ceremonies and feasts in connection with the goose hunt. The Goose Dance, or *Niskisimowin*, was an important Lowland Cree spiritual ceremony and feast. The Goose Dance was held to show respect for the geese, and to maintain a spiritual link between geese and humans.[20] Drawing upon James Isham's account of a ceremonial goose feast near York Factory in the 1730s and other, later, ethnographic accounts, anthropologist David Meyer concluded that "the Goose Dance was simply the most elaborate of those ceremonies dedicated to the spirits of the food animals. The elaboration of this ceremony reflects the high esteem for waterfowl, and especially geese, held by the Cree. To some extent this may relate to the fact that the geese returned each spring at a critical point in the lives of those Cree."[21] However, the Goose Dance appears to have been quite distinct from the HBC's goose-hunting feast. The Goose Dance was celebrated upon the arrival of the geese, and feasting on geese was a central focus of the ceremony. In contrast, the HBC goose-hunting ceremony was a preparatory feast in which other foods, especially European provisions, were provided as an encouragement to the Lowland Cree goose hunters prior to the arrival of the geese.

Special gifts were presented to the Homeguard Cree leaders who participated in the goose hunts. These men, called captains of the goose hunt, were usually expert hunters and also possessed considerable influence over other Homeguard Cree hunters.[22] Although these leaders were rewarded by the HBC for their service as goose hunters, many received gifts from the company long after they had reached old age and were no longer productive hunters. At Albany Fort, a number of successive leaders among the goose hunters lived to old age and retained their rank as captains until death. For example, a man known as the "Indian Doctor" received gifts from the company for thirty years between 1711 and 1741. In his latter years he hunted very little, but the company continued to give him presents equal to the rank of captain in recognition of his influence over the other Homeguard Cree goose hunters. Another Albany Fort Homeguard Cree goose-hunt captain, named Pinnitakie, collected gifts from the company after he had lost his sight. The Albany Fort district report identified Pinnitakie as "the old Northern leader, nearly blind, has a good deal of influence among the Indians—hunts but little himself."[23] The captains received coats, hats, and other fancy clothing signifying their rank, and they also obtained extra supplies of brandy, tobacco, and other goods, which they often redistributed among their followers.

Shortly after the feast, most Homeguard Cree left the plantation and entered the marshes, where they set up camps, or "goose tents," as they were called by the HBC. The goose tents were located in traditionally productive staging areas. Around York Factory, goose tents were usually pitched near Fourteens River, Cross Creek, French Creek, and the Point of Marsh. In the vicinity of Albany Fort, goose tents were generally established at the marshes on either side of the mouth of the Albany River. Around Severn House, goose tents were also set up on both sides of the river, and they were known as the North and South goose tents. The HBC usually sent some of their own men to the goose tents to help with the hunt. Although a few actually shot geese, most of the company men were engaged in salting the geese and packing them into wooden casks or barrels. Women, children, and elderly people accompanied the hunters. The role of women was especially important in preparing geese for future use by drying and smoking, and in taking care of feathers and quills that were later sold to the company or used to decorate clothing and other items. Women also assisted in transporting the geese from the marsh to the HBC posts. In the spring of 1772 at Albany Fort, many women were sick or lame, and Chief Factor Humphrey Marten lamented that he was forced to employ eight of his men on that duty.[24]

Henry Ellis, who visited York Factory in 1746-47, provided a good description of the Lowland Cree goose hunt.

> There is a certain Season when these Birds are expected on their Journey Northward, and they are expected at York Fort and Churchill near at the same time, for which Reason, at both Places they call the New-Moon nearest the twenty-fifth of March, or the Spring Moon with us, the Goose Moon. To kill the Geese both Factory Servants and Indians go out to the Swamps, and there build themselves what they call a Stand, which is a Parcel of Bows stuck up, and they sit within them waiting for the Geese, never going in Pursuit of them; when the Geese come near they call to them, imitating the Cackle of the Geese so well, that the Geese will answer, and on the continuing to Call them, the Geese will wheel and come nearer the Stand. There is usually but one in a Stand, and while he is lureing the Geese, he keeps motionless the whole Time, and on his Knees with his Gun cock'd, but does not fire until he can plainly see the Eyes of the Geese, and the Geese are going from him; when the first Gun is discharg'd, he dexterously picks up another Gun, that lies ready, and fires that also: What Geese he kills, he usually puts up with Sticks in such a Manner as to represent them like alive, for a Decoy to others; they also make sometimes sham Decoys, about their Stands. As there are some Days in every Season, in which there are greater Flights of Geese, than what they are on other Days, a single Indian will on one of those Days kill two Hundred. They also decoy the Ducks to shoot them, but that is done by whistling.
>
> The Factories have a great Dependence upon the Geese for their Subsistance; when the Season is approaching, they send their Servants out in several Parties to Places where the Geese most frequent: A Number

of Indians also going with each Party, who come down to be hired for that Purpose. These Servants stay out from the Factories all the Season; and being provided with Salt and Casks, shall in some favourable Years, salt up three or four thousand Geese.[25]

George Barnston recorded the following description of a Homeguard Cree goose hunter: "The hunter is stationed in what is called a stand—a space from four to five feet square, enclosed by willow twigs and long grass stalks—from which he fires, with forms of geese or 'decoys' set up a short distance in his front. The geese fly toward these, when he gives out their peculiar call, and frequently he has his wife, or son, or grown-up daughter, to load the discharged gun for him, while he fires with the loaded."[26]

James Isham also provided a detailed account of the Homeguard Cree goose hunt.

> These Natives are good Mark's men with their Gun, tho not to Compare to Some of our own Country men, their antient way being only Bow's and Spear's—Knowing nothing of the Effects of a fowling piece tell the English settled in these parts;—their game is Chiefly Running, or Standing, Excep't those Indians that Keep's constant attendance to the factory's in the Seasons, who Kils most flying Killing 100 Geese and upwards of a Day Each man in a Stand,—Which stand is a little Brush or wood put round Breast high wherein they sitt, and as the geese fly's by in Ranges they Call them within a shott if a mile of and having two Guns by them, will as they come towards them Kill oft'n 3 or a 4 at a Shott, and so as they go from them Kill as many more with the other gunn, at the same time Keep calling and Loading that if the flock Consists of 20 Geese hee'l besure to have them all,—they will oft'n Kill a Great many at a Shott Rising, Creeping along with their gun at their Shoulder, thro woods and Swamp's, tell they think they are nigh a Nuff then start foreward which occations the Geese to Rise upon the wing, when he watches the time, takes them as they rise killing 20 or 30 at a shott and Sometimes more.[27]

Isham's assertion that some of the company men were better goose hunters than the Homeguard Cree is not supported by HBC records. Andrew Graham said that Lowland Cree hunters "surpass us in the use of the gun, which is a European accomplishment."[28] In later years, some HBC men became proficient goose hunters. For example, at York Factory in the spring of 1791, two company men named Thomas and Sutherland killed 630 geese.[29] However, as early as 1713, Anthony Beale, Chief Factor at Albany Fort, commented on his dependence on the Homeguard Cree to hunt geese for the company. Beale was forced to give the Cree hunters extra presents to encourage them to hunt geese, because none of his men were able to kill geese.[30] Edward Umfreville noted that "they shoot them flying, and are so very dexterous at this sport, that a good hunter will kill, in times of plenty, fifty or sixty in a day."[31] The HBC tried occasionally to train its own men to hunt geese, but these experiments met with limited success. For example, in the spring of 1749, George Spence, Chief Factor at Albany Fort, reported on April 8 that "our Indian Hunters pitched their tents in ye North and South Marshes, and agreeable to Your Honours Orders contained in ye 4th paragraph of your general letter of 1748, I have sent 9 of our men along with ye Indians in order to learn to kill geese." However, nine days later, he reported that "3 of our men who were along with ye Indians learning to kill geese, desired to return home, having fired away all their powder and shot, and killed nothing."[32]

The HBC provided all the essential hardware to the Lowland Cree goose hunters. The guns, called "fowling pieces" by Isham, were loaned to the Homeguard Cree who agreed to hunt for the company. Each Homeguard Cree goose hunter used at least two firearms, according to contemporary descriptions of the hunt. The fowling pieces may have been of a different type from the ordinary trade guns, and perhaps they were specially made for the goose hunt. The company's armourers were kept busy cleaning and repairing these guns before, during, and after each hunt. The HBC also supplied the Cree hunters with other necessary items, such as gunpowder, powder horns, shot, gunflints, and gunworms. The Homeguard Cree quickly became expert marksmen with European firearms. In 1716, James Knight, who was in charge of York Factory, observed that "there is no man knows how to use guns better than the Indians."[33]

Nicolas Jeremie reported that the French traders "send out the natives to hunt, giving them a pound of powder and four pounds of lead [shot] for twenty ducks or brant, and these they have to bring to the fort."[34] According to Andrew Graham, the HBC gave one pound of gunpowder and one pound of shot for twenty geese. In addition, the Homeguard Cree hunters were paid the equivalent of one made beaver in value of other trade goods for every twenty geese they gave to the company. Edward Umfreville reported that the payment for geese was one made beaver for every ten geese.[35] The actual rate appears to have varied over time and between posts. Unfortunately, the HBC account books did not consistently record this type of information. Several account books that provided detailed information on the provision trade indicated that the value paid for migratory waterfowl was variable, and likely represented differences in the quality of the birds. For example, the Albany Fort account books in the 1770s indicate that one made beaver was paid for ten to twenty-four ducks, and six to eight geese.[36] However, the HBC account books indicate that the value was much higher near the end of the pre-1782 period. At York Factory, the rate was about five geese for one made beaver in goods. At Severn House, the rate was even higher. Between 1779 and 1781, the value of one made beaver in goods was paid for two to three geese.

The HBC expected a certain number of geese for every measure of powder and shot that was given to the goose hunters, but accepted less if the geese were scarce. In the fall of 1769 near Albany Fort, Humphrey Marten, Chief Factor, explained that "the geese being not so plenty this fall as usual, the Indians could not bring in the usual numbers for the powder and shot."[37] The HBC account books recorded the company's expenditures on the goose hunts, and these data provide an insight into the growing importance of the provision trade. At Albany Fort, ninety to 590 kilograms of gunpowder, 365 to 590 kilograms of shot, and 300 to 1600 flints were used in the spring and fall goose hunts. The figures for York Factory were about half and at Severn about one-third of the Albany expenditures. At Albany and Severn, the fall goose hunts were more expensive on average than the spring hunts. There was no significant difference in the seasonal goose hunt expenditures at York Factory.[38] The expenditures on the goose hunts at Albany Fort show a steady growth, but those at York Factory peaked in the 1750s before declining toward 1782. The trade goods obtained by the Homeguard Cree goose hunters included brandy, tobacco, cloth, blankets, and many other goods. A comparison of the amounts of essential (ie., gunpowder, gunshot, flints, etc.) and non-essential items expended by the HBC on the goose hunts reveals the growing importance of the non-essential items. By 1782, the value of non-essential goods expended on the fall goose hunt at Albany Fort had risen to 33 percent, and at York Factory to more than 50 percent. Although brandy and tobacco accounted for much of the increase, other goods, such as cloth and hardware, had also become necessary goose-hunt expenditures.

Compared to the goose-hunt data from the nineteenth century, the harvest levels before 1782 were low. At Albany Fort, the numbers of geese procured in the spring goose hunt averaged about 2000. The numbers at York Factory ranged from a few hundred to over 5000, while the Severn spring goose hunt brought in an average of about 500 geese. Comparable figures for the fall goose hunts were not recorded by the HBC traders, but a comparison of expenditures indicates that about equal numbers would have been obtained.[39] Thus, total goose harvests from the three HBC posts averaged about 15,000 geese per year.

The relatively low numbers of geese killed by the Homeguard Cree for the company before 1782 can be explained by a number of factors. A significant factor was the availability of other food and commercial resources during the goose-hunting seasons. Caribou, especially in the areas around York Factory and Severn House, attracted the attention of many Lowland Cree. Another factor was the relatively low numbers of HBC men employed at the coastal trading posts before 1782. For example, the average workforce at York Factory was about forty, about thirty-five at Albany Fort, and usually nine men stationed at Severn House. In 1727-28, 3023 salted and fresh geese were consumed by twenty-four men stationed at York Factory, an average of 126 geese per man.[40] At Albany Fort in 1717-18, a total of 3066 geese was consumed by twenty-seven HBC men, or an average of 114 geese per individual.[41]

The goose hunts also generated other products that were traded to the HBC. Feathers and quills were traded by the women. Goose feathers were valued at one made beaver for ten pounds of feathers, although the weight was often difficult to measure. Joseph Isbister, who was in charge of Albany Fort in 1756, commented, "We packed some fall feathers and took as much care as possible to pick out all dirt and pieces of goose skins, cloded and wet feathers which ye Indians put amongst them to make them weighty for they are great cheats."[42] The value of goose quills varied from post to post. At York Factory and Severn House, one made beaver was paid for 2000 goose quills. At Albany Fort, the rate was 500 quills for one made beaver. The numbers of feathers and quills traded at Albany Fort increased gradually to about 820 kilograms of feathers and 80,000 quills per year by 1782. The trade at York Factory maintained an average of about 300 kilograms of feathers and 15,000 quills in the pre-1782 period. Like the trade in geese, the trade in quills and feathers was far below that which developed in the nineteenth century.

In addition to migratory waterfowl, caribou became a major resource in the Lowland Cree provision trade. However, commercial caribou hunting, like the goose hunt, was slow to develop. In the early fur-trade period, the Lowland Cree contributed mainly by building fences for the European traders to snare caribou that migrated near the posts. Large-scale commercial hunting developed in the latter half of the eighteenth century, in response to the expansion of the HBC's inland fur-trade operations. Caribou fences, or hedges, were built by the Lowland Cree along the migration routes of the caribou. Nicolas Jeremie recorded an early description of caribou hedges built by the Lowland Cree near the mouth of the Hayes River: "The natives make barriers of trees, heaped one on the other, leaving openings at intervals, and across these they stretch snares, and in this way they catch many."[43] Near York Factory, most caribou hedges were built along the edge of the Hayes River, to take advantage of the thicker tree growth that camouflaged the hedge and snares. One hedge, known as the upper hedge, was located on the left bank of the Hayes River about twenty-six kilometres above York Factory. The middle hedge was also located on the left bank, midway between the upper hedge and the factory. Another fence, known as the lower hedge, was built on the right bank of the Hayes River between Ten Shilling Creek and French Creek.

The Lowland Cree who built caribou hedges for the HBC were paid small wages for their efforts. For example, in 1718, a group of Homeguard Cree who built a hedge near York Factory were paid three pounds of Brazil tobacco, five pounds of shot, and one pound of decorative glass beads.[44] However, many participated in these projects when other pursuits were unavailable, or at times when sick, old, widowed, or orphaned Indians were temporarily dependent on the company. For example, a caribou hedge that was built in the fall of 1751 about five kilometres upriver from York Factory, one quarter of a mile in length, employed the "lame Indian men, widows and children who has none to look after them."[45] Two years later, the hedge was lengthened by a work party composed of ten HBC men and "some Indians" who also set thirty snares in the hedge. In the summer of 1763, Ferdinand Jacobs, Chief Factor at York Factory, employed thirteen Homeguard Cree for four days rebuilding a caribou hedge. They built 1150 metres of new hedge, for which they were paid one made beaver each per day. Jacobs also reported that he had to provide food and tobacco for them and their families, and give the men a "drink of liquor" after each day's work. In the summer of 1770, a number of Lowland Cree were once again employed to repair the caribou hedge. Ferdinand Jacobs noted, "I have now Six Indian men at work to repair our Deer Hedge and put our Deer Snares in good Order against the Deer crosses, as I can not spare our own men for that Service, the Indians being better acquainted with that kind of work, and for which I Pay Each man a beaver a day."[46]

The caribou hedges were usually used during the spring migration and occasionally caught large numbers of caribou, but most caribou were harvested during the fall migration by spearing them in river crossings. Henry Ellis remarked that the Lowland Cree near York Factory "attack them [caribou] in the Water, and kill prodigious Numbers, which they bring down on Floats to the Factories."[47] Naturalist Thomas Pennant said, "The Indians also kill great numbers during the seasons of migration, watching in their canoes, and spearing them while passing over the rivers of the country, or

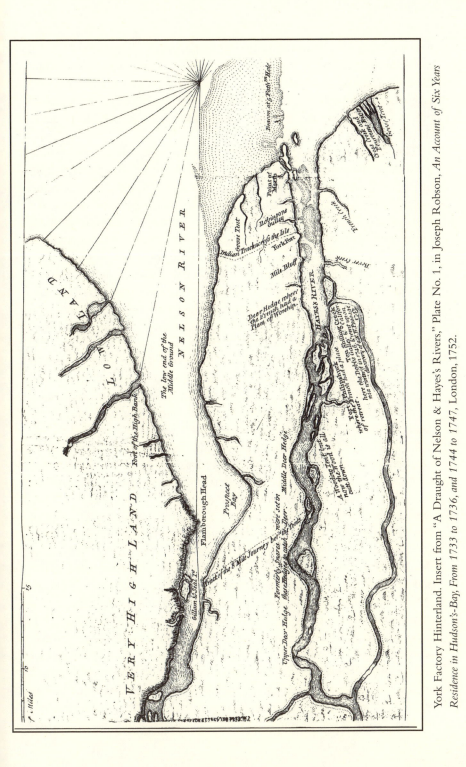

York Factory Hinterland. Insert from "A Draught of Nelson & Hayes's Rivers," Plate No. 1, in Joseph Robson, *An Account of Six Years Residence in Hudson's-Bay; From 1733 to 1736, and 1744 to 1747*, London, 1752.

from island to island; for they swim most admirably well....They often kill multitudes for the sake of their tongues only; but generally they separate the flesh from the bones, and preserve it by drying it in the smoke: they also save the fat, and sell it to the English in bladders, who use it instead of butter. The skins are also an article of commerce, and used in London by the Breeches-makers."[48]

The commercial trade in caribou products began with sales of caribou tongues, which were prized year-round because they contained rich reserves of fat when other parts of the caribou were lean. The Lowland Cree also preferred to trade caribou tongues because they were easy to transport to the posts, and they could be quickly cured to prevent them from spoiling. Humphrey Marten, who was in charge of York Factory in 1776, stated that the HBC paid one made beaver for ten caribou tongues, and three made beaver for a whole caribou. Since it was much easier to transport thirty tongues than a whole caribou carcass, the Lowland Cree preferred to trade the former item. Although caribou tongues figured prominently in feasts and gift-giving ceremonies in the early European fur-trade period, a large-scale commercial trade in caribou tongues began to develop at York Factory in the 1740s, where the numbers of caribou tongues traded varied from as low as 100 to more than 1500 each year. Most tongues were traded during the fall hunt in the months of August and September. Large numbers of caribou tongues were occasionally brought in to York Factory in the summer; for example, in July 1741, 135 tongues were traded at the factory, and in July 1749, 132 tongues were traded.[49] Occasionally, Lowland Cree hunters brought hundreds of tongues in a single visit to York Factory. In August 1769, Ferdinand Jacobs, Chief Factor at York Factory, reported that "several Canoos of Indians came here to Trade Parchment Deer Skins and from whom I Received 390 Dryed Deers Tongues, 30 bladders of Fatt, 30 Young Geese, 2 Sides of Dryed Venison and 4 Bundles of Pemmycon for which I Paid them."[50]

The trade in other caribou products was slower to develop because of the difficulty in transporting heavy loads of meat to the posts. One of the best places to hunt caribou in the fall was along the lower Nelson River. However, the Lowland Cree found it difficult to transport the products of their hunt to York Factory because of the often dangerous water conditions along the coast between the Nelson and Hayes rivers. During the early years at York Factory, the HBC men were aware of the caribou resource that was seasonally available in the vicinity of the lower Nelson River, but they also understood the difficulty of obtaining caribou from that area. On August 17, 1740, James Isham noted that "several familys of Indians came from ye North River to trade Deer skins, fatt and tongues, having kill'd a pretty many Deer, But ye Northw. wind making such a surf along port nelson shore that they can not bring itt to ye factory before itt spoil'd. I can not spare 2 men to go to port nelson to salt Deers flesh; if I could I might gett a great quantity of ye best meat."[51]

The HBC traders at York Factory made several attempts to develop a caribou trade directly with the Lowland Cree along the lower Nelson River. The first attempt was initiated by James Isham on July 21, 1748, when he sent John Hughes and two Homeguard Cree families in the company's sloop to the Nelson River with a tent and instructions to collect country provisions. Hughes was provided with casks, salt, and fishing nets, and he established a camp at Flamborough Head on the lower Nelson River. However, he was able to collect only one cask of salted caribou flesh, and that was lost when the boat that had been sent to pick up the cargo hit a rock "coming over the flatts" and sank. Isham persisted in his plan to develop a caribou trade and, in 1749, his men erected a log building at Flamborough Head, which was named Cumberland Fort. E.E. Rich has suggested that Cumberland Fort was built in response to the British Parliamentary Enquiry of 1749, which was critical of the HBC's lack of exploration and settlement inland from Hudson Bay.[52] However, Cumberland House, which was re-named Flamborough House, served as a seasonally occupied, provision-collection depot and not as a springboard to further interior developments. In 1750, the HBC men stationed at Flamborough House procured five casks of salted venison and a quantity of caribou fat.[53] In 1751, one cask of salted venison and three casks of salted geese were collected.[54] In 1759, Flamborough House reached its peak production of three hogsheads (a large cask containing 280 to 630 litres) of salted venison.[55] However, even this amount was well below the company's expectations, and could not justify the expense of maintaining the provision post. In November of 1759, Flamborough House was abandoned.[56]

In the 1760s, the HBC traders at York Factory began to pursue a more active campaign to obtain caribou from the Lowland Cree hunters, and sent small parties of company men to the Lowland Cree camps for the specific purpose of trading caribou. On January 27, 1761, James Isham sent two men with trade goods and enough provisions to last two months to camp at the mouth of the Steel River "to wait the Crossing [of] the Deer."[57] The caribou provision trade grew into a productive enterprise for the Lowland Cree and groups of Northern Ojibway who began to participate in this trade in the 1760s. Annually, the company purchased more than 300 whole caribou, 1300 tongues, and quantities of other products, such as sides, briskets, rumps, heads, hearts, ruhiggan, and pemmican.

York Factory Caribou Trade, 1747–1781

Year	Caribou (whole)	Tongues	Heads	Hearts	Sides	Fat (bladders)	Pemmican (bundles)	Ruhiggan (bundles)	Dried Venison
1747	122	185	28		251			1	
1748	14	148							
1751	106	279	129		120	23			
1752	29	126	39		20		2		
1754	71	548	174		38	44		7	
1756	45	565	4		77	16		30	
1757	87	457	55		168	58		36	
1759	94	565	227		63	88		8	
1760	89	916		16	318	326	2	29	
1761	59	920	42	2	186			66	
1762	84	516	20	5	271	121		3	
1763	93	754	37	57	300	53	10	35	30
1764	125	880	33	16	611	24	44		
1765	191	412	142	70	470	161	2		
1766	258	430	254			50			
1767	380	856	188	182	382	145			
1769	249	827	192	12	108	225		2	
1770	112	1492	243	33	195	347	16	2	11
1771	273	1254	271	59	123	290	2		
1773	111	1150	60		194	288			
1774	150	850	98		85				
1775	203	620	364	12	200	236			
1777	124	1370	88	18	274	70	304		
1778	99	299	23	25	28	14			
1779	312	688	452	191	69	10		2	
1780	385	1090	120	41	77	240			
1781	98	259	110	34	49	660	60	60	600

In the vicinity of Albany Fort, the caribou hunt was focussed on Akimiski Island. The HBC traders at Albany Fort tried on a number of occasions to open up a commercial trade with the Lowland Cree hunters on the island. The first record of such a venture was made on June 12, 1727, when Joseph Adams was sent from Albany Fort to explore Akimiski Island with a group of Homeguard Cree. Adams was impressed with the caribou resource on the island, and in 1733, he attempted to develop a summer caribou trade. On July 3 that year, Adams sent some men in the company's sloop to trade caribou meat from the Lowland Cree hunters on the island. That venture proved unfruitful, and the HBC men returned two weeks later with only two casks of venison. In the summer of 1746, Joseph Isbister tried again to develop a caribou trade on the island. He sent some men in the sloop to Akimiski Island, but nine days later they returned frustrated, having traded only "ye quantity of two deers of fresh meat and five deers dried."[58] Isbister persisted, and sent a sloop there again in the summer of 1747. This time the HBC men succeeded, and Isbister noted on their return to Albany Fort on July 16, 1747, that "they brought a great quantity of venison from ye Indians on Viner's [Akimiski] Island."[59] Despite this success, the caribou trade did not become a major enterprise for the Albany Fort traders. Thereafter, the Albany traders limited their involvement to encouraging the Indian hunters to bring a share of their bounty to trade at the fort. An indirect measure of the growing participation of the Lowland Cree in the caribou provision trade can be found in the number of caribou skins traded at the coastal posts. By 1760, the total caribou skin trade amounted to nearly 2000 skins. Most of the trade took place at York Factory and, to a lesser extent, at Severn House. Since caribou skins were prime in the fall, most of the trade took place during and after the fall migration.

The Lowland Cree also traded substantial quantities of fish to the European traders. When the HBC re-established Albany Fort in 1692, an elderly Lowland Cree man was employed as a fisherman. James Knight, who was in charge of Albany Fort in 1693, reported that "an old Indian caught all our fish last fal,"[60] and he paid one coat, three skeins of twine, two nets, and one worn hatchet for the fish. However, the HBC traders came to rely less on the Indians for fish, as their own men became proficient in seining and setting nets in the vicinity of the posts.

The HBC also attempted to develop a trade in a product known as isinglass, derived from the air bladder of sturgeon. The inner membrane of the air bladder contained a gelatinous substance that was used in the production of high-quality glue, and as a fining agent for beer, wine, and liquor. Isinglass was used by the Lowland Cree as a glue and a binding agent for paint. James Isham observed that "the Glue the Natives saves out of the Sturgeon is Very strong and good, they use itt in mixing with their paint, which fixes the Colours' so they never rub out."[61] In 1694, the HBC's governing committee in London wrote to Chief Factor James Knight at Albany Fort, "We should be glad you could procure us some Isinglass being only the sound [air bladder] of sturgeon dryed, wee are Informed great quantitys may be had, that Comodity is also very currant here."[62] Despite the company's persistent attempts to stimulate an isinglass trade, the Lowland Cree could not be persuaded to bring sturgeon bladders for trade.[63] Sturgeon eggs, or caviar, were also a product much in demand in Europe, but the HBC was unable to discover the appropriate technology for preparing the eggs. The caviar trade in Europe was a closely guarded industry, and the HBC did not develop the necessary contacts or partnerships with caviar merchants to make the trade in sturgeon eggs a profitable venture. Sturgeon and other fish eggs were consumed by Lowland Cree, who considered them to be a great delicacy. David Masty, an Eastmain Cree, commented that "fish eggs are considered a delicacy to Native people. They are mixed with flour, lard, salt and baking powder, called Wa–koy–kunow, in Cree. Fish eggs are dried and, in times of need, they are soaked in water until they are soft and used to make Wa–koy–kunow. Dried fish can also be boiled and eaten."[64]

Sturgeon fisheries in the Hudson Bay lowlands were generally located in upper sections of the rivers, out of the reach of the HBC fishermen. Most sturgeon traded at the coastal posts were brought by Half-Homeguard Cree or upland people, who caught them on their way down to trade at the posts. HBC inland travellers, such as Matthew Cocking, reported that upland traders caught sturgeon on their way to and from York Factory. Spears were commonly used, but nets and guns were also employed to catch these fish. Sturgeon were also brought to York Factory for trade by Lowland Cree from the Nelson River. In 1717, James Knight was informed by several people about a sturgeon fishing station located about eighty kilometres up the Nelson River.[65] Knight failed in his attempts to develop a fishing station there, and an HBC sturgeon fishery did not develop at York Factory, or, indeed, at any of the other coastal trading posts. Sturgeon represented an additional item of trade, and also a supply of fresh provisions for the upland Indian traders. Most of the sturgeon were traded at York Factory from late May to early July, which coincided with the spawning runs. The arrival of Cree fishermen with a supply of fresh sturgeon to trade was greeted with considerable enthusiasm by the HBC traders. At York Factory on July 29, 1781, Humphrey Marten traded twenty-five sturgeon from two canoes of

"Bungeeze [Northern Ojibway]," and commented that it was "a noble supply of fresh provisions as both English and Indians are tired of salt food."[66]

The Lowland Cree occasionally hunted and sold beluga, or white, whales to the European fur traders, but this trade did not develop into a major industry. On August 31, 1715, James Knight reported from York Factory that he had traded a "white whale that the Indians had kill'd,"[67] and on May 25, 1718, Henry Kelsey paid the value of four made beaver for a white whale that had been killed by the Homeguard Cree.[68] HBC personnel encouraged the Lowland Cree to trade white whales for domestic purposes because oil rendered from these animals was needed to keep lamps burning in the posts. The HBC also attempted to develop a commercial trade in whale oil near York Factory, but Lowland Cree fishermen could not be persuaded to harvest sufficient quantities to make the trade profitable.[69] The danger and difficulty involved in hunting white whales may have been a deterrent. Alternative forms of employment in subsistence and commercial harvesting activities would have made the prospect of hunting white whales a marginal concern. Like the white whale, seals were occasionally bought by the fur traders for their blubber, which was used as a fuel for the lamps in the coastal posts. The demand for whale or seal blubber was relatively moderate, but it was a necessary trade item.[70] For example, when, on October 22, 1772, a large seal was traded by the Homeguard Cree at Albany Fort, Humphrey Marten noted that it was "very acceptable as we have not a drop of lamp oil in the fort."[71]

The involvement of the Lowland Cree in the provision trade gradually increased during the pre-1782 period. By 1781, Humphrey Marten, who was in charge of York Factory, remarked that "I Humbly inform your Honours [HBC Board of Governors in London] that the homeguard hunting indians have brought to this Fort since last August a large quantity of very good provisions and that they are in general very willing to oblige and assist an englishman."[72]

Transportation

Prior to the establishment of inland trading posts, the opportunities for employment in transport-related activities were limited to carrying letters and other correspondence between the coastal posts. According to Andrew Graham, the payment for carrying these packets varied roughly with the distance between the posts. The following chart shows the rates paid by the HBC to lowland Indians for this packet service.

HBC Prices for Packet Service

Trading Posts	Distance	Rate (MB)
Churchill Fort to York Factory	210 km	24 MB
York Factory to Severn House	240 km	30 MB
Severn House to Albany Fort	620 km	50 MB
Albany Fort to Moose Fort	120 km	15 MB
Moose Fort to Eastmain House	100 km	15 MB

These rates reflected the average prices paid for these packet services during Andrew Graham's term of employment with the HBC. In earlier times, the prices paid for these services were considerably lower. For example, a packet that was carried from Albany Fort to York Factory in 1720 cost the company only twenty-one made beaver.[73] The goods received in payment amounted to one gun (nine MB), two and a half kilograms of gunpowder (three MB), one blanket (six MB), and one and one-half metres of cloth (three MB). In the summer of 1742, an Albany River Lowland Cree was paid only eighteen made beaver for carrying a packet to York Factory.[74]

The delivery of packets between trading posts, and especially the long-distance trips between Albany Fort and York Factory, were generally conducted by Homeguard Cree who were travelling between the posts for other purposes. In delivering these packets, the Lowland Indians followed a route known as *kayash iskinow*, or "the ancient path."[75] This path followed stranded beach ridges that paralleled the coast of Hudson Bay. Usually, the Homeguard Cree packetmen moved slowly between the posts, taking their families and sometimes larger groups along with them. Many packets between Albany and York took several months or longer to deliver. For example, an Albany River Homeguard Cree named Blind Jack set off with a packet from Albany Fort on May 18, 1727, and delivered it three months later to York Factory on August 20, 1727. Blind Jack apparently wintered near York Factory and took a return packet to Albany Fort the next summer. The return trip also took three months.[76] The trip between Albany and York could be accomplished in far less time,[77] but it is evident that the journey was usually performed at a leisurely pace, with hunting, fishing, and gathering being the main pursuits. The delivery of packets, although relatively infrequent in the pre-1782 period, was a service that the HBC traders depended upon for important information from fellow traders. When Andrew Graham found out that some Lowland Cree had not received full payment for delivering packets between Severn House and York Factory, he "apologized to them as a mistake and directly made up the Defficiency. Let us always deal equitably with the Natives which must tend to the Companys interests and our own credit."[78]

The first post inland from the coast of Hudson Bay was Henley House, located about 250 kilometres upriver from Albany Fort, near the confluence of the Kenogami River. Built in 1743, Henley House served mainly as a watch post until 1775.[79] Despite its limited role and small complement of employees (an average of seven or eight men), a transportation system developed to supply the post with provisions and other necessary goods. The transport link offered employment opportunities to the lowland Indians who lived near Albany Fort. During much of the pre-1782 period, employment opportunities for the Lowland Cree in transporting goods were limited, but beginning in 1774, with the establishment of Cumberland House inland from York Factory, the participation of the Lowland Cree in the annual boat brigades increased. As early as 1778, the dependency of the HBC traders on Cree labour to transport goods between York Factory and Cumberland House created problems for Humphrey Marten, who was in charge of York Factory.

> The Indians excessively troublesome for brandy, notwithstanding they have had two large feasts already, they say they will not assist in carrying goods or bringing them down, except their demands are complyed with, what to do I know not, I strive to do my best yet I fear with feasts and payment for carrying goods up, also for hunting for our men in coming down, a thousand beaver in goods will not satisfy them, this joyned to the great quantity of bread, prunes and other provisions they consume, as they must all be fed, and well fed too (and they eat not a little) makes it exceedingly expensive.[80]

European Diseases

The European fur traders who came to work at posts along the coast of Hudson Bay were impressed with the general health and physical strength of the Lowland Cree. For example, James Isham wrote in 1743 that "the Natives in these parts are of an incredible strong constitution both men and women,"[81] and in 1768, Andrew Graham, who was in charge of Severn House, similarly observed that "they are of a strong constitution both men and women."[82] William Falconer, who was stationed at Severn House in 1766, wrote, "They are of a middling stature and very proportionable, few deformed and scarce any of them fat,"[83] and Edward Umfreville, who had been stationed at Severn House and York Factory from 1771 to 1783, also wrote that "their constitutions are strong and healthy, and their disorders few."[84] The impression of a healthy, robust Lowland Cree population, given by European writers in the mid-eighteenth century, was probably a reflection of the state of their health compared with that of Europeans at the time. However, "disorders" were few but not absent. Graham and Falconer listed the diseases as "the flux" (dysentery), "consumption, and pain in the breast," or "Country distemper" (probably tuberculosis), the "King's Evil" (scrofula), and venereal disease. Significantly, none of the HBC fur traders noted above reported the presence or past history of highly infectious and deadly diseases such as measles, whooping cough, or smallpox. Both Graham and Falconer noted that smallpox was not known among the Lowland Cree.

However, statements by Graham and Falconer that smallpox had never been present among the Lowland Cree is contrary to the speculations of scholars of historical demography and epidemiology. Demographer Henry F. Dobyns postulated that smallpox introduced into Mexico by Spaniards in the period from 1520 to 1524 became a pandemic spreading throughout North America and affecting "all or very nearly all Native Americans."[85] He also speculated that wave after wave of smallpox epidemics subsequently swept across parts of North America, including one in 1738-39 that was said to have reached Hudson Bay.[86] Medical geographer Jody Decker agreed with Dobyns, and suggested that an earlier smallpox epidemic also affected the Lowland Cree around York Factory in 1721.[87] The records of the HBC traders in the eighteenth century do not provide much support for the presence of smallpox in the Hudson Bay lowlands before 1782. Chief Factor Henry Kelsey said that smallpox was present at York Factory in 1721, but it is apparent from the various descriptions made by Kelsey that smallpox was not the cause of the illness first reported in the fall of 1721 among the family of a Lowland Cree leader known as "Old Captain." On September 23, 1720, Kelsey wrote that "the Capt's. son in law from the N. side of Port Nelson [arrived] saying the Capt. & most of his family very sick and desire to be fetcht hither till they recover."[88] They were cared for near York Factory throughout the winter, but on December 28, Kelsey reported that the old leader was "very bad and vomits blood continually."[89] On March 23, 1721, six months after the sickness was first reported, Kelsey concluded that the disease afflicting the Old Captain and his family was smallpox. He wrote that "2 of the Captain's family came here for food and say he and some others are very ill, altho most of the Indians that have lain here all Winter have had the Small Pox which I never saw among the home Indians before."[90] On April 14, 1721, Kelsey was visited by "one Indian [who] came from the Capt. And saies he is like to

Dye and sent for a Watch to look att, one of my wearing Coates and a Blanket for a Winding shett [sheet] if he dies. I insert this to lett your Honours [HBC Governing Committee in London] see the superstitious humours of these people."[91] The Old Captain appeared at York Factory on May 1, 1721, leading a group of sixty Lowland Cree. Kelsey noted that "he is in a very bad condition and thinks of Dying."[92] His ill health gradually became worse and, on November 26, Kelsey reported, "The Captain is over-spread with a leperousy and that his leggs and arms are wasted very much." Finally, on January 29, 1722, the Old Captain died near York Factory.[93]

Given the various descriptions, it is very unlikely that the lingering illness that led to the death of the Old Captain was smallpox. Some symptoms, such as the vomiting of blood, may have led Kelsey to believe smallpox was the cause, but the haemorrhagic form of smallpox would surely have resulted in death within days or weeks. In addition, if smallpox was indeed active in the York Factory area, it would have resulted in more deaths in the family or extended kin group of the Old Captain. Although some family members were reported to be sick during the sixteen months of the Old Captain's illness, none died. In fact, Kelsey did not report a single death among any of the Lowland Cree or others who visited York Factory. The exact nature of the Old Captain's illness may never be known, but smallpox probably was not involved.[94]

In 1737 and 1738, smallpox was spread along the French trade routes into the interior west of Lake Superior. Historical geographer Paul Hackett has traced the origin and diffusion of this disease epidemic, and noted that it may have reached the area around York Factory in the winter of 1738-39. On February 26, 1739, James Isham, who was Chief Factor at York Factory, reported "very Remarkable Sickness, and casualtys is very much [present among] our Indian Hunters this year."[95] However, Isham did not mention smallpox in his daily journal or in his larger volume of observations. Sickness and even death from diseases such as the common cold and tuberculosis were not uncommon among the Lowland Cree by the mid-eighteenth century, but the spread of highly infectious and virulent diseases such as smallpox was probably unknown before the summer of 1782.

A review of all the HBC records from the period of initial settlement to 1782 indicates that the Lowland Cree suffered from occasional outbreaks of infectious diseases transmitted by European traders. Although relatively few Lowland Cree died from diseases before 1782, significant negative effects were recorded by the HBC traders. In general, diseases that were transmitted during the winter were less widespread because of the dispersed distribution of the population. In summer, when people were engaged in long-distance travel for trade, and populations were more concentrated at communal fishing or hunting camps, the epidemic diseases were able to spread over large areas and affect greater numbers of people.

The HBC made efforts to screen out employees who were infected with disease, but these precautions were not always successful. This was particularly true for HBC men who were infected with venereal disease. For example, in the fall of 1732, Robert Tomlins died at York Factory and Chief Factor Thomas Macklish noted that "he had been 26 days under a salivation, had been under the care of severall in England for cure of the Pox [likely syphilis], before he came unto York Factory."[96] In the fall of 1764 at York Factory, one HBC man died of "the Pox" and another was sick but recovered.[97] Syphilis and other venereal diseases spread quickly to the Lowland Cree by HBC men who had sexual relations with women around the bay-side posts.[98] Andrew Graham observed that venereal disease among the Lowland Cree "originated from an intercourse with the European traders in Hudson's Bay, and from the people of Canada, who traverse the Lakes and the interior parts of that extensive continent in quest of furs."[99]

"Country distemper," a term commonly used to denote tuberculosis, was reported to be fairly common in the Lowland Cree population by the mid-eighteenth century. William Falconer observed that "it continues 12 hours or more at a time and is an excessive pain, but never proves mortal."[100] Andrew Graham, writing about the country distemper, speculated that it was caused by "cold air being drawn into the lungs, and constraining the vessels throughout that organ." Graham noted that "perspiration is extremely difficult and painful, yet I never heard of any dying of it."[101] Scrofula, a type of tuberculosis affecting the lymphatic glands, was also a common illness among the Lowland Cree.[102]

In the summer of 1751, an unusual and remarkably severe disease epidemic was detected in the York Factory area. The disease was first reported by James Isham on June 13, when he wrote that "14 Indians very bad upon the plantation of a sort of measells, they are taking at first with violent colds, coughs, sore throats, swell faces, and very full of spotts."[103] Two days later, twenty Lowland Cree were immobilized by the disorder. By June 17, most of the "home Indians" were so sick that they were not able to move from the plantation. The sickness cleared quickly (most Lowland Cree had recovered by June 24) and no deaths were reported near York Factory, but the epidemic appears to have persisted inland. An indication of its geographic transmission was reported on July 2, 1751, when a large group of "Misineepee" [Churchill River Cree] and "Stone Indians" [Assiniboine] arrived at York Factory and informed Isham that many more were forced to turn back because of sickness.[104] While it is interesting to speculate that the sickness was caused by a measles epidemic, the fact that no deaths were reported makes it difficult to make such an identification. Paul Hackett concluded that the disease was, in fact, measles, and that it probably originated in the south among the equestrian Plains Indians. It spread northward through Aboriginal trade routes and eventually reached York Factory in 1751.[105]

In many cases, the source and type of disease that afflicted the Lowland Cree can not be deduced from the HBC reports. Often, the HBC traders were not eyewitnesses to the events, but noted the effects of the disease from verbal reports. For example, on November 19, 1732, three Lowland Cree arrived at Albany Fort and informed Joseph Adams that there was "a great sickness among them,"[106] but nothing else was recorded to enable an identification of the disease. The common cold and influenza were rarely lethal among the HBC traders, but the Lowland Cree sometimes succumbed to these endemic European diseases. On January 6, 1741, a "Hective Fever" among the Lowland Cree near Albany Fort was responsible for the death of at least one child.[107] At York Factory on June 30, 1752, James Isham remarked that "most of ye home Indian men, women and children bad of a cough and sore throats."[108] This outbreak may have been transmitted from HBC men stationed at York Factory who were also sick with symptoms of the common cold. Reports of sickness from colds were frequent during the 1750s. James Isham reported in July 1753 that two women and a child had died from colds near Flamborough House (Nelson River), and that many people in the interior had died from the same sickness.[109] In March 1754, he recorded the deaths of six Lowland Cree near York Factory, which he attributed to "a consumption or Hective fever."[110] A similar disease outbreak was noted in the Albany Fort records in 1753-54. In the fall of 1753, Joseph Isbister noted that "many of our Indians are laid up with a great Cold which has put them off from shooting [geese] and also creates a slow fever."[111] Between September 22 and October 1, 1753, five Lowland Cree died near Albany Fort. In the summer of 1757, reports of sickness and mortality abounded near York Factory, and in a two-day period in June, fifteen people died. The sickness apparently spread upland. James Isham noted on August 19, 1757, "Sad news, Indians inland dropping off surprizingly."[112] It continued throughout the winter of 1757-58, and in the summer of 1758, Isham reported that six men, and twelve women and children had died among the Nelson River Cree.[113] In the summer of 1777, Humphrey Marten, who was in charge of York Factory, reported "many of the English and Indians bad with sore throats, violent coughs and difficulty of breathing."[114]

By far the most deadly disease in the post-European-contact period to affect the Lowland Cree was the smallpox epidemic of 1782-83. Unlike most of the previous disease outbreaks, which appear to have originated from the European traders who were stationed at the coastal posts, this smallpox epidemic was transmitted from the south by upland traders who visited the coastal region. It is generally believed that the smallpox epidemic began in 1779 in the south, possibly originating as far south as Mexico, and spread northward along Aboriginal trade routes.[115] Historian Arthur Ray has traced the transmission routes of the epidemic northward through the prairie region to the Saskatchewan River.[116] Paul Hackett has shown that two routes of transmission followed war parties: one from the Shoshone or Snake Nation into the western Canadian plains; and the other from the Missouri River Nations into the eastern Canadian plains.[117]

The smallpox reached Cumberland House, an HBC trading post on the lower Saskatchewan River, after being transmitted by Aboriginal people from the South Saskatchewan River who had visited smallpox-infected Mandan villages for trade in the summer of 1781. On December 11, 1781, HBC traders at Cumberland House reported that some people had been infected with smallpox.[118] Throughout the winter of 1781-82, the epidemic continued to spread among the Northern Ojibway and Upland Cree who lived in the hinterland of Cumberland House. The stage was set for northward transmission of the disease when the spring thaw broke the ice on the rivers and allowed canoe traffic down to Hudson Bay.

Paul Hackett has traced in detail the spread of the smallpox epidemic to York Factory in the summer of 1782.[119] He pointed out that the disease was transmitted along the Saskatchewan River by a returning war party who had encountered sick and dying Shoshoni warriors in the Red Deer River valley. A group of Northern Ojibway, known as Bungee or Lake Indians by the HBC traders, traded at Cumberland House in the winter of 1781-82, and were the first to carry the disease into the Hudson Bay lowlands. On June 10, 1782, a trading party of Northern Ojibway in sixteen canoes arrived at York Factory, and informed Matthew Cocking that "a violent disorder has raged among their people which they describe as an eruption on the skin."[120] Several of their leaders had died and many others were dangerously ill. They had become infected shortly after one of their people had visited Cumberland House in the winter.[121] This particular party probably became infected after the initial outbreak, since it is doubtful that the smallpox virus could have persisted throughout the cold winter months.[122] William Tomison met a few of the same Northern Ojibway on his trip down to York Factory from Cumberland House, and he reported that most of the group (people travelling in fourteen of the sixteen canoes) had died from smallpox. Tomison brought two of the survivors back to York Factory on July 2, 1782, and Cocking confirmed that they were pock-marked and suffering from the disease.

On June 23, 1782, a small group of Nelson River Cree, three women and three children, arrived at York Factory. They reported that among five families who wintered together, all the others except one other woman and four children had died. One of the women told Cocking that she and her husband had gone to Cumberland House during the winter, accompanied by four Northern Ojibway who belonged to the group noted above. Like the Northern Ojibway, the Nelson River Cree women provided a similar description of the disease outbreak, confirming that it was a smallpox epidemic. They told of "their Husbands that died of a violent breaking out upon them all over their bodies and within the mouth and throat."[123] The women also became sick, but were able to recover and return home.

During the rest of the summer of 1782, most of the upland people who arrived at York Factory were either sick or had been infected with smallpox. Many related shocking accounts of the deaths of most of their relatives and friends. Matthew Cocking took measures to prevent the smallpox from spreading to the Lowland Cree near the factory. The sick people were immediately quarantined in tents set apart from the others. The buildings and compound around the factory were meticulously cleaned. Cocking sent his own Native family and a lame man who had been staying at York Factory over the river to shield them from the disease and to keep any other Lowland Cree from crossing over the river to the factory. He also sent word to his men who were whaling near the mouth of the Nelson River to warn the Lowland Cree nearby to stay away.

Despite these efforts at York Factory, smallpox was easily transmitted to the Lowland Cree. For example, several infected Northern Ojibway were allowed into the factory on June 11, when Cocking was away for a brief visit with his family. Other infected Northern Ojibway were inadvertently allowed into the factory during the summer. Cocking sent letters to Severn House, Albany Fort, and Moose Factory, warning the HBC men to "keep their Home Indians out of the way of any strangers," but these letters were sent on August 13, more than two months after the disease had been detected.[124] By the time the letters reached Albany Fort, the smallpox epidemic had already been transmitted to the Albany River Lowland Cree.

The second diffusion route from the Missouri River spread the smallpox epidemic toward the southern Hudson Bay lowlands along the Albany

River trade route. The first news of the epidemic reached Gloucester House on May 25, 1782. Three Northern Ojibway leaders, named Captain Abbitywabino and lieutenants Netawekemisack and Countisquie,[125] arrived at Gloucester House with a group of followers in ten canoes. Captain Abbitywabino reported that many of his people had already died from the disease.[126] On June 22, 1782, a group of Ojibway from Rainy Lake visited Gloucester House, and John Kipling, who was in charge for the HBC, wrote that "there is a great mortality among the Indians and that most of the Indians in and near the raney Lake is dead, and that the assineybols [Assiniboine] country is depopulated."[127] These long-distance visitors may have inadvertently helped to spread the smallpox epidemic into the Albany River basin. The smallpox spread widely in the region north and west of Lake Superior known as the Little North. By the spring of 1783, most of the people who lived near Sturgeon Lake, east of Lake Nipigon, were reported dead. Among the dead was Captain Abbitywabino. Many deaths were reported among the people around Gloucester House in the summer of 1783. John Kipling, who was in charge of Gloucester House, noted that "there has hardly been an Indian in but what has lost some part of their in that Cruel Disorder."[128] Transmission of the smallpox down the Albany River to the coastal Lowland Cree is difficult to ascertain. Paul Hackett concluded that smallpox did not spread beyond Pashkokogan Lake, located upriver from Gloucester House. However, the records from Albany Fort during the summer make note of a remarkable sickness among the Lowland Cree. The first upland people arrived at Albany Fort on May 2, 1782, and although nothing unusual was noted about these visitors, Thomas Hutchins reported on the same day that sickness and death afflicted the Lowland Cree near the fort. In a letter to Edward Jarvis, who was in charge of Moose Fort, Hutchins reported "a great Sickness and Mortality amongst them particularly the children which quite disheartens the whole."[129] Later that month, he noted that "a poor child died on the plantation, this is the 7th of the Natives who have died this spring and several are still very ill."[130] By June 5, twelve Lowland Cree had died near Albany Fort. During the rest of the summer, other sick upland people arrived at Albany Fort, increasing the probability that the epidemic was spread to other Lowland Cree.

If the smallpox epidemic reached Albany Fort in the summer of 1783, its impact may have been accelerated by harsh living conditions during the previous winter when food was scarce and sickness prevalent among the Albany River Lowland Cree. Thomas Hutchins, who was in charge of Albany Fort in the summer of 1782, reported that there was "a universal famine and sickness prevailing amongst the Natives during the whole winter [1781–82]."[131] The busy summer trading period at Albany Fort attracted people from all directions, thereby increasing the risk of widespread transmission of the smallpox to neighbouring Lowland Cree. However, the records at Moose Fort indicate that the disease did not affect the Lowland Cree who lived in the vicinity of that post.

Among the oral traditions of the Lowland Cree is one about a disease epidemic at the mouth of the Ekwan River.[132] The identification of the disease can be deduced from various descriptions of the symptoms spoken of in the oral tradition, including severe headaches, stomach pains, vomiting, and a fever followed by chills. After the first symptoms appeared, people died within twenty-four to forty-eight hours. These are symptoms and effects typically associated with acute haemorrhagic smallpox, the type thought to have been involved in the 1782–83 epidemic. Although the oral tradition identified the disease as bubonic plague and spread by the HBC traders to the Lowland Cree, all the other accounts fit with the historical descriptions of the smallpox epidemic. According to the oral tradition, the HBC traders made efforts to quarantine the Lowland Cree population. It was said that "Trading Post officials sent out messengers to the native summer camps, instructing them not to come to the settlement."[133] Despite these precautions, hundreds of people travelled to the post and contracted the disease, and then visited the summer gathering place at the mouth of the Ekwan River. The oral tradition about the effect of the epidemic is compelling:

> People died at the rate of one person per family per day, the first day. Within a few more days, three out of each family of five died each day. Those who had tried to leave the settlement [Albany Fort] before getting the disease arrived at the festival ground barely alive, only to die a few hours or a day later. Those who survived the killing stage of the disease were too weak to help those who were dying. Within three days, half of the tee-pees were quiet, with no life, no sign of life from them.
>
> What sign of life there was came from those who wailed in pain or those who mourned for their loved ones and the dead. And there was that sound that was heard in the atmosphere, the exact sound from the village in the spring [a wailing in the clouds was heard during the spring before the epidemic].[134]

Unfortunately, details about the spread of smallpox among the Lowland Cree near York Factory are unavailable because of the French capture and destruction of the post on September 1, 1782. However, York Factory was rebuilt the following year and subsequent records indicate that the smallpox caused significant mortality among the Lowland Cree who lived in the hinterland of the factory. Although exact figures were not recorded, the HBC traders noted the deadly consequences of the epidemic. For example, in the spring of 1786, Marten wrote that "I gave the usual presents to 45 Indians, great and small for the goose hunt. In the above number of Indians are no more than 5 real hunters; and ten grown women, such havoc hath death made amongst the elderly Indians, for I well remember when we could number 16 good men hunters besides stout boys. Consequently the ravages made by death are much more detrimental to your Honours interest than those made by the Enemy."[135]

To the north of York Factory, the smallpox epidemic probably reached Churchill Fort by Upper Churchill River and Nelson River Cree who traded there in the summer of 1782. It is likely that the Chipewyan were also agents of transmission of the smallpox epidemic to the Churchill Fort area. Trader Alexander Mackenzie reported that the people who lived north of Lac la Ronge (probably Chipewyan) carried the disease eastward to the area near Churchill Fort in the spring of 1782.[136] Although details of the transmission of the disease were not recorded by the HBC traders at Churchill Fort before the French also destroyed that post, the after-effects were described by Samuel Hearne when he re-established Churchill in the fall of 1783. According to him, more than half the Lowland Cree near Churchill Fort died during the epidemic, reducing the population from sixty-nine to thirty-two.[137]

The smallpox epidemic did not reach as far as Severn House, located at the mouth of the Severn River. The HBC trade there tapped a fairly small hinterland that was remote from the main trade routes going to York Factory and Albany Fort. The relative isolation of the Severn River trade may have deterred the spread of smallpox to the area. Also, the HBC was able to take preventative measures to protect the local Lowland Cree population. News of the smallpox at York Factory was communicated in a letter dated August 12, 1782, from William Falconer at York to Peter Willrige, who was temporarily in charge at Severn. Delivered by two York Factory Lowland Cree on August 21, Falconer's letter gave specific orders to quarantine the people in the area.

> The purport of this is to advise you that the small Pox having been communicated to the Natives about Cumberland House, and the upper Settlement [Hudson House] have almost entirely rooted them, and the Pungees have also caught the infection, are most of them (that belong to this place) either dying or dead. You will therefore keep a strict look out, that none of the Homeguards come to the factory, but keep them at a

proper distance so that none of the Pungees that come for debt may have any communication with them. Should you find the disorder has attacked any of them, do all in your power for their preservation, if the Englishmen have been handling any person that may have had the small Pox, you must be careful that they shift, wash and air their Cloaths as well as themselves ere they go near one of the homeguards, by this prudent precaution the homeguards here are preserved. I solicit you most earnestly to adhere to this advice, as not only the Company's Interest, but our own preservation depend now on the homeguards safety.[138]

Smallpox was not reported in the immediate vicinity of Severn House, but the disease did take a toll on the Lowland Cree and Northern Ojibway who lived upriver. Soon after the river ice broke in the spring of 1783, the full extent of the epidemic inland became clear. On April 14, 1783, two families (probably Northern Ojibway) arrived at Severn House, and they had "seen but one Indian during the winter, that they are all dead inland, these are very deeply marked with the small pox, one of them has lost all his children by it except one poor boy, which is both blind and lame, and they have been obliged to haul him all the winter."[139] The number of deaths actually reported at Severn House was low, but other indirect reports suggest that the rate of mortality was quite high among the inland Severn River Lowland Cree. For example, the 1784 spring goose hunt was attended by very few Lowland Cree, and Falconer explained that "we have but 5 or 6 men that can be called Hunters, but loaded with swarms of widdows, orphans and infirm creatures."[140]

Deaths from disease continued in the coastal area near Albany Fort in the fall and winter of 1782-83. Unlike York Factory and Churchill Fort, which were both destroyed by the French, Albany Fort was spared and a continuous record of events is available to shed light on the effects of the epidemic in the area. On September 12, 1782, two Lowland Cree died on the plantation near the fort. One week later, another died, and Edward Jarvis, who was in charge of Albany Fort, wrote that "the Natives who are much disheartened by the mortality which still rages among them: a fine young Indian having died this night, which makes 3 since my arrival and several more are taken sick."[141] During that winter, many Lowland Cree arrived at Albany Fort accompanied by sick and dying people. Many came to the post to trade for medicine from the company store in desperate efforts to save family members and others. Jarvis was kept busy during the winter, supplying food and caring for sick and dying people. In November, he noted: "22 Indians young and old on the plantation to feed, besides widows. Orphans and distressed children."[142] By December 1, the number had grown to sixty-seven, including sixteen families plus widows and orphans.

HBC reports indicate that the smallpox epidemic spread among the Lowland Cree who lived along the Attawapiskat and Ekwan rivers. Two Lowland Cree leaders from that area arrived at Albany Fort on May 11, 1783. Jarvis reported that "Lt. Earchyekeshick, Saquot and their gangs came in 13 canoes, but poorly gooded having had many deaths in their families."[143] The epidemic also affected the HBC employees because the usual supplies of country provisions were unavailable. In March, with "two men sick, five convalescent, ye scurvy begins to make its appearance. Unfortunate country, once so healthy and abounding in provisions even in my remembrance is now quite contrary having not a single days partridges been served to the men ye whole winter."[144]

The after-effects of the smallpox epidemic continued to be felt near Albany Fort throughout the 1783-84 season. Many suffered from food shortages as sickness and death disrupted the usual activities of the Lowland Cree. Grief among affected families was also a factor in reducing the Albany River Lowland Cree to a state of starvation. On March 8, 1784, Edward Jarvis observed that "Captain Questach and family came in without a single fur of any kind in a most pitiable condition, he fairly cried with joy at having reached the fort which he never expected."[145] Several weeks later, Jarvis received news of similar conditions among the Lowland Cree who lived north of the Albany River: "I have received the disagreeable news of several deaths among some of the best Indians; Lt. Earchyekeshick having lost his eldest son is inconsolable and cannot even pay his debt, and Saquot's family were all starving."[146] On August 9, 1784, Jarvis noted that "Captain Assup came in so poor that many of his young fellows could not even pay their debts; they tell of numerous deaths among the Indians around them by an epidemical disorder which from their description should seem to be the smallpox, which I fear has made its way from the northward."[147] On June 15, 1784, Jarvis wrote, "Departed this life Captain Questach, Captain of our Goose hunters, he has been declining ever since the famine he underwent in the winter." On June 16, Captain Questach was buried near Albany Fort, and Jarvis "with all the Indians on the plantation attended the remains of old Captain Questach to a wooden tomb built in a very permanent manner; he was buried with more solemnity and ceremony than ever I saw upon like occasion; Gave him the colour half mast high; In the evening the Indians made a grand feast upon the occasion and kept their guns firing all night."[148]

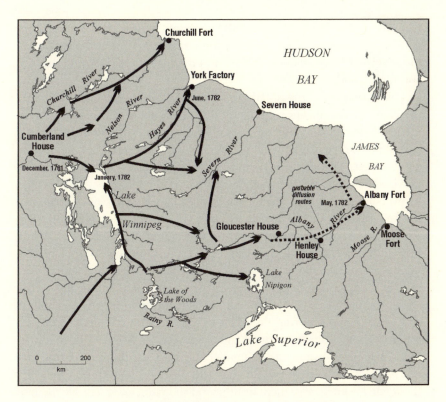

Diffusion of Smallpox into the Lowlands, 1782-83

By the fall of 1784, the acute physical suffering seems to have run its course near Albany Fort, but many of the Lowland Cree had not yet recovered from the psychological damage that had resulted from so many deaths. They concluded that "God was angry with their country," in order to explain the tragic sequence of events triggered by the smallpox epidemic.[149] The effects of the epidemic continued to be felt by the Albany River Lowland Cree as late as 1785. On March 13 that year, Edward Jarvis noted that "this is the third year of famine at Albany."[150]

An assessment of the impact of the smallpox epidemic on the Lowland Cree can be made from the quantitative and qualitative information provided by HBC traders. Humphrey Marten's enumeration of Lowland Cree goose hunters at York Factory in the spring of 1786 indicated that eleven of sixteen men, about two-thirds, had died from smallpox.[151] Samuel Hearne calculated that 54 percent of the Lowland Cree near Churchill Fort died from smallpox. Similar demographic information is not available from Severn House or Albany Fort, but the descriptions of death and suffering in the aftermath of the epidemic indicate that a great mortality took place. In addition to the high mortality during the epidemic, the survivors faced many hardships in procuring food, clothing, shelter, and trade goods.

Calvin Martin has suggested that Aboriginal people generally attributed the cause of the smallpox epidemic to a "conspiracy of the beasts."[152] In other words, animals were the cause of their sickness and death, and Aboriginal people retaliated by killing them in numbers exceeding sustainable harvest levels. The HBC traders did not record such sentiments among the Lowland Cree, and it was decades later that animal populations were thinned by over-hunting in the region. However, the Lowland Cree did attribute a spiritual cause to the smallpox epidemic, which may have been linked to animal agents. Andrew Graham wrote an account of an interview with a Lowland Cree regarding the spirit world, who told Graham, "I believe there is a Whittico, the author and contrivor of every mischief and misfortune, the occasion of sickness, death and famine; and is continually on the watch to hurt me. And that he has many servants who are enemies to me, and walking about during the night in the similitude of a dog, wolf and other ravenous animals, to injure and plague me."[153] William Falconer provided a similar account of the connection between the spirit world and disease: "The evil Spirit whom they stile Whitico they think can afflict them with sickness, give them health, food and raiment, or deprive them of either, and take away life when he pleases; they say he has many small Whiticos under him, whom he sends to plague them, when he does not chuse to come himself."[154]

The Lowland Cree also had an extensive knowledge of natural medicines and believed in the power of certain individuals to possess supernatural healing powers. Lowland Cree healers included those who administered herbal remedies, and others who invoked spiritual assistance to physically remove the disease from the body. The latter were routinely dismissed by the HBC traders as frauds or tricksters. Andrew Graham called them jugglers or conjurers, and speculated that they practised "several tricks of sleight hand ... and a thousand other pranks."[155] The herbal doctors were viewed with less scepticism by the HBC traders, probably because their methods were more similar to accepted European health-care practices. These healers, or *tuckathin*, had an extensive knowledge of medicinal plants and traded widely for certain herbs known to cure ailments. Every year a trade was carried on for roots and herbs brought by Aboriginal people from the upland country. In addition to Aboriginal remedies, some Lowland Cree healers incorporated European medicines into their practice.

Graham observed that "besides the knowledge of plants and herbs that grow in the country, he usually procures a trunk with medicines at the factory, which gives great satisfaction to himself, and engages the esteem of others."[156] The Lowland Cree also made use of sweat lodges to cure illness. Graham described the construction of sweat lodges and the ritual of smoking tobacco during the sweat, and noted that "when the person has sweat as much as he chooses sometimes the house is let to cool gradually, and he will scrape off the sweat. At other times he will come directly out and roll himself in the snow, or plunge into the river without any bad consequence from a conduct so extraordinary."[157] Jody Decker believes the latter practice could have increased mortality rates during the smallpox epidemic, because "high temperatures accompanying many infectious diseases such as smallpox could be lowered so dramatically by such actions that shock and death ensued."[158]

It is difficult to measure the success or failure of Lowland Cree attempts to stem the onslaught of the smallpox epidemic, since most of the coping with the disease took place far away from the HBC traders who wrote about the epidemic. However, the oral tradition from Ekwan River provides an interesting account of the response to the disease epidemic. In addition to unsuccessful attempts to quarantine the sick people, elders at the traditional summer gathering place at the mouth of the Ekwan River instructed the younger people to gather bear oil, which was used as a traditional emetic remedy. The bear oil was fed to people showing early signs of the disease, and the induced vomiting was said to have stopped the spread of the disease. The use of the bear-oil remedy was initiated after half the population had already succumbed to the disease, but the dying stopped soon after. The effectiveness of purging the stomach with bear oil as a cure for smallpox may be questioned, but the fact that the deaths stopped undoubtedly gave support to traditional medicinal knowledge against a seemingly unstoppable and alien contagion.

Overall, the rate of mortality among the Lowland Cree was high, probably 50 percent or higher in some areas. However, families and individuals survived the disease and gave rise to new generations. HBC traders marvelled at the rate of recovery, a development that also mitigated in favour of their own future well-being. Humphrey Marten wrote from York Factory on June 18, 1786, that "we have now 15 Indians to feed, the greatest number of them are thriving boys and girls and bid fair to repopulate this dismally depopulated Country."[159]

8.
The Lowland Cree in the Fur Trade, 1783-1821

Fur Trade

The smallpox epidemic of 1782-83 had a significant negative impact on the involvement of the Lowland Cree in the fur trade. The impact was widespread throughout the area affected by the disease, and the HBC account books reported the magnitude of the reduction in furs for several years thereafter. For example, the total Albany Fort fur returns (including inland posts) dropped from 9052 made beaver in 1782-83, to 6975 made beaver in 1783-84. In the summer of 1782, Thomas Hutchins, who was in charge of Albany Fort, already noted the decline in the fur trade, and that "they [Lowland Cree] flocked to the factory for support and assistance inasmuch that the Albany home Tribe produced 1200 Made Beaver less than in former years."[1] At York Factory, the decline was more precipitous, with the total value of furs dropping from 12,837 made beaver in 1781-82 to 2832 made beaver in 1783-84.[2] The Severn House fur returns fell from 4066 made beaver in 1781-82 to 2418 made beaver in 1783-84.

The decline in the fur trade caused directly by the deaths of Lowland Cree fur trappers and hunters was amplified by the common practice of throwing away possessions, including furs, by grieving relatives. Edward

Jarvis, who was in charge of Albany Fort in 1784, explained, "I have not now 3000 MBeaver in the Fort, and I believe not 200 Beaver skins in the whole, the Indians having universally either been obliged to eat them or throw them away, the effects of their grief for many deaths among them."[3] On October 7, 1797, two Lowland Cree arrived at Severn House and Thomas Thomas observed that they "had, in consequence of the death of their brother, thrown away every article which they had taken in debt (this is their common manner of showing sorrow at the loss of a friend or relation) they were now wholly destitute of necessaries."[4] In the summer of 1799, a large group of Lowland Cree in twenty canoes arrived at York Factory with no furs to trade. According to Joseph Colen, "The death of a son of the Chief who was the principal hunter, early in the fall, stopped the whole party from killing furs—this is too frequently the case with Indians."[5] On January 15, 1810, William Cook, who was in charge of York Factory, noted that "3 Natives [arrived at the factory] from a party of homeguards tenting in Foxes Lake ... very little exertion appears to have gone forwards in this family owing to the Death of their Leader."[6] In 1821, Thomas Vincent, who was in charge of Albany Fort, noted that a Homeguard Cree named Sheshequon had brought in a poor trade, because "according to the Indian custom when a Death takes place amongst em, a gloom remains for a considerable time; this has been the case with him last winter, his wife paid the Debt of Nature last summer."[7]

High mortality rates and lingering sickness because of malnutrition and other after-effects among Lowland Cree hunting groups necessitated adaptive strategies, and the role of women became critical to the survival of some groups. For example, in 1790, three Severn River Lowland Cree families who had wintered together arrived at Severn House with several sick people, including the principal hunters. The HBC trader noted that they brought only seventy-five made beaver in furs, and these were "chiefly trapt by the women."[8]

The smallpox epidemic temporarily interrupted the HBC's inland operations, but within a few years after the epidemic the network of inland trading posts rapidly expanded. As a result, few upland traders visited the coastal trading posts after 1782. The establishment of a network of inland trading posts made the long, difficult trips by canoe to the bay unnecessary to obtain HBC trade goods. John McNab, who was in charge of Albany Fort in 1795, recalled that the last "real uplander" to visit the fort was a man named Muscowenatauga, who made the trip in 1782. McNab observed that since Muscowenatauga's visit, "not a single beaver has been brought to the Fort by an uplander."[9] In addition to reducing the volume of furs, the inland expansion of the HBC also affected the composition of the furs received at the coastal posts, since only locally available animals were harvested for the coastal trade. The HBC records at Albany Fort in the post-1782 period provided a breakdown of the furs traded at each of the posts, and this information sheds light on the Lowland Cree fur trade in that period. The Lowland Cree traded mainly at Albany Fort, Henley House, and Martins Fall. The Homeguard Cree contributed most of the furs at Albany Fort, and the Half-Homeguard Cree were major suppliers at Henley House and, to a lesser extent, Martins Fall.

The fur trade during the period 1783 to 1821 throughout the northwestern interior of the continent was affected by extreme competition between the HBC and various fur companies based in the St. Lawrence River valley that eventually amalgamated to form the North West Company (NWC). The peak period of fur-trade activity occurred between 1790 and 1810, when record numbers of fur traders and trading posts were in operation.[10] The fur trade in the Hudson Bay lowlands was not immune to the intensive competition that developed between the HBC and NWC in that period.

Although French and later Canadian fur traders from the St. Lawrence River valley made periodic forays into the Hudson Bay lowlands before 1782, there was little sustained competition within the region (except in the hinterland of Moose Factory) until after 1783. In 1784, Canadian fur traders began to intercept Lowland Cree hunters as far north as the Nelson River. On September 5, 1784, a large group of Nelson River Cree arrived at York Factory with very few furs. They told Humphrey Marten they had been forced to trade with the "Pedlars."[11] On June 2, 1786, a group of Homeguard Cree who traded at York Factory acknowledged that they had previously traded with the Canadians.[12] The Canadian trading post was located a few days' journey upriver from York Factory, in the middle track, which was the route from the Saskatchewan River that followed Cross Lake, Bigstone River, and Fox River to the Hayes River. The exact location of this post is uncertain, but it may have been situated on Cross Lake. In 1789-90, a Canadian post operated on Gull Lake, about 200 kilometres inland from York Factory. This was probably Gull Lake on the lower Nelson River. This lake was depicted on Philip Turnor's map of the Churchill, Nelson, and Hayes rivers in 1779.[13] In 1791, several Nelson River Cree arrived at York Factory with more information about the Canadian competition: "The Canadian traders are so numerous, no Indian can rest with his family without having one or more of these people continually visiting them and collecting their furrs as soon as killed."[14] In 1793, the Canadian traders built a post near *Pathepow neepee*, or Deep Water Lake (Oxford Lake). Joseph Colen was especially concerned about the impact of this post because it was "in the centre of the wintering grounds of my Home Guard up this river."[15] In 1796, the HBC traders at York Factory learned about a Canadian trading post on the Jack River (near present Norway House), which, Joseph Colen remarked, was "almost in the Centre of York Fort Home Guard Hunters."[16] The strategy of the Canadian traders was to keep the York Factory men pinned down to the lower country to prevent the HBC from establishing posts in more profitable places like the Athabasca country. Along the Nelson River, Canadian traders were very active in 1792-93. Joseph Colen observed that "the Canadian masters declare that their expenditure of goods last season has been double the value of the Furrs collected by them. They are liberal in distributing their Liquor among the Natives below to keep the Honourable Company's servants in action, and to prevent their being employed in places where greater profit arises, which enables them to do much in opposing the lower settlements."[17]

As a result of intensive competition, HBC and Canadian traders urged the Lowland Cree and other subarctic people to kill as many fur bearers as possible, especially beaver. By 1805, the fur-trade competition in the upper country had reached its peak, and the stress on the fur resources was clearly evident. On the borders of the lowlands, new techniques were employed to maximize fur returns. For example, Canadian fur traders employed Aboriginal people from the St. Lawrence valley to hunt and trap furs. These people, mainly Iroquois from the Montreal region, were employed specifically to hunt beaver. HBC traders reported the impact of Iroquois trappers as early as 1802-03. John McNab, who was in charge of York Factory that year, learned from HBC inland traders that "these Iroquois are adding greatly to the failure of our exertions inland, they are now some hundreds who winter and summer in the best beaver grounds, are regularly agreed to the Canadian masters who pay them 10 livres for every pound of beaver skin and have them bound not to trade one with us under a penalty of them giving them 10 skins (for nothing) for every one they barter with us."[18] On May 16, 1805, Lowland Cree from the Martins Fall area reported that Iroquois employed by the Canadian traders "hunt up all the Beaver."[19] Upriver from Martins Fall, the HBC traders noted the extreme competition for furs. John Hodgson commented that "there is now such an increase in Traders from Canada, that it is with great difficulty to get a skin from the Natives, unless a man is constantly with them to take the Beaver out of the hole."[20]

As beaver populations dwindled in the early 1800s, Canadian traders encouraged neighbouring upland people to hunt in the lowlands. For

example, in 1815-16, the HBC traders reported that numbers of Northern Ojibway who lived near Lake Nipigon had hunted beaver near Martins Fall. William Thomas, who was in charge of the Martins Fall trading
post, remarked that "it is the policy in the Canadians sending their Indians into this part to hunt for were they to remain on their own lands
their hunts would be trifling."[22] John Davis, who was in charge of Martins Fall post in 1819, observed that the local people complained of the
encroachment of Uplanders from the south on their hunting grounds,
and that "the Canadian Indians had come down on their grounds in the
fall of the year and had since left them and carried off all the Beaver in
these parts."[22]

A South East View of Albany Factory, A Winter View, by William Richards, watercolour,
1804-1811 (PAM, HBCA, P-118).

By the early 1800s, the beaver resource in the Hudson Bay lowlands had declined to very low numbers. In 1810, William Cook, who was in charge of York Factory, remarked that he had received "very few Beaver skins—indeed these animals are nearly extirpated in the low country."[23] Cook noted that the Lowland Cree who lived in the area between York Factory and Oxford House traded very few beaver skins, which "proves the poverty of the latter country at the same time that it assures us of the truth of the Indians assertion that the Beaver being annihilated."[24] By 1812, he said "the scarcity of furs in all directions around the Factory is without a parallel."[25] Steel beaver traps, which have often been cited as a primary cause of beaver depletion, came into use in the York Factory area after the beaver populations had declined. The first evidence of these traps in the HBC journals was noted in the winter of 1814-15.[26]

The Albany Fort district report for 1815-16 listed the names of the Lowland Cree who traded at the post. That report also enumerated the value of the furs brought by each hunter, and the proportion of beaver skins in the returns. The total value of furs in 1815-16 amounted to 3189 made beaver and the value of beaver skins was 1004 made beaver, or less than one-third of the total returns. Some Lowland Cree hunters brought in relatively large quantities of beaver skins while others brought in few or none. For example, the hunter identified as Missiscape traded 107 beaver skins from a total of 147 made beaver value in furs. Others, such as Weemeshoes, brought in very few beaver skins (eleven) with the rest of the furs that amounted to 102 made beaver. HBC trader Jacob Corrigal pointed out in 1818 that the hunters who brought in greater numbers of beaver skins were Half-Homeguard Cree who lived farther away from the coast. In contrast, the coastal Homeguard Cree who lived near Albany Fort brought in mainly marten skins, which, Corrigal noted, were "the principal fur animal near the coast."[27]

The fur returns at Albany Fort continued to decline through the 1817-18 season, as many Albany River Lowland Cree traded at Severn House. Some of the hunters who traded furs at Albany Fort were women, an indication that the role of women in Lowland Cree society was more complex than their portrayal in the existing literature. In 1819-20, the Albany Fort fur returns began to increase, which reflected in large measure the return of Lowland Cree hunters who had previously traded at Severn House.

In 1819, John Work, who was in charge of Severn House, observed that "the beaver are decreasing in number annually. The Indians complain that few beaver are to be got anywhere near the sea coast.... The Indians assign two reasons for the deficiency in beaver, some say that the country is entirely hunted up, which I believe is the case in some places near the coast. Others again affirm that in some parts of the District [inland] beaver are still pretty numerous, but on the account of the great quantity of snow which entirely filled up the small rivers and creeks so that the haunts of the beaver could not be found."[28] The beaver population near Henley House was reported to have declined greatly by 1821. In the area around Martins Fall, the HBC traders also noted the decline in beaver. Jacob Corrigal, who was in charge of Martins Fall post in 1824, said that "Beaver are now very much exhausted in this quarter,"[29] and he compared the beaver returns in 1812, 1823, and 1824 to illustrate the substantive decline in beaver in the area.

Beaver Trade at Martins Fall Post, 1812, 1823,1824

Skin Type	1812	1823	1824
large beaver	1684	750	257
small beaver	900	409	75
total	2584	1159	332

The decline in beaver in the lowlands was noticed by the HBC traders because of the impact on its commercial business, but the Lowland Cree were also deprived of a significant food resource.[30]

The HBC and Canadian traders escalated their use of liquor substantially in the period between 1783 and 1821 as an incentive to increase the production of furs. In 1786, Humphrey Marten, who was in charge of York Factory, explained, "It is impossible for me to prevent them from getting liquor.... Indeed your Honours servants are obliged to give them a little occasionally to form a friendship with them or keep an old one up."[31] In 1793, Joseph Colen, who was in charge of York Factory, wrote extensively about the rising liquor trade that was spurred on by competition with Canadian traders.

> These Canadian Traders are so artful, it is impossible to keep the few skins the Indians procure from them, as they attend their tents with liquor, and collect the produce of their hunt almost immediately on animals being killed. This induced the Indians to remove their Tents to a greater distance from these enterprizing Traders and nearer to the Factory, while others who cannot refrain from liquor employ their young men hunting to purchase a supply, by which many are kept almost in a continual state of intoxication.[32]

Five months later, he wrote:

> I am in hopes they are now convinced that it is not in their interest to
> trade their Winter furrs with the Canadians for liquor. But their liberality
> to Indians in this article has made them a depraved race, and their whole
> time is taken up in drinking. The number of Natives who have fallen
> victims to intoxication within these two years past are many, and should
> the Natives [Canadians] continue their practice of carrying their strong
> spirits to the tents of Natives I much fear the whole country will soon be
> depopulated.[33]

The rapid increase in the use of liquor by fur traders in the Hudson Bay
lowlands paralleled the liquor trade in the upland region.[34] Most of the
liquor was given to the Lowland Cree free, in the form of gifts; very little
liquor was traded directly for furs. The liquor trade peaked in 1794-95,
when 1237 gallons of brandy were used in the Albany Fort hinterland. By
comparison, the total amount of liquor used before 1763, when large numbers of upland traders were involved in the fur trade at Albany Fort, never
exceeded 400 gallons per year.[35]

Although over-hunting was a major cause of the depletion of beaver
and other fur bearers, unusual weather patterns in the period between
1783 and 1821 contributed to the stress on animal populations. William
Falconer, who was in charge of Severn House in 1784-85, noted that "we
have had the mildest weather and least snow ever known by the oldest
Native living."[36] According to Lowland Cree reports at York Factory in
1793, many beaver were killed during widespread flooding that occurred
during the spring of 1792.[37] In the fall of 1793, a prolonged drought was
blamed for killing many beaver near York Factory. Joseph Colen reported:

> All the Natives complain this winter of a scarcity of Beaver, which they
> impute to the shoalness of the water in the Rivers in the Fall of the year
> which drained the water from their Houses that on opening them it has
> not been infrequent this winter to find all the Beaver it contained dead....
> Should this calamity prove universal over this extensive country, which
> God prevent, it is to be feared many of those valuable animals will fall
> victim to want more than by the hand of the hunter—instinct teaches
> them to avoid the snares of the latter, as it rarely happens that the whole
> family of a Beaver House is destroyed, their subteranious communica-
> tions being so artfully contrived as to baffel the most experienced hunter;
> one or more generally escape, by which its species has been hitherto
> preserved, but a few seasons of Drought would entirely destroy the whole
> race.[38]

Fire was another factor contributing to the reduction in the numbers of animals in the region. Fuelled by drought, fires swept through the area near York Factory in the summer of 1794. On July 9, Joseph Colen observed that "the fire upwards continue with unabated violence. The Factory and for miles below is surrounded by clouds of smoak, and the sun appears thro' it like unto a Ball of fire."[39] On July 28 that year, he reported that fires had been burning for five weeks, and that "great indeed must have been the destruction of animals by this devouring element and many score miles of woodland laid waste."[40] The drought that began in the fall of 1793 continued for several years. George Sutherland, who was in charge of York Factory in the summer of 1795, noted that the water level in the Hayes River was extremely low, and "an Instance of this kind was never known before at this place."[41] Massive fires also burned near York Factory in the summer of 1799.

Unusual weather conditions continued to prevail in the early 1800s.[42] In the winter of 1806-07, remarkably mild temperatures were experienced near York Factory. John McNab observed that "so mild weather at so late a period was never before witnessed by the oldest native about the Factory, and there are two now on the plantation who well remember two vessels sent on discovery wintering in Ten Shilling Creek."[43] Severe drought was noted again in the summer of 1808 near York Factory. The HBC men who worked the boat brigades on the Hayes River noted the low water levels, and James Halcro reported that "he has been 18 years going up and down the river, and never saw it so shoal."[44]

By 1795, the combination of drought, fires, and competition from nearby Canadian traders had reduced the beaver population around York Factory to very low numbers. The Lowland Cree who traded at York Factory brought very few beaver skins, and George Sutherland commented that many had not hunted beaver. In 1796, many of the Lowland Indians reported that beaver were very scarce throughout their hunting grounds.

Calvin Martin has suggested that epidemic diseases were responsible for the decline in beaver populations throughout the subarctic region of North America.[45] However, the HBC documents from the Hudson Bay lowlands provide no evidence that disease directly contributed to the decline in beaver populations. Anthropologist Robert Brightman's study of the Upland Rock Cree of the Churchill River pointed to increased rates of predation and higher efficiency of European goods, especially steel beaver traps, as the principal factors in the decline of beaver and other animals in the upland region.[46] Again, this is only a small part of the story. Instead, in the Hudson Bay lowlands, the prolonged and unusually dry weather, and related fires, had a disruptive effect on the entire ecosystem of the lowlands. In 1799, the Lowland Cree near York Factory reported that "the coast is so impoverished they cannot provide food for their families and wish to get into a more plentiful country."[47] In the winter of 1799-1800, animals of all kinds were scarce near York Factory. Despite the general decline in animal resources in the lowlands, a few areas continued to support healthy animal populations. These were remote from the main areas of fur-trade competition. For example, caribou and moose were reported to be plentiful in the Attawapiskat area in 1820. Increased rates of predation, spurred on by intensive fur-trade competition, together with extreme environmental stress in the late eighteenth century, appear to have been the main factors in thinning animal populations in the lowlands.

A Man & his Wife Returning with a Load of Partridges from their Tent, by William Richards, watercolour, 1804-1811 (PAM, HBCA, P-116).

The Lowland Cree Provision Trade, 1783-1821

At Albany Fort, many Homeguard Cree goose hunters were reluctant to hunt for the company in the aftermath of the smallpox epidemic. Edward Jarvis, who was in charge of Albany Fort, noted an instance in the fall of 1784, when "eight canoes of Indians came in to the hunt, among the rest Old Wittituckye to take debt, having left his family and sons behind in a plentiful country terrified at the remembrance of the last years famine; so that we need to try every means for provisions they being without dispute the best goose hunters at Albany."[48] Jarvis later confirmed that Wittituckeye's family, along with several others, decided to remain far away from Albany Fort, about halfway to Severn House in the so-called "Deer Country." Wittituckeye explained that he would not hunt geese because he wished to remain in a "more plentiful country."[49] This was undoubtedly a reference to the caribou resource that was more plentiful along the northern coast near Cape Henrietta Maria.

The rapid expansion of the HBC inland fur trade after 1783 increased the company's dependency on country provisions. The large increases in resident labourers, the expansion of the HBC transport network, and the seasonal influx of inland traders required substantially greater quantities of provisions.[50] The caribou provision trade in the northern parts of the Hudson Bay lowlands increased rapidly as the HBC expanded its fur-trade operations inland. The HBC traders encouraged the Lowland Cree to hunt caribou, and offered increasingly large rewards to obtain more caribou meat. These activities also drew in numbers of Lowland Cree from the Albany River area. The Northern Ojibway who survived the smallpox epidemic also continued to hunt caribou near York Factory. In the fall of 1814, William Cook reported that "Bungee Indians" hunted caribou along the Pennycutaway River, about fifty kilometres above the factory.[51] According to Cook, the name "Pennycutaway" was an anglicized version of the Indian name, *Oo-pootha-cah-to-way*, meaning the "gnawing of beavers."

In a move to expedite the collection of caribou meat, fat, tongues, and skins, the HBC traders at York Factory re-established a caribou provision post in 1790 at Flamborough Head on the Nelson River. Joseph Colen described the post as "a substantial log tent about a mile beyond where the old Factory stood,"[52] rebuilt to "serve as a store room to receive venison from the Natives in the summer." By the end of the summer, the HBC had collected 4700 kilograms of caribou meat at that post. In 1793, the York Factory traders stepped up their efforts to obtain caribou meat by posting several men at the Fourteens Goose Tent to remain all summer and trade caribou meat from the Lowland Cree. In 1794, the York Factory men built Gordon House at a place on the Hayes River (along a stretch of the river known then as the Hill River) called The Rock. That post functioned as a provision-collection depot and as a forward supply post for the boat brigades on the Hayes River. In the fall of 1809, the HBC sent men to a number of caribou-crossing places along the Nelson River to trade caribou meat from the Lowland Cree hunters. In the fall of 1810, the York Factory traders built a provision post at Deers Island in the Nelson River. Deers Island was located near the mouth of the Nelson River, about thirty kilometres above the Seal Islands, and it was known as the first crossing place on the Nelson River.[53] The Deers Island post was established to procure caribou meat in the fall and early winter. William Cook observed that "our attention is chiefly directed to the Winter Deer which never fail to migrate to these parts in the month of November."[54] Procuring caribou meat at that time of the year was advantageous because it could be frozen for later use.

By 1800, the intense hunting pressure made the movements of the caribou herds less predictable, and hunting efforts less successful. John Ballenden, who was in charge of York Factory in 1800-01, commented that "during my residence now in your Honours Service for 30 years, I have never observed the Indians so distressed for snow shoes as this, the poor creatures that arrived this day had snow shoes entirely made of boards, without the least netting in them, the first instance of this kind I have seen."[55] In 1807, the scarcity of caribou near York Factory was a major cause for concern of both the Lowland Cree and HBC traders. John McNab remarked that "the oldest among them saying they never saw such a summer of scarcity, or the deer to fail so long and so universally,"[56] and "last year [1806] coming down the [Hayes] river its banks were strewed with the carcasses of deer—now one cannot be got for the maintenance of their former destroyers."[57]

Caribou continued to be scarce near York Factory in the summer of 1808. Many Lowland Cree sought relief at the factory, and John McNab was concerned about his ability to feed the visitors and his own men. He wrote that "last summer they [Lowland Cree] said was the scarcest ever known at York—what may they now say of this?"[58] Unusually large kills of caribou were reported near York Factory in 1811-12. The wintering over of a large group of Red River settlers at the mouth of the Nelson River greatly increased the demand for caribou meat. In addition, the settlers were willing to pay more than the HBC, and this competition fuelled the caribou hunt by the Lowland Cree. In 1813, however, the situation near York Factory had grown worse. Cook noted "the prevailing scarcity of last winter both as to provisions and furs, the like of which was never known."[59]

The magnitude of the caribou hunt in the lowlands during the period from 1783 to 1821 can be measured by examining the HBC's caribou-skin trade. The impact of the smallpox epidemic temporarily dampened the upward trend in the caribou trade that had begun before 1782, but the post-smallpox readjustment was rapid and, by the 1790s, the trade in caribou skins had increased to record levels. The caribou-skin trade at Severn House peaked in 1792-93, with a total of 2666 skins. The decline in the trade thereafter was fairly rapid, and after 1811-12, no caribou skins were received at Severn House. The pattern at York Factory was similar, but the trade peaked about a decade later with 3417 skins traded in 1804-05. The decline in the caribou-skin trade at York Factory was even more precipitous than that at Severn House and, by 1811-12, had also reached its nadir.

The tactics employed by the HBC traders to obtain greater supplies of caribou put pressure on Lowland Cree hunters to harvest caribou far in excess of the numbers killed before 1783. In addition to supplying caribou during the spring and fall migrations, the Lowland Cree were recruited to hunt caribou year-round for the HBC posts. The change toward year-round hunting can be seen in the amounts of venison traded at York Factory. Before 1783, very little venison or other caribou products were traded in the middle of summer or during the winter months. This pattern began to change after 1783 and, at the height of the caribou trade in the early 1800s, the Lowland Cree supplied these products year-round to the HBC traders at York Factory.

By 1815, the caribou herds had been reduced to such low numbers that the Lowland Cree found it difficult to secure enough for their own food requirements. William Cook, who was in charge of York Factory in 1815, observed that "no dependence can be placed upon supplies of meat [caribou]. The Indians tho good Hunters can scarcely support themselves."[60] In 1827, Simon McGillivray Jr., who was in charge of Severn House, reported that caribou were generally unavailable near the post and "the means of procuring subsistence is very limited at Severn House, and were it not for the Wild Fowl, that are killed Spring and Autumn, it would be impossible to maintain a post there."[61] McGillivray noted that only seven caribou tongues, 268 kilograms of venison, fifty-three kilograms of "half-dry meat," and four kilograms of dried venison were traded at Severn House in 1826-27.

Several visitors to the York Factory region after 1830 made note of the remarkable decline in the caribou and the resulting impact on the Lowland Cree. John McLean, who visited York Factory in 1837, offered the following account of the demise of the caribou:

Not many years ago this immense part of the country was periodically visited by immense herds of rein-deer; at present there is scarcely one to be found. Whether their disappearance is owing to their having changed the course of their migrations, or to their destruction by the natives, who waylaid them on their passage, and killed them by hundreds, is a question not easily determined. It may be they have only forsaken this part of the country for a time, and may yet return in as great numbers as ever: be that as it may, the present want to which the Indians are subject, arises from the extreme scarcity of those animals, whose flesh and skins afforded them food and clothing. Their subsistence is now very precarious; derived principally from snaring rabbits and fishing; and rabbits also fail periodically.[62]

Thomas Simpson, who resided at York Factory from 1836 to 1839, blamed over-hunting by the Lowland Cree for the decline in caribou.

Near York Factory, in 1831, this propensity [over-hunting by Indians], contrary to all the remonstrances of the gentlemen of that place, led to the indiscriminate destruction of a countless herd of reindeer, while crossing the broad stream of the Haye's River, in the height of summer. The natives took some of the meat for present use, but thousands of carcasses were abandoned to the current, and infected the river banks, or floated out into Hudson's Bay, there to feed the sea-fowl and the Polar bear. As if it were a judgement for this barbarous slaughter, in which women and even children participated, the deer have never since visited that part of the country in similar numbers.[63]

Sir John Richardson later recounted a similar story, but he gave the year 1833 as the year of the reputed slaughter.

The reindeer that visit Hudson's Bay travel southward toward James's Bay in spring. In the year 1833, vast numbers of them were killed by the Cree Indians at a noted pass three or four days march above York Factory. They were on their return northward, and were crossing Hayes River in incredible multitudes. The Indians, excited by the view of so many animals thronging into the river, committed the most unwarranted slaughter; man, woman, and child rushed into the water and stabbed the poor deer wantonly, letting most of the carcasses float down the stream or putrify on the beach, for they could use only a small number of those they slew. From that date the deer did not use the pass until last year [1848], when a few resumed their old route, and were suffered to go unmolested, the Indians not being prepared for their coming.[64]

Simpson and Richardson attributed the disappearance of the caribou to a single massive slaughter. However, it is more likely that these accounts referred to the last large-scale caribou hunt that took place near York Factory, and that the demise of the caribou in the Hudson Bay lowlands was rooted in the eighteenth century, when the caribou provision and skin trade was initiated by the HBC. The actual disappearance of the caribou took place over decades, with much of the damage occurring in the 1790s, at the peak of fur-trade activity in the lowlands.[65]

The over-exploitation of caribou by the Lowland Cree (and Northern Ojibway) appears contrary to the many historical accounts of their respect for animals. However, it is also apparent that the Lowland Cree did not perceive their increasing harvest of the caribou resource to be responsible for the decline in the caribou population. In fact, there is ample evidence to suggest that the opposite was true. The widespread belief among the Lowland Cree that killing more caribou would result in larger numbers returning in the future was recorded by several European observers. For example, in 1720, the HBC trader at Churchill Fort remarked on "it being a Superstition amongst them the more [caribou] they kill, the plentier they are."[66] Robert Brightman has documented other historical references to the same belief among the Lowland Cree and neighbouring subarctic Aboriginal people: "The availability of animals to hunters and trappers was understood as subject to ritual influence, but the idea that hunting pressure could reduce species populations in the long term and on a large scale was absent. Instead, when killed, butchered, consumed, and disposed of with "respect," animals were understood to regenerate or to be reborn in proportion to the numbers killed."[67]

Brightman explained that:

> The game shortages occurred because Crees conceived the moose, caribou, and beaver as infinitely renewable resources whose numbers could neither be reduced by overkilling nor managed by selective hunting. This was why it was appropriate to kill large numbers of animals and retrieve only delicacies and also to kill as many animals as possible for commercial purposes. And when the new technology and market increased rates of predation to levels that caused populations to decline, the Crees continued to hunt indiscriminately because they did not initially construe the two processes to be related.[68]

Although the Lowland Cree believed that the caribou they killed would return to replenish the stock, the hunting of caribou beyond the limit of sustainable harvest was also linked to the HBC's policy of exerting pressure on the Lowland Cree to supply increasing quantities of skins and meat. By 1821, the massive caribou herds had been thinned to the point of near extinction, and a major Lowland Cree resource was no longer available.[69]

In the southern parts of the Hudson Bay lowlands, near Albany Fort and Moose Fort, the HBC came to depend on greater production from the Lowland Cree goose hunts in order to facilitate inland expansion. In 1784, Edward Jarvis at Albany observed that the goose hunt was "the very hinge [upon which] our upland business must turn."[70] The numbers of geese killed annually for the HBC are available for some years at Albany Fort. For example, in 1786-87, the HBC received 9539 geese; in 1795-96 the HBC harvest was 7832 geese; and in 1805-06 the yield was 7848 geese. Salted geese were also used to provision some of the inland trading posts. For example, in the spring of 1790, 1000 geese were sent to Henley House.[71]

A major problem in attracting the Lowland Cree to hunt geese for the HBC was the growing inability of the company to provide reciprocal supplies of food to the Lowland Cree in times of need. Edward Jarvis recorded the following speech made by an Albany River Lowland Cree hunter in 1784: "To be sure we will [not] exert ourselves in killing you plover when you will not give us flour, and if you will not let us have your english provisions we wont hunt for you."[72] The Lowland Cree realized that the HBC needed more supplies of country provisions to develop their inland trading networks, and used this knowledge to gain more from the company. The Albany River Lowland Cree who hunted geese for the HBC demanded more goods from the company in return for their services. Liquor was an item that became indispensable in conducting the Albany goose hunts. In the fall of 1785, Edward Jarvis commented that "it is a pity we had not more hunters or those few we have would refrain from drinking while they fly, but I find it impossible to prevent it as they say Brandy is the chief inducement for their hunting at all."[73]

The HBC employed increasingly greater resources in the goose hunts near Albany Fort during the period from 1783 to 1821. In 1812, the HBC traders at Albany Fort built a post at the mouth of Capusco Creek. Called the Capusco Goose Tent, it was described as a "log tent" and it was designed to increase the number of geese, feathers, and quills obtained by the company. By 1815, the HBC traders had redoubled their efforts by building a second goose tent at the mouth of Chickney Creek. Although Albany Fort's inland trade was significantly reduced after 1810, demand for country provisions remained high. The establishment of a timber operation at Moose Factory required substantial supplies of country provisions, especially geese. In the summer of 1814, twenty-seven casks of salted geese were shipped from Albany Fort, and in 1815, 4000 geese were supplied to Moose Factory.[74]

The growing importance of geese in the provision requirements of the HBC can be seen in the company's expenditures on the goose hunts. At Albany Fort, the annual expenditure more than doubled from 623 made beaver in 1781-82, to 1400 made beaver in 1797-98. The trade in goose quills and feathers provided another indicator of the increased emphasis on the goose hunt at Albany Fort. The trade in goose quills grew from an average of 53,600 per year in the 1770s, to over 90,000 in the first decade of the 1800s. The increase in the feather trade rose from an average of 673 kilograms in the 1770s, to 828 kilograms in the first decade of the 1800s. These increases are even more significant if the decrease in the Homeguard Cree population after the smallpox epidemic is taken into account.

Despite the growing demand for geese at the HBC posts, many of the Lowland Cree were generally uninterested in hunting geese while other resources, especially caribou, were abundant. In 1792, Joseph Colen tried unsuccessfully to persuade a group of Lowland Cree to hunt geese for the company. The situation became critical in 1794, and twelve families of Churchill Homeguard Cree (formerly York Factory Homeguard Cree) were sent to York Factory to hunt geese.[75] These families had previously lived near York Factory and, after the spring goose hunt, refused to return to Churchill. The HBC was powerless to dictate where they should live, and as Joseph Colen remarked, "[they] tell me if I attempt to force them, they have it in their power to prevail on many of their Relations (with whom they would wish to remain) to accompany them to Canadian settlements."[76] The significant decline in animal populations in the Hudson Bay lowlands, beginning in the early 1800s, shifted a greater focus on the goose hunts as a means of subsistence and commerce. By 1821, the production of geese at the coastal trading posts was far greater than ever before. At Albany Fort, the average number of geese harvested by the Homeguard Cree goose hunters had reached 15,000 per year.[77]

Transportation

In addition to employment in the provision trade, many Lowland Cree became more deeply involved in the HBC's transportation system in the period between 1783 and 1821. The employment of Lowland Cree in the boat brigades was critical to the inland expansion of the HBC. On June 7, 1790, John McNab reported that three Lowland Cree men had deserted

Departure of the second colonist transport from York Fort to Rock Fort, Sept. 6, 1821, by Peter Rindisbacher, watercolour on pencil with pen and ink outline (PAC, Y.F.3.0–1).

the boat brigade between Albany Fort and Henley House, and he acknowledged that "dependence on Indians is too precarious but cannot possibly be avoided."[78] At the peak of Albany Fort's inland trade in the 1790s, more than eighty Lowland Cree, including men, women, and children, were employed on the boat brigades.[78] Payment for work on the boat brigades was almost entirely made up of liquor. At the height of Albany Fort's inland trading in 1796, the use of liquor was a necessary but evil requirement. John McNab, who was in charge of Albany Fort, reported that the Lowland Cree who worked on the boat brigades were "drunk and troublesome," and added that it was "a sad circumstance where the Inland existence depends on their aid."[80] However, the reduction of Albany's inland trading network in the late eighteenth century reduced the opportunities for Lowland Cree to work on the boat brigades. By 1800, the number of Lowland Cree employed on the Albany River boats had declined to twenty-three people. The major retrenchment of the Albany inland trading posts in 1810 caused further reductions in the involvement of Lowland Cree in the boat brigades.

A network of inland trading posts from Severn House was slow to develop, and the HBC invested few resources to sustain the limited number of posts established upriver from Severn House. At York Factory, the boat brigades were a vital link in the HBC's competition with the NWC in the area known as the Great North (the area north and west of Lake Winnipeg). The Lowland Cree provided important labour for the development of the transport network between the coast and Lake Winnipeg, which was the inland hub of the transportation system. Unlike the Albany River boat brigades that declined in the early 1800s, the York Factory brigades continued to be active up to and after 1821.

The delivery of packets between the coastal trading posts became a more important service in the post-1782 period. With the expansion of inland trading posts, and increasing competition from Canadian fur traders, communication between the major coastal supply posts was essential. Correspondence between the coastal and inland posts also required a delivery service. The packet service provided year-round employment opportunities for a growing number of Lowland Cree. The payment for delivery services also increased after 1782. For example, the price for delivery between Albany Fort and Severn House in 1790 amounted to forty-four made beaver.[81] In 1784, two Lowland Cree were paid 100 made beaver for delivering packets between York Factory and Cumberland House.[82]

The Lowland Cree also became more involved in providing other services and products to the fur traders in the period between 1783 and 1821. They were encouraged to bring in more fish, ptarmigan, snowshoe hare, and other local food resources on a year-round basis, and products such as snowshoes, sleds, and leather for shoes were all in greater demand in the period of inland fur-trade expansion.

Epidemic Diseases

After the smallpox epidemic of 1782–83, occasional disease outbreaks occurred among the Lowland Cree but none produced mortality rates that approached the magnitude of the smallpox epidemic.[83] However, several significant disease outbreaks in the period between 1783 and 1821 were noted by the HBC traders. During the winter of 1792-93, an unidentified disease caused a number of deaths among the Lowland Cree near York Factory, and during the winter of 1794-95, many Albany River Lowland Cree suffered from an unidentified disease. In the winter of 1795-96, an unidentified disease spread throughout the Homeguard Cree population near Severn House. Many came to the post for medicine and provisions, and on February 2, 1796, 113 people described as "sick and starving" gathered at the plantation near Severn House.[84] An epidemic disease near Albany Fort in the fall of 1796 may have been connected with the sickness among the Severn River Lowland Cree. On September 5, 1796, about 200 Lowland Cree were encamped near Albany Fort and John NcNab noted that there was "an epidemical catarrh raging among us . . . many of the men [HBC] and natives in great affliction."[85] On September 7, McNab observed "many Indians affected with the catarrh and dangerously ill—such hot sultry weather [90 degrees fahrenheit] at this period is not remembered by the oldest Indian."[86] The disease outbreak claimed the lives of at least five Lowland Cree, and the sickness lingered among the people who stayed near the post until October of that year.

Outbreaks of colds and influenza occasionally affected the Lowland Cree. For example, in the winter of 1797-98, many Lowland Cree complained of flu-like symptoms. On April 27, 1798, John McNab remarked that several Lowland Cree who visited the post were "affected with febrile complaints, by their account epidemical among them."[87] In the summer of 1801, an unusual sickness appeared among the Lowland Cree and some of the HBC men at Albany Fort. John Hodgson described the disease as an "Epidemical disorder" that "appears to be like the yellow fever."[88] Although Hodgson reported that many Lowland Cree, especially children, were dangerously ill, only one death was recorded.

In 1819 and 1820, measles and whooping cough epidemics spread into the York Factory area and caused significant mortality rates among the Lowland Cree. These diseases originated in cities along the northeastern Atlantic seaboard and spread into the area north of Lake Superior along major fur-trade routes.[89] The measles epidemic was transmitted to the Lowland Cree who lived near York Factory by HBC employees who were infected in the Red River colony. These men worked on the transport brigades between the colony and York Factory, and probably transmitted the disease to Lowland Cree who were employed on the brigades along the lower section of the transport route. The disease was first reported by Sir John Franklin, who visited York Factory in the fall of 1819. Franklin noted that the Lowland Cree who lived in the vicinity of the factory were "suffering under the combined afflictions of hooping cough and measles."[90] He also reported the presence of the disease among the Lowland Cree near Oxford House, which he visited on September 28, 1819. Franklin observed that "a few Crees were at this time encamped in front of the fort. They were suffering under the combined maladies of hooping cough and measles, and looked miserably dejected."[91] Robert Hood, who accompanied Franklin, reported "a number of Indian tents were pitched near the house [Oxford House], and the dreadful ravages of hooping cough, and the measles had filled them with lamentation and despair. The poor creatures felt so deeply the loss of their relations, that they forsook their hunting occupations and starvation brought them to the border of the lake, where without much trouble they obtained fish."[92]

The HBC traders at York Factory noted the effects of whooping cough, but did not specifically identify measles among the Lowland Cree. On July 7, 1819, James Swain, who was in charge of York Factory, noted "a number of Natives and children afflicted with the Hooping cough, it has been brought from Red River and seems highly contagious."[93] By July 13, the epidemic had spread, and "all the Indian women and children about the place [were] dangerously ill with the Hooping cough." As late as August 4, 1819, the epidemic was still raging. Swain noted: "All the Indians and women and children seriously indisposed with Chincough."[94] Paul Hackett has recently pointed out that Franklin's identification of whooping cough and measles among the Lowland Cree at York Factory and Oxford House was probably a more accurate indication of the spread of the measles epidemic than the HBC reports.

Unlike the smallpox epidemic in 1782–83, the measles epidemic in 1819 did not spread through a large portion of the Lowland Cree population. Infection appears to have been localized near York Factory, which was the terminus for the Red River transport brigades. Although the epidemic spread widely throughout the Little North, it was not transmitted north into the lower Severn River or Albany River watersheds within the Hudson Bay lowlands. Hackett has traced the diffusion of the measles epidemic along the fur-trade transport routes in the Little North and he concluded that the travel times between the point of origin of the disease (Fort William) and the northern outposts along the margins of the Hudson Bay lowlands were too long to sustain and transmit the disease.[95] In addition, mortality rates appear to have been much lower than those recorded for the earlier smallpox epidemic. While the smallpox epidemic spread slowly among the

Lowland Cree, the outbreak of measles was brief and recovery rates appeared to have been much higher than during the smallpox epidemic.

Lowland Cree Population Dynamics

The depletion of caribou, beaver, and other animals in the Hudson Bay lowlands caused significant population movements of Lowland Cree within and outside the region in the period between 1783 and 1821. Following

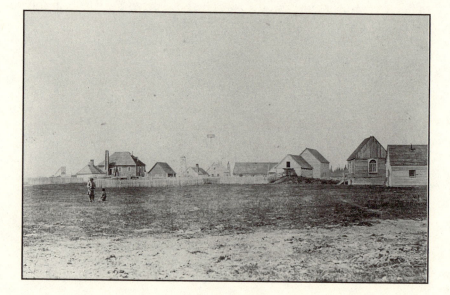

Albany, c. 1867–1868. Photograph: Bernard Rogan Ross (PAM, HBCA 363-a-6/5).

the 1782-83 smallpox epidemic, many Albany River Lowland Cree shifted their range farther northward toward Severn House. Although Edward Jarvis blamed this northward movement on the reduction in the standard of trade for goods at Severn House, he acknowledged the impact of the smallpox epidemic.[96] A Cree hunter who intended to move north told Jarvis, "Do not urge us to hunt geese when there are really none to kill, but let us have our debts and get as far as we can from the Factory to the northward where deer are plenty and we <u>can</u> live [underlined in original]."[97] Jarvis was concerned about the migration of many of the best goose hunters. In his journal, he outlined the negative impact of these developments:

> Without we can procure Country provisions for the mother settlement [Albany Fort] and Henley, we can never keep the Europeans for Gloster and inland—these families [those who moved north] are beyond dispute the very best goose hunters belonging to Albany and seldom killed us less than 1400 sometimes 1600 nay more Geese—the loss of Furrs is nothing since whether at Albany or Severn the Company will assuredly get them, and tho' I am not totally imenible to pecuniary emoluments, would readily part with their furr hunts to Severn to get their goose hunts at Albany; for the loss of so much provisions is <u>not</u> to be remedied but by an extraordinary indent of provisions from Europe, which after we get it is neither so good for the men's health, so agreeable to their humour, nor probably so cheap to the Company—I repeat it that I would rather lose their furrs than have the apparently extensive rising prospects at Gloster dispersed by the want of that sinew of expedition, <u>Provision</u> [underlined in original].[98]

Another problem associated with the northward migration of Albany River Lowland Cree toward Severn was the reduction in leather traded at Albany Fort. Most of the leather traded there came from the so-called northern tribes who hunted caribou between Albany and Severn. With many of them trading at Severn after 1783, the loss of the caribou leather trade was also detrimental to the business at Albany Fort. Edward Jarvis noted "another great evil that arises from their going to Severn which is the scarcity of shoe leather without which the inland business cannot go on."[99] An examination of the Albany Fort account books confirms the reduction in the number of caribou skins after 1783. From 1775 to 1783, the shipments from Albany Fort to Europe contained 199 caribou skins, while from 1784 to 1794, only seventeen caribou skins were packed. The attraction of the caribou hunt in the area near Cape Henrietta Maria was confirmed by George Sutherland, who delivered a packet between Albany Fort and Severn House in the summer of 1785. Sutherland reported that many Albany River Lowland Cree were "all wallowing among deer's flesh much nigher Albany than this place [Severn House]."[100] In 1788, Edward Jarvis explained that the reason Albany River Lowland Cree had shifted their range northward was "because the Deer are so numerous and easy come at the Northward which they prefer to hunting geese in our cold marshes."[101]

By 1815, growing numbers of Albany River Lowland Cree had moved north toward Cape Henrietta Maria. By that time the caribou had been depleted, but the movement of these Albany River Lowland Cree was motivated by better fishing grounds in that area. Jacob Corrigal, who was in charge of Albany Fort in 1815, was "apprehensive that none or very few of the Northern Indians will attend the Goose Hunt this fall, George Sutherland [an Indian] and Missiseepe has come in, who tells me that they left them all to the Northward of the Cape [Henrietta Maria] in the Deer Country at a fine Lake for fishing where they intend to pass the Fall and winter."[102]

The migration of Albany River Lowland Cree toward Severn caused some Severn River Lowland Cree to shift their range farther north, toward York Factory. Several families of Severn River Lowland Cree moved to the York Factory area in 1790. In 1796, a number of Severn Homeguard Cree joined the York Factory Homeguard Cree during the fall goose hunt. In the spring of 1797, six families who formerly hunted near Severn House and Albany Fort hunted geese near York Factory. In 1803, a mixed group of Severn and Albany Homeguard Cree arrived at York Factory, intending to live in the area. John McNab, who was in charge of York Factory and had previously worked at Albany Fort, remarked that "among them 6 of Albany Choice hunters, old acquaintances, several of them requests to stay here, say they have wintered at Severn with many more of their Albany companions now there."[103] In the fall of 1803, several Albany River Lowland Cree traded at York Factory and spent the winter in the area.[104]

In the spring of 1799, thirty Cree goose hunters were identified by name in the York Factory records. Of these, fifteen were Severn River Homeguard Cree, who killed 815, or 63 percent, of the 1297 geese harvested. By 1807, some Severn River Lowland Cree had become prominent leaders at York Factory. On October 16, 1807, John McNab reported that "2 Indians came down the river for medicine to the oldest Indian belonging to York—they say he is very ill ... his progeny are numerous and consequential, he was a hunter at Severn when first founded [1759] by the late Mr. Marten."[105] There was also a shift in Lowland Cree population away from Churchill Fort and toward York Factory in the period between 1783 and 1821. Some were attracted back to their former homelands to become goose hunters in place of the York Factory Homeguard Cree goose hunters who died during the smallpox epidemic. There was also pressure to move away from the Churchill River area after 1782 because of the influx of Chipewyan who moved closer to Churchill Fort. By 1821, all but a few of the Lowland Cree had moved away from Churchill to the York Factory area. In 1820, the Lowland Cree male population near Churchill Fort included two elderly men, eight young men and youths, and two or three boys.[106]

In the 1790s, some groups of Lowland Cree in the hinterland of York Factory began to migrate out of the lowlands. The establishment of inland trading posts along the transport route between York Factory and Lake Winnipeg attracted Lowland Cree, especially those who were regarded as Half-Homeguard Cree at York Factory. The employment of Lowland Cree on the boat brigades also promoted an inland population shift for families

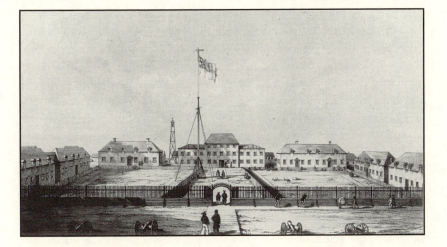

York Factory, 1853 (PAM, HBCA, P114).

who were involved in that business. Historian Raymond Beaumont remarked that the southward movement of Lowland Cree was "in response to privation at York Factory and the promise of a better life elsewhere."[107] Several HBC fur traders noted the southward drift of Lowland Cree along the Nelson and Hayes rivers into the upland region. In 1793, some of the Half-Homeguard Cree who previously traded at York Factory had moved farther inland and wintered near Chatham House on the upper Nelson River.[108] In 1794, the combination of declining resources near York Factory and the lure of Canadian traders caused some of the York Factory Homeguard Cree to move farther inland. Joseph Colen reported, "They say that the scarcity of animals on the coast of late years has distressed their families—when they were here during the summer, which obliged them to remove to a more plentiful country, a great distance from the factory, that bringing their families with them would prevent the conveyance of furs. Therefore the men intend in future to come down in turns, while others remain to kill supplies for their families."[109] Colen later remarked, "Indeed Natives who have been long in habits of hunting near the factory, have told me in plain terms that these risks [food shortages] would be avoided in future, by disposing of their skins near their Hunting Ground."[110]

The Lowland Cree who moved near the inland trading posts came to be identified as Homeguards for each particular post. For example, those who coalesced near Henley House at the confluence of the Albany and Kenogami rivers were usually called Henley House Homeguards. The establishment of Oxford House in 1798 attracted a number of Lowland Cree who were formerly known as York Factory Homeguard Cree. Anthropologist Christopher Hanks observed that "the formation of the Oxford House Band was the result of the depot requiring natives to provide provisions and labor for transporting goods to and from the interior....Therefore, the Oxford House Band is the result of the historic late eighteenth and early ninetenth century interaction between the fur trade and native groups and was not an *in situ* development of the aboriginal population."[111]

By 1812, the migration of Lowland Cree away from York Factory was in full swing. William Cook reported that a group of so-called "Eastern Indians" planned to move farther inland in the fall, and that some of the Nelson River Lowland Cree intended to give up their "Old Haunts" to "go inland in the Fall and to winter about the Lakes in the mid Country."[112] By 1815, some of the Hayes River Lowland Cree who formerly resided near York Factory were living near Lake Winnipeg. James Sutherland, who was in charge of the HBC's Norway House District (then called Jack River), made the following observations:

This last year their were 26 families who traded at this post, among them 34 men and lads capable of Hunting, but their numbers always vary as they wander from one district to another as their capricious fancy leads them. Part of these Indians are from the sea coast about York Factory and the other from the headwaters of the Severn River. The original inhabitants of this place seem to have all emigrated to the Westward within this few years back, several families have left this place and gone to Swan River and Cumberland House, the poverty of the country for animals enduce them to leave their native soil.[113]

Some Lowland Cree migrated as far away as the Cumberland House district near the upper Saskatchewan River. In 1815, Alexander Kennedy, who was in charge of Cumberland House, noted "about one hundred and ten families on this District at present, nearly half of whom are newcomers from York Factory, North River, and what we call the Rat Country being to the northward of Cumberland where the lands are getting so poor as to induce the Indians to leave it."[114]

The conditions that forced many Lowland Cree to migrate also affected the Northern Ojibway who lived along the margins of the Hudson Bay lowlands. J.F. Wright, who conducted a geological survey around Island Lake in 1927, learned about the history of the area from the local HBC fur trader, S.J.C. Cumming. Wright reported that the Island Lake post "was outfitted from Severn and was in operation in 1824, but a few years later was abandoned on account of the scarcity of fur-bearing animals, fish and game. The Indians were forced to leave the lake and migrated to Oxford House, Trout Lake, and Little Grand Rapids."[115]

The HBC tried to discourage the movement of Lowland Cree between coastal posts. HBC traders were advised not to trade with Indians who received debts from other posts. However, this strategy had its shortcomings because the traders were often unaware of the extent of the debts that individual Indians had incurred at other posts. In 1790, Joseph Colen attempted to establish this strategy at York Factory and encouraged his fellow traders to do the same, because "would every master follow the same plan it would be a considerable saving annually to the Honourable Company and prevent the low Country Natives from rambling."[116] Despite Colen's determination to stop the Lowland Cree from "rambling," he was unable to dictate where they should live. On April 6, 1790, Colen was unable to convince a group of Severn House Homeguard Cree to return to that post: "If I did not agree to their visiting York, in future, there were other places they could carry their furrs, and where they would be acceptable—said they were free and have liberty to go ware they pleased, and were they used well, they would stay."[117] The competition that developed between coastal trading posts was exploited by the Lowland Cree. As fur-trade competition increased, attracting Indians to trade at each post became more difficult. HBC traders offered increasingly large gifts to Lowland Cree leaders who could bring more followers to trade at their posts. Some Lowland Cree leaders attracted followers by giving gifts to encourage other Indians to leave their usual post. For example, in 1786, a Severn River Lowland Cree leader named Waukescicoat gave gifts to Albany River Lowland Cree to attract them to trade at Severn. These gifts included a gun, two blankets, a coat, and brandy.[118] Edward Jarvis observed that "the Severn Indian Captain [Waukescicoat] would be glad to increase his consequence by gaining the Albany [Lowland Cree] to trade at Severn even supposing he was not desired [by William Falconer] to do it."[119]

1821

The merger of the North West Company and Hudson's Bay Company in 1821 brought an end to fur-trade competition throughout much of the northwestern interior of North America. However, the effects were not immediately significant in the Hudson Bay lowlands. North West Company traders never established a foothold in the region, and even along the southern fringe many of their trading posts had been withdrawn years before 1821. The new company did enact a number of policies that gradually had an impact on the Lowland Cree. The closure of redundant trading posts in the upland hinterland meant that Cree hunters had limited options to sell their furs and provisions. The company also attempted to restrict the movement of the Lowland Cree by ordering its traders to limit credit to local hunters. Some Cree families responded to these new measures by opting out of the fur-trade economy. For example, Thomas Vincent reported in 1825 that the Lowland Cree in the Winisk River area were living comfortably without trading for supplies with the company. Vincent explained that they had become disgusted with the company trader at Severn House "for the last 3 years and live idly and easy at fishing stations, seldom are in want of food and warmly apparelled in Furs."[120] This situation had changed little in 1834, when George Barnston reported that the Winisk River Lowland Cree still lived independently of the company. He wrote, "Having procured a blanket, an ax, and a hook, he becomes forthwith miserably independent. Day after day finds him seated at a hole in the Ice, angling for pike, to the full gratification of all that is indolent in his disposition, but in perfect mocking of the Trader's wishes."[121]

Conclusion

It is now clear that the Hudson Bay Lowland Cree, far from being creations of the European fur trade, occupied the region for thousands of years before the arrival of the newcomers. Their own oral traditions recounted for generations that their ancestors had always lived there, and bore witness to the arrival of the first Europeans. The oral traditions also told about battles against Iroquois raiders before the fur traders came to build posts along the coast of Hudson Bay. The prevailing view in the literature, however, portrayed the lowlands as a no-man's land until the fur-trade posts were built. Scholars had based this view on the misconception that the environment was too harsh to permit year-round living by Aboriginal people. They also thought that technologically superior European trade goods attracted the Cree to move into the lowlands from original homelands located to the south in the more sheltered forest of the Canadian Shield country. Building on this premise, scholars advanced the view that permanent occupation was possible only after the Europeans arrived and only in the shelter of the fur-trade posts. The Lowland Cree were thus depicted as relatively recent arrivals who moved into the lowlands after Europeans established trading posts.

Archaeological discoveries in the 1970s and 1980s proved that the Lowland Cree oral traditions were right. Radiocarbon dating confirmed that people had occupied the lowlands for thousands of years. Further investigations concluded that human occupation was year-round, and analyses of artifacts linked the original people directly to the Lowland Cree. A number of archaeological sites were littered with caribou bones, indicating that the sites had been used for generations as hunting camps. Ancient fish weirs were also uncovered in sites that revealed they had been used year-round for thousands of years. The archaeological discoveries reconstructed a way of life focussed on seasonally abundant resources and pointed to external relations with neighbouring Aboriginal peoples. This complex world was far from the *terra nullius* depicted in the scholarly literature.

A re-examination of early European records affirms that the Lowland Cree lived in the region at the time of contact. French missionary records indicated that the Lowland Cree were actively engaged in an early and extensive network of trade that linked with Aboriginal middlemen and Europeans in the St. Lawrence valley. The St. Lawrence valley trading connection with the Lowland Cree intensified in the mid-seventeenth century, after Iroquois war parties severed east-west transport routes and forced western fur supplies to be re-routed from the upper Great Lakes to James Bay and then southeast to the St. Lawrence River. Raids by Iroquois war parties deep into the lowlands failed to disrupt the trade networks. The establishment of trading posts along the coast of Hudson Bay and James Bay in the late seventeenth century built on pre-existing fur-trade routes, and the Lowland Cree were poised to become strategic intermediaries between other Aboriginal fur producers and European traders.

When Europeans first arrived, the Lowland Cree were engaged in warfare with their northern neighbours: the Chipewyan and Inuit. European guns gave a tactical advantage to Lowland Cree warriors who were emboldened to travel hundreds of kilometres in search of victims and prisoners. While other factors were involved, the fur trade and access to European goods promoted an intensification of traditional warfare patterns. Lowland Cree warriors were bold and aggressive, characteristics that belie the meek and inoffensive Homeguard Cree portrayed in the literature. They were also peacemakers who engaged in long-distance diplomatic journeys to secure alliances and promote commercial exchanges.

Weapons of war were also used with enhanced success against animals, and Cree warriors became expert marksmen with guns in hunting caribou, geese, and other game. As a result, the thundering herds of caribou that annually journeyed to coastal calving grounds were thinned to precariously low numbers in the early nineteenth century by intensive hunting for meat and hides. The decline in caribou was one of a number of ecological changes precipitated by hunting pressures during the fur-trade period. Beaver, although never abundant in the lowlands, were over-hunted to the point of near extinction by the beginning of the nineteenth century. In addition to increased hunting pressure, unusually severe weather conditions in the late eighteenth century appear to have contributed to changing animal populations.

The territory of the Lowland Cree was not significantly affected by the fur trade. Although the Hudson's Bay Company acquired a Royal Charter granting exclusive rights to the lowlands and a vast surrounding territory, the Lowland Cree did not sell or give away any of their land. The traders were not interested in gaining ownership of the land, apart from the small areas occupied by their trading posts. For their part, the Lowland Cree were not averse to the building of trading posts on their land as long as they benefitted from these developments. Lowland Cree raids into Inuit and Chipewyan lands were not motivated by the acquisition of territory. There were encroachments within the southern parts of Lowland Cree territory by groups of Northern Ojibway, who moved into the area in the mid-eighteenth century. In time, a mixed Ojibway and Cree dialect appeared among groups along the edges of the lowlands.

The Lowland Cree were described as healthy and strong by early European observers, but contact with the newcomers brought new and deadly diseases. Lacking biological immunity to such infectious diseases as smallpox and measles, the Lowland Cree suffered incredible mortality rates when these contagions first appeared among them. The routes of disease transmission followed traditional trade routes throughout North America, and many epidemics originated in the east and south at colonial population centres. This was true of the devastating 1782-83 smallpox epidemic that began some four years earlier in the Spanish settlements near Mexico, and then spread northward through a complex Aboriginal trade network to eventually reach the Lowland Cree. Some diseases came directly from Europe with the men on trans-Atlantic ships recruited to work at the coastal trading posts. The impact of infectious diseases went far beyond the initial mortality rates, as the loss of many able-bodied men and women caused long-term suffering of families who depended upon the skills of all members for their livelihood and comfort.

The Lowland Cree developed an intricate web of relationships with the European fur traders. The term "Homeguard" was used to describe the people who came to live in close proximity to the coastal trading posts and became employed as goose hunters and seasonal labourers. Coined by HBC traders, and first recorded by Andrew Graham, the term "Homeguard Cree" was picked up by historians and used in a pejorative way to denote people who depended on the assistance of European traders. The fur-trade records paint a more complex picture of the life of the Lowland Cree. While they occasionally came to the posts in search of temporary food and shelter, they were more often the providers of much-needed food resources for the traders. They also performed the important work of labourers on the boat brigades and couriers of mail between the bay-side posts. While some who lived near the posts were known as Homeguards, others, designated Half-Homeguards, lived at a distance from the posts and only visited periodically to exchange furs and provisions for European goods. These people maintained an independent way of life patterned after generations of living off the land using traditional knowledge. Overall, the Lowland Cree proved resilient in their encounters with European fur traders. Despite major changes such as the decline in the great caribou herds in the lowlands, they continued to hunt, fish, and harvest other resources of the land and water as their ancestors had done for countless generations. The Muskekowuck Athinuwick continue to be the original people of the great swampy land.

Endnotes

Introduction

1. Arthur S. Morton, *A History of the Canadian West to 1870-71: Being a History of Rupert's Land (the Hudson's Bay Company's Territory) and of the North-West Territory (Including the Pacific Slope)*, ed. Lewis G. Thomas (Toronto: University of Toronto Press, 1973), 129.

2. Edwin E. Rich, *Hudson's Bay Company, 1670-1870* (Toronto: McClelland and Stewart Ltd., 1960), 496.

3. Flora Beardy and Robert Coutts, eds., *Voices from Hudson Bay: Cree Stories from York Factory* (Montreal and Kingston: McGill-Queen's University Press, 1996).

Chapter 1

1. In addition to the major division between the bedrock of the Hudson Bay lowlands and the upland Canadian Shield, local outcroppings of different geological formations are responsible for a few other rapids in the lowlands. For example, the Whiteseal Falls and the Limestone Rapids in the Severn River are caused by the contact between two different geological formations that bisect the river at those places. See Jean-Luc Pilon, *Washahoe Inninou Dahtsuounoaou: Ecological and Cultural Adaptation Along the Severn River in the Hudson Bay Lowlands of Ontario*, Conservation Archaeology Report, Northwestern Region, Report No. 10 (Kenora: Ontario Ministry of Citizenship and Culture, 1987), 6.

2. Robert Bell, "Report on the Country Between Lake Winnipeg and Hudson's Bay, 1878," in *Geological Survey of Canada Report of Progress for 1877-78* (Montreal: Dawson Brothers, 1879), 7CC.

3. Robert Bell, "Albany River: Lake Abazotikitchewan to Mouth of Kenogami River," in *Ontario Bureau of Mines Annual Report,* vol. 21, 2 (1912), 85.

4. I.P. Martini, "Geomorphological Features of the Ontario Coast of Hudson Bay," *Naturaliste Canadien* 109, 3 (1982): 421, cited in Pilon, *Washahoe*, 7.

5. Bell, "Report on the Country," 25CC.

6. Robert Bell, "Report on an Exploration of Portions of the At-ta-wa-pish-kat and Albany Rivers, Lonely Lake to James' Bay," in *Annual Report of the Geological and Natural History Survey of Canada,* vol. 2 (1887), 32G.

7. W.J. Wilson, "Reconnaissance Surveys of Four Rivers South-West of James Bay," in *Geological Survey of Canada, Summary Report for 1902-03*, vol. 15 (1903), 233A.

8. W.C. Noble and J.W. Pollock, "Archaeology of the Hawley Lake Area, Hudson Bay Lowlands, Ontario," in *Canadian Archaeological Association – Collected Papers, March 1975*, Archaeological Research Report No. 6 (Toronto: Ontario Ministry of Culture and Recreation, Historical Sites Branch, 1975), 79.

9. Pilon, *Washahoe,* 20.

10. When the HBC established Churchill Fort in 1717, the Lowland Cree and Western Hudson Bay Inuit were engaged in periodic warfare. The area between the Nelson and Churchill rivers was an unoccupied buffer zone. James Knight remarked that "we have no Indians on this side [north] of Portnellson River but the 2 as are with me." See James Knight, *The Founding of Churchill: Being the Journal of Captain James Knight, Governor-in-Chief in Hudson Bay, from the 14th of July to the 13th of September, 1711*, ed. James F. Kenney (Toronto: J.M. Dent and Sons, Ltd, 1932), 140.

11. The name *Nottaway* was used by the Lowland Cree to describe their enemies. Daniel Francis and Toby Morantz pointed out that the first European map to depict the Nottaway River, the Franquelin map of 1699, identified it as the "River of the Iroquois." They also noted that oral traditions collected by J.M. Cooper at Rupert House indicated that the Nottaway River was named after the Iroquois who came down the river on raiding parties. See Daniel Francis and Toby Morantz, *Partners in Furs: A History of the Fur Trade in Eastern James Bay, 1600-1870* (Montreal and Kingston: McGill-Queen's University Press, 1983), 21.

12. HBCA, E.2/9, fo. 83.

13. HBCA, B.198/a/3, April 9, 1762, fo. 25. The term *Misckick* appears to have been a phonetic variation of *Muskekowuck*, which means "swampy ground." Graham's list of words in the Lowland Cree language indicated that the name for a level country was *Muscuti Tuski*, a name that was later applied more commonly to the interior prairie region. See Andrew Graham, *Andrew Graham's Observations on Hudson's Bay, 1767-91*, ed. Glyndwr Williams (London: The Hudson's Bay Record Society, 1969), 208.

14. HBCA, B.239/a/42, May 19, 1757, fo. 46. Early scientific observers who visited the western Hudson Bay lowlands also noted the use of the term "plains" to describe the region. In 1886, Robert Bell conducted a geological survey of the lower Albany River and observed that "the country on either side [of the Albany River] is quite flat.... In some parts, it is so open as to be called plains" (Bell, "Report on an Exploration," 32G).

15. James Isham explained that the term *A'thin new* meant "an Indian." See James Isham, *James Isham's Observations on Hudsons Bay, 1743, and Notes and Observations on a Book Entitled A Voyage to Hudson Bay in the Dobbs Galley, 1749*, ed. E.E. Rich (London: The Hudson's Bay Record Society, 1949), 17. Andrew Graham used the plural form, *Athinuwick*, which he translated as "Indians" (Graham, *Andrew Graham's Observations*, 15B). David Pentland, an Algonquian linguist, commented that the term *ininiw* was used as a self-designation by Cree speakers. See David H. Pentland, "Synonymy of the West Main Cree," in *Handbook of North American Indians*, vol. 6, *Subarctic*, ed. June Helm (Washington: Smithsonian Institution, 1981), 227.

16. Pentland, "Synonymy," 227.

17. The terms "nation" and "tribe" were used interchangeably by European fur traders to describe the Lowland Cree. "Nation" was more commonly applied to the larger grouping of Cree speakers, and "tribe" was used to describe regional subdivisions.

18. K.G. Davies, ed., *Letters From Hudson Bay, 1703-40* (London: The Hudson's Bay Record Society, 1965), 45.

19. HBCA, B.198/a/11, June 22, 1769, fo. 31d.

20. HBCA, B.198/a/47, January 13, 1796, fo. 21.

21. Toby Morantz, *An Ethnohistoric Study of Eastern James Bay Cree Social Organization, 1700-1850*, Mercury Series, Canadian Ethnology Service Paper No. 88 (Ottawa: National Museum of Man, 1983), 38. M. de Bacqueville de la Potherie, who visited the French trading post at the mouth of the Hayes River in 1698, observed that "the tribe that lives nearest the fort [Fort Bourbon] are the Ouenebigonhelinis, which means 'the people of the sea shore'" (see J.B. Tyrrell, ed., *Documents Relating to the Early History of Hudson Bay* [Toronto: The Champlain Society, 1931], 262). Andrew Graham recorded the name *Winipeg Athinuwick*, which signified the people of the seaside, or coast of Hudson Bay (Graham, *Andrew Graham's Observations*, 192). Isham translated the Lowland Cree word *We ne pek* as meaning "the Sea or oeacean" (Isham, *James Isham's Observations*, 5). David Pentland explained that "the Cree word wi-nipe-k 'foul water, salt water' refers primarily to Hudson Bay" (Pentland, "Synonymy," 229). J.W. Anderson, an HBC fur trader who worked in the Hudson Bay lowlands in the early twentieth century, noted the basic division of the Lowland Cree into Coasters and Inlanders: "The James Bay Crees divided themselves into two distinct classes depending on whether they lived on the shores of James Bay or gained their livelihood in the interior up one or other of the various rivers. The coast Indians called themselves Winni-pay-ko-ininew and the inlanders were Noo-che-mik-ininew but in common English usage they were known as 'coasters' and 'inlanders.'" See J.W. Anderson, *Fur Trader's Story* (Toronto: The Ryerson Press, 1961), 126.

22. In 1967, John Macfie, who worked for the Ontario Department of Lands and Forests (now Ministry of Natural Resources), noted the significance of the unique ecological zone along the Hudson Bay coast: "The coast Crees, drawing their livelihood from these contrasting elements, have developed a way of life distinct from that of the main body of eastern Canada's Algonkian tribes." See John Macfie, "The Coast Crees," *The Beaver* 47,1 (1967): 15.

23. HBCA, B.239/a/75, August 10, 1778, fo. 58.

24. HBCA, B.239/a/105, June 13, 1801, fo. 47d.

25. HBCA, B.239/d/18, fo. 8.

26. The term "tribe" was also a European appellation. It was commonly used to describe groups of Aboriginal people who spoke the same language and were linked by social, cultural, political, and other customary traditions. European fur traders who worked in the lowlands often used the term to describe groups of people who occupied specific regional territories. Other terms, such as "gangs" and "bands," were also used as substitutes for "tribes."

27. Tyrrell, *Documents Relating*, 263.

28. Graham, *Andrew Graham's Observations*, 192. Pentland translated the Cree word *omaske-ko-w* as "muskeg person, swamp person" (see Pentland, "Synonymy," 227). John

Honigmann, who conducted an anthropological study of the people who lived near the mouth of the Attawapiskat River, commented that there was a distinction between the coastal and inland people. However, the generic term for self-identification was *omooskekowak*, which he translated as "Swampy Cree." See John J. Honigmann, "Foodways in a Muskeg Community: An Anthropological Report on the Attawapiskat Indians," unpublished report of Department of Northern Affairs and National Resources, 1948, p. 19. John Long also observed that the Albany and Moose River Lowland Cree term for self-designation was *omaskekowak*, meaning "swamp or muskeg person." See John S. Long, "'Shaganash': Early Protestant Missionaries and the Adoption of Christianity by the Western James Bay Cree, 1840-1893," unpublished PhD dissertation, University of Toronto, 1986, 15.

29. HBCA, E.2/5, fo. 4d.

30. Pentland, "Synonymy," 229.

31. Graham observed that the Aboriginal name for the Hayes River near York Factory was *Penesewichewan Sepee* (Graham, *Andrew Graham's Observations*, 209). Pentland explained that the name translated as "flows-down-the-bank river" (Pentland, "Synonymy," 269).

32. Graham noted that the Aboriginal name for firesteel was *Apit* (Graham, *Andrew Graham's Observations*, 209). La Potherie explained that about fourteen leagues (roughly seventy kilometres) upriver from its mouth, the Hayes River was known as *Apitsibi*, which he translated as "the river of arrow flints" (Tyrrell, *Documents Relating*, 260).

33. On his journey inland from York Factory in 1774, Matthew Cocking observed that "all Hills are [called] Chuckitanah, from which the river receives its name" (HBCA, B.239/a/72, July 11, 1774, fo. 2d).

34. Tyrrell, *Documents Relating*, 382.

35. HBCA, B.239/d/7, fo. 7d (1714).

36. HBCA, B.3/d/1, fo. 15d.

37. John Oldmixon, "The History of Hudson's Bay," in *Documents Relating to the Early History of Hudson Bay*, ed. J.B. Tyrrell (Toronto: The Champlain Society, 1931), 391.

38. HBCA, B.3/d/3, fo. 9; B.3/d/6, fo. 16; B.3/d/11, fo. 17; and B.3/d/13, fo. 12d.

39. HBCA, B.3/a/73, fos. 2-4.

40. HBCA, B.3/a/89, July 14, 1789, fo. 49d.

41. HBCA, B.198/a/37, July 20, 1787, fo. 4d.

42. HBCA, B.198/a/37, May 18, 1788, fo. 34d.

43. HBCA, B.198/a/37, February 25, 1788, fo. 25.

44. HBCA, B.198/a/39, February 22, 1790, fo. 21d.

45. HBCA, B.239/e/1, fo. 5d.

46. HBCA, B.198/e/1, fo. 8d.

47. HBCA, B.135/e/1, fo. 4d.

48. HBCA, B. 16/e/1, fo. 6d.

49. HBCA, B. 16/e/1, fo. 7.

50. HBCA, B.154/e/1, fo. 6. Robert Brightman's study of the Upland Rock Cree of the Churchill River basin noted a similar pattern of territorial flexibility and resource sharing: "The evidence contained in post reports from the early 1800s suggests that individual hunting groups were associated at any given time with a vaguely delimited range but that they moved often and that no exclusive tenure was recognized." See Robert Brightman, *Grateful Prey: Rock Cree Human-Animal Relationships* (Berkeley: University of California Press, 1993), 272. Charles Bishop studied the Northern Ojibway of the Osnaburgh House area (upper Albany River), and noted that "although band members tended to hunt in the same general region each year, resources belonged to those who came first, even when they were within the region inhabited by another band." See Charles Bishop, "The Emergence of the Hunting Territories among the Northern Ojibwa," *Ethnology* 60, 1 (1970): 11.

51. Graham, *Andrew Graham's Observations*, 191-193.

52. Modern linguists use the term "Cree" for the language spoken by the people denominated the Keishkatchewan Nation by Graham. Cree is derived from a larger language base called Algonquian. Those who live in the Hudson Bay lowlands speak a dialect commonly referred to as Swampy Cree. Other regional dialects include Woods Cree and Plains Cree. Among the Swampy Cree, some linguists have identified sub-dialects known as Western and Eastern Swampy Cree. The speakers of these sub-dialects live on either side of a boundary line that bisects the lowlands roughly halfway between the Severn and Winisk rivers. See Richard Rhodes and Evelyn Todd, "Subarctic Algonquian Languages," in *Handbook of North American Indians*, vol. 6, *Subarctic*, ed. June Helm (Washington: Smithsonian Institution, 1981), 53. Dialect divisions between the Lowland Cree were not recognized by European observers in the seventeenth, eighteenth, and early nineteenth centuries. These differences may have developed later in the nineteenth or twentieth century.

53. HBCA, E.2/5, fo. 4d.

54. John McLean, *John McLean's Notes of a Twenty-Five Year's Service in the Hudson's Bay Territory* (Toronto: The Champlain Society, 1932), 194.

55. William Falconer, "Severn House Journal, 1768-69," unpublished manuscript in National Archives of Canada, MG 19, D2, July 8, 1769. Paul Kane, who visited Norway House in the summer of 1846, commented, "The Indians belong to the Mas-ka-gau tribe, or 'Swamp Indians,' so called from their inhabiting the low swampy land which extends the whole way from Norway House to Hudson's Bay." Kane, who had travelled among the Upland Cree who lived in the prairie region, was not impressed with the physical features or the language of the Lowland Cree living in the vicinity of Norway House. He observed that the Lowland Cree were "rather diminutive in comparison with those who inhabit the plains.... Their language somewhat resembles the [Plains] Cree, but is not so agreeable in sound." See Paul Kane, *Wanderings of an Artist Among the Indians of North America from Canada to Vancouver Island and Oregon, Through the Hudson's Bay Company's Territories and Back Again* (Toronto: The Radisson Society of Canada, Ltd., 1925), 71.

56. John West, *The Substance of a Journal During a Residence at the Red River Colony, British North America, in the Years 1820-23* (Vancouver: Alcuin Society, 1967), 16.

57. Modern linguists agree that the Cree language spoken by the people who live in the Moose River basin is closely related to the dialect of the Albany River Lowland Cree (see Rhodes and Todd, "Subarctic Algonquian Languages," 55).

58. HBCA, B.3/d/5, fo. 15d.

59. HBCA, B.3/a/30, fo. 23.

60. HBCA, E.2/4, fo. 80d.

61. Henry Kelsey, *The Kelsey Papers*, ed. Arthur Doughty and Chester Martin (Ottawa: King's Printer, 1929), 2; Glyndwr Williams, ed., *Hudson's Bay Miscellany, 1670-1870* (London: The Hudson's Bay Record Society, 1975), 51.

62. Arthur S. Morton, *A History of the Canadian West to 1870-71: Being a History of Rupert's Land (the Hudson's Bay Company's Territory) and of the North-West Territory (Including the Pacific Slope)*, ed. Lewis G. Thomas (Toronto: University of Toronto Press, 1973), 153.

63. John E. Foster, "The Home Guard Cree and the Hudson's Bay Company: The First Hundred Years," in *Approaches to Native History in Canada: Papers of a Conference held at the National Museum of Man, October, 1976*, Mercury Series, History Division Paper No. 25, ed. D.A. Muise (Ottawa: National Museum of Man, 1977), 51.

64. HBCA, E.2/7, fo. 16d.

65. HBCA, E.2/4, fo. 80d.

66. Henry Ellis, *An Account of a Voyage for the Discovery of a North-West Passage by Hudson's Streights, to the Western and Southern Ocean of America,* vol. 1 (New York: Johnson Reprint Corporation, 1968), 178.

67. In 1755, Joseph Isbister recommended that the HBC re-establish Henley House near the confluence of the Kenogami River because French fur traders were settled nearby. Isbister stated that leaving Henley House unoccupied "will leave the french at full liberty to carry off all the Trade of ye Bay, not only by intercepting all the upland Indians but also to take off all our home and Sea Indians by reason they go as far inland as Henley to catch goods" (HBCA, B.3/a/47, March 6, 1755, fos. 24-24d).

68. HBCA, B.3/a/41, May 22, 1750, fo. 22.

69. English and French trading posts operated intermittently at the mouth of the Moose River from 1673 to 1696. The HBC re-established Moose Fort in 1730.

70. HBCA, B.42/a/1, September 12, 1718, fo. 23.

71. Ellis, *An Account of a Voyage*, vol. 1, 180-181.

72. HBCA, B.198/a/23, June 4, 1779, n.p.

73. HBCA, B.239/a/21, October 21, 1776, fo. 5d.

74. HBCA, B.3/a/12, fo. 9.

75. Historical geographer Guy Joubert divided the Homeguard Cree into three groups: the Sedentary, Semi-Sedentary, and Occasional Homeguards. The Sedentary Homeguard Cree were people who remained at the post year-round. These included several families who were employed as hunters by the HBC, and sick, elderly, and other needy people. The Semi-Sedentary Homeguard Cree referred to the remainder of the Homeguard population who wintered near the trading post and hunted seasonally for the company. The Occasional Homeguard Cree included the Half-Homeguard Cree and other upland Indian people, such as the Northern Ojibway,

who lived in areas adjacent to the Hudson Bay lowlands. See J. Guy R. Joubert, "The Homeguard Indians of the Hudson Bay Lowland in the Eighteenth Century: A Case Study of Severn House," unpublished BA Honours thesis, University of Manitoba, 1984, pp. 28-37.

76. HBCA, B.3/a/2, October 26, 1706, fo. 12.

77. HBCA, B.3/d/17, fo. 11.

78. HBCA, B.3/a/9, fo. 3. The composition of Miskemote's family group is difficult to reconstruct, but the HBC records indicate that Macklish's comments in the fall of 1715 were not entirely accurate. When Miskemote arrived at Albany Fort on December 11, 1715, his "family" included six individuals. In the fall of 1716, Miskemote and his wife cared for a grandchild while they stayed at Albany Fort. On January 27, 1718, Miskemote arrived at Albany Fort with two women and two boys. Macklish may have considered the members of Miskemote's extended family to be too few, or too young, to be able to support him and his wife and the three widows.

79. HBCA, B.3/a/9, January 26, 1716, fo. 6d.

80. HBCA, B.3/d/27, fo. 10d. The HBC introduced a currency system based on the value of a single prime beaver skin, known as a "made beaver." All other goods were valued in relationship to the made beaver.

81. Miskemote's disability was attributed to gout. On February 16, 1717, Miskemote was reported to be "dangerously sick of the gout" (HBCA, B.3/a/9, fo. 19). On December 23, 1718, he was carried into the fort because he was "lame of the Gout" (HBCA, B.3/a/9, fo. 47). Shortly after learning of Miskemote's death, Joseph Myatt commented that "he lived to a good old age, but at the same time, I think I never saw a European more afflicted with the Gout than he hath been for this several years past" (HBCA, B.3/a/10, September 12, 1721, fo. 4). Although gout appears to have been a rare ailment among the Indian population, another case was noted among the Albany Homeguard Indians in 1724, when Richard Staunton reported there was an old man called "Sucutash who is lame with the gout and rhumattisme" (HBCA, B.3/a/12, fo. 31d).

82. HBCA, B.3/a/4, fo. 34d.

83. William Falconer, "Remarks on the Natives near the Cost of Hudson's Bay and Straits, with some remarks on the Climate, etc.," unpublished ms copy in the National Archives of Canada, MG 19, D2, vol.1, part 2, n.d., 33.

84. HBCA, B.198/a/20, September 23, 1775, fo. 6d.

85. HBCA, B.239/a/65, fo. 16.

86. Falconer, "Remarks on the Natives," 20.

87. Graham, *Andrew Graham's Observations*, 170.

88. The views of Leacock and others who have promoted the idea of an egalitarian, leaderless Aboriginal society have been recently challenged by other scholars. For example, Toby Morantz documented leadership patterns among the Indians of eastern James Bay at the time of early European fur-trade contact. Morantz argued that the HBC practice of recognizing captains among the eastern James Bay Indians was rooted in a pre-existing leadership system. She concluded that "the trading captain system was an overlay, a stratum grafted onto the existing traditional, subsistence-oriented structures." See Toby Morantz, "Northern Algonquian concepts of status and

leadership reviewed: a case study of the eighteenth-century trading captain system," *Canadian Review of Sociology and Anthropology* 19, 4 (1982): 495. This study of the Hudson Bay Lowland Cree supports Morantz's assessment that leadership roles fostered by European fur traders were rooted in pre-existing leadership structures.

89. Toby Morantz, "Old Texts, Old Questions: Another Look at the Issue of Continuity and the Early Fur-Trade Period," *Canadian Historical Review* 73, 2 (1992): 192, 179.

90. This leader is not to be confused with another man named The Swan who was noted in the York Factory journals about the same time. The Swan who visited York Factory was also a great leader, but he was a Missinepee Cree who lived in the upper Churchill River area. James Knight noted the arrival at York Factory of several "Mishenipee Indians," including "The Swan" or "Waupisoo," in June of 1715 (HBCA, B.239/a/1, June 19, 1715, fo. 42). It is improbable that Wapesew could have travelled from Albany Fort back to the upper Churchill River and then down to York Factory between March and June.

91. HBCA, B.3/a/6, March 14 and 18, 1715, fo. 11. James Settee, who grew up at Split Lake, recorded a large gathering of Lowland Cree at the mouth of the Nelson River in the fall of 1823. Settee attended the assembly with his grandfather, whose birthplace was near the mouth of the Nelson River but who had relocated to Split Lake. Settee observed, "We saw a large camp. The whole plantation of the mouth of the Nelson River was full of lodges of deer skins as white [as] white cloth. Hundreds of Indians had assembled from Churchill, Severn and moose Factory from James' Bay York Factory. All the Head men came and greeted my grand Father and took him to a large Tent prepared for us. My grand Father had been elected as the Chief of all tribes living on the seacoast, he was called the Little Englishman." See Jennifer S.H. Brown, "James Settee and his Cree Tradition: An Indian Camp at the Mouth of Nelson River Hudsons Bay," in *Actes du Huitieme Congres des Algonquinistes*, ed. William Cowan (Ottawa: Carleton University, 1977), 39. This large assembly was not reported in the HBC archival records. Charles Tuttle, who visited the Hudson Bay lowlands and adjacent uplands in 1884, noted that one man, who lived in the area of the upper Nelson River, was considered to be the leader of a large population: "An old chief who lives on the banks of the Nelson [River], about three hundred miles above York, who is at the head of two or three hundred families." See Charles R. Tuttle, *Our North Land: Being a Full Account of the Canadian North-West and Hudson's Bay Route, together with a Narrative of the Experiences of the Hudson's Bay Expedition of 1884* (Toronto: C. Blackett Robinson, 1885), 378.

92. The term "captain" was used by fur traders to distinguish prominent leaders. Leaders of lesser rank were usually denominated "lieutenants."

93. Pierre Esprit Radisson, "Relation of the Voyage of Pierre Esprit Radisson, to the North of America, in the years 1682 and 1683," in *Report of the Minister of Agriculture for the Dominion of Canada, 1895,* Canada Sessional Paper No. 8a (Ottawa, 1896), 67.

94. HBCA, B.3/d/1, fo. 15d.

95. HBCA, B.135/d/2, fo. 8.

96. Graham, *Andrew Graham's Observations*, 170.

97. HBCA, B.3/d/5, fo. 15d.

98. HBCA, B.3/a/13, May 25, 1725.

99. HBCA, B.3/a/61, May 28, 1769, fo. 35d.

100. HBCA, B. 3/a/84, April 22 and 23, 1785, fos. 34d and 35.

101. HBCA, B.3/a/88, May 16, 1787, fo. 30d.

102. HBCA, B.3/a/84, May 3, 1785, fo. 36d.

103. HBCA, B.3/a/97, August 19, 1796, fo. 31.

104. HBCA, B.239/a/35, August 13, 1751, fo. 2d.

105. HBCA, B.42/a/1, November 5, 1718, fo. 29.

106. HBCA, B.42/a/1, May 8, 1719, fo. 45.

107. Ellis, *An Account of a Voyage*, vol. 1, 228-229.

108. Falconer, "Remarks on the Natives," 20.

109. Graham, *Andrew Graham's Observations*, 269.

110. Ibid., 192.

111. According to Samuel Hearne, sixty-nine Homeguard Cree lived in the vicinity of Churchill before the smallpox epidemic (Martha McCarthy, *Churchill: A Land-Use History, 1782-1930,* Microfiche Report Series, No. 219 [Ottawa: Parks Canada, 1985], 83). Guy Joubert estimated that the pre-epidemic population of Homeguard Cree near Severn House was between seventy-five and 100 people (Joubert, "The Homeguard Indians," 32).

112. John Foster stated, "Although population figures are tenuous at best, learned 'guesstimates' indicate a slow but steady increase in population over the years following initial contact" (Foster, "The Home Guard Cree," 55). Unfortunately, Foster provided no substantive evidence to support this view, other than a reference to Charles Bishop's undocumented assertion of "marked population growth among both the Ojibwa and Cree between the seventeenth and nineteenth centuries." See Charles Bishop, "Ojibwa, Cree, and the Hudson's Bay Company in Northern Ontario: Culture and Conflict in the Eighteenth Century," in *Western Canada Past and Present*, ed. A.W. Rasporich (Calgary: McClelland and Stewart West, 1975), 154.

113. Graham, *Andrew Graham's Observations*, 330.

114. HBCA, B.3/e/15, fo. 3.

115. Ibid.

116. HBCA, B.239/e/1, fo. 5d.

117. HBCA, B.42/e/2, fo. 6.

118. HBCA, B.198/e/6, fo. 8.

119. HBCA, B.135/e/3, fos. 7-9.

Chapter 2

1. John S. Long, "'Shaganash': Early Protestant Missionaries and the Adoption of Christianity by the Western James Bay Cree, 1840-1893," unpublished PhD dissertation, University of Toronto, 1986, p. 25.

2. Reuben G. Thwaites, *The Jesuit Relations and Allied Documents*, vol. 51 (Cleveland: Burrows Brothers, 1896-1901), 57.

3. Arthur S. Morton, *A History of the Canadian West to 1870-71: Being a History of Rupert's Land (the Hudson's Bay Company's Territory) and of the North-West Territory (Including the Pacific Slope)*, ed. Lewis G. Thomas (Toronto: University of Toronto Press, 1973), 30-32.

4. Ibid., 3.

5. William L. Morton, *Manitoba: A History* (Toronto: University of Toronto Press, 1957), 14.

6. Walter M. Hlady, "Indian Migrations in Manitoba and the West," *Papers of the Manitoba Historical and Scientific Society* 3, 17 (1960-61): 26.

7. The pottery artifacts were initially reported in the archaeological literature by James V. Wright in 1968: "Two rim sherds recovered by Dr. Robert Bell of the Geological Survey of Canada (National Mus. Can. Records) at the mouth of the Nelson River both relate to the Blackduck focus." See his "The Boreal Forest," in *Science, History and Hudson Bay*, vol. 1, ed. C.S. Beals (Ottawa: Department of Energy, Mines and Resources, 1968), 66.

8. W.A. Kenyon, *The History of James Bay 1610-1686: A Study in Historical Archaeology*, Archaeology Monograph 10 (Toronto: Royal Ontario Museum, 1986), 45.

9. The view that the lowlands lacked sufficient resources for Aboriginal people to subsist in the region was reinforced by other scholars. For example, Jean Trudeau remarked that "the limited availability of country food [in the Hudson Bay lowlands] made the introduction of flour, lard and tea supplied by the trader in return for pelts highly desirable." See Jean Trudeau, "The Cree Indians," in *Science, History and Hudson Bay*, vol. 1, ed. C.S. Beals (Ottawa: Department of Energy, Mines and Resources, 1968), 130.

10. K.C.A. Dawson, *Albany River Survey, Patricia District, Ontario, September, 1976*, Mercury Series, Archaeological Survey of Canada, Paper No. 51 (Ottawa: National Museum of Man, 1976), 79.

11. Ibid.

12. Henry Ellis, *An Account of a Voyage for the Discovery of a North-West Passage by Hudson's Streights, to the Western and Southern Ocean of America*, vol. 1 (New York: Johnson Reprint Corporation, 1968), 185.

13. Walter M. Hlady, "Manitoba – The Northern Woodlands," in *Ten Thousand Years: Archaeology in Manitoba*, ed. Walter M. Hlady (Altona: D.W. Friesen and Sons Ltd., 1970), 95.

14. William J. Mayer-Oakes, *Archaeological Investigations in the Grand Rapids, Manitoba, Reservoir, 1961-62*, Occasional Paper No. 3, Department of Anthropology (Winnipeg: University of Manitoba Press, 1970), 354.

15. William N. Irving and John Tomenchuk, "Archaeology of the Brant River, Polar Bear Park, Ontario, 1972: A Preliminary Report," *Ontario Archaeology* 22 (1974): 41.

16. W.C. Noble and J.W. Pollock, "Archaeology of the Hawley Lake Area, Hudson Bay Lowlands, Ontario," in *Canadian Archaeology Association – Collected Papers, March 1975*, Archaeological Research Report No. 6 (Toronto: Ontario Ministry of Culture and Recreation, Historical Sites Branch, 1975), 88.

17. Ibid., 89.

18. Ibid., 95.

19. K.C.A. Dawson, "Prehistory of the Interior Forest of Northern Ontario," in *Boreal Forest Adaptations: The Northern Algonkians,* ed. A.T. Steegmann Jr. (New York: Plenum Press, 1983), 55.

20. Christopher G. Trott, "Report of the Constance Lake Historical Research Project, 1977," unpublished manuscript, Ontario Ministry of Culture and Recreation, 1978, p. 52.

21. Ibid., 64.

22. Norman James Williamson, "The Constance Lake Historical Project, Phase II, 1978," unpublished manuscript, Ontario Ministry of Culture and Recreation, 1979, p. 71.

23. David K. Riddle, "Archaeological Survey of the Albany River, Year 2: Triangular Lake to Washi Lake," in *Studies in West Patricia Archaeology No. 2: 1979-1980,* ed. C.S Reid and W.A. Ross (Toronto: Ontario Ministry of Culture and Recreation, Historical Planning and Research Branch, 1981), 208, 256.

24. James V. Wright, "Prehistory of the Canadian Shield," in *Handbook of North American Indians,* vol. 6, *Subarctic,* ed. June Helm (Washington: Smithsonian Institution, 1981), 88.

25. David K. Riddle, "An Archaeological Survey of Attawapiskat Lake, Ontario," *Studies in West Patricia Archaeology, No. 3, 1980-81,* ed. W.A. Ross (Toronto: Ontario Ministry of Citizenship and Culture, 1982), 29, 110.

26. Scott Hamilton, "Archaeological Investigations at the Wapekeka Burial Site (FlJj-1)," unpublished report, Lakehead University,1991, p. 71.

27. Dale R. Russell, "The Effects of the Spring Goose Hunt on the Crees in the Vicinity of York Factory and Churchill River in the 1700's," in *Proceedings of the Second Congress, Canadian Ethnology Society,* vol. 2, Mercury Series, Canadian Ethnology Service Paper No. 28, ed. Jim Freeman and Jerome H. Barkow (Ottawa: National Museum of Man, 1975), 422.

28. Charles A. Bishop, "Demography, Ecology and Trade among the Northern Ojibwa and Swampy Cree," *The Western Canadian Journal of Anthropology* 3, 1 (1972): 66.

29. Patrick J. Julig, "Human Use of the Albany River from Preceramic Times to the Late Eighteenth Century," unpublished MA thesis, York University, 1982, pp. 80-81.

30. Ibid., 89.

31. Patrick J. Julig, "Prehistoric Site Survey in the Western James Bay Lowlands, Northern Ontario," in *Boreal Forest and Sub-Arctic Archaeology,* ed. C.S. Reid, Occasional Papers of the London Chapter of the Ontario Archaeological Society, No. 6, 1988, p. 130.

32. Jean-Luc Pilon, *Washahoe Inninou Dahtsuounoaou: Ecological and Cultural Adaptation Along the Severn River in the Hudson Bay Lowlands of Ontario,* Conservation Archaeology Report, Northwestern Region, Report No. 10 (Kenora: Ontario Ministry of Citizenship and Culture, 1987), 139.

33. Ibid., 1.

34. Ibid., 71.

35. Ibid., 82.

36. Kenneth R. Lister, "Provisioned at Fishing Stations: Fish and the Native Occupation of the Hudson Bay Lowland," in *Boreal Forest and Sub-Arctic Archaeology,* ed. C.S. Reid,

Occasional Publications of the London Chapter of the Ontario Archaeological Society, No. 6, 1988, pp. 72-99.

37. Pilon, *Washahoe Inninou Dahtsuounoaou,* 105.

38. Other archaeologists now support Pilon's conclusions. For example, in 1991, Donald Clark summarized the pre-European distribution of the Cree people, whose geographic range included the Hudson Bay lowlands. See Clark, *Western Subarctic Prehistory,* Archaeological Survey of Canada (Hull: Canadian Museum of Civilization, 1991), 135. James V. Wright revised his earlier views in 1987, when he included the lowlands in a map depicting the distribution of Cree between AD 500 and European contact. See Wright, "Cultural Sequences, AD 500 – European Contact," in *Historical Atlas of Canada,* vol. 1, *From the Beginning to 1800,* ed. R. Cole Harris (Toronto: University of Toronto Press, 1987), plate 9.

39. Jean-Luc Pilon, "Culture, History and Ethnicity in the Hudson Bay Lowlands," in *Boreal Forest and Sub-Arctic Archaeology,* ed. C.S. Reid, Occasional Publications of the London Chapter of the Ontario Archaeological Society, 1988, p. 100.

40. Ibid., 108.

Chapter 3

1. "Ojibway," "Ojibwa," and "Chippewa" are variations of the same name that has been used to describe a large group of people who have common cultural traditions and speak the same language. Although regional dialects of the Ojibway language exist, the basic language group occupies a large territory that surrounds much of the Great Lakes watershed. The name Chippewa has been used in the United States, while Ojibwa or Ojibway has been the common appellation in Canada. The name "Saulteaux," originally applied by French visitors to the Ojibway people who lived in the Sault Ste. Marie area, has also been commonly applied to these people. Their self-designation is *Anishinabae,* which means "the people."

2. HBCA, E.2/9, fo. 83; HBCA, B.123/e/14, fo. 3d.

3. Warren was told by Ojibway elders that the migration took place about eight generations before his time (1852). "From the manner in which they estimate their generations, they may be counted as comprising a little over half the full term of years allotted to mankind, which will materially exceed the white man's generation. The Ojibways never count a generation as passed away until the oldest man in the family has died, and the writer assumes from these, and other facts obtained through observation and inquiry, forty years as the term of an Indian generation" (William W. Warren, *History of the Ojibway People* [St. Paul: Minnesota Historical Society Press, 1984], 90). According to this formula, the date of the migration was about AD 1530.

4. Warren, *History of the Ojibway People,* 91.

5. Ibid., 82.

6. Charles Bishop suggested that the Assiniboine occupied the area west of Lake Superior at the time of European contact. See his *The Northern Ojibway and the Fur Trade: An Historical and Ecological Study* (Toronto: Holt, Rinehart and Winston, 1974), 4-5. However, other scholars have presented persuasive arguments against this position. Clinton Wheeler provided evidence in his essay "The Historic Assiniboine: A

Territorial Dispute in the Ethnohistoric Literature (in *Actes du Huitieme Congres des Algonquinistes,* ed. William Cowan) to show that the Assiniboine lived south of Lake Winnipeg when French fur traders first visited Lake Superior. The Assiniboine were long-distance traders and warriors who also travelled to Hudson Bay to trade with the HBC. In his unpublished MA thesis, University of Manitoba, entitled "Warfare Patterns of the Assiniboine to 1809," Gary Doige conducted an extensive review of the early historical documents and Assiniboine oral traditions, and he concluded that the "territorial heartland of the protohistorical Assiniboine lay in the Lake Winnipeg-lower Red River valley region" (p.45).

Harold Hickerson suggested that, beginning about 1660, the Ojibway migrated westward in order to better position themselves as middlemen in the European fur trade developing in the St. Lawrence valley and on Hudson Bay (see his "Land Tenure of the Rainy Lake Chippewa at the Beginning of the 19th Century," p. 44; and *The Chippewa and Their Neighbours,* p. 66). Charles Bishop believed that some Northern Ojibway began to move north of Lake Superior in the 1680s as a result of European fur-trade pressures, and completed their expansion about 1770, but his view has been rejected by a number of scholars. Edward Rogers and Mary Black Rogers were among the first to propose that the Northern Ojibway occupied the area north of Lake Superior before the arrival of European fur traders (see their article "Who Were the Cranes? Groups and Group Identity Names in Northern Ontario," in *Approaches to Algonquian Archaeology,* ed. Margaret Hanna and Brian Kooyman). Adolph Greenberg and James Morrison, in "Group Identities in the Boreal Forest: The Origin of the Northern Ojibway," suggested that the apparent post-European-contact migration of the Northern Ojibway was due to the changing names used in French and English accounts.

7. Louis F.R. Masson, comp., "An Account of the Athabasca Indians by a Partner of the North West Co., 1795," unpublished manuscript, 4, National Archives of Canada, 1795.

8. HBCA, B.156/a/13, fo. 61.

9. James H. Howard, *The Plains Ojibwa or Bungi: Hunters and Warriors of the Northern Prairies, with Special Reference to the Turtle Mountain Band* (Vermillion: University of South Dakota Anthropological Papers, no. 1, 1965), 9. S.M. Shrofel and H.C. Wolfart explained that the modern usage of the term *nahkawewak* is a Cree verb, meaning "they speak Saulteaux." See S.M. Shrofel and H.C. Wolfart, "Aspects of Cree Interference in Island Lake Ojibwa," in *Papers of the Eighth Algonquian Conference,* ed. William Cowan (Ottawa: Carleton University, 1977), 157.

10. HBCA, E.2/7, fo. 17.

11. HBCA, B.211/a/1, January 31, 1780, fo. 30d.

12. HBCA, B.123/e/14, fo. 4. The name "Bungee" was still used in the nineteenth century to describe Northern Ojibway who lived east of Lake Winnipeg. James Stewart, an HBC trader at Berens River, recalled that the Indian people "went under the name of Bungays, a name I have not heard of in any other part of the country." See his "Rupert's Land Indians in the Olden Time," in *Annual Archaeological Report for Ontario, 1904, Appendix to the Report of the Minister of Education* (Toronto: L.K. Cameron, 1905), 89.

13. Charles Bishop, *The Northern Ojibwa*, 16n. Bishop cited George Barnston's 1839 report on the Martins Fall district as the source, but Barnston did not refer to begging (HBCA, B.123/e/14).

14. HBCA, B.51/e/1, fo. 15d. In her book on the Ojibwa of western Canada (*The Ojibwa of Western Canada, 1780-1870* [Winnipeg: University of Manitoba Press, 1994], xvi-xvii), Laura Peers cited Fidler's report and added information from James Isham's vocabulary of Northern Ojibway words that confirm Fidler's interpretation of the origin of the name Bungee. During the late nineteenth century, the term was used to describe the unique speech of descendants of English, Scottish, and Orkney fur traders and their Lowland Cree or Northern Ojibway wives who settled in the Red River Colony. See, for example, Eleanor Blain, "Speech of the Lower Red River Settlement," in *Papers of the Eighteenth Algonquian Conference,* ed. William Cowan (Ottawa: Carleton University, 1987), 23. Margaret Stobie explained that the term was originally applied to Northern Ojibway, but by the 1840s it was also applied to Lowland Cree who migrated south to the Norway House area. See Margaret Stobie, "Backgrounds of the Dialect Called Bungi," *Papers of the Historical and Scientific Society of Manitoba,* Series 3 (24): 68-69.

15. HBCA, B.123/e/14, fo. 3d.

16. Warren explained that the Ojibway were "divided into several grand families or clans, each of which is known and perpetuated by a symbol of some bird, animal, fish, or reptile which they denominate the Totem or Do-daim (as the Ojibways pronounce it) and which is equivalent, in some respects, to the coat of arms of the European nobility." See William W. Warren, *History of the Ojibway People* (St. Paul: Minnesota Historical Society Press, 1984), 34-35.

17. Duncan Cameron, "The Nipigon Country," in *Les Bourgeois de la Compagnie du Nord-ouest: Recits de voyages, letters, et rapports inedits relatifs au Nord-ouest canadien,* vol. 2, ed. Louis F.R. Masson (New York: Antiquarian Press, 1960), 246. Alanson Skinner noted the following animal-named clans among the Northern Ojibway: "at Lac Seul, deer, moose, bear, beaver, pelican; at Osnaburgh, sturgeon, sucker, loon, caribou; and at Fort Hope, moose, sturgeon, loon, crow (raven?), goose, duck. The snake and kingfisher clans were also reported, and the Indians admitted there were more, the names of which they did not know." See Alanson Skinner, *Notes on the Eastern Cree and Northern Saulteaux* (New York: Anthropological Papers of the American Museum of Natural History, 1911), 150.

18. HBCA, B.3/a/98, July 17, 1797, fo. 46.

19. HBCA, B.155/e/1, fo. 3d.

20. Skinner, *Notes on the Eastern Cree and Northern Saulteaux,* 56.

21. The Jack Indians were first reported at Albany Fort on May 17, 1729 (HBCA, B.3/a/17, fo. 21). Joseph Adams, who was in charge of Albany Fort in 1730, noted that the Jack Indians came from the north (HBCA, B.3/a/18, June 19, 1730, fo. 18d). Their leader was a man named Putchekeechuck (HBCA, B.3/a/19, June 3, 1731, fo. 20; B.3/a/21, May 14, 1733, fo. 17d). The name Jack Indians was not used by the HBC traders after 1733, but Putchekeechuck and his followers continued to trade at Albany Fort for many years, under the name Severn or Seaside Indians.

22. HBCA, B.239/a/22, June 12, 1741, fo. 35d.

23. David Pentland made a linguistic connection between an Indian named Ashkee Ethinu, who visited York Factory in 1719, and a Northern Ojibway named Missinekegick, who lived in the Cumberland House area in 1774. Pentland remarked, "It is thus possible that there had been Ojibwa speakers in the Cumberland House area for 50 years before they were first noticed by the traders." See David Pentland, "The Ashkee Indians," in *Papers of the Sixteenth Algonquian Conference,* ed. William Cowan (Ottawa: Carleton University, 1985), 158.

24. James Isham, *James Isham's Observations on Hudsons Bay, 1743, and Notes and Observations on a Book Entitled A Voyage to Hudsons Bay in the Dobbs Galley, 1749,* ed. E.E. Rich (London: The Hudson's Bay Record Society, 1949), 112.

25. HBCA, B.239/a/68, fo. 41d.

26. HBCA, B.239/a/70, fo. 35.

27. HBCA, B.239/a/79, July 8, 1781, fo. 43.

28. HBCA, E.2/4, fo. 81.

29. Andrew Graham, *Andrew Graham's Observations on Hudson's Bay, 1767-91,* ed. Glyndwr Williams (London: The Hudson's Bay Record Society, 1969), 280, 281.

30. HBCA, B.239/a/71, fo. 30.

31. HBCA, E.2/7, fo. 17.

32. HBCA, E.2/9, fo. 83.

33. HBCA, B.123/e/14, fo. 5. Alanson Skinner remarked, "Between Agumiska [Akimiski Island] and York, the Ojibway, who originally dwelt inland along the north shore of Lake Superior, have worked northward to the headwaters of the Attawapiscat River in pursuit of furs, since the advent of the Hudson's Bay Company, forming a northern wedge, as it were, projecting into the Cree domains" (Skinner, *Notes on the Eastern Cree and Northern Saulteaux,* 11).

34. HBCA, B.283/e/1, fo. 4. As early as 1800, William Sinclair, who was in charge of Oxford House, reported that the local Lowland Cree were afraid to travel into the neighbouring "Bungee Country" (HBCA, B.239/b/66, February 29, 1800, fo. 106).

35. HBCA, B.93/e/3, fo. 3.

36. Cameron, "The Nipigon Country," 241, 242.

37. HBCA, B.117/e/5, fo. 1d.

38. HBCA, B.123/e/14, fo. 4.

39. HBCA, B.239/a/86, fo. 56d; HBCA, B.239/a/92, June 9, 1792, fo. 33; June 17, 1792, fo. 34; August 22, 1792, fo. 4. Tension between the Lowland Cree and Northern Ojibway persisted despite the close links that developed between the two groups. For example, a man named Chucky, who was murdered by a Lowland Cree near Severn House in the fall of 1774, was described as "a stout man, of about 24 years of age, of upland extraction, and always hated by the low country natives, tho' apparently not ill-natured, he was the best goose hunter belonging to this place" (HBCA, B.198/a/19, October 2, 1774, fo. 8d). Chucky, who was probably a Northern Ojibway, had married a Lowland Cree woman and resided among his wife's family near the coast. He was murdered by his wife's uncle.

40. Sydney Augustus Keighley, Renee Fossett Jones, and David Kirkby Riddle, *Trader, Tripper, Trapper: The Life of a Bay Man* (Winnipeg: Rupert's Land Research Centre, 1989), 122. Keighley later revised his assessment of the identity of the people who were known as the Bungee when he visited the HBC post called Big Beaver House on the Winisk River, located about 160 kilometres south of Big Trout Lake. Keighley wrote that "the natives here we called simply the eastern tribe. Later I came to identify these people as the Bungee. Their ways were very different from the Big Trout People, who looked down on them because of some of their customs" (*Trader, Tripper, Trapper*, 126).

41. Peter Jacobs, *Journal of the Reverend Peter Jacobs, Indian Wesleyan Missionary from Rice Lake to the Hudson's Bay Territory and Returning, Commencing May, 1852, With a Brief Account of His Life* (New York: n.p., 1858), 46.

42. John McLean, *John McLean's Notes of a Twenty-five Year's Service in the Hudson's Bay Territory* (Toronto: The Champlain Society, 1932), 132.

43. HBCA, B.129/e/7, fo. 3.

44. Albert P. Low, "Preliminary Report on an Exploration of Country From Lake Winnipeg to Hudson Bay," in *Geological and Natural History Survey of Canada Annual Report (1886),* vol.2, new series, 5F–16F (Montreal: Dawson Brothers, 1887), 13F.

45. William McInnes, "The Headwaters of the Winisk and Attawapiskat Rivers," *Sessional Papers of Canada,* No. 26, Summary Report of the Geological Survey of Canada, 1909, p. 47.

46. J.C. Boileau Grant, "Anthropometry of the Cree and Saulteaux Indians in Northeastern Manitoba," *National Museum of Canada Bulletin* 59 (1929): 1. In the summer of 1930, Irving Hallowell noted the influence of the Lowland Cree language on the speech of the Northern Ojibway who lived at Island Lake: "Linguistically, the Island Lake natives may be characterized by calling them Saulteaux or, better perhaps, Saulteaux-Ojibwa, indicating more clearly by this hyphenated term the close relationship of their language to Ojibwa proper. Locally, they are said to speak a mixed dialect of Saulteaux and Cree....The linguistic base at Island Lake may very well be Saulteaux-Ojibwa with an overlay of Cree due to modern conditions. On the other hand, it is not impossible that a much older contact with Cree-speaking peoples has affected the language much more deeply than a superficial inspection would indicate, since the Saulteaux of this region may have been marginal to Cree bands for a considerable period, because to the south and east we find only Saulteaux spoken today." See A. Irving Hallowell, "Notes on the Material Culture of the Island Lake Saulteax," *Journal de Societe des Americanistes, Paris,* 30 (1938): 131–132.

47. Evelyn M. Todd, "A Grammar of the Ojibwa Language: The Severn Dialect," unpublished PhD dissertation, University of North Carolina, 1971, 1.

48. Ibid., 265.

49. H. Christoph Wolfart, "Boundary Maintenance in Algonquian: A Linguistic Study of Island Lake, Manitoba," *American Anthropologist* 75 (1973): 1317.

50. Shrofel and Wolfart, "Aspects of Cree Interference," 164.

51. A. Irving Hallowell, *The Ojibwa of Berens River, Manitoba: Ethnography into History,* ed. Jennifer S.H. Brown (Fort Worth: Harcourt Brace Jovanovich College Publishers, 1992), 22.

52. HBCA, B.154/e/1, fo. 5d.

53. Edward S. Rogers, "Cultural Adaptations: The Northern Ojibwa of the Boreal Forest, 1670-1980," in *Boreal Forest Adaptations: The Northern Algonkians,* ed. A. Theodore Steegmann, Jr. (New York: Plenum Press, 1983), 90.

54. David Thompson, *David Thompson's Narrative of His Explorations in Western America,* ed. J.B. Tyrrell (Toronto: The Champlain Society, 1916), 48-49. The oral history of Upland Cree westward migration as related by Saukamappee is not covered in Dale Russell's review of the literature relating to the eighteenth-century Western Cree. Russell concluded there was little evidence to support the prevailing view that the European fur trade influenced a "western invasion" by the Cree in the eighteenth century (see Dale Russell, *Eighteenth-Century Western Cree and Their Neighbours,* Mercury Series paper 143 [Ottawa: Canadian Museum of Civilization, Anthropological Survey of Canada, 1991]). However, Saukamappee's account and others noted in this book indicate quite clearly that the fur trade indeed played a role in shaping the course of Cree migrations.

55. HBCA, B.16/e/1, fo. 6d.

56. HBCA, B.239/a/2, fo. 50.

57. HBCA, B.239/a/2, August 22, 1716, fos. 54d-55.

58. HBCA, B.239/a/3, May 19, 1717, fo. 49.

59. HBCA, B.239/a/32, June 25, 1749, fo. 34d.

60. HBCA, B.239/a/86, May 31, 1786, fo. 38.

61. HBCA, B.198/a/28, August 19, 1783, fo. 26d.

62. HBCA, B.198/a/2, September 22, 1760, fo. 42d.

63. HBCA, B.3/a/13, June 3, 1725, fo. 29.

64. HBCA, B.3/a/47, fo. 1d. Woudbe was a captain of the Albany River Homeguard Cree. In 1755, he was involved in the murders of HBC men at Henley House. George Rushworth, who was stationed at Albany Fort, remarked that Woudbe "paid his debts by robbing the upland Indians of there goods which I have seen him do it" (HBCA, A.11/2, September 8, 1755, fo. 173).

65. Pentland explained that the name *Oupeshepou* was probably derived from a term meaning "one who uses a [fish] weir." See David H. Pentland, "Synonymy of the East Main Cree," in *Handbook of North American Indians,* vol. 6, *Subarctic,* ed. June Helm (Washington: Smithsonian Institution, 1981), 205. Modern English-speaking scholars have commonly used the term "East Main Cree," despite acknowledging that their language is more closely related to that spoken by Naskapi and Montagnais Indians to the east and south. See, for example, Richard A. Rhodes and Evelyn M. Todd, "Subarctic Algonquian Languages," in *Handbook of North American Indians,* vol. 6, *Subarctic,* 55.

66. Richard J. Preston, "East Main Cree," in *Handbook of North American Indians,* vol. 6, *Subarctic,* ed. June Helm (Washington: Smithsonian Institution, 1981), 196.

67. Truman Michelson, "Indian Language Studies on James and Hudson's Bays, Canada," in *Explorations and Field-Work of the Smithsonian Institution in 1935* (Washington: Smithsonian Institution, 1936), 75.

68. Toby Morantz, *An Ethnohistoric Study of Eastern James Bay Cree Social Organization, 1700-1850,* Mercury Series, Canadian Ethnology Service Paper No. 88 (Ottawa: National Museum of Man, 1983), 54.

69. HBCA, B.3/a/28, July 3, 1739, fo. 4.

70. HBCA, B.182/a/7, fo. 43.

Chapter 4

1. Joan B. Townsend, "Firearms Against Native Arms: A Study in Comparative Efficiencies with an Alaskan Example," *Arctic Anthropology* 20, 2 (1983).

2. Andrew Graham, *Andrew Graham's Observations on Hudson's Bay, 1767-91,* ed. Glyndwr Williams (London: The Hudson's Bay Record Society, 1969), 172.

3. Daniel Francis, "Les Relations entre Indiens et Inuit dans L'est de la baie d'Hudson, 1700-1840," *Etudes/Inuit Studies* 3,2 (1979): 73.

4. This explanation was common among other Aboriginal people over a wide geographic area. The Chipewyan attributed sickness and death to the magical powers of their enemies. Samuel Hearne reported, "When any of the principle Northern Indians [Chipewyan] die, it is generally believed that they are conjured to death, either by some of their own countrymen, by some of the southern Indians [Lowland and Upland Cree], or by some of the Esquimaux." See Samuel Hearne, *A Journey from Prince of Wales's Fort in Hudson's Bay to the Northern Ocean, 1769-1770-1771-1772,* ed. Richard Glover (Toronto: The Macmillan Company of Canada Ltd, 1958), 216-217.

5. William Coats, who was employed by the HBC from 1727 to 1751, explained that Inuit captives were given to the Ottawa, who, in turn, handed them over to the Five Nations Iroquois. He observed that "these powerful people [Ottawa] are such a terror to the servile tribes, that although they do not constantly go annually a Usquemow hunting for their bloody inhumane sacrifice, those poor creatures [Lowland Cree] do this for them, or are sure to be that sacrifice for themselves; and these, when procured, are to be tendered to the heads of the five nations of Iroquois, or Eliquoes, to be distributed to these very Notawais, or Otawais." See William Coats, *The Geography of Hudson's Bay: Being the Remarks of Captain W. Coats, in Many Voyages to that Locality, Between the Years 1727 and 1751,* ed. John Barrow (London: The Hakluyt Society, 1852), 56-57.

6. The pre-European-contact territory of the Western Hudson Bay Inuit has been difficult to determine because of the lack of archaeological data, but Brenda L. Clark suggested that they occupied the coastal area as far south as Churchill River, beginning about AD 1200 (see her "Thule Occupation of West Hudson Bay," in *Thule Eskimo Culture: An Anthropological Retrospective,* ed. Allen P. McCartney, Mercury Series, Archaeological Survey of Canada Paper No. 88 [Ottawa: National Museum of Man, 1979], 89, 96). Ernest Burch postulated that the Western Hudson Bay Inuit migrated to the Hudson Bay coastal area from the Coppermine Region in the seventeenth century. Drawing upon linguistic and archaeological data, Burch concluded, "The migrants were numerous enough to assimilate and/or exterminate their predecessors" (Ernest Burch, "The Thule-Historic Eskimo Transition on the West Coast of Hudson Bay," in *Thule Eskimo Culture,* 202). Burch and James G.E. Smith suggested that the

territory occupied by the Western Hudson Bay Inuit about 1718 included only a small stretch of coastline from Eskimo Point (north of the Seal River) to Chesterfield Inlet. See Ernest Burch and James G.E. Smith, "Chipewyan and Inuit in the Central Subarctic, 1613-1977," *Arctic Anthropology* 16, 2 (1979): 79.

7. Nicolas Jeremie, *Twenty Years of York Factory, 1694-1714: Jeremie's Account of Hudson Strait and Bay*, ed. R. Douglas and J.N Wallace (Ottawa: Thornburn and Abbott, 1926), 18.

8. Coats, *The Geography of Hudson's Bay*, 35.

9. HBCA, B.239/a/2, July 29, 1716, fo. 49. Inuit boats, called umiaks, were very large, according to the Lowland Cree. Inuit umiaks reportedly carried thirty to fifty Inuit men and their families. Ernest Burch suggested that Knight was engaged in "an exercise in fantasy" because Burch believed that the Inuit did not occupy any part of the western coast of Hudson Bay in the seventeenth and early eighteenth centuries (see Burch, "Caribou Eskimo Origins: An Old Problem Reconsidered," *Arctic Anthropology* 15, 1 [1978]: 12). While Knight may have exaggerated certain elements of what he saw or was told by the Lowland Cree, it is unlikely that so many other European observers would have fabricated accounts of Inuit on the western coast of Hudson Bay in that period.

10. Jeremie, *Twenty Years of York Factory*, 21-22. The signs of habitation that Munk found nearby may have been remains of Inuit encampments. According to Clark's archaeological study, the Inuit camps at the mouth of the Churchill River would have been occupied only in summer. "It is doubtful the Inuit would have wintered at Churchill because the nature of the sea ice along the coast south of Eskimo Point is very poor for ice hunting methods" (Clark, "Thule Occupation of West Hudson Bay," 96). Burch suggested that the charcoal pictographs found by Munk were probably made by the Lowland Cree. However, the other artifacts, such as stone dwellings, were probably made by the Inuit (see Burch, "Caribou Eskimo Origins," 4-5). It is conceivable that the artifacts were left by both Lowland Cree and Inuit, suggesting that both groups periodically occupied the area.

11. James Isham, *James Isham's Observations on Hudsons Bay, 1743, and Notes and Observations on a Book Entitled A Voyage to Hudsons Bay in the Dobbs Galley, 1749,* ed. E.E. Rich (London: The Hudson's Bay Record Society, 1949), 181. When James Knight built a trading post for the HBC at the mouth of the Churchill River in 1717, he found the remains of a large Inuit encampment at a place called Esqimaux Point (present Eskimo Point). It appeared that about 300 to 400 Inuit had wintered at this point. They had built umiaks nearby and hunted white whales. A fight had broken out here in the spring of 1717 between the Inuit and a small group of Chipewyan who had left York Factory to return to their homelands following a peace mission. See James Knight, *The Founding of Churchill: Being the Journal of Captain James Knight, Governor-in-Chief in Hudson Bay, from the 14th of July to the 13th of September, 1717,* ed. James F. Kenney (Toronto: J.M. Dent and Sons Ltd., 1932), 116-117, 142. Archaeological investigations at Seahorse Gully have revealed extensive remains of Inuit occupation in the pre-European-contact period. See Orysia Luchak, "Prince of Wales's Fort in the 18th Century: An Analysis of Trade, Construction, and Sloop Voyages Northward," Manuscript Report Number 243, Parks Canada (Ottawa: Department of Indian and Northern Affairs, 1978), 12-14.

12. Joseph Robson, *An Account of Six Years Residence in Hudson's Bay, from 1733 to 1736 and 1744 to 1747* (Toronto: S.R. Publishers Ltd., Josh Reprint Corporation, 1965), 64. Robson's observation that the Inuit preferred to encamp on points of land near the open sea was the same as the account made by Lowland Cree who spoke with James Knight in the summer of 1716. Knight remarked that, according to the Lowland Cree, "they [Inuit] Allways make there Tents upon points of head Lands that they see any body before they come to them so they Launch their Boats and get to Sea" (HBCA, B.239/a/2, August 2, 1716, fo. 50).

13. Graham, *Andrew Graham's Observations*, 213-214. Most contemporary observers attributed the withdrawal northward of the Inuit from the Churchill River area to hostility with the Lowland Cree and the Chipewyan, who were better equipped with European firearms. The HBC refused to trade firearms to the Inuit until the latter part of the eighteenth century, and only small numbers of firearms were available to the Inuit thereafter (Graham, *Andrew Graham's Observations,* 236).

14. Ibid., 236.

15. Jeremie, *Twenty Years of York Factory,* 16.

16. HBCA, B.239/a/2, August 2, 1716, fo. 50.

17. HBCA, B.239/a/29, April 9, 1747, fo. 25d. Accounts of Inuit near the mouth of the Severn River continued to be recorded in the early twentieth century. In 1928, S.J.C. Cumming, an HBC trader, reported "the story being that women of a wandering Eskimo tribe were captured near Severn, on Hudson Bay, many years ago, and were taken inland by the Indians" (see S.J.C. Cumming, "HBC Posts, Keewatin District: No. 11 – Island Lake Post," *The Beaver,* Outfit 259, 3 [1928]: 117).

18. Burch and Smith downplayed the warfare between the Lowland Indians and the Western Hudson Bay Inuit during the fur-trade period. They commented that "the Cree were anything but belligerent vis-à-vis the Caribou Inuit, with whom they had almost no direct contact" (Burch and Smith, "Chipewyan and Inuit in the Central Subarctic," 77). However, they recognized that linguistic evidence pointed to a different conclusion. The Inuit word for Lowland Cree was *unaalit,* a term that means "belligerent" or "competitive."

19. HBCA, B.239/a/2, August 2, 1716, fo. 50.

20. HBCA, B.239/a/2, April 29, 1716, fo. 25.

21. Jeremie, *Twenty Years of York Factory,* 21.

22. Robert Janes downplayed the impact of the hostility between Lowland Cree and Inuit in the area around the mouth of the Churchill River. Although he pointed to examples of "no man's land" areas elsewhere in the subarctic, he stated, "No information was found, however, that would indicate the presence of such a buffer zone in southern Keewatin during the eighteenth and nineteenth centuries." See Robert Janes, "Indian and Eskimo Contact in Southern Keewatin: An Ethnohistorical Approach," *Ethnohistory* 20,1 (1973): 47. Janes, and Burch and Smith, portrayed the territory near the mouth of the Churchill River as occupied by the Chipewyan Indians at the time of first European fur-trade contact (Burch and Smith, "Chipewyan and Inuit in the Central Subarctic," 79). However, the HBC archival documents clearly indicate that the territory of the Chipewyan was far removed from Churchill Fort when that post was established in 1717.

23. Burch dismissed the HBC accounts of the withdrawal of Inuit northward as a result of the acquisition of European firearms by Indians. However, he incorrectly focussed on the Chipewyan Indians as the people who drove the Inuit north (Burch, "Caribou Eskimo Origins," 11). The HBC accounts refer more specifically to the Lowland Cree as the agents of this warfare. Viewed from this perspective, the HBC accounts of Inuit withdrawal northward because of Lowland Cree attacks cannot be discredited in the manner employed by Burch (1978), and Burch and Smith (1979).

24. Henry Ellis, *An Account of a Voyage for the Discovery of a North-West Passage by Hudson's Streights, to the Western and Southern Ocean of America,* vol. 2 (New York: Johnson Reprint Corporation, 1968), 43-44. Burch and Smith incorrectly attributed this statement to Chipewyan-Inuit warfare (Burch and Smith, "Chipewyan and Inuit in the Central Subarctic," 80).

25. HBCA, B.239/d/10, fo. 53d.

26. Robson, *An Account of Six Years Residence,* 63.

27. John Oldmixon, "The History of Hudson's Bay," in *Documents Relating to the Early History of Hudson Bay,* ed. J.B. Tyrrell (Toronto: Champlain Society, 1931), 381-382.

28. Coats, *The Geography of Hudson's Bay,* 61.

29. Daniel Francis and Toby Morantz, *Partners in Furs: A History of the Fur Trade in Eastern James Bay, 1600-1870* (Montreal and Kingston: McGill-Queen's University Press, 1983), 75.

30. HBCA, B.3/d/2, fo. 12d.

31. HBCA, B.3/a/2, fos. 27d and 30.

32. HBCA, B.3/a/16, fo. 18.

33. HBCA, B.3/a/18, fo. 17d.

34. HBCA, B.135/a/5, fos. 17d, 21.

35. HBCA, B.3/a/24, fos. 27, 31d.

36. HBCA, B.135/a/6, fo. 13.

37. HBCA, B.3/a/24, August 1, 1736, fo. 32d.

38. HBCA, B.3/d/45, fo. 7d.

39. HBCA, B.3/a/38, fo. 5.

40. HBCA, B.3/a/77a, fo. 26d.

41. The Lowland Cree may have intended to kill the Inuit boy in retribution for the sickness and deaths caused by the smallpox epidemic in 1782-83 (HBCA, B.3/a/81, fo. 24). John Easter later became an apprentice with the HBC and entered the service of the company in 1788 (HBCA, B.3/d/99, fo. 5d).

42. HBCA, B.3/a/28, fo. 4.

43. HBCA, B.3/a/47, June 6, 1755, fo. 37d.

44. HBCA, B.3/a/49, fo. 30; HBCA, B.3/a/50, fo. 1.

45. HBCA, B.3/a/59, fo. 34.

46. HBCA, B.3/a/62, fo. 27d.

47. HBCA, B.3/a/66, fo. 19d. In a letter to Andrew Graham, who was in charge of Severn House, Marten remarked that "most of our Indians are going on an Esquimau

hunt, being invited thereto by the Moose Fort Indians" (HBCA, B.198/a/18, May 26, 1774, fo. 31d). There may have been more than one war party that set out from the Albany River area in 1774. Thomas Hutchins reported that "in June last [1774] ten of the best Indian men went from hence to warr with the Esquimaux in defiance of every perswasion and remonstrance to the contrary" (HBCA, A.11/3, September 15, 1774, fo. 200).

48. HBCA, B.3/a/66, fo. 33d.

49. HBCA, B.198/a/19, fo. 27.

50. HBCA, B.3/a/74, fo. 21d.

51. HBCA, B.3/a/78, fo. 22d.

52. HBCA, B.3/a/80, fo. 21.

53. HBCA, B.198/a/45, fo. 4.

54. HBCA, B.198/a/47, fo. 28d.

55. HBCA, B.3/a/92, fo. 27.

56. HBCA, B.86/a/46, fo. 19.

57. Graham, *Andrew Graham's Observations*, 174.

58. Ibid., 226.

59. Ibid., 219.

60. Edward Chappell, *Narrative of a Voyage to Hudson Bay* (Toronto: Coles Publishing Company, 1970), 110.

61. Graham, *Andrew Graham's Observations*, 174.

62. Alanson Skinner, *Notes on the Eastern Cree and Northern Saulteaux*, vol. 9,1 (New York: Anthropological Papers of the American Museum of Natural History, 1911), 78-79.

63. Claude C. Le Roy Bacqueville de la Potherie, "Letters of La Potherie [1700]," in *Documents Relating to the Early History of Hudson Bay*, ed. J.B. Tyrrell (Toronto: The Champlain Society, 1931), 233.

64. Ellis, *An Account of a Voyage*, 46.

65. Francis, "Les Relations entre Indiens et Inuit," 79-80.

66. Graham, *Andrew Graham's Observations*, 195.

67. Jeremie, *Twenty Years of York Factory*, 20. *Maskegon* was substituted by the English translators for the original French term *Savanois*.

68. HBCA, B.239/a/1, May 6, 1716, fo. 26d.

69. A.S. Morton expressed a negative assessment of the role of the Lowland Cree in this peace initiative when he asked, "What likelihood was there that a rabble of Crees armed with guns could meet those who had been hitherto their victims in a council of peace?" See A.S. Morton, *A History of the Canadian West to 1870-71: Being a History of Rupert's Land (the Hudson's Bay Company's Territory) and of the North-West Territory (Including the Pacific Slope)*, ed. Lewis G. Thomas (Toronto: University of Toronto Press, 1973), 132.

70. HBCA, B.239/d/9, fo. 4.

71. HBCA, B.239/d/7, fo. 8; HBCA, B.239/d/7, fo. 9.

72. HBCA, B.239/d/8, fo. 6.

73. HBCA, B.239/a/3, May 6, 1717, fo. 46d.

74. HBCA, B.239/a/2, May 10, 1716, fo. 29d.

75. HBCA, B.239/a/2, May 8, 1716, fo. 28d.

76. HBCA, B.239/a/3, fo. 41.

77. HBCA, B.239/a/3, April 20, 1717, fos. 41d, 42.

78. HBCA, B.239/d/9, fo. 7.

79. HBCA, B.239/d/10, fo. 52.

80. HBCA, B.239/a/3, May 6, 1717, fo. 46d.

81. HBCA, B.239/a/3, June 5, 1717, fo. 54; June 6, 1717, fo. 54d.

82. HBCA, B.42/a/4, fo. 23.

83. James G.E. Smith, "Chipewyan, Cree and Inuit Relations West of Hudson Bay, 1714–1955," *Ethnohistory* 28, 2 (1981): 141.

84. Coats, *The Geography of Hudson's Bay*, 32.

85. Isham, *James Isham's Observations*, 312.

86. Francis and Morantz, *Partners in Furs*, 19.

87. Reuben G. Thwaites, *The Jesuit Relations and Allied Documents*, vol. 46 (Cleveland: Burrows Brothers, 1896-1901), 287-291.

88. Ibid., vol. 47, 151-153.

89. Ibid., vol. 56, 183.

90. Oldmixon, "The History of Hudson's Bay," 385.

91. Thwaites, *The Jesuit Relations*, vol. 59, 39.

92. Christopher G. Trott, "Report of the Constance Lake Historical Research Project, 1977," unpublished manuscript, Ontario Ministry of Culture and Recreation, 1978, pp. 64-65.

93. James Wesley, *Stories from the James Bay Coast* (Cobalt, ON: The Highway Bookshop, 1993), 9.

94. C. Douglas Ellis, ed. and trans., *âtalôhkâna nêsta tipâcimôwina: Cree Legends and Narratives from the West Coast of James Bay* (Winnipeg: University of Manitoba Press, 1995), 177.

95. Gilles Havard, *La Grand Paix de Montreal de 1701: Les Voies dela Diplomatie Franco-Amerindienne* (Montreal: Recherches Amerindiennes au Quebec, 1992), 189.

96. Victor P. Lytwyn, "A Dish with One Spoon: The Shared Hunting Ground Agreement in the Great Lakes and St. Lawrence Valley Region," in *Papers of the Twenty-Eighth Algonquian Conference,* ed. David H. Pentland (Winnipeg: University of Manitoba Press, 1997).

97. New York Colonial Documents, *Documents Relative to the Colonial History of the State of New York,* ed. E.B. O'Callaghan, vol. 9 (Albany: Weed, Parsons, 1853-1857), 722.

98. J.B Tyrrell, ed., *Documents Relating to the Early History of Hudson Bay* (Toronto: The Champlain Society, 1931), 24.

99. HBCA, B.239/d/6.

100. HBCA, B.3/a/1, fo. 50d.

101. The locations of the French fur-trade posts are difficult to pinpoint because the HBC traders relied on vague information conveyed by Indians. On May 3, 1716, Aboriginal traders reported that the French had built a post on the Albany River, located about seven days' travel by canoe upriver from Albany Fort. This may have been in the area near the confluence of the Albany and Kenogami rivers, where the HBC later built Henley House (HBCA, B.3/a/9, fo. 10d). In the summer of 1732, upland traders reported that there were two French posts on the Albany River (HBCA, B.3/a/20, June 7, 1732, fo. 25). After the HBC established Henley House in 1743, the French withdrew from that area of the Albany River but they still maintained posts upriver. Aboriginal people reported that the nearest French post was about 250 kilometres upriver, probably near the site of the future HBC post named Gloucester House (HBCA, B.3/a/37, May 7, 1746, fo. 38). In 1754, a report was received at Albany that French traders had been within eighty kilometres of the sea coast between Albany Fort and York Factory. This may have referred to French traders on the lower Severn River (HBCA, B.3/a/46, June 6, 1754, fo. 31d). Another report in 1716 described a French trading post located about eight days' paddle by canoe up the Moose River. This may have been the French post on Lake Abitibi (see Conrad E. Heidenreich and Francoise Noel, "Trade and Empire, 1697-1739," in *Historical Atlas of Canada,* vol. 1, *From the Beginning to 1800,* ed. R.C. Harris [Toronto: University of Toronto Press, 1987], plate 39).

102. HBCA, B.3/a/4, March 24, 1713, fo. 26.

103. HBCA, B.3/a/4, June 3, 1713, fo. 34d.

104. HBCA, B.3/a/9, May 25, 1716, fo. 26; B.3/a/13, June 3, 1725, fo. 29.

105. HBCA, B.3/a/12, September 22, 1723, fo. 5d.

106. HBCA, B.3/a/17, May 7, 1729, fo. 20.

107. HBCA, B.3/a/17, fos. 22d, 23.

108. HBCA, B.3/a/35, May 17, 1744, fo. 30d. The same fear was expressed about attacks by the *Attawawas,* a name that was generally used to describe the Ottawa, an Algonquian-speaking group who lived around Lake Huron. In 1778, Thomas Hutchins, who was in charge of Albany Fort, reported: "The Attawawas still seem to harbour an hostile intent … they frighten all our Indians out of their wits being esteemed cannibals" (HBCA, A.11/4, March 14, 1778, fo. 71d).

109. HBCA, B.198/a/35, June 4, 1787, fo. 36d.

Chapter 5

1. Andrew Graham, *Andrew Graham's Observations on Hudson's Bay, 1767-91,* ed. Glyndwr Williams (London: The Hudson's Bay Record Society, 1969), 166.

2. These were probably barren ground caribou. However, scientific classification of these animals has been problematic since the herds disappeared in the nineteenth century. According to Samuel Hearne, the lowland caribou was much larger than the barren ground caribou he observed northwest of Churchill Fort. See Samuel Hearne, *A*

Journey from Prince of Wales's Fort in Hudson's Bay to the Northern Ocean, 1769-1770-1771-1772, ed. Richard Glover (Toronto: The Macmillan Company of Canada Ltd., 1958), 145. Following Hearne, others classified the Hudson Bay lowland animals as woodland caribou. Foremost in this regard were John Richardson (see his *Fauna Boreali-Americana; or the Zoology of the Northern Parts of North America* [London: John Murray, 1829], 250) and Edward Preble (in *A Biological Investigation of the Hudson Bay Region* [Washington: US Department of Agriculture, Division of Biological Survey, 1902], 41). However, other investigators have challenged these conclusions. For example, J.B. Tyrrell identified the lowland animals as barren ground caribou. See J.B. Tyrrell, "Hudson Bay Exploring Expedition, 1912," in *Twenty-Second Annual Report of the Bureau of Mines (Ontario)* 12, 1 (1913), 178. A.W.F. Banfield's landmark study of the barren ground caribou also concluded that the lowland herds were that species. Unlike previous investigators who relied on Hearne's description of size differences, Banfield was the first to focus on migration patterns and herd size as indicators of caribou taxonomy. Banfield concluded that "the range of the barren-ground caribou formerly extended eastward along the shore of Hudson Bay as far as Cape Henrietta Maria and that Hearne and Preble erroneously believed these to be woodland caribou." See A.W.F. Banfield, *Preliminary Investigation of the Barren Ground Caribou,* Wildlife Management Bulletin, Series 1, No. 10A (Ottawa: Department of Northern Affairs and Natural Resources, 1954), 12.

Francis Harper attempted to reconcile the differing opinions on the identification of the lowland caribou, and concluded: "Possibly chief reliance should be placed upon the testimony of such high authorities as Hearne, Richardson, and Preble when they refer to the animals as Woodland Caribou. Furthermore, none of the early writers identify them unequivocally as the Barren Ground species. It remains fairly evident that long ago some species of Caribou in great numbers did actually cross these rivers in a southerly direction in the spring, pass the summer on coastal tundra east of York Factory, and return northward or northwestward in late summer or autumn. Whichever species it was, it represented a segment of the population that must have become reduced to utterly insignificant numbers, if not entirely extirpated, some decades ago. In any event, it does not seem very likely that we shall ever be able to reconstruct the actual movements of the 'incredible multitudes' in the York Factory region of more than a century ago." See Francis Harper, *The Barren Ground Caribou of Keewatin* (Lawrence: University of Kansas, 1955), 9-10. John Kelsall's detailed study of the barren ground caribou in 1968 was also inconclusive about the identification of the caribou that historically visited the lowlands. However, Kelsall admitted, "some of the earliest reported movements were so large that they must have involved migratory [barren ground caribou] herds." See John Kelsall, *The Migratory Barren-Ground Caribou of Canada* (Ottawa: Queen's Printer, 1968), 61. According to the oral history of Lowland Indians living near the mouth of the Attawapiskat River in the 1940s, "The brush caribou (locally called 'deer') ('hatik'), once fairly plentiful along the west coast of James Bay, has all but disappeared from the country." See John J. Honigmann, "Foodways in a Muskeg Community: An Anthropological Report on the Attawapiskat Indians," unpublished report for the Department of Northern Affairs and National Resources, 1948, p.161.

3. Nicolas Jeremie noted that the paths made by the caribou "form a closer net work than the streets of Paris." See Nicolas Jeremie, *Twenty Years of York Factory, 1694-1714:*

Jeremie's Account of Hudson Strait and Bay, ed. R. Douglas and J.N. Wallace (Ottawa: Thornburn and Abbott, 1926), 22.

4. HBCA, B.239/a/88, March 29, 1788, fo. 33d.

5. Jeremie, *Twenty Years of York Factory*, 22.

6. Ibid.

7. Gabriel Marest, "Letter from Father Marest, Missionary of the Company of Jesus, to Father de Lamberville of the Company of Jesus, Overseer of the Missions of Canada," in *Documents Relating to the Early History of Hudson Bay*, ed. J.B. Tyrrell (Toronto: The Champlain Society, 1931), 127.

8. Claude C. LeRoy Bacqueville de la Potherie, "Letters of La Potherie [1700]," in *Documents Relating to the Early History of Hudson Bay*, ed. J.B. Tyrrell (Toronto: The Champlain Society, 1931), 221.

9. T.S. Drage, *An Account of a Voyage for the Discovery of a North-West Passage by the Hudson's Streights, to the Western and Southern Ocean of America Performed in the Years 1746 and 1747, in the Ship California, Capt. Francis Smith, Commander*, vol. 2 (New York: S.R. Publishers Ltd., and Johnson Reprint Corporation, 1968), 17.

10. David Thompson, *David Thompson's Narrative of His Explorations in Western America*, ed. J.B. Tyrrell (Toronto: The Champlain Society, 1916), 100.

11. Oral traditions from York Factory elders indicate that men and women hunted caribou. Amelia Saunders (nee Stoney), who was born at Fort Severn and lived at York Factory, recalled that she used to hunt caribou, and that "we hunted a lot, just like the men. We were taught this as we were growing up." See Flora Beardy and Robert Coutts, eds., *Voices from Hudson Bay: Cree Stories from York Factory* (Montreal and Kingston: McGill-Queen's University Press, 1996), 44.

12. The significance of traditional caribou crossing sites was noted by A.W.F. Banfield: "The location of well-used migration crossing points was of great importance to natives and European explorers relying on the barren-ground caribou for their existence on the tundra and in the sub-Arctic forests" (Banfield, *Preliminary Investigation*, part 1, p. 14). According to Bryan Gordon, caribou water crossings have been important places for hunting by Indians for thousands of years. He suggested that "caribou aggregation, predictable habits and relative ease in killing suggest that North American Palaeo-Indians would have utilized water crossings in a manner similar to that of the Upper Palaeolithic hunters of Europe." See Bryan Gordon, "Prehistoric Chipewyan Harvesting at a Barrenland Caribou Water Crossing," *The Western Canadian Journal of Anthropology* 7, 1 (1977): 81.

13. See, for example, HBCA, B.239/a/10, March 22, 1728, fo. 16d (60 miles); B.239/a/13, March 26, 1731, fo. 17 (20 miles); B.239/a/13, March 30, 1731, fo. 17 (40 miles); B.239/a/17, March 26, 1735, fo. 19 (40 miles); B.239/a/25, March 19, 1744, fo. 18 (20 miles); B.239/a/28, April 7, 1747, fo. 25d (20 miles); B.239/a/35, March 27, 1752, fo. 26 (34 miles); and B.239/a/42, March 18, 1757, fo. 34 (50 miles).

14. Edwin E. Rich, ed., *Cumberland House Journals and Inland Journal, 1775-82*, vol. 1 (London: The Hudson's Bay Record Society, 1951), 4.

15. HBCA, B.198/a/19, fo. 32.

16. HBCA, B.198/a/11, fo. 24.

17. William Coats, *The Geography of Hudson's Bay: Being the Remarks of Captain W. Coats, in Many Voyages to that Locality, Between the Years 1727 and 1751*, ed. John Barrow (London: The Hakluyt Society, 1852), 43. Today, the connection between caribou herds and Akimiski Island appears to have been lost. The name is said to mean "the land across" (John Long, personal communication to the author).

18. Coats, *The Geography of Hudson's Bay*, 60. In the summer of 1887, Albert P. Low conducted a geological survey of Akimiski Island, and reported that the island was easily accessible by canoe at low tide, when the distance from the mainland to the northern tip of the island was less than a mile. See Albert P. Low, *Report on Explorations in James' Bay and Country East of Hudson Bay, Drained by the Big, Great Whale and Clearwater Rivers* (Montreal: William Foster Brown and Co, 1888), 25J.

19. Jean-Luc Pilon, *Washahoe Inninou Dahtsuounoaou: Ecological and Cultural Adaptation Along the Severn River in the Hudson Bay Lowlands of Ontario,* Conservation Archaeology Report, Northwestern Region, Report No. 10 (Kenora: Ontario Ministry of Citizenship and Culture, 1987), 71.

20. James Isham, *James Isham's Observations on Hudsons Bay, 1743, and Notes and Observations on a Book Entitled A Voyage to Hudsons Bay in the Dobbs Galley, 1749*, ed. E.E. Rich (London: The Hudson's Bay Record Society, 1949), 152-153.

21. HBCA, B.239/a/4, April 26, 1718, fo. 20d.

22. HBCA, B.239/a/78, fo. 40.

23. HBCA, B.239/a/87, July 26, 1787, fo. 45.

24. Beardy and Coutts, *Voices from Hudson Bay*, 3. John Honigmann, who studied the Lowland Cree at Attawapiskat on the western coast of James Bay in the mid-twentieth century, also noted the absence of night fishing with torches in their Aboriginal culture, and said the use of fishing torches was "taught to the Indians by personnel of the Hudson's Bay Company." See John J. Honigmann, "The Attawapiskat Swampy Cree: An Ethnographic Reconstruction," in *Anthropological Papers of the University of Alaska*, ed. R. Sleinbach and J.W.Van Stone (Fairbanks: University of Alaska Press, 1956), 37.

25. Ernest S. Burch, "The Caribou/Wild Reindeer as a Human Resource, *American Antiquity* 37, 3 (1972): 343.

26. Timothy Ball's study of HBC archival records at York Factory and Churchill Fort between 1715 and 1851 indicated that "it appears that the birds [geese] relate their migratory decisions primarily to one climatic variable, namely wind direction. The warming conditions would be expected with a south wind in these latitudes and are therefore not the controlling factor." See Timothy Ball, "The Migration of Geese as an Indicator of Climate Change in the Southern Hudson Bay Region Between 1715 and 1851," *Climate Change* 5, 1 (1983): 86. It should be noted that Ball's data for the first sighting of geese at York Factory do not correspond with the figures I obtained from the York Factory records.

27. HBCA, B.198/a/29, May 15, 1784, fo. 32d.

28. HBCA, B.198/a/37, May 7, 1788, fo. 33.

29. HBCA, B.239/a/3, fo. 47d.

30. HBCA, B.198/a/48, fo. 36d.

31. HBCA, B.239/a/17, May 10, 1735, fo. 23d.

32. HBCA, B.239/a/90, May 30, 1790, fo. 44d.

33. HBCA, B.239/a/24, fo. 22d.

34. Marest, "Letter from Father Marest," 127.

35. Bacqueville de la Potherie, "Letters of La Potherie," 221.

36. Graham, *Andrew Graham's Observations*, 41.

37. Ibid., 47.

38. HBCA, B.3/a/2, fo. 27.

39. Graham, *Andrew Graham's Observations,* 42.

40. Ibid., 43.

41. Isham, *James Isham's Observations*, 120–121.

42. Graham, *Andrew Graham's Observations*, 43.

43. George Barnston, "Recollections of the Swans and Geese of Hudson's Bay," *The Canadian Naturalist and Geologist* 6,5 (1861): 340.

44. Isham, *James Isham's Observations*, 127; Graham, *Andrew Graham's Observations,* 48.

45. Barnston, "Recollections," 338.

46. Graham, *Andrew Graham's Observations*, 48.

47. HBCA, B.3/239/a/8, April 15, 1723, fo. 44d.

48. Charles Bishop, "The First Century: Adaptive Changes among the Western James Bay Cree between the Early Seventeenth and Early Eighteenth Centuries," in *The Subarctic Fur Trade: Native Social and Economic Adaptations,* ed. Shepard Krech, III (Vancouver: University of British Columbia Press, 1984), 31.

49. Dale Russell, "The Effects of the Spring Goose Hunt on the Crees in the Vicinity of York Factory and Churchill River in the 1700's," in *Proceedings of the Second Congress, Canadian Ethnology Society*, vol. 2, ed. Jim Freeman and Jerome H. Barkow, Mercury Series, Canadian Ethnology Service Paper No. 28 (Ottawa: National Museum of Man, 1975), 422.

50. Honigmann, "The Attawapiskat," 32.

51. Pilon, *Washahoe,* 35.

52. Graham, *Andrew Graham's Observations*, 41.

53. HBCA, B.239/a/101, July 25, 1798, fo. 42.

54. Isham, *James Isham's Observations*, 41.

55. Luke Fox, *North-west Fox or Fox from the North-west Passage* (New York: S.R. Publishers Ltd., 1965), 216.

56. Pierre Esprit Radisson, *The Explorations of Pierre Esprit Radisson, from the Original Manuscript in the Bodleian Library and the British Museum*, ed. Arthur Adams (Minneapolis: Ross and Haines, 1961), 146.

57. Edward Umfreville, *The Present State of Hudson's Bay: Containing a Full Description of that Settlement, and the Adjacent Country; and Likewise of the Fur Trade with Hints for its Improvement*, ed. W. Stewart Wallace (Toronto: The Ryerson Press, 1954), 90. William McInnes conducted geological surveys of the Winisk and Attawapiskat rivers in 1905,

and he provided a good summary of the fish that were available in those rivers: "Whitefish and sturgeon are the best food fishes, and occur in most of the lakes. Both are taken in nets, and the latter also by spearing from scaffolds built out over rapids in the rivers. Dore [pickerel] and pike are also generally distributed over the whole area, and form an important source of food supply, though the sucker among the fishes, like the rabbit among the mammals, holds the most important place, as it can be caught everywhere, not only in the larger lakes but also in the smaller ponds and streams. Brook trout were actually caught [by the surveying party] only in the Winisk river near its mouth, and in the streams running into the Albany river, but were seen in the rapids below Weibikwei; the Indians assert that they occur also in the lake itself. Lake trout were caught in large numbers in Trout Lake at the head of the Severn river, but are not found in either the Winisk or Attawapiskat rivers." See William McInnes, "Report on a Part of the Northwest Territories of Canada Drained by the Winisk and Upper Attawapiskat Rivers" (Ottawa: Department of Mines, Geological Survey Branch, 1909), 45. J.B. Tyrrell, who conducted a geological survey of the Hayes and Severn rivers in 1912, commented that "fish form the staple food of the inhabitants of this country. The principal kinds so used are trout, whitefish, tullibee [lake herring] and suckers" (Tyrrell, "Hudson Bay Exploring Expedition," 180). Archelaus Beardy, who was born at York Factory in 1912, recalled that ciscoes (another name for lake herring) were caught in the fall (Beardy and Coutts, *Voices from Hudson Bay*, 13).

58. Lake sturgeon were sometimes taken with a gun. Matthew Cocking observed that Lowland Cree who accompanied him on an inland journey in 1774 killed sturgeon with guns in the Chuckitanah (Hill) River (HBCA, B.239/a/72, July 10, 1774, fo. 2d). In their study of the Weagamow Ojibway who live on the border of the lowlands, Black and Rogers commented that "the technology for securing fish was more complex than that employed in hunting and gathering. It consisted of hooks, gaffs, spears, traps, jack lights, and even arrows … in the old days, people sometimes gathered at small rapids during the spring and used clubs and their hands to catch walleye and suckers." See Mary Black and Edward Rogers, "Subsistence Strategy in the Fish and Hare Period, Northern Ontario: The Weagamow Ojibwa, 1880-1920," *Journal of Anthropological Research* 3, 1 (1976): 6-7. The use of lights in night fishing or hunting was not mentioned in the records before 1821.

59. Graham, *Andrew Graham's Observations*, 122. David Massan, who was born at Big Trout Lake in 1915 and moved to York Factory in 1930, recalled that people used to depend on weirs to catch fish. "They would build weirs and trap the fish. That's what they survived on. Oh, there used to be lots of fish caught in these weirs. People would just throw the fish out onto the riverbank! They used the weirs until the river started freezing. That's when they had to be on guard, at this time of the year. When the boxes filled up they would freeze together if no one was there to take them out. These boxes used to fill up so fast—that's how much fish there was. Some fish were kept in the water and a net was used to pull them ashore. They were usually stored for the winter so the people wouldn't go hungry" (Beardy and Coutts, *Voices from Hudson Bay*, 9-10).

60. Kenneth R. Lister, "Provisioned at Fishing Stations: Fish and the Native Occupation of the Hudson Bay Lowland," in *Boreal Forest and Sub-Arctic Archaeology*, ed. C.S. Reid, Occasional Publications of the London Chapter of the Ontario Archaeological Society, no. 6, 1988, p. 75.

61. HBCA, B.198/e/1, fo. 4d. In the summer of 1905, William McInnes conducted geological surveys on the Winisk and Attawapiskat rivers, and reported that "in the spring, camped close to a rapid on one of the larger streams, they [Indians] live on fish, principally carp [suckers], caught automatically by a michiken or fish-weir, crossing the stream at the rapid" (McInnes, "The Headwaters," 79).

62. HBCA, B.3/a/67, March 8 and 10, 1774, fos. 3d, 4d.

63. Richard Beardy, who was born at York Factory in 1915, recalled that seine nets were used in the summer. He said, "Fishing was the most important source of survival during the summer. They would put the net out in the river with people at each end and slowly drag it to shore, catching the fish as they dragged the net" (Beardy and Coutts, *Voices from Hudson Bay*, 11).

64. HBCA, B.3/e/8, fo. 3.

65. HBCA, B.135/a/8, fo. 6.

66. Chief Thomas Fiddler and James E. Stevens, *Killing the Shamen* (Moonbeam: Penumbra Press, 1985), 5.

67. Umfreville, "The Present State," 90.

68. Graham, *Andrew Graham's Observations*, 118.

69. HBCA, B.3/a/34, June 12, 18, fos. 44d, 46d.

70. Graham, *Andrew Graham's Observations*, 118.

71. HBCA, B.239/a/30, fo. 28.

72. Isham, *James Isham's Observations*, 168.

73. HBCA, B.86/a/33, July 29, 1780, fo. 48d; B.86/e/1, fo. 2.

74. HBCA, B.234/a/1, fo. 7.

75. Isham, *James Isham's Observations*, 81, 155-156.

76. John D. Cameron, who was in charge of the HBC's post at Lac la Pluie (later named Fort Frances) in 1826, described the Ojibway method of preparing sturgeon pemmican: "They cut up [sturgeon flesh] in flakes and dry over a slow fire, after which they pound the dried flakes between stones until it becomes like a kind of spunge; this with the oil they gather; affords them a rich and substantial food of which they are very fond" (HBCA, B.105/e/6, fo. 4). James Sutherland, who explored the region around Lake St. Joseph on the Upper Albany River in 1784, encountered a Canadian fur trader who subsisted on sturgeon ruhiggan (HBCA, B.78/a/9, May 31, 1784, fo. 7).

77. Graham, *Andrew Graham's Observations*, 118-119.

78. Ibid., 122.

79. Ellis, *An Account of a Voyage*, 32.

80. Some species of geese, such as brant geese, stayed along the Hudson Bay and James Bay coasts, breeding on coastal islands. Many Canada geese also stayed in the lowlands to breed, but they were scattered throughout the vast area, and a focussed hunt for geese was not possible during the summer period.

81. HBCA, B.239/a/3, April 13, 1717, fo. 40d.

82. HBCA, B.239/a/14, fo. 24.

83. HBCA, B.198/a/9, June 22, 1775, fo. 40d; B.198/a/21, April 15, 1777, fo. 20.

84. HBCA, B.198/a/21, fo. 21.

85. HBCA, B.239/a/76, July 25, 1779, fo. 58d.

86. HBCA, B.198/a/78, July 19, 1780, fo. 40.

87. HBCA, B.3/a/14, fo. 26d.

88. William Falconer, "Remarks on the Natives near the Cost of Hudson's Bay and Straits, with some remarks on the Climate, etc," unpublished manuscript copy in the National Archives of Canada, MG 19, D2, vol. 1, part 2, n.c., p.38. The hard work done by Cree women was recalled by Mary Redhead, who was born in 1920 at York Factory. She said, "The women didn't mind working in those days. There wasn't anything hard about it. No hesitating. It was something that was done daily. No, the women never complained. Strange, aye? That's how it was" (Beardy and Coutts, *Voices from Hudson Bay*, 44).

89. Isham, *James Isham's Observations*, 155-156.

90. Graham, *Andrew Graham's Observations*, 31.

91. HBCA, B.239/a/19, fo. 12d.

92. HBCA, B.239/a/26, fo. 8d.

93. HBCA, B.198/a/58b, June 21, 1819, fo. 13.

94. HBCA, B.239/a/20, fo. 10.

95. HBCA, B.239/a/24, fo. 7.

96. Graham, *Andrew Graham's Observations*, 47.

97. HBCA, B.3/a/13, fo. 36.

98. Graham, *Andrew Graham's Observations*, 83.

99. Although many HBC employees came from the Orkney Islands with a tradition of fishing, they were not as proficient as Cree fishermen. This point was made clear on a number of occasions in HBC journals. For example, on July 19, 1768, Humphrey Marten, Chief Factor at Albany Fort, noted that "an Indian came in with Fish, altho I have had a Net down some time yet cannot get a Fish" (HBCA, B.3/a/60, fo. 29).

100. HBCA, B.239/a/33, fo. 37d.

101. HBCA, B.239/a/33, fos. 39d-40.

102. The reasons why white whales visited river estuaries in summer is not well understood. There is no apparent connection with reproductive biology because white whales usually breed during April and May. HBC whalers who worked on the Eastmain believed that the white whales moved into these areas because they craved access to fresh water. Andrew Graham also remarked that "in spring they are so desirous to get into the rivers that we observe them playing in the Bay close to the entrance of them: nay, they swim under the ice, and play in open holes in the river, before the ice takes its departure" (Graham, *Andrew Graham's Observations*, 116).

103. Graham, *Andrew Graham's Observations*, 115-116.

104. David Massan recalled that white whales were still caught in the early twentieth century near Port Nelson and used for oil and dog food (Beardy and Coutts, *Voices from Hudson Bay*, 11).

105. HBCA, B.239/a/33, fo. 41.

106. Graham, *Andrew Graham's Observations*, 116.

107. HBCA, B.239/a/8, fo. 54d.

108. HBCA, B.198/a/1, fos. 27d-28.

109. HBCA, B.198/a/1, fos. 29d, 30.

110. Falconer, "Remarks on the Natives," 13.

111. Amelia Saunders recalled that berries were an important food source. She said, "Oh, we ate a lot of berries! These were always part of the diet, like meat. Soon as the berries were ready we would all get together and pick them" (Beardy and Coutts, *Voices from Hudson Bay*, 39).

112. HBCA, B.239/a/33, August 6, 1750, fo. 43.

113. HBCA, B.3/a/9, fo. 58d.

114. Graham, *Andrew Graham's Observations*, 133.

115. The vegetation of the Hudson Bay lowlands and the significance of the region's resources as habitat for caribou is discussed in detail by Peter A.J. Brokx, "The Hudson Bay Lowland as Caribou Habitat," unpublished MA thesis, University of Guelph, 1965.

116. Isham, *James Isham's Observations*, 155.

117. HBCA, B.3/a/9, fo. 13d.

118. HBCA, B.239/a/8, fo. 23.

119. HBCA, B.239/a/73, fo. 3d.

120. Graham, *Andrew Graham's Observations*, 15.

121. Albert Hill, who was born in 1905 at Puskwatenak (Manitoba) and lived at York Factory from 1926, noted that people would build rafts in spring and sell the timber to the company (Beardy and Coutts, *Voices from Hudson Bay*, 24).

122. HBCA, B.239/a/36, fo. 38.

123. Isham, *James Isham's Observations*, 102.

124. Graham, *Andrew Graham's Observations*, 172.

125. HBCA, B.239/a/33, fo. 39d, 40.

126. HBCA, B.239/a/2, August 6, 1716, fo. 51d.

127. HBCA, B.239/a/5, fo. 81.

128. HBCA, B.198/a/16, fo. 43.

129. HBCA, B.198/a/18, fo. 29d.

130. HBCA, B.239/a/27, fo.2.

131. Beardy and Coutts, *Voices from Hudson Bay*, 8.

132. HBCA, B.3/a/63, October 1, 1770, fo. 6d.

133. HBCA, B.198/a/8, fo. 6d.

134. HBCA, B.3/a/2, fo. 24.

135. HBCA, B.3/a/38, fo. 18d.

136. HBCA, B.3/a/39, fo. 22d.

137. HBCA, B.3/a/17, fo. 10d.

138. "Moose" is an Algonquian word that means "eater of twigs," but the same species of animal in Europe was called elk. The early European fur traders referred to the moose as elk, and this has caused some confusion because the North American *wapiti* also became known as elk.

139. Andrew Graham explained that it was uncommon to receive "green" or fresh moose meat because of the long distance that the meat had to be transported to reach the coastal factories. He added, "The nose is esteemed a great delicacy. I have received several times a present of a few of them from leading Indians" (Graham, *Andrew Graham's Observations*, 17).

140. Charles A. Bishop, "Demography, Ecology and Trade Among the Northern Ojibwa and Swampy Cree," *The Western Canadian Journal of Anthropology* 3,1 (1972): 59.

141. Parchment beaver gradually replaced coat beaver as the type of beaver fur desired by the traders. This was largely the result of changes in the English hatting industry that made it easier to remove the guard hairs from parchment skins. Parchment beaver skins were also easier to grade and transport, and these factors combined to make coat beaver less desirable by the end of the eighteenth century.

142. Graham, *Andrew Graham's Observations*, 22.

143. Isham, *James Isham's Observations*, 144.

144. Graham, *Andrew Graham's Observations*, 11.

145. Ibid., 276.

146. Summer hunting for beaver was easier than in winter, especially after the introduction of the gun. The HBC found it difficult to persuade the Lowland Cree not to kill beaver in the summer. The company's London directors advised their traders to burn the summer beaver skins before the eyes of the Indians, but the traders found it difficult to use such tactics (Isham, *James Isham's Observations*, xxi). Gradually, summer beaver skins were weaned out of the trade, but the Lowland Cree continued to hunt beaver in the summer for their own use. Despite the protests of the HBC, fresh beaver flesh was occasionally brought in as a trade item in the summer, an indication that beaver hunting was not exclusively an activity directed by the fur trade.

147. Graham, *Andrew Graham's Observations*, 11.

148. Isham, *James Isham's Observations*, 144.

149. Andrew Graham and James Isham differed in their views about the consumption of otters by the Lowland Cree. Graham noted that otters were eaten, while Isham held that otters were not (Graham, *Andrew Graham's Observations*, 12; Isham, *James Isham's Observations*, 165).

150. HBCA, B.3/a/10, October 9, 1721, fo. 8.

151. HBCA, B.3/b/2, May 22, 1745, fo. 18d.

152. Graham, *Andrew Graham's Observations*, 31.

153. HBCA, B.239/a/30, fo. 10.

154. HBCA, B.198/a/29, fo. 3d. Polar bear flesh was not popular at York Factory by the twentieth century, but Alex Ouscan, who was born at Wapinayo (White Partridge)

Creek, recalled that polar bears used to be part of the diet in earlier times. He said, "A long time ago people ate polar bear. They didn't throw away the meat. They'd eat the whole bear. They would dry the meat and render down the fat for oil" (Beardy and Coutts, *Voices from Hudson Bay*, 39).

155. Banfield suggested that these population cycles may be due to migration patterns of the snowshoe hare. See A. W.F. Banfield, *The Mammals of Canada* (Toronto: University of Toronto Press, 1974), 82.

156. Graham, *Andrew Graham's Observations*, 109. Joseph Saunders, who was born in 1907 at Kaskatamagun (Manitoba) and lived at York Factory, recalled that even the intestine of the willow ptarmigan was eaten (Beardy and Coutts, *Voices from Hudson Bay*, 39).

157. HBCA, B.239/a/73, February 3, 1776, fo. 28d.

158. HBCA, B.3/a/35, fo. 1d.

159. HBCA, B.239/a/75, April 7, 1778, fo. 35d.

160. HBCA, B.3/a/51, April 23, 1759, fo. 26d.

161. HBCA, B.198/a/11, fo. 23d.

162. HBCA, B.239/a/90, April 12, 1790, fo. 34.

163. Graham, *Andrew Graham's Observations*, 106. Mary Redhead recalled that people at York Factory also used to eat owls and seagulls (Beardy and Coutts, *Voices from Hudson Bay*, 8).

164. HBCA, B.3/a/1, October 21, 1705, fo. 10d.

165. The liver of the burbot contains a large amount of Vitamin D. See W.B. Scott and E.J. Crossman, *Freshwater Fishes of Canada* (Ottawa: Department of Fisheries and Oceans, 1979), 645.

Chapter 6

1. Samuel de Champlain, *The Works of Samuel de Champlain*, vol. 1, ed. H.P. Biggar (Toronto: The Champlain Society, 1922-36), 123-124.

2. Ibid., vol. 1, 74.

3. Ibid., vol. 3, 105.

4. W.A. Kenyon, *The History of James Bay 1610-1686: A Study in Historical Archaeology*, Archaeology Monograph 10 (Toronto: Royal Ontario Museum, 1986), 1.

5. Luke Fox, *North-west Fox or Fox from the North-west Passage* (New York: S.R. Publishers Ltd., 1965), 100.

6. Ibid., 118.

7. Ibid., 119.

8. Jens Munk, *The Journal of Jens Munk, 1619-20* (Toronto: The Royal Ontario Museum, 1980), 20.

9. John Long speculated that the event may have referred to a later meeting at a different location near the Albany River. See John Long, "Narratives of Early Encounters between Europeans and the Cree of Western James Bay," *Ontario History* 80, 3 (1988): 230, 231.

10. Fox, *North-west Fox,* 216.

11. Thomas James, *The Dangerous Voyage of Captain Thomas James, In his intended Discovery of a North West Passage into the South Sea* (Toronto: Coles Publishing Ltd., 1973), 102.

12. Ibid., 104.

13. Reuben G. Thwaites, *The Jesuit Relations and Allied Documents*, vol. 11 (Cleveland: Burrows Brothers, 1896-1901), 197, 199.

14. Ibid., vol. 18, 229.

15. Ibid., vol. 46, 249.

16. Ibid., vol. 21, 123.

17. Ibid., vol. 44, 243.

18. Ibid., vol. 33, 67.

19. Ibid., vol. 45, 229.

20. Ibid., vol. 44, 237. For a detailed examination of the locations of these and other trade routes, see Nellis M. Crouse, *Contributions of the Canadian Jesuits to the Geographical Knowledge of New France, 1632-1675* (Ithaca: Cornell Publishing and Printing Company, 1924), 139-168.

21. Thwaites, *The Jesuit Relations*, vol. 45, 229.

22. Ibid., vol. 44, 249.

23. Ibid., vol. 45, 225.

24. Ibid., 229.

25. Ibid., vol. 56, 203.

26. Ibid., vol. 46, 265.

27. Ibid., 275.

28. Ibid., 287, 289.

29. Ibid., vol. 47, 153.

30. Pierre Esprit Radisson, *The Explorations of Pierre Esprit Radisson, from the Original Manuscript in the Bodleian Library and the British Museum,* ed. Arthur Adams (Minneapolis: Ross and Haines, 1961), 111.

31. Ibid., 140.

32. Radisson's claim that he reached James Bay has been rejected by some scholars. Grace Lee Nute said there was insufficient time during the journey to allow Radisson to travel to James Bay. See her *Caesars of the Wilderness: Medard Chouart, Sieur des Groseilliers and Pierre Esprit Radisson, 1618-1710* (New York and London: D. Appleton-Century, 1943) 66.

33. Radisson, *The Explorations,* 147.

34. Thwaites, *The Jesuit Relations,* vol. 55, 123.

35. Nute, *Caesars of the Wilderness,* 118.

36. Upland traders, including the "Captain of the Tabittee [Abitibi] Indians," were also among the people who met the HBC traders. The leader of the Abitibi Indians traded about 250 skins, but promised to bring more if the HBC built a permanent post at the mouth of the Moose River.

37. Nute, *Caesars of the Wilderness,* 392.

38. For a detailed examination of this disease epidemic, see F.J. Paul Hackett, "'A Very Remarkable Sickness': The Diffusion of Directly Transmitted, Acute Infectious Diseases in the Petit Nord, 1670-1848," unpublished PhD dissertation, University of Manitoba, 1999, pp. 107-112.

39. Nute, *Caesars of the Wilderness,* 291-292. This account was reported by a crew member named Paul Mercer. Radisson's party reached the mouth of the Nelson River on September 14, 1670.

40. Ibid., 384.

41. Pierre Esprit Radisson, "Relation of the Voyage of Pierre Esprit Radisson, to the North of America, in the years 1682 and 1683," in *Report of the Minister of Agriculture for the Dominion of Canada, 1895,* Canada Sessional Paper No. 8a, Ottawa, 1896, pp. 11, 13.

42. Ibid., 77.

43. Ibid., 39.

44. Ibid., 67.

45. Ibid., 69.

46. Ibid.

47. Ibid., 75.

48. Nute, *Caesars of the Wilderness,* 225.

49. New York Colonial Documents, *Documents Relative to the Colonial History of the State of New York,* vol. 9, ed. E.B. O'Callaghan (Albany: Weed, Parsons, 1853-1857), 286.

50. A Cree oral tradition from the Albany River area recalls that "at times smoke could be seen on the horizon on the Bay. We heard later that it was the English and the French battling with each other to gain control of the land of the Indian, all this land of the James and Hudson Bay area" (John Long, "Narratives of Early Encounters," 234).

51. Nicolas Jeremie, *Twenty Years of York Factory, 1694-1714: Jeremie's Account of Hudson Strait and Bay,* ed. R. Douglas and J.N. Wallace (Ottawa: Thornburn and Abbott, 1926), 39.

52. HBCA, B.239/a/2, August 22, 1716, fo. 55.

Chapter 7

1. Andrew Graham, *Andrew Graham's Observations on Hudson's Bay, 1767-91,* ed. Glyndwr Williams (London: The Hudson's Bay Record Society, 1969), 315.

2. Ibid., 276.

3. The "debt" system, or advancing credit to the Lowland Cree, was introduced very early in the HBC fur trade. Joseph Isbister, who was in charge of Albany Fort in 1741, explained that "as to our Home Indians, it [debt system] was introduced att first as a bridle to bring them more dependent on the settlement for our necessary subsistence" (HBCA, A.11/2, September 6, 1741, fo. 106d).

4. Graham, *Andrew Graham's Observations,* 299.

5. HBCA, B.3/a/47, February 18, 1755, fo. 20.

6. Michael Payne, *The Most Respectable Place in the Territory: Everyday Life in Hudson's Bay Company Service York Factory, 1788 to 1870* (Ottawa: National Historic Parks and Sites, Canadian Parks Service, Environment Canada, 1989), 136.

7. Gabriel Marest, "Letter from Father Marest, Missionary of the Company of Jesus, to Father de Lamberville of the Company of Jesus, Overseer of the Missions of Canada," in *Documents Relating to the Early History of Hudson Bay,* ed. J.B. Tyrrell (Toronto: The Champlain Society, 1931), 127.

8. Claude C. Le Roy Bacqueville de la Potherie, "Letters of La Potherie [1700]," in *Documents Relating to the Early History of Hudson Bay*, ed. J.B. Tyrrell (Toronto: The Champlain Society, 1931), 221.

9. HBCA, B.3/d/11, fo. 17.

10. HBCA, B.135/a/4, May 9, 1734, fo. 16d.

11. HBCA, B.3/a/13, May 3, 1725, fo. 24.

12. HBCA, B.239/a/100, June 6, 1797, fo. 21d.

13. HBCA, B.3/a/13, May 4, 1725, fo. 24.

14. James Isham, *James Isham's Observations on Hudsons Bay, 1743, and Notes and Observations on a Book Entitled A Voyage to Hudsons Bay in the Dobbs Galley, 1749*, ed. E.E. Rich (London: The Hudson's Bay Record Society, 1949), 76-77.

15. HBCA, B.3/a/33, September 24, 1742, fo. 4d.

16. HBCA, B.3/a/16, fo. 15, April 19, 1728. The custom still continues, but other prizes are substituted for the bottle of brandy. In the spring of 1992, the prize for the first goose killed near the Lowland Cree community of Fort Severn (formerly Severn House) was a .22 rifle, three boxes of shells, and $100 cash (Wawatay, "First Goose Guess," *Wawatay News* [May 7, 1992]: 16).

17. HBCA, B.3/a/20, fo. 20, April 10, 1732.

18. HBCA, B.3/a/30, April 23, 1741, fo. 40.

19. HBCA, B.3/a/28, fo. 19.

20. David Meyer, "Waterfowl in Cree Ritual—The Goose Dance," in *Proceedings of the Second Congress, Canadian Ethnology Society*, ed. Jim Freeman and Jerome H. Barkow, Mercury Series, Canadian Ethnology Service Paper No. 28 (Ottawa: National Museum of Man, 1975), 437.

21. David Meyer, "The Goose Dance in Swampy Cree Religion," *Journal of the Canadian Church Historical Society* 33, 1 (1991): 118.

22. Brian Craik's study of the social and political organization of the goose hunt by Aboriginal people on the east coast of James Bay included the following comments about leadership patterns: "The hunters appeal to particular men among them to suggest where they should hunt. Men of families who have roots on the coast are relied upon to fill the role of *goose boss.* These men not only suggest *where* the hunt is to be, but provide the knowledge of *how* to hunt there [italics in original]." See Brian Craik, "The Formation of a Goose Hunting Strategy and the Politics of the Hunting Group," in *Proceedings of the Second Congress, Canadian Ethnology Society,* ed. Jim Freeman and Jerome H. Barkow, Mercury Series, Canadian Ethnology Service Paper No. 28 (Ottawa: National Museum of Man, 1975), 454.

23. HBCA, B.3/e/12, fo. 7.

24. HBCA, B.3/a/64, May 14, 1772, fo. 32.

25. Henry Ellis, *An Account of a Voyage for the Discovery of a North-West Passage by Hudson's Streights, in the Western and Southern Ocean of America*, vol. 2 (New York: Johnson Reprint Corporation, 1968), 30-31.

26. George Barnston, "Recollections of the Swans and Geese of Hudson's Bay," *The Canadian Naturalist and Geologist* 6, 5 (1861): 341.

27. Isham, *James Isham's Observations*, 117-119.

28. Graham, *Andrew Graham's Observations*, 294.

29. HBCA, B.239/a/91, May 28, 1791, fo. 23.

30. HBCA, B.3/a/4, April 6, 1713, fo. 27d.

31. Edward Umfreville, *The Present State of Hudson's Bay: Containing a Full Description of that Settlement, and the Adjacent Country; and Likewise of the Fur Trade with Hints for its Improvement*, ed. W. Stewart Wallace (Toronto: The Ryerson Press, 1954), 20.

32. HBCA, B.3/a/40, fo. 19d.

33. HBCA, B.239/a/2, fo. 62.

34. Nicolas Jeremie, *Twenty Years of York Factory, 1694-1714: Jeremie's Account of Hudson Strait and Bay*, ed. R. Douglas and J.N. Wallace (Ottawa: Thornburn and Abbott, 1926), 38.

35. Umfreville, *The Present State*, 20.

36. HBCA, B.3/d/81, fos. 12-12d; B.3/d/85, fo. 14.

37. HBCA, B.3/a/62, October 17, 1769, fo. 6d.

38. Dale Russell asserted that the spring goose hunt was more important than the fall goose hunt. See Dale R. Russell, "The Effects of the Spring Goose Hunt on the Crees in the Vicinity of York Factory and Churchill River in the 1700's," in *Proceedings of the Second Congress, Canadian Ethnology Society*, ed. Jim Freeman and Jerome H. Barkow, Mercury Series, Canadian Ethnology Service Paper No. 28 (Ottawa: National Museum of Man, 1975), 422. However, the HBC records indicated that the fall hunt was usually more important. Geese killed in the fall were needed to provision the fur traders during the long winter period when other food resources, especially caribou, were less reliable. Edward Jarvis, who was in charge of Albany Fort in 1786, explained that "the spring is not the season for an advantageous goose hunt, but the Autumn [underlined in original]" (HBCA, B.3/a/87, fo. 4d).

39. Arthur Dobbs's critique of the HBC included information on the goose hunt at Albany Fort. According to testimony from former company employees who had worked in the area during the 1730s, the average spring goose hunt at Albany produced about 1300 geese for the company and about 3000 geese were obtained in the fall. See Arthur Dobbs, *An Account of the Countries Adjoining to Hudson's Bay in the North-west Part of America* (New York: Johnson Reprint Corporation, 1967), 53.

40. HBCA, B.239/a/10, fos. 29d-36d.

41. HBCA, B.3/a/26, fo. 8d.

42. HBCA, B.3/a/48, April 12, 1756, fo. 24.

43. Jeremie, *Twenty Years of York Factory*, 22.

44. HBCA, B.239/a/4, August 3, 1718, fo. 33.

45. HBCA, B.239/a/35, September 24, 1751, fo. 8.

46. HBCA, B.239/a/62, July 16, 1770, fo. 48.

47. Ellis, *An Account of a Voyage*, 182-183.

48. Thomas Pennant, *Arctic Zoology* (New York: Arno Press Inc., 1974), 26, 27.

49. HBCA, B.239/a/22 and 32.

50. HBCA, B.239/a/61, fo. 50.

51. HBCA, B.239/a/22, fo. 4d.

52. Edwin E. Rich, *Hudson's Bay Company, 1670-1870*, vol. 1 (Toronto: McClelland and Stewart, 1960), 583-585.

53. HBCA, B.239/a/34, fo. 5d.

54. HBCA, B.239/a/35, fo. 3.

55. HBCA, B.239/a/41, August 5, 1759, fo. 41.

56. A rumour that French forces planned to attack York Factory was cited as a reason for abandoning Flamborough House. All the men and goods were removed from the post, but it was not demolished. This is curious since there was an apparent fear that the French might use it as a base of operation (Graham, *Andrew Graham's Observations*, 251n). The structure stood until the summer of 1766, when it burned to the ground. Andrew Graham speculated that some of the local Lowland Cree were to blame (HBCA, B.239/a/54, July 27, 1766, fo. 42).

57. HBCA, B.239/a/48, fo. 16d.

58. HBCA, B.3/a/37, July 21, 1746, fo. 51.

59. HBCA, B.3/a/38, fo. 32d.

60. HBCA, B.3/d/2, fo. 13.

61. Isham, *James Isham's Observations*, 168-169.

62. Edwin E. Rich, ed., *Hudson's Bay Copy Booke of Letters, Commissions, Instructions Outward, 1688-1696* (London: Hudson's Bay Record Society, 1957), 231-232.

63. The processing of sturgeon bladders into isinglass required considerable care and effort. The delicate inner membranes had to be carefully peeled away and sun-dried before packing them and transporting them to the posts. The low price offered by the HBC for isinglass may have been a factor in preventing a trade in that product. For example, in 1815, George Holdsworth's report on the Berens River district concluded that "another class of productions is Isinglass which might be procured in considerable quantities if its value could allow more liberal encouragement to be given to the Indians for procuring it" (HBCA, B.16/e/1, fo. 4). James Sutherland, who was in charge of the HBC's Jack River (Norway House) District in 1815, offered a similar view of the isinglass trade: "A quantity of isinglass might be got but it is doubtful whether it would pay the expense of procuring it. The price we can afford to pay for it will not induce the Natives to clean and cure it as it ought to be" (HBCA, B.154/e/1, fo. 3d). For more information about isinglass, see Holzkamm, Lytwyn, and Waisberg, "Rainy River Sturgeon: An Ojibway Resource in the Fur Trade Economy," *The Canadian Geographer* 32, 3 (1988): 194-205.

64. David Masty, "Traditional Use of Fish and Other Resources of the Great Whale River Region," *Northeast Indian Quarterly* 7,4 (1991): 14.

65. HBCA, B.239/a/3, February 2, 1717, fo. 22.

66. HBCA, B.239/a/79, fo. 48.

67. HBCA, B.239/a/1, August 31, 1715, fo. 52d.

68. HBCA, B.239/a/4, fo. 23d.

69. The HBC made plans as early as 1742 to develop a commercial whale fishery at York Factory (Rich, *Hudson's Bay Company*, vol. 1, 540). The whale fishery actually began in 1750, when the HBC hired a whale harpooner and commissioned a whaling sloop named the *Whale* (HBCA, B.239/a/33, May 24, 1750, fo. 32d). However, the first attempt at whale fishing by the HBC proved unproductive. In the summer of 1752, only twenty-two whales were caught and the harpooner was subsequently relieved of his duties (HBCA, B.239/a/35, July 24, 1752, fo. 40d; Rich, *Hudson's Bay Company*, vol. 1, 621). A second whale fishery at York Factory was organized in 1766. A harpooner was hired who had previously worked in the Greenland whale fishery, but once again the numbers of whales caught failed to live up to the company's expectations (HBCA, A.11/115, fo. 96). In the period after 1766, whale fishing was attempted periodically by the HBC in the Hayes and Nelson rivers, but these ventures produced limited results. Andrew Graham believed that the failure of the commercial white whale fishery near York Factory was due to poor organization. Graham noted that the harpooners who were hired by the company spent too much time in "building unnecessary out-houses, and scheming daily fruitless and wild undertakings" (Graham, *Andrew Graham's Observations*, 260). The company also attempted to establish a bowhead whale fishery north of Churchill, but that, too, ended in failure. A relatively more successful venture was the bowhead whale trade with the Inuit north of Churchill. See Orysia J. Luchak, "Prince of Wales's Fort in the 18th Century: An Analysis of Trade, Construction and Sloop Voyages Northward," Manuscript Report Number 243, Parks Canada, Department of Indian and Northern Affairs, 1978, pp. 79-110.

70. Statistics on the numbers of seals traded by the HBC were not kept regularly in the account books. The post journals recorded some of the transactions involving seals. For example, in the fall of 1723, eight seals were traded at Albany Fort (HBCA, B.3/a/12, September 15, 23, 25, October 15, 1723, fos. 5, 5d, and 8).

71. HBCA, B.3/a/65, fo. 15d.

72. HBCA, B.239/a/79, May 2, 1781, fo. 31.

73. HBCA, B.3/d/28, fo. 12d.

74. HBCA, B.3/d/50, fo. 10.

75. John Macfie, "The Ancient Path," *The Beaver* 69,2 (1989): 62.

76. HBCA, B.239/a/10, fos. 2d and 23d; B.3/a/17, fo. 3d.

77. A Lowland Cree man and his wife took a packet from York Factory to Albany Fort in less than seven weeks in the summer of 1735 (HBCA, B.239/a/18, August 11, 1735, fo. 1d; B.3/a/24, September 25, 1735, fo. 4d). In 1770, an urgent trip from Severn House to Albany Fort was done in eighteen days by William Tomison and a Lowland Cree guide (Macfie, "The Ancient Path," 69).

78. HBCA, B.198/a/15, March 5, 1772, fo. 22.

79. Henley House was destroyed twice: in 1755 and 1759. It was rebuilt in 1766 (see Victor P. Lytwyn, *The Fur Trade of the Little North: Indians, Pedlars, and Englishmen East of Lake Winnipeg, 1760-1821* [Winnipeg: Rupert's Land Research Centre, 1986], 7-8, 22-23).

80. HBCA, B.239/a/75, July 23, 1778, fo. 54.

81. Isham, *James Isham's Observations*, 96.

82. HBCA, E.2/4, fo. 38.

83. Falconer, "Remarks on the Natives," 20.

84. Umfreville, *The Present State*, 19.

85. Henry F. Dobyns, *Their Number Become Thinned: Native American Population Dynamics in Eastern North America* (Knoxville: University of Tennessee Press, 1983), 13.

86. Ibid., 15.

87. Jody F. Decker, "'We Should Never be Again the Same People': The Diffusion and Cumulative Impact of Acute Infectious Diseases Affecting the Natives on the Northern Plains of the Western Interior of Canada, 1774-1839," unpublished PhD dissertation, York University, 1989, p. 59.

88. HBCA, B.239/a/6, fo. 3.

89. HBCA, B.239/a/6, fo. 9d.

90. HBCA, B.239/a/6, fo. 15.

91. HBCA, B.239/a/6, fo. 17.

92. HBCA, B.239/a/6, fo. 18d.

93. HBCA, B.239/a/7, fo. 7d.

94. Paul Hackett speculated that Henry Kelsey was correct in identifying the disease as smallpox. He noted a case of sickness and starvation among one group in November 1722, and attributed it to the after-effects of smallpox.

95. HBCA, B.239/a/21, fo. 23d.

96. HBCA, B.239/a/14, fo. 8d.

97. HBCA, B.239/a/53, fo. 8d, 9.

98. Jennifer Brown pointed out that the official HBC policy forbade sexual relations between company employees and Aboriginal women. However, she also noted that before 1770 there were at least fifteen instances of HBC men and Aboriginal women in sexual relationships. See Jennifer S.H. Brown, *Strangers in Blood: Fur Trade Company Families in Indian Country* (Vancouver: University of British Columbia Press, 1980), 52.

99. Graham, *Andrew Graham's Observations*, 144. Percy Mathews, who was employed as a medical doctor at York Factory from 1864 to 1884, remarked that syphilis was "one of the predisposing causes of disease generally among the York Indians....The disease is locally known as the 'Nelson River Complaint,' and among the Indians 'Muchetas-pinawin'—literally, bad disease." See Percy Mathews, "Notes on Diseases among the Indians Frequenting York Factory, Hudson's Bay," *Canadian Medical and Surgical Journal* (1885): 462-463.

100. Falconer, "Remarks on the Natives," 34.

101. Graham, *Andrew Graham's Observations*, 143.

102. Mathews commented that "Scrofula, without tubercle, so far as it refers to glandular swellings, more or less ulcerations and indolent abcesses, is far from uncommon" (Mathews, "Notes on Diseases," 452).

103. HBCA, B.239/a/34, fo. 38d.

104. Ibid.

105. F.J. Paul Hackett, "'A Very Remarkable Sickness': The Diffusion of Directly Transmitted, Acute Infectious Diseases in the Petit Nord, 1670-1848," unpublished PhD dissertation, University of Manitoba, 1999, pp. 151-158.

106. HBCA, B.3/a/21, fo. 8.

107. HBCA, B.3/a/31, fo. 20. Mathews observed that pneumonia sometimes spread among the Lowland Cree as an epidemic disease: "This may instance the epidemic form that disease assumes in small isolated places like York. When the surroundings, mode of living, and nature of food are very much the same, individual susceptibilities seem to be done away with, and disease then takes a generally aggressive character" (Mathews, "Notes on Diseases," 451).

108. HBCA, B.239/a/35, fo. 35d.

109. HBCA, B.239/a/36, fo. 37.

110. HBCA, B.239/a/37, fo. 17d.

111. HBCA, B.3/a/46, fo. 6d.

112. HBCA, B.239/a/42, fo. 41.

113. HBCA, B.239/a/44, fo. 31.

114. HBCA, B.239/a/74, fo. 37.

115. Decker, "We Should Never," 73.

116. Arthur J. Ray, *Indians in the Fur Trade: Their Role as Trappers, Hunters, and Middlemen in the Lands Southwest of Hudson Bay, 1670-1870* (Toronto: University of Toronto Press, 1974), 105-107.

117. Hackett, "A Very Remarkable Sickness," 190.

118. HBCA, B.49/a/11, fo. 4.

119. Hackett, "A Very Remarkable Sickness," 192-196. Cole Harris has recently traced the smallpox epidemic westward to the Pacific coast, and assessed its impact among the Salish peoples in the area around the Strait of Georgia. See R. Cole Harris, "Voices of Disaster: Smallpox around the Strait of Georgia in 1782," *Ethnohistory* 41,4 (1994): 591-626.

120. HBCA, B.239/a/80, fo. 63.

121. HBCA, B.239/a/80, fo. 64.

122. Steadman Upham reported that the "lower limit of survivability" of the smallpox virus is reached at about zero degree Celsius. See Steadman Upham, "Smallpox and Climate in the American Southwest," *American Anthropologist* 88,1 (1986): 120.

123. HBCA, B.239/a/80, fo. 69.

124. HBCA, B.239/a/80, fo. 94.

125. The HBC designated leaders using military rank of captain or lieutenant. The captain was usually the senior leader of a trade group, but the rank was also given to leaders of the goose hunt. For more information about Lowland Cree leadership, see Charles Bishop, "The First Century: Adaptive Changes among the Western James Bay Cree between the Early Seventeenth and Early Eighteenth Centuries," in *The Subarctic Fur Trade: Native Social and Economic Adaptations*, ed. Shepard Krech III (Vancouver: University of British Columbia Press, 1984); and Toby Morantz, "Northern Algonquian concepts of status and leadership reviewed: a case study of the eighteenth-century trading captain system," *Canadian Review of Sociology and Anthropology* 19,4 (1982): 482-501.

126. HBCA, B.78/a/7, fo. 21.

127. HBCA, B.78/a/7, fo. 24.

128. HBCA, B.78/a/8, fo. 25d.

129. HBCA, B.135/b/12, fos. 26d-27.

130. HBCA, B.3/a/80, fo. 20d.

131. HBCA, A.11/4, fos. 154d-155.

132. Louis Bird, "The Wailing in the Clouds," *The Northern Review* (Summer 1993): 35-43.

133. Ibid., 39.

134. Ibid., 41.

135. HBCA, B.239/a/86, fo. 30.

136. Alexander Mackenzie, *The Journals and Letters of Sir Alexander Mackenzie*, ed. W. Kaye Lamb (Cambridge: The University Press, 1970), 76.

137. HBCA, B.42/b/26, fo. 3d.

138. HBCA, B. 198/a/28, fo. 3.

139. HBCA, B.198/a/28, fo. 15.

140. HBCA, B.198/a/29, fo. 44d.

141. HBCA, B.3/a/81, fo. 1.

142. HBCA, B.3/a/81, fo. 8d.

143. HBCA, B.3/a/81, fo. 24.

144. HBCA, B.3/a/81, fo. 21.

145. HBCA, B.3/a/82, fo. 21.

146. HBCA, B.3/a/82, fo. 23.

147. HBCA, B.3/a/82, fo. 46d.

148. HBCA, B.3/a/82, fo. 38.

149. HBCA, B.3/a/83, fo. 2.

150. HBCA, B.198/a/29, fo. 42d.

151. HBCA, B.3/a/84, fo. 27d.

152. HBCA, B.239/a/86, fo. 30.

153. Calvin Martin, *Keepers of the Game: Indian-Animal Relationships and the Fur Trade* (Berkeley: University of California Press, 1978), 108.

154. Graham, *Andrew Graham's Observations*, 160.

155. Falconer, "Remarks on the Natives," 21.

156. Graham, *Andrew Graham's Observations*, 161.

157. Ibid., 162.

158. Ibid., 164.

159. Decker, "We Should Never," 170.

160. HBCA, B.239/a/86: fo. 41d.

Chapter 8

1. HBCA, A.11/4, June 22, 1782, fo. 155.

2. York Factory and Severn House were abandoned for the 1782-83 season because of an attack by a French naval force in the fall of 1782.

3. HBCA, B.198/a/29, June 5, 1784, fo. 42d.

4. HBCA, B.198/a/49, fo. 11.

5. HBCA, B.239/a/101, June 11, 1799, fo. 33.

6. HBCA, B.239/a/116, fo. 10.

7. HBCA, B.3/e/7, fo. 8.

8. HBCA, B.198/a/38, April 20, 1789, fo. 28d.

9. HBCA, B.3/a/96, June 13, 1795, fo. 45d.

10. See D. Wayne Moodie, et. al, "Competition and Consolidation, 1760-1825," plate 61, in *Historical Atlas of Canada*, vol. 1, *From the Beginning to 1800*, ed. R.C. Harris (Toronto: University of Toronto Press, 1987); also plate 62, "Trading Posts, 1774-1821"; also plate 65, "Peoples of the Boreal Forest and Parkland."

11. HBCA, B.239/a/82, fo. 48d.

12. HBCA, B.239/a/86, fo. 38d.

13. HBCA, G.2/11, reproduced in Richard I. Ruggles, *A Country So Interesting: The Hudson's Bay Company and Two Centuries of Mapping, 1670-1870*, plate 12 (Montreal and Kingston: McGill-Queen's University Press, 1991).

14. HBCA, B.239/a/91, June 19, 1791, fo. 25.

15. HBCA, B.239/a/95, March 17, 1793, fo. 22d. S.J.C. Cumming, an HBC trader who was in charge of Oxford House in 1929, explained the meaning of its Lowland Cree name: "The lake is known to the Indians as *Pinapowinapheek Sagahagin*, meaning Deep Hole Lake. This name is derived from a small inlet off the northwest end of the lake, which is so deep as to be popularly supposed to be bottomless by the Indians of the district." See S.J.C. Cumming, "HBC Posts, Keewatin District: No. 11 – Oxford House," *The Beaver*, Outfit 260, 1 (1929): 225.

16. HBCA, B.239/a/99, May 31, 1796, fo. 14.

17. HBCA, B.239/a/95, June 3, 1793, fo. 32.

18. HBCA, B.239/a/107, July 6, 1803, fo. 33.

19. HBCA, B.3/a/107, May 16, 1805, fo. 14d.

20. HBCA, B.3/a/107, July 3, 1805, fo. 28d. After the amalgamation of the XY Company with the North West Company in 1805, many Canadian traders were left unemployed. Some of these so-called freemen remained to hunt and trap furs on their own. In 1808, Peter Fidler, an HBC inland trader, reported he met "a number of Canadians, between 20 and 30, under the denomination of free men; they had all served the NWCo, after leaving their service had gone down to Canada and being free of their former masters had agreed among themselves to return to the interior country to hunt (chiefly Beaver) for themselves" (HBCA, B.239/a/114, June 25, 1808, fo. 27). A number of freemen were active in the lowlands. For example, on August 1, 1809, a man named George Brown, who was described as a "half Canadian," arrived at Albany Fort to trade furs (HBCA, B.3/a/111, fo. 19d). Another Canadian freeman who hunted near Albany Fort with his family was Jean Baptiste Rousseau (HBCA, B.3/a/113, January 20, 1810, fo. 7d).

21. HBCA, B.78/e/2, fo. 4.

22. HBCA, B.123/e/1, fos. 3-3d.

23. HBCA, B.239/a/116, May 9, 1810, fo. 17d. According to retrospective comments made by HBC traders, beaver were once relatively abundant in the Hudson Bay lowlands. Alexander Kennedy, who was in charge of Albany Fort in 1826-27, observed that "beavers have been once numerous throughout this District" (HBCA, B.3/e/13, fo. 2), and George Barnston, who was in charge of the HBC post at Martins Fall in 1839, remarked that the nearby "swamps" were "rich in Beaver in days of Yor" (HBCA, B.123/e/14, fo. 5).

24. HBCA, B.239/a/117, June 5, 1811, fo. 7d.

25. HBCA, B.239/a/118, April 9, 1812, fo. 10d.

26. HBCA, B.239/a/121, December 23, 1814, fo. 11d.

27. HBCA, B.145/e/6, fo. 4d.

28. HBCA, B.198/e/2, fo. 2d.

29. HBCA, B.123/e/8, fo. 4.

30. After 1821, the HBC attempted to prohibit the killing of beaver in order to allow the beaver population to replenish. The imposition of bans on the trade in beaver skins did not have the desired effect because the Lowland Cree continued to kill beaver for food. In 1827, the HBC trader at Island Lake reported that "when conversing with the natives on this subject they at once admitted the advantages to be derived from preserving the Beaver, but an old man acutely observed 'would you allow beaver to live and your children to starve, is it not hard to see one swimming before your canoe while your son is crying for something to eat—but since it is your desire to preserve the Beaver, says old Eganescum, I will make a bargain with you; I last summer found eight Beaver Houses, and I have taken from you thirty skins in debt, now the beaver in these lodges will pay my debt, and feed my children, part of the winter, but since you wish to preserve them, throw away [my] debt, and support my family for the winter, and on these conditions I will allow the Beaver to live.' This was a kind of reasoning I was not prepared to answer, and for which our minutes of council had made no provisions" (HBCA, B.283/e/1, fos. 4d-5). HBC conservation measures

slowly nursed the beaver populations in the Hudson Bay lowlands to their former levels.

31. HBCA, B.239/a/86, July 17, 1786, fo. 47d.

32. HBCA, B.239/a/95, March 17, 1793, fo. 22d.

33. HBCA, B.239/a/95, August 7, 1793, fos. 44d-45.

34. There was a rapid increase in the liquor trade by Albany Fort upland traders in the Little North. At its peak, in 1798-99, the volume of brandy exceeded 2500 gallons. See Victor P. Lytwyn, *The Fur Trade of the Little North: Indians, Pedlars, and Englishmen East of Lake Winnipeg, 1760-1821* (Winnipeg: Rupert's Land Research Centre, 1986), 124.

35. Arthur J. Ray and Donald Freeman, *'Give Us Good Measure': An Economic Analysis of Relations Between the Indians and the Hudson's Bay Company Before 1763* (Toronto: University of Toronto Press, 1978), 132-135.

36. HBCA, B.198/a/31, February 26, 1785, fo. 26d.

37. HBCA, B.239/a/95, March 17, 1793, fo. 22d.

38. HBCA, B.239/a/96, March 6, 1794, fo. 17d.

39. HBCA, B.239/a/96, fo. 44.

40. HBCA, B.239/a/96, July 28, 1794, fo. 48d.

41. HBCA, B.239/a/97, June 9, 1795, fo. 24d.

42. Unusual weather patterns were also reported in the interior of the Little North. In 1804-05, a widespread drought occurred, which lowered water levels and made canoe travel difficult. See Lytwyn, *The Fur Trade of the Little North,* 109; and D.D. Kemp, "The Drought of 1804-05 in Central North America," *Weather* 37, 2 (1982): 34-41.

43. HBCA, B.239/a/113, fo. 6. The first Europeans to spend the winter in the area of York Factory did so in 1682-83. If the account referred to the first winter, the Lowland Cree people who provided this information to McNab could not have actually witnessed the arrival of the Europeans, but related an oral tradition of that event. It is more likely, however, that the reference was to the *Dobbs Galley* and the *California* wintering in Ten Shilling Creek in 1745-46.

44. HBCA, B.239/a/114, June 24, 1808, fo. 26d.

45. Calvin Martin, "Wildlife Diseases as a Factor in the Depopulation of the North American Indian," *The Western Historical Quarterly* 7, 1 (1976): 48-62.

46. Robert Brightman, *Grateful Prey: Rock Cree Human-Animal Relationships* (Berkeley: University of California Press, 1993), 280.

47. HBCA, B.239/a/101, July 8, 1799, fo. 39.

48. HBCA, B.3/a/82, August 21, 1784, fo. 48.

49. HBCA, B.3/a/83, fo. 6.

50. The size of the HBC labour force increased substantially after 1783. The pre-epidemic labour force was about 200 men, and by 1795 that figure had tripled to about 600 men. See Moodie, et al., "Peoples of the Boreal Forest and Parkland," plate 65, in *Historical Atlas of Canada.*

51. HBCA, B.239/a/121, October 7, 1815, fo. 3.

52. HBCA, B.239/a/90, May 7, 1790, fo. 41.

53. HBCA, B.239/a/117, September 22, 1810, fo. 2.

54. HBCA, B.239/a/117, September 22, 1810, fo. 2d.

55. HBCA, B.239/a/105, December 16, 1800, fo. 18.

56. HBCA, B.239/a/113, July 17, 1807, fo. 15.

57. HBCA, B.239/a/113, July 13, 1807, fo. 28d. While the migrations of the caribou became less predictable, herd sizes remained relatively large into the first decade of the nineteenth century. William Cook described large herds of caribou crossing the Nelson River in the spring of 1812, and noted that some of the "straggling herds" numbered 500 to 600 caribou (HBCA, B.239/a/118, April 3, 1812, fo. 9d).

58. HBCA, B.239/a/114, August 16, 1808, fo. 17.

59. HBCA, B.239/a/120, August 17, 1813, fo. 28.

60. HBCA, B.239/e/1, fo. 4d.

61. HBCA, B.198/e/7, fo. 1.

62. John McLean, *John McLean's Notes of a Twenty-Five Year's Service in the Hudson's Bay Territory* (Toronto: The Champlain Society, 1932), 195.

63. Thomas Simpson, *Narrative of the Discoveries on the North Coast of America; Effected by the Officers of the Hudson's Bay Company During the Years 1836-39* (London: Richard Bentley, 1843), 76.

64. John Richardson, *Arctic Searching Expedition: A Journal of a Boat-Voyage through Rupert's Land and the Arctic Sea, in Search of the Discovery Ships under Command of Sir John Franklin* (New York: Greenwood Press, 1969), 290.

65. The caribou did not actually disappear from the region, but they were reduced to such low numbers that few were available for trade to the HBC. By the latter part of the nineteenth century, the numbers of caribou began to increase, as shown by the HBC records of caribou meat traded at York Factory. For example, in 1873-74, 24,675 pounds of fresh venison (equivalent to 300 caribou) were traded at York Factory, and in 1878-79 the amount was 27,348 pounds (341 caribou) (HBCA, B.239/a/182, fos. 10 and 121d). The caribou have continued to increase in the twentieth century, and one herd known as the Pen Island herd currently migrates to the Severn River area each summer. The Pen Island herd numbers about 4000 animals, and their annual movements approximate the migration routes of the great herds of earlier times. See John Dadds, "Far-Flung Caribou Pose a Mystery," *Aski* (Winter 1988): 12.

66. HBCA, B.42/a/1, April 30, 1720, fo. 76.

67. Robert Brightman, "Conservation and Resource Depletion: The Case of the Boreal Forest Algonquians," *The Question of the Commons: The Culture and Ecology of Communal Resources*, ed. Bonnie J. McCay and James M. Acheson (Tucson: The University of Arizona Press, 1987), 131-132.

68. Brightman, *Grateful Prey*, 280.

69. The depletion of these significant food and commercial resources may have influenced the rise of a Lowland Cree spiritual revival movement in 1842-43. The movement was led by Abishabis, a Lowland Cree from the Severn River area. Abishabis, who proclaimed himself a prophet and advocated a return to Aboriginal

ways of life, adapted Aboriginal spiritual beliefs and Christian ideas obtained from missionaries who were active in the area around Norway House. However, Jennifer Brown has pointed out that the depletion of traditional resources in the Hudson Bay lowlands was a significant factor in spreading the views of Abishabis widely throughout the region. Brown concluded that the rise of this spiritual movement was "surely related to current ecological and fur trade conditions." See Jennifer Brown, "The Track to Heaven: The Hudson Bay Cree Religious Movement of 1842-43," in *Papers of the Thirteenth Algonquian Conference*, ed. William Cowan (Ottawa: Carleton University Press, 1982), 56. Drawing upon HBC records, Brown was able to show that food and commercial resources continued to be in short supply at the time of this Lowland Cree spiritual revival. John Long noted that part of the prophecy contained references to caribou that were described as "innumerable, amazingly fat, gigantic and delicious beyond conception." See John Long, "The Cree Prophets: Oral and Documentary Accounts," *Journal of the Canadian Church Historical Society* 31, 1 (1989): 4. This prophetic belief suggested a return to earlier times when caribou were abundant in the Hudson Bay lowlands. Abishabis's influence as a prophet was short-lived, however, and he was killed near Severn House in the fall of 1843.

70. HBCA, B.3/a/83, fo. 6.

71. HBCA, B.3/z/2, fo. 303; HBCA, B.3/d/106, fo. 68d; HBCA, B.3/d/117, fo. 59d; HBCA, B.3/a/91, May 15, 1790, fo. 26d.

72. HBCA, B.3/a/83, fo. 7.

73. HBCA, B.3/a/86, October 4, 1785, fo. 2d.

74. HBCA, B.3/a/117a, July 4, 1814, fo. 18d; HBCA, B.3/a/118, April 13, 1815, fo. 25.

75. HBCA, B.239/a/96, May 14, 1794, fo. 23d.

76. HBCA, B.239/a/96, June 2, 1794, fo. 26.

77. HBCA, B.3/e/8, fo. 1. The numbers of geese annually traded by the Lowland Cree to the HBC at the coastal posts continued to rise after 1821. In 1823, Angus Bethune, who was in charge of Albany Fort, remarked that 10,000 to 15,000 geese per year was considered a good trade (HBCA, B.3/e/8, fo. 1). By the mid-nineteenth century, that number had doubled. George Barnston estimated that the average annual harvest by the Lowland Cree at Albany Fort was about 30,000 geese. At Moose Factory, about 10,000 geese were procured by the HBC each year, and the combined annual goose harvest at Severn House, York Factory, and Churchill Fort was about 20,000 geese. See George Barnston, "Recollections of the Swans and Geese of Hudson's Bay," *The Canadian Naturalist and Geologist* 6, 5 (1861): 343. The trade in goose feathers and quills also continued to increase in the post-1821 period. The increase was especially large at Albany Fort, where feathers and quills came to represent a significant portion of the overall trade. For example, the average trade in feathers and quills at Albany Fort in the 1860s was about six times higher than the trade figures for the 1790s.

78. HBCA, B.3/a/91, June 7, 1790, fo. 28d.

79. HBCA, B.3/a/97, May 24, 1796, fo. 24d.

80. HBCA, B.3/a/97, May 18, 1796, fo. 23d.

81. HBCA, B.3/d/100, fo. 16d.

82. HBCA, B.239/a/82, June 5, 1784, fo. 36.

83. William Ewart concluded that tuberculosis and influenza were the principal diseases causing mortality among the Lowland Cree near York Factory in the nineteenth century. See William B. Ewart, "Causes of Mortality in a Subarctic Settlement (York Factory, Manitoba), 1714-1946," *Canadian Medical Association Journal* 129 (1983): 573.

84. HBCA, B.198/a/47, fo. 25d.

85. HBCA, B.3/a/97, fo. 33d.

86. HBCA, B.3/a/97, fo. 34.

87. HBCA, B.3/a/101, fo. 18d.

88. HBCA, B.3/a/104, July 23, 1801, fo. 20d; July 30, 1801, fo. 24.

89. Paul Hackett, "The 1819-20 Measles Epidemic: Its Origins, Diffusion and Mortality Effects upon the Indians of the Petit Nord," unpublished MA thesis, University of Manitoba, 1991, pp. 59-60.

90. John Franklin, *Narrative of a Journey to the Shores of the Polar Sea in the Years 1819, 20, 21, and 22* (London: John Murray Co., 1823), 25.

91. Ibid., 37.

92. Robert Hood, *To the Arctic by Canoe, 1819-21: The Journal and Paintings of Robert Hood, Midshipman with Franklin*, ed. C. Stuart Houston (Montreal: McGill–Queen's University Press, 1974) 31.

93. HBCA, B.239/a/126, fo. 31d.

94. HBCA, B.239/a/126, fos. 32d and 34d.

95. Hackett, "The 1819-20 Measles Epidemic," 99.

96. Beginning in 1783, the price of goods, called the standard of trade, was revised at Severn House to approximately the same level as the rate provided at Albany Fort. Prior to 1783, the price of trade goods at Severn House and York Factory had been significantly higher. For example, guns, which had been selling at fourteen made beaver each, were reduced to ten to twelve made beaver, and the price of blankets was cut from seven to six made beaver. Most other trade goods, including cloth, gunpowder, and shot, were also lowered to the rate that applied at Albany Fort (B.198/d/34, fos. 6-6d; B.198/d/36, fos. 6-7d). Edward Jarvis explained that "the difference of standard before I believe was a great motive for their attachment here" (HBCA, B. 3/a/83, fo. 6d).

97. HBCA, B.3/a/83, fo. 2.

98. HBCA, B.3/a/83, fo. 6d.

99. HBCA, B.3/a/87, fo. 4d.

100. HBCA, B.198/a/31, July 17, 1785, fo. 54d.

101. HBCA, B.198/a/37, June 26, 1788, fo. 43.

102. HBCA, B.3/a/118, September 5, 1815, fo. 38.

103. HBCA, B.239/a/107, July 11, 1803, fo. 22.

104. HBCA, B.239/a/109, September 6, 1803, fo. 1d.

105. HBCA, B.239/a/114, fo. 8d.

106. Martha McCarthy, *Churchill: A Land-Use History, 1782-1930*, Microfiche Report Series, No 219 (Ottawa: Parks Canada, 1985), 85.

107. Raymond M. Beaumont, "Origins and Influences: The Family Ties of the Reverend Henry Budd," *Prairie Forum* 17, 2 (1992): 179-180.

108. HBCA, B.239/a/95, June 3, 1793, fo. 32.

109. HBCA, B.239/a/96, May 27, 1794, fo. 25.

110. HBCA, B.239/a//100, fo. 9d.

111. Christopher Hanks, "The Swampy Cree and the Hudson's Bay Company at Oxford House," *Ethnohistory* 29, 2 (1982): 103.

112. HBCA, B.239/a/118, July 24, 1812, fo. 20; HBCA, B.239/a/118, June 12, 1812, fo. 16.

113. HBCA, B.154/e/1, fo. 5d.

114. HBCA, B.49/e/1, fo. 4d.

115. J.F. Wright, "Island Lake Area, Manitoba," in *Summary Report of the Canadian Geological Survey*, part B, Ottawa, 1927, p. 56.

116. HBCA, B.239/a/90, February 12, 1790, fo. 22d.

117. HBCA, B.239/a/90, April 6, 1790, fos. 32d-33.

118. HBCA, B.3/a/86, April 1, 1786, fo. 20d.

119. HBCA, B.3/a/87, fo. 5. The migration of Lowland Cree away from the York Factory area, which began in the 1790s, continued after 1821. Some of the Lowland Cree who settled in the Norway House area around 1800 moved farther south and west. By 1831, the first wave of migrants to the Norway House area had moved farther away. Donald Ross, who was in charge of Norway House, remarked, "The Indians attached to this place, are now reduced to four or five families—they have for some years past been gradually moving off towards Moose Lake, Swan River and Red River, countries that have of late abounded in Muskrats, and where at all times the means of living are easier acquired and a better quality than in this quarter which produces scarcely any other than fish" (HBCA, B.154/e/4, fo. 1d). HBC Governor George Simpson blamed the settlers in the Red River colony for enticing the Lowland Cree to migrate southward to the Red River valley. In 1835, he commented, "The happy tidings of cheap ale and civilization at Red River have quite unhinged their minds, and occasioned their migrating thither in large bodies, where they find employment from the Settlers, which is chiefly paid in ale. This migration of Indians to Red River is now going on to an alarming extent, not from Island Lake only, but from York, Norway House, Severn and Cumberland likewise. While they were few in number, they were mild, timid and inoffensive, but now that they begin to feel their strength, they assume a very different tone, and are disposed to rule over the Saulteaux, the original proprietors of the river, and will in a very short time consider themselves on a footing with the half breeds [Metis], and treat the whites as intruders" (HBCA, D.4/102, fos. 42d-43).

120. HBCA, B.3/e/10, fo. 4d.

121. HBCA, B.234/e/1, fo. 2d. From 1821 until the latter part of the nineteenth century, the HBC held a monopoly in the fur trade throughout much of the Canadian subarctic. Company traders were discouraged from extending credit to "strange Indians" who lived outside the district boundaries of each trading post. The HBC also attempted to implement other business practices designed to keep Indian hunters and

their families from moving into new territories. Monopoly conditions also increased the profits obtained by the HBC traders. In his study of the fur trade in northern Manitoba, Frank Tough observed that "the Company could 'whipsaw' the Indian trapper by reducing the buying price of furs and increasing the selling price of trade goods.... Monopoly prices were central to a debt system which served to maintain both the marginal and dutiful trappers as fur producers." The northward expansion of "free traders" in the late nineteenth century provided alternative markets, and Tough pointed out that the Lowland Cree quickly adapted to the new fur-trade conditions. See Frank Tough, "Indian Economic Behaviour, Exchange and Profits in Northern Manitoba during the Decline of Monopoly, 1870–1930," *Journal of Historical Geography* 16, 4 (1990): 389.

Bibliography

Hudson's Bay Company Archives (HBCA), Winnipeg, Manitoba

A.11/series	London Correspondence
B.3/a/series	Albany Fort Journals
B.3/b/series	Albany Fort Correspondence
B.3/d/series	Albany Fort Account Books
B.3/e/series	Albany Fort District Reports
B.3/z/series	Albany Fort Miscellaneous
B.16/e/series	Berens River District Reports
B.42/a/series	Churchill Fort Journals
B.42/e/series	Churchill Fort District Reports
B.49/e/series	Cumberland House District Reports
B.51/e/1	Fort Dauphin District Report, 1820
B.54/a/1	Duck Lake (Severn R.) Post Journal, 1797-98
B.78/a/series	Gloucester House Journals
B.78/e/series	Gloucester House District Reports
B.86/a/series	Henley House Journals
B.86/e/series	Henley House District Reports
B.88/a/series	Hulse House Journals
B.93/e/series	Island Lake District Reports
B.105/e/6	Lac la Pluie District Report, 1825-26
B.117/e/5	Long Lake District Report, 1832-33
B.123/a/series	Martins Fall Post Journals
B.123/e/series	Martins Fall District Reports
B.129/e/7	Michipicoten District Report, 1829-30
B.135/a/series	Moose Fort Journals

B.135/d/series	Moose Fort Account Books
B.135/e/series	Moose Fort District Reports
B.145/e/6	New Brunswick House District Report, 1817–18
B.154/e/series	Norway House District Reports
B.155/e/series	Osnaburgh House District Reports
B.156/a/series	Oxford House Journals
B.182/a/series	Rupert House Journals
B.198/a/series	Severn House Journals
B.198/e/series	Severn House District Reports
B.211/a/1	Sturgeon Lake Journal, 1779–80
B.234/a/series	Winisk Post Journals
B.239/a/series	York Factory Journals
B.239/b/series	York Factory Correspondence
B.239/d/series	York Factory Account Books
B.239/e/series	York Factory District Reports
B.283/e/series	Gods Lake District Reports
D.4/series	Governor George Simpson's London Correspondence
E.2/series	Andrew Graham's Observations
G.2/11	Map by Philip Turnor, 1779

General Bibliography:

Anderson, J.W.

1961 *Fur Trader's Story.* Toronto: The Ryerson Press.

Arima, Eugene Y.

1984 "Caribou Eskimo." In *Handbook of North American Indians.* Volume 5, *Arctic,* edited by David Damas. Washington: Smithsonian Institution.

Bacqueville de la Potherie, Claude C. Le Roy

1931 "Letters of La Potherie [1700]." In *Documents Relating to the Early History of Hudson Bay,* edited by J.B. Tyrrell. Toronto: The Champlain Society.

Ball, Timothy

1983 "The Migration of Geese as an Indicator of Climate Change in the Southern Hudson Bay Region Between 1715 and 1851." *Climatic Change* 5, 1: 85–93.

Banfield, A.W.F.

1954 *Preliminary Investigation of the Barren Ground Caribou.* Wildlife Management Bulletin, Series 1, No. 10A. Ottawa: Department of Northern Affairs and National Resources, National Parks Branch, Canadian Wildlife Service.

1961 *A Revision of the Reindeer and Caribou, Genus Rangifer.* Bulletin No. 177, Biological Series No. 66. Ottawa: National Museum of Canada.

1974 *The Mammals of Canada.* Toronto: University of Toronto Press.

Barger, W.K.

1979 "Inuit-Cree Relations in the Eastern Hudson Bay Region." *Arctic Anthropology* 16, 2: 59-75.

Barnston, George

1861 "Recollections of the Swans and Geese of Hudson's Bay." *The Canadian Naturalist and Geologist* 6, 5: 337-344.

Beardy, Flora, and Robert Coutts, eds.

1996 *Voices from Hudson Bay: Cree Stories from York Factory.* Montreal and Kingston: McGill-Queen's University Press.

Beaumont, Raymond M.

1992 "Origins and Influences: The Family Ties of the Reverend Henry Budd." *Prairie Forum* 17, 2: 167-200.

Bell, Robert

1879 "Report on the Country Between Lake Winnipeg and Hudson's Bay, 1878." In *Geological Survey of Canada Report of Progress for 1877-78.* Montreal: Dawson Brothers.

1887 "Report on an Exploration of Portions of the At-ta-wa-pish-kat and Albany Rivers, Lonely Lake to James' Bay." *Annual Report of the Geological and Natural History Survey of Canada* 2 (new series): 5G-38G.

1912 "Albany River: Lake Abazotikitchewan to Mouth of Kenogami River." *Ontario Bureau of Mines Annual Report* 21, 2: 84-86 (originally published in the *Report of the Geological Survey of Canada, 1871-72*: 109-112).

Bird, Louis

1993 "The Wailing in the Clouds." *The Northern Review* (Summer): 35-43.

Bishop, Charles A.

1970 "The Emergence of the Hunting Territories among the Northern Ojibwa." *Ethnology* 60,1:1-15.

1972 "Demography, Ecology and Trade Among the Northern Ojibwa and Swampy Cree." *The Western Canadian Journal of Anthropology* 3,1: 58-71.

1974 *The Northern Ojibwa and the Fur Trade: An Historical and Ecological Study.* Toronto: Holt, Rinehart and Winston.

1975 "Ojibwa, Cree, and the Hudson's Bay Company in Northern Ontario: Culture and Conflict in the Eighteenth Century." In *Western Canada Past and Present*, edited by A.W. Rasporich. Calgary: McClelland and Stewart West.

1982 "The Indian Inhabitants of Northern Ontario at the Time of Contact: Socio-Territorial Considerations." In *Approaches to Algonquian Archaeology,* edited by M.G. Hanna and B. Kooyman. Calgary: University of Calgary Press.

1983 "The Western James Bay Cree: Aboriginal and Early Historic Adaptations." *Prairie Forum* 8, 2: 147-155.

1984 "The First Century: Adaptive Changes among the Western James Bay Cree between the Early Seventeenth and Early Eighteenth Centuries." In *The Subarctic Fur Trade: Native Social and Economic Adaptations,* edited by Shepard Krech III. Vancouver: University of British Columbia Press.

Black, Mary B., and Edward S. Rogers

1976 "Subsistence Strategy in the Fish and Hare Period, Northern Ontario: The Weagamow Ojibwa, 1880-1920." *Journal of Anthropological Research* 3,1: 1-43.

Blain, Eleanor

1987 "Speech of the Lower Red River Settlement." In *Papers of the Eighteenth Algonquian Conference,* edited by William Cowan. Ottawa: Carleton University.

1991 "Dependency: Charles Bishop and the Northern Ojibwa." In *Aboriginal Resource Use in Canada: Historical and Legal Aspects,* edited by Kerry Abel and Jean Friesen. Winnipeg: University of Manitoba Press.

Brightman, Robert

1987 "Conservation and Resource Depletion: The Case of the Boreal Forest Algonquians." In *The Question of the Commons: The Culture and Ecology of Communal Resources,* edited by Bonnie J. McCay and James M. Acheson. Tucson: The University of Arizona Press.

1993 *Grateful Prey: Rock Cree Human-Animal Relationships.* Berkeley: University of California Press.

Brokx, Peter A.J.

1965 "The Hudson Bay Lowland as Caribou Habitat." Unpublished MA thesis, University of Guelph.

Brown, Jennifer S.H.

1977 "James Settee and his Cree Tradition: An Indian Camp at the Mouth of Nelson River Hudsons Bay." In *Actes du Huitieme Congres des Algonquinistes,* edited by William Cowan. Ottawa: Carleton University.

1980 *Strangers in Blood: Fur Trade Company Families in Indian Country.* Vancouver: University of British Columbia Press.

1982 "The Track to Heaven: The Hudson Bay Cree Religious Movement of 1842-43." In *Papers of the Thirteenth Algonquian Conference,* edited by William Cowan. Ottawa: Carleton University.

Burch, Ernest S. Jr.

1972 "The Caribou/Wild Reindeer as a Human Resource." *American Antiquity* 37, 3: 339-368.

1978 "Caribou Eskimo Origins: An Old Problem Reconsidered." *Arctic Anthropology* 15, 1: 1-35.

1979 "The Thule-Historic Eskimo Transition on the West Coast of Hudson Bay." In *Thule Eskimo Culture: An Anthropological Retrospective,* edited by Allen P. McCartney. Mercury Series, Archaeological Survey of Canada Paper No. 88. Ottawa: National Museum of Man.

Burch, Ernest S. Jr., and James G.E. Smith

1979 "Chipewyan and Inuit in the Central Subarctic, 1613-1977." *Arctic Anthropology* 16, 2: 76-101.

Campbell, Bill

c. 1909 "The Diary of Big Bill Campbell." Unpublished manuscript, Toronto Public Library.

Cameron, Duncan

1960 "The Nipigon Country." In *Les Bourgeois de la Compagnie du Nord-ouest: Recits de voyages, lettres et rapports inedits relatifs au Nord-ouest canadien.* Volume 2, edited by Louis F.R. Masson. New York: Antiquarian Press (originally published in 1889-90).

Canada

1974 *The National Atlas of Canada.* Fourth Edition (revised). Toronto: The Macmillan Company of Canada Limited (in association with the Department of Energy, Mines and Resources and Information Canada, Ottawa).

Carlson, Roy L., and James V. Wright

1987 "Prehistoric Trade." In *Historical Atlas of Canada.* Volume 1, *From the Beginning to 1800,* edited by R. Cole Harris. Plate 14. Toronto: University of Toronto Press.

Catchpole, A.J.W., D.W. Moodie, and B. Kaye

1970 "Content Analysis: A Method for the Identification of Dates of First Freezing and First Breaking from Descriptive Records." *The Professional Geographer* 22, 5: 252-257.

Champlain, Samuel de

1922-36 *The Works of Samuel de Champlain,* 5 volumes, edited by H.P. Biggar. Toronto: Champlain Society.

Chappell, Edward

1970 *Narrative of a Voyage to Hudson Bay.* Toronto: Coles Publishing Company (originally published in 1817 by J. Mawman, London).

Clark, Brenda L.

1979 "Thule Occupation of West Hudson Bay." In *Thule Eskimo Culture: An Anthropological Retrospective,* edited by Allen P. McCartney. Mercury Series, Archaeological Survey of Canada Paper No. 88. Ottawa: National Museum of Man.

Clark, Donald W.

1991 *Western Subarctic Prehistory*. Archaeological Survey of Canada. Hull: Canadian Museum of Civilization.

Coats, William

1852 *The Geography of Hudson's Bay: Being the Remarks of Captain W. Coats, in Many Voyages to that Locality, Between the Years 1727 and 1751*, edited by John Barrow. London: The Hakluyt Society.

Craik, Brian

1975 "The Formation of a Goose Hunting Strategy and the Politics of the Hunting Group." In *Proceedings of the Second Congress, Canadian Ethnology Society*. Volume 2, edited by Jim Freeman and Jerome H. Barkow. Mercury Series, Canadian Ethnology Service Paper No. 28. Ottawa: National Museum of Man.

Crouse, Nellis M.

1924 *Contributions of the Canadian Jesuits to the Geographical Knowledge of New France, 1632-1675*. Ithaca: Cornell Publishing and Printing Company.

Crowe, Charles S.

1887 "Letter from Charles S. Crowe, York Factory, 15 June 1887, to Alexander Matheson at Rat Portage." Unpublished letter, Matheson Papers. Toronto: Toronto Public Library.

Cumming, S.J.C.

1928 "HBC Posts, Keewatin District: No. 11 - Island Lake Post." *The Beaver,* Outfit 259, 3: 116-117.

1929 "HBC Posts, Keewatin District: No. 11 - Oxford House." *The Beaver,* Outfit 260, 1: 225.

Currie, Campbell, and Harold C. Hanson

1957 "The Kill of Wild Geese by the Natives of the Hudson-James Bay Region." *Arctic* 10, 4: 211-229.

Curtis, Edward S.

1970 *The North American Indian*. Volume 18. New York: Johnson Reprint Corporation (originally published in 1928).

Dadds, John

1988 "Far-Flung Caribou Pose a Mystery." *Aski,* Winter: 12.

D'Anglure, Bernard Saladin

1984 "Inuit of Quebec." In *Handbook of North American Indians*. Volume 5, *Arctic*, edited by David Damas. Washington: Smithsonian Institution.

Davies, K.G., ed.

1965 *Letters From Hudson Bay, 1703-40.* London: The Hudson's Bay Record Society.

Dawson, K.C.A.

1976 *Albany River Survey, Patricia District, Ontario, September 1976.* Mercury Series, Archaeological Survey of Canada, Paper No. 51. Ottawa: National Museum of Man.

1976 "Historic Populations of Northwestern Ontario." In *Papers of the Seventh Algonquian Conference, 1975,* edited by W. Cowan. Ottawa: Carleton University.

1983 "Prehistory of the Interior Forest of Northern Ontario." In *Boreal Forest Adaptations: The Northern Algonkians,* edited by A.T. Steegmann Jr. New York: Plenum Press.

Dean, W.G.

1957 "Human Geography of the Lower Albany River Basin." *Geographical Bulletin* 10: 54-76.

Decker, Jody F.

1989 "'We Should Never be Again the Same People': The Diffusion and Cumulative Impact of Acute Infectious Diseases Affecting the Natives on the Northern Plains of the Western Interior of Canada, 1774-1839." Unpublished PhD dissertation, York University.

Dobbs, Arthur

1967 *An Account of the Countries Adjoining to Hudson's Bay in the North-west Part of America.* New York: Johnson Reprint Corporation (originally published in 1744 by J. Robinson, London).

Dobbs, W. Stewart

1906 "The Region South of Cape Tatnam, Hudson Bay." In *Summary Report for 1905.* Geological Survey of Canada, Sessional Papers, No. 26.

Dobyns, Henry F.

1983 *Their Number Become Thinned: Native Animal Population Dynamics in Eastern North America.* Knoxville: University of Tennessee Press.

Doige, Gary B.

1989 "Warfare Patterns of the Assiniboine to 1809." Unpublished MA thesis, University of Manitoba.

Drage, T.S.

1968 *An Account of a Voyage for the Discovery of a North-West Passage by the Hudson's Streights, to the Western and Southern Ocean of America Performed in the Years 1746 and 1747, in the Ship California, Capt. Francis Smith, Commander,* 2 volumes, reprint edition. New York: S.R. Publishers Ltd., and Johnson Reprint Corporation (originally published in 1749 by Jollife, Corbett and Clarke, London).

Ellis, C. Douglas, ed. and transl.

1995 *âtalôhkâna nêsta tipâcimôwina: Cree Legends and Narratives from the West Coast of James Bay.* Winnipeg: University of Manitoba Press.

Ellis, Henry

1968 *An Account of a Voyage for the Discovery of a North-West Passage by Hudson's Streights, to the Western and Southern Ocean of America,* 2 volumes. New York: Johnson Reprint Corporation (originally published in 1748 by Jollife, Corbett and Clarke, London).

Ewart, William B.

1983 "Causes of Mortality in a Subarctic Settlement (York Factory, Manitoba), 1714-1946." *Canadian Medical Association Journal* 129: 571-574.

Fahlgren, J.E.J., and Geoffrey Matthews

1985 *North of 50: An Atlas of Far Northern Ontario.* Toronto: University of Toronto Press.

Falconer, William

1768-69 "Severn House Journal, 1768-69." Unpublished manuscript, National Archives of Canada, MG 19, D2.

n.d. "Remarks on the Natives near the Cost of Hudson's Bay and Straits, with some remarks on the Climate, ect." Unpublished manuscript copy, National Archives of Canada, MG 19, D2, Volume 1, Part 2.

Faries, R., and E.A. Watkins

1938 *A Dictionary of the Cree Language spoken by the Indians in the Provinces of Quebec, Ontario, Manitoba, Saskatchewan and Alberta.* Toronto: The General Synod of the Church of England in Canada.

Fiddler, Thomas (Chief), and James E. Stevens

1985 *Killing the Shamen.* Moonbeam: Penumbra Press.

Fisher, Anthony D.

1969 "The Cree of Canada: Some Ecological and Evolutionary Considerations." *Western Canadian Journal of Anthropology* 1: 7-18.

Forbis, R.G., and W.C. Noble

1985 "Archaeology." In *The Canadian Encyclopedia.* Volume 1. Edmonton: Hurtig Publishers.

Foster, John E.

1977 "The Home Guard Cree and the Hudson's Bay Company: The First Hundred Years." In *Approaches to Native History in Canada: Papers of a Conference held at the National Museum of Man, October, 1975,* edited by D.A. Muise. Mercury Series, History Division Paper No. 25. Ottawa: National Museum of Man.

Fox, Luke

1965 *North-west Fox or Fox from the North-west Passage.* New York: S.R. Publishers, Ltd (originally published in 1635 by B. Alsop and T. Fawcett, London).

Francis, Daniel

1979 "Les Relations entre Indiens et Inuit dans L'est de la baie d'Hudson, 1700-1840." *Etudes/Inuit Studies* 3, 2: 73-83.

Francis, Daniel, and Toby Morantz

1983 *Partners in Furs: A History of the Fur Trade in Eastern James Bay, 1600-1870.* Montreal and Kingston: McGill-Queen's University Press.

Franklin, John

1823 *Narrative of a Journey to the Shores of the Polar Sea in the Years 1819, 20, 21, and 22.* London: John Murray Co.

George, Peter J., and Richard J. Preston

1987 "'Going in Between': The Impact of European Technology on the Work Patterns of the West Main Cree of Northern Ontario." *Journal of Economic History* 47, 2: 447-460.

Gillespie, Beryl C.

1981 "Major Fauna in the Traditional Economy." In *Handbook of North American Indians.* Volume 6, *Subarctic*, edited by June Helm. Washington: Smithsonian Institution.

Godfrey, W.E.

1986 *The Birds of Canada.* Revised edition. Ottawa: National Museums of Canada.

Gordon, Bryan C.

1977 "Prehistoric Chipewyan Harvesting at a Barrenland Caribou Water Crossing." *The Western Canadian Journal of Anthropology* 7, 1: 69-83.

Graham, Andrew

1969 *Andrew Graham's Observations on Hudson's Bay, 1767-91*, edited by Glyndwr Williams. London: The Hudson's Bay Record Society.

Grant, J.C. Boileau

1929 "Anthropometry of the Cree and Saulteaux Indians in Northeastern Manitoba." *National Museum of Canada Bulletin 59.* Ottawa.

Greenberg, Adolph M., and James Morrison

1982 "Group Identities in the Boreal Forest: The Origin of the Northern Ojibwa." *Ethnohistory* 29, 2: 75-102.

Gunn, Donald

1880 *History of Manitoba from the earliest settlement to 1835.* Ottawa: Maclean, Roger.

Hackett, F.J. Paul

1991 "The 1819-20 Measles Epidemic: Its Origins, Diffusion and Mortality Effects upon the Indians of the Petit Nord." Unpublished MA thesis, University of Manitoba.

1999 "'A Very Remarkable Sickness': The Diffusion of Directly Transmitted, Acute Infectious Diseases in the Petit Nord, 1670-1848." Unpublished PhD dissertation, University of Manitoba.

Hallowell, A. Irving

1938 "Notes on the Material Culture of the Island Lake Saulteaux." *Journal de Societe des Americanistes, Paris* 30 (new series): 129-140.

1992 *The Ojibwa of Berens River, Manitoba: Ethnography into History,* edited by Jennifer S.H. Brown. Fort Worth: Harcourt Brace Jovanovich College Publishers.

Hamilton, Scott

1991 "Archaeological Investigations at the Wapekeka Burial Site (FlJj-1)." Unpublished report, Lakehead University.

Hanks, Christopher

1982 "The Swampy Cree and the Hudson's Bay Company at Oxford House." *Ethnohistory* 29, 2: 103-115.

Harper, Francis

1955 *The Barren Ground Caribou of Keewatin.* Lawrence: University of Kansas.

Harris, R. Cole

1994 "Voices of Disaster: Smallpox around the Strait of Georgia in 1782." *Ethnohistory* 41, 4: 591-626.

Harris, R.C., ed.

1987 *Historical Atlas of Canada.* Volume 1, *From the Beginning to 1800,* edited by R.C. Harris. Toronto: University of Toronto Press.

Havard, Gilles

1992 *La Grand Paix de Montréal de 1701: Les Voies de la Diplomatie Franco-Amérindienne.* Montréal: Recherches Amérindiennes au Québec.

Hearne, Samuel

1958 *A Journey from Prince of Wales's Fort in Hudson's Bay to the Northern Ocean, 1769-1770-1771-1772,* edited by Richard Glover. Toronto: The Macmillan Company of Canada Ltd. (first published in 1795).

Heidenreich, Conrad E.

1971 *Huronia: A History and Geography of the Huron Indians, 1600-1650.* Toronto: McClelland and Stewart.

1987 "The Great Lakes Basin, 1600-1653." In *Historical Atlas of Canada*. Volume 1, *From the Beginning to 1800,* edited by R.C. Harris. Plate 35. Toronto: University of Toronto Press.

Heidenreich, Conrad E., and Francoise Noel

1987 "Trade and Empire, 1697-1739." In *Historical Atlas of Canada*. Volume 1, *From the Beginning to 1800,* edited by R.C. Harris. Plate 39. Toronto: University of Toronto Press.

Hickerson, Harold

1967 "Land Tenure of the Rainy Lake Chippewa at the Beginning of the 19th Century." *Smithsonian Contributions to Anthropology* 2, 4: 40-63.

1988 *The Chippewa and their Neighbours: A Study in Ethnohistory.* Revised edition, edited by Jennifer S.H. Brown and Laura L. Peers. Prospect Heights: Waveland Press (originally published in 1970).

Hlady, Walter M.

1960-61 "Indian Migrations in Manitoba and the West." *Papers of the Manitoba Historical and Scientific Society,* Series 3, 17: 24-53.

1970 "Manitoba—The Northern Woodlands." In *Ten Thousand Years: Archaeology in Manitoba,* edited by Walter M. Hlady. Altona: D.W. Friesen and Sons Ltd.

Hodge, F.W., ed.

1913 *Handbook of Indians in Canada.* Appendix to the Tenth Report of the Geographic Board of Canada, Ottawa.

Holzkamm, Tim E., Victor P. Lytwyn, and Leo G. Waisberg

1988 "Rainy River Sturgeon: An Ojibway Resource in the Fur Trade Economy." *The Canadian Geographer* 32, 3: 194-205.

Honigmann, John J.

1948 "Foodways in a Muskeg Community: An Anthropological Report on the Attawapiskat Indians." Unpublished report, Department of Northern Affairs and National Resources, Ottawa (distributed by the Northern Co-ordination and Research Centre in 1961).

1956 "The Attawapiskat Swampy Cree: An Ethnographic Reconstruction." In *Anthropological Papers of the University of Alaska,* edited by R. Leinbach and J.W. Van Stone. Fairbanks: University of Alaska Press.

1981 "West Main Cree." In *Handbook of North American Indians.* Volume 6, *Subarctic,* edited by June Helm. Washington: Smithsonian Institution.

Hood, Robert

1974 *To the Arctic by Canoe, 1819-21: The Journal and Paintings of Robert Hood, Midshipman with Franklin,* edited by C. Stuart Houston. Montreal: McGill-Queen's University Press.

Howard, James H.

1965 *The Plains Ojibwa or Bungi: Hunters and Warriors of the Northern Prairies, with Special Reference to the Turtle Mountain Band.* Anthropological Papers, no. 1. Vermillion: University of South Dakota.

Innis, Harold A.

1930 *The Fur Trade in Canada.* Toronto: University of Toronto Press.

Irving, William N., and John Tomenchuk

1974 "Archaeology of the Brant River, Polar Bear Park, Ontario, 1972: A Preliminary Report." *Ontario Archaeology* 22: 33–60.

Isham, James

1949 *James Isham's Observations on Hudsons Bay, 1743, and Notes and Observations on a Book Entitled A Voyage to Hudsons Bay in the Dobbs Galley, 1749,* edited by E.E. Rich. London: The Hudson's Bay Record Society.

Jacobs, Peter

1858 *Journal of the Reverend Peter Jacobs, Indian Wesleyan Missionary from Rice Lake to the Hudson's Bay Territory and Returning. Commencing May, 1852, With a Brief Account of his Life.* New York: Published for the Author.

James, Thomas

1973 *The Dangerous Voyage of Captain Thomas James, In his intended Discovery of a North West Passage into the South Sea.* Toronto: Coles Publishing Ltd. (reprinted from a 1740 edition by O. Payne, London; originally published in 1633).

Janes, Robert R.

1973 "Indian and Eskimo Contact in Southern Keewatin: An Ethnohistorical Approach." *Ethnohistory* 20, 1: 39–54.

Jenness, Diamond

1960 *The Indians of Canada.* Fifth edition. Bulletin 65, Anthropological Series No. 15. Ottawa: National Museum of Canada (originally published in 1932).

Jeremie, Nicolas

1926 *Twenty Years of York Factory, 1694-1714: Jeremie's Account of Hudson Strait and Bay,* edited by R. Douglas and J.N. Wallace. Ottawa: Thornburn and Abbott (translated from the French edition of 1720).

Joubert, J. Guy R.

1984 "The Homeguard Indians of the Hudson Bay Lowland in the Eighteenth Century: A Case Study of Severn House." Unpublished BA Honours thesis, University of Manitoba.

Judd, Carol

1983 "Housing the Homeguard at Moose Factory, 1730-1982." *The Canadian Journal of Native Studies* 3,1: 23-37.

1984 "Sakie, Esquawenoe, and the Foundation of a Dual-Native Tradition at Moose Factory." In *The Subarctic Fur Trade: Native Social and Economic Adaptations*, edited by Shepard Krech III. Vancouver: University of British Columbia Press.

Julig, Patrick J.

1982 "Human Use of the Albany River from Preceramic Times to the Late Eighteenth Century." Unpublished MA thesis, York University.

1988 "Prehistoric Site Survey in the Western James Bay Lowlands, Northern Ontario." In *Boreal Forest and Sub-Arctic Archaeology*, edited by C.S. Reid. Occasional Publications of the London Chapter of the Ontario Archaeological Society, No. 6.

Kane, Paul

1925 *Wanderings of an Artist Among the Indians of North America from Canada to Vancouver Island and Oregon, Through the Hudson's Bay Company's Territories and Back Again.* Toronto: The Radisson Society of Canada Ltd. (originally published in 1858).

Keighley, Sydney Augustus, Renee Fossett Jones, and David Kirkby Riddle

1989 *Trader, Tripper, Trapper: The Life of a Bay Man.* Winnipeg: Rupert's Land Research Centre.

Kelsall, John P.

1968 *The Migratory Barren-Ground Caribou of Canada.* Ottawa: Queen's Printer.

Kelsey, Henry

1929 *The Kelsey Papers,* edited by Arthur G. Doughty and Chester Martin. Ottawa: King's Printer.

Kemp, D.D.

1982 "The Drought of 1804-05 in Central North America." *Weather* 37, 2: 34-41.

Kenyon, W.A.

1986 *The History of James Bay 1610-1686: A Study in Historical Archaeology.* Archaeology Monograph 10. Toronto: Royal Ontario Museum.

Knight, James

1932 *The Founding of Churchill: Being the Journal of Captain James Knight, Governor-in-Chief in Hudson Bay, from the 14th of July to the 13th of September, 1717,* edited by James F. Kenney. Toronto: J.M. Dent and Sons Ltd.

Knight, Rolf

1965 "A Re-examination of Hunting, Trapping, and Territoriality among the Northeastern Algonkian Indians." In *Man, Culture, and Animals*, edited by Andrew Leeds and

Andrew P. Vayda. Publication No. 78. Washington: American Association for the Advancement of Science.

Kroeber, Alfred L.

1939 *Cultural and Natural Areas of Native North America*. Berkley: University of California Press.

Leacock, Eleanor B.

1954 "The Montagnais 'Hunting Territory' and the Fur Trade." In *American Anthropological Association Memoir*. Volume 78. Washington.

Lister, Kenneth R.

1988 "Provisioned at Fishing Stations: Fish and the Native Occupation of the Hudson Bay Lowland." In *Boreal Forest and Sub-Arctic Archaeology*, edited by C.S. Reid. Occasional Publications of the London Chapter of the Ontario Archaeological Society, No. 6.

Long, John S.

1986 "'Shaganash': Early Protestant Missionaries and the Adoption of Christianity by the Western James Bay Cree, 1840-1893." Unpublished PhD dissertation, University of Toronto.

1988 "Narratives of Early Encounters between Europeans and the Cree of Western James Bay." *Ontario History* 80, 3: 227-245.

1989 "The Cree Prophets: Oral and Documentary Accounts." *Journal of the Canadian Church Historical Society* 31,1: 3-13.

Low, Albert P.

1887 "Preliminary Report on an Exploration of Country From Lake Winnipeg to Hudson Bay." In *Geological and Natural History Survey of Canada Annual Report (1886)*. Volume 2 (new series). Montreal: Dawson Brothers.

1888 *Report on Explorations in James' Bay and Country East of Hudson Bay, Drained by the Big, Great Whale and Clearwater Rivers*. Montreal: William Foster Brown and Co.

Lowie, Robert H.

1920 *Primitive Society*. New York: Boni and Liveright.

Luchak, Orysia J.

1978 "Prince of Wales's Fort in the 18th Century: An Analysis of Trade, Construction, and Sloop Voyages Northward." Manuscript Report Number 243. Ottawa: Parks Canada, Department of Indian and Northern Affairs.

Lytwyn, Victor P.

1984 *York Factory Native Ethnohistory: A Literature Review and an Assessment of Source Material*. Microfiche Report Series, no. 162. Ottawa: Parks Canada.

1986 *The Fur Trade of the Little North: Indians, Pedlars, and Englishmen East of Lake Winnipeg, 1760-1821*. Winnipeg: Rupert's Land Research Centre.

1987 "Transportation in the Petit Nord." In *Historical Atlas of Canada*. Volume 1, *From the Beginning to 1800,* edited by R.C. Harris. Plate 63. Toronto: University of Toronto Press.

1997 "A Dish with One Spoon: The Shared Hunting Ground Agreement in the Great Lakes and St. Lawrence Valley Region." In *Papers of the Twenty-Eighth Algonquian Conference,* edited by David H. Pentland. Winnipeg: University of Manitoba Press.

Macfie, John

1967 "The Coast Crees." *The Beaver* 47, 1: 13-15.

1989 "The Ancient Path." *The Beaver* 69, 2: 62-63.

Macfie, John, and Basil Johnston

1991 *Hudson Bay Watershed: A Photographic Memoir of the Ojibway, Cree, and Oji-Cree.* Toronto: Dundurn Press.

Mackenzie, Alexander

1970 *The Journals and Letters of Sir Alexander Mackenzie,* edited by W. Kaye Lamb. Cambridge: The University Press.

Marest, Gabriel

1931 "Letter from Father Marest, Missionary of the Company of Jesus, to Father de Lamberville of the Company of Jesus, Overseer of the Missions of Canada." In *Documents Relating to the Early History of Hudson Bay,* edited by J.B. Tyrrell. Toronto: The Champlain Society.

Martin, Calvin

1976 "Wildlife Diseases as a Factor in the Depopulation of the North American Indian." *The Western Historical Quarterly* 1: 48-62.

1978 *Keepers of the Game: Indian-Animal Relationships and the Fur Trade.* Berkeley: University of California Press.

Martini, I.P.

1982 "Geomorphological Features of the Ontario Coast of Hudson Bay." *Naturaliste Canadien* 109, 3: 415-429.

Mason, Leonard

1967 "The Swampy Cree: A Study in Acculturation." In *Anthropology Papers of the National Museum of Canada, Number 13.* Ottawa: Department of the Secretary of State.

Masson, Louis F.R., comp.

1795 "An Account of the Athabasca Indians by a Partner of the North West Co., 1795." Unpublished manuscript, National Archives of Canada.

Masty, David Sr.

1991 "Traditional Use of Fish and Other Resources of the Great Whale River Region." *Northeast Indian Quarterly* 7, 4: 12-15.

Mathews, Percy W.

1885 "Notes on Diseases among the Indians Frequenting York Factory, Hudson's Bay." *Canadian Medical and Surgical Journal*: 449-465.

Mayer-Oakes, William J.

1970 *Archaeological Investigations in the Grand Rapids, Manitoba, Reservoir, 1961-62.* Occasional Paper No. 3, Department of Anthropology. Winnipeg: University of Manitoba Press.

McCarthy, Martha

1985 *Churchill: A Land-Use History, 1782-1930.* Microfiche Report Series, No. 219. Ottawa: Parks Canada.

McInnes, William

1906 "The Headwaters of the Winisk and Attawapiskat Rivers." *Sessional Papers of Canada.* Summary Report of the Geological Survey of Canada, Sessional Paper No. 26, pp. 76-80.

1909 "Report on a Part of the Northwest Territories of Canada Drained by the Winisk and Upper Attawapiskat Rivers." Ottawa: Department of Mines, Geological Survey Branch.

McLean, John

1932 *John McLean's Notes of a Twenty-Five Year's Service in the Hudson's Bay Territory.* Toronto: The Champlain Society.

Meyer, David

1975 "Waterfowl in Cree Ritual – The Goose Dance." In *Proceedings of the Second Congress, Canadian Ethnology Society.* Volume 2, edited by Jim Freeman and Jerome H. Barkow. Mercury Series, Canadian Ethnology Service Paper No. 28. Ottawa: National Museum of Man.

1991 "The Goose Dance in Swampy Cree Religion." *Journal of the Canadian Church Historical Society* 33,1: 107-118.

Michelson, Truman

1936 "Indian Language Studies on James and Hudson's Bays, Canada." In *Explorations and Field-Work of the Smithsonian Institution in 1935.* Washington: Smithsonian Institution.

Moodie, D. Wayne, A. J. W. Catchpole, and Kerry Abel

1992 "Northern Athapaskan Oral Traditions and the White River Volcano." *Ethnohistory* 39, 2: 148-171.

Moodie, D. Wayne, Victor P. Lytwyn, and Barry Kaye

1987 "Trading Posts, 1774-1821." In *Historical Atlas of Canada.* Volume 1, *From the Beginning to 1800,* edited by R. C. Harris. Toronto: University of Toronto Press.

Moodie, D. Wayne, Barry Kaye, Victor P. Lytwyn, and Arthur J. Ray

1987 "Peoples of the Boreal Forest and Parkland." In *Historical Atlas of Canada*. Volume 1, *From the Beginning to 1800*, edited by R.C. Harris. Toronto: University of Toronto Press.

Moodie, D. Wayne, Victor P. Lytwyn, Barry Kaye, and Arthur J. Ray

1987 "Competition and Consolidation, 1760-1825." In *Historical Atlas of Canada*. Volume 1, *From the Beginning to 1800*, edited by R.C. Harris. Toronto: University of Toronto Press.

Mooney, James

1913 "Maskegon." In *Handbook of Indians of Canada*. Ottawa: C.H. Parmelee, King's Printer (published as an Appendix to the Tenth Report of the Geographic Board of Canada; originally published by the Bureau of American Ethnology in 1907).

Morantz, Toby

1978 "The Probability of Family Hunting Territories in Eighteenth Century James Bay: Old Evidence Newly Presented." In *Papers of the Ninth Algonquian Conference*, edited by William Cowan. Ottawa: Carleton University.

1982 "Northern Algonquian concepts of status and leadership reviewed: a case study of the eighteenth-century trading captain system." *Canadian Review of Sociology and Anthropology* 19, 4: 482-501.

1983 *An Ethnohistoric Study of Eastern James Bay Cree Social Organization, 1700-1850.* Mercury Series, Canadian Ethnology Service Paper No. 88. Ottawa: National Museum of Man.

1992 "Old Texts, Old Questions: Another Look at the Issue of Continuity and the Early Fur-Trade Period." *Canadian Historical Review* 73, 2: 166-193.

Morrison, Allan

c. 1825 "History of the Fur Trade in the Northwest." Typescript copy from original manuscript in Minnesota Historical Society Archives, Allan Morrison Papers, M878, St. Paul.

Morse, Eric W.

1979 *Fur Trade Canoe Routes of Canada: Then and Now.* Second edition. Toronto: University of Toronto Press (originally published in 1969).

Morton, Arthur S.

1973 *A History of the Canadian West to 1870-71: Being a History of Rupert's Land (the Hudson's Bay Company's Territory) and of the North-West Territory (Including the Pacific Slope).* Second edition, edited by Lewis G. Thomas. Toronto: University of Toronto Press (originally published in 1939).

Morton, William L.

1957 *Manitoba: A History.* Toronto: University of Toronto Press.

Munk, Jens

1980 *The Journal of Jens Munk, 1619-20.* Toronto: The Royal Ontario Museum (adapted from the original published in 1624, and reprinted in English in 1897 under the title *Danish Arctic Expeditions, 1615 to 1620,* edited by C.C.A. Gosch, London: The Hakluyt Society).

Nelson, George

1988 *"The Orders of the Dreamed": George Nelson on Cree and Northern Ojibwa Religion and Myth, 1823,* edited by Jennifer S.H. Brown and Robert Brightman. Winnipeg: University of Manitoba Press.

New York Colonial Documents (NYCD)

1853-1857 *Documents Relative to the Colonial History of the State of New York,* 15 volumes, edited by E.B. O'Callaghan. Albany: Weed, Parsons.

Nicks, John

1985 "David Thompson." In *Dictionary of Canadian Biography.* Volume 8, edited by Frances G. Halpenny. Toronto: University of Toronto Press.

Noble, W.C., and J.W. Pollock

1975 "Archaeology of the Hawley Lake Area, Hudson Bay Lowlands, Ontario." In *Canadian Archaeological Association - Collected Papers, March 1975.* Archaeological Research Report No. 6. Toronto: Ontario Ministry of Culture and Recreation, Historical Sites Branch.

Norton, William

1989 *Explorations in the Understanding of Landscape: A Cultural Geography. Contributions to Sociology, Number 77.* New York: Greenwood Press.

Nute, Grace Lee

1943 *Caesers of the Wilderness: Medard Chouart, Sieur des Groseilliers and Pierre Esprit Radisson, 1618-1710.* New York and London: D. Appleton-Century.

Oldmixon, John

1931 "The History of Hudson's Bay." In *Documents Relating to the Early History of Hudson Bay,* edited by J.B. Tyrrell. Toronto: Champlain Society (originally published in 1708).

Payne, Michael

1989 *The Most Respectable Place in the Territory: Everyday Life in Hudson's Bay Company Service York Factory, 1788 to 1870.* Ottawa: National Historic Parks and Sites, Canadian Parks Service, Environment Canada.

Peers, Laura L.

1994 *The Ojibwa of Western Canada, 1780-1870.* Winnipeg: University of Manitoba Press.

Pennant, Thomas

1974 *Arctic Zoology*. New York: Arno Press Inc. (originally published in 1784-85 by H. Hughes, London).

Pentland, David H.

1981 "Synonymy of the West Main Cree." In *Handbook of North American Indians*. Volume 6, *Subarctic*, edited by June Helm. Washington: Smithsonian Institution.

1981 "Synonymy of the Northern Ojibwa." In *Handbook of North American Indians,* Volume 6.

1981 "Synonymy of the East Main Cree." In *Handbook of North American Indians,* Volume 6.

1981 "Synonymy of the Attikamek (Tete de Boule)." In *Handbook of North American Indians,* Volume 6.

1981 "Synonymy of the Western Woods Cree." In *Handbook of North American Indians,* Volume 6.

1985 "The Ashkee Indians." In *Papers of the Sixteenth Algonquian Conference,* edited by William Cowan. Ottawa: Carleton University.

Pike, Warburton

1892 *The Barren Ground of Northern Canada*. London: Macmillan and Co.

Pilon, Jean-Luc

1981 "An Archaeological Reconnaissance Along the Lower Severn River, Northwestern Ontario." Unpublished manuscript, Ontario Ministry of Citizenship and Culture.

1982 "Excavations Along the Lower Severn River, Northwestern Ontario." Unpublished manuscript, Ontario Ministry of Citizenship and Culture.

1984 "Archaeological Investigations in the Rocksands Area, Severn River, Northwestern Ontario - 1983." Unpublished manuscript, Ontario Ministry of Citizenship and Culture.

1984 "Oussinaougouk and Trails West: An Example of Prehistoric Culture Change in the Southern Hudson's Bay Lowlands." *Arch Notes* (May/June): 38-39.

1987 *Washahoe Inninou Dahtsuounoaou: Ecological and Cultural Adaptation Along the Severn River in the Hudson Bay Lowlands of Ontario*. Conservation Archaeology Report, Northwestern Region, Report No. 10. Kenora: Ontario Ministry of Citizenship and Culture.

1988 "Culture, History and Ethnicity in the Hudson Bay Lowlands." In *Boreal Forest and Sub-Arctic Archaeology,* edited by C.S. Reid. Occasional Publications of the London Chapter of the Ontario Archaeological Society, No. 6.

1990 "Historic Native Archaeology Along the Lower Severn River, Ontario." *Canadian Journal of Archaeology* 14: 123-141.

Preble, Edward A.

1902 *A Biological Investigation of the Hudson Bay Region*. Washington: U.S. Department of Agriculture, Division of Biological Survey, North American Fauna No. 22, Government Printing Office.

Preston, Richard J.

1981 "East Main Cree." In *Handbook of North American Indians.* Volume 6, *Subarctic,* edited by June Helm. Washington: Smithsonian Institution.

Radisson, Pierre Esprit

1896 "Relation of the Voyage of Pierre Esprit Radisson, to the North of America, in the years 1682 and 1683." In *Report of the Minister of Agriculture for the Dominion of Canada, 1895.* Canada Sessional Paper No. 8a. Ottawa.

1961 *The Explorations of Pierre Esprit Radisson, from the Original Manuscript in the Bodleian Library and the British Museum,* edited by Arthur Adams. Minneapolis: Ross and Haines (originally published in 1885).

Ray, Arthur J.

1974 *Indians in the Fur Trade: Their Role as Trappers, Hunters, and Middlemen in the Lands Southwest of Hudson Bay, 1670-1870.* Toronto: University of Toronto Press.

1976 "Diffusion of Diseases in the Western Interior of Canada, 1830-1850." *The Geographical Review* 66: 139-157.

1982 "York Factory: The Crises of Transition, 1870-1880." *The Beaver* (outfit 313) 2: 26-31.

1984 "Periodic Shortages, Native Welfare, and the Hudson's Bay Company, 1670-1930." In *The Subarctic Fur Trade: Native Social and Economic Adaptations*, edited by Shepard Krech III. Vancouver: University of British Columbia Press.

Ray, Arthur J., and Donald Freeman

1978 *'Give Us Good Measure': An Economic Analysis of Relations Between the Indians and the Hudson's Bay Company Before 1763.* Toronto: University of Toronto Press.

Reeves, Randall R., and Edward Mitchell

1987 *History of White Whale (Delphinapterus leucas) Exploitation in Eastern Hudson Bay and James Bay.* Canadian Special Publication of Fisheries and Aquatic Sciences, No. 95. Ottawa: Department of Fisheries and Oceans.

Rhodes, Richard A., and Evelyn M. Todd

1981 "Subarctic Algonquian Languages." In *Handbook of North American Indians.* Volume 6, *Subarctic,* edited by June Helm. Washington: Smithsonian Institution.

Rich, Edwin E.

1960 *Hudson's Bay Company, 1670-1870,* 3 volumes. Toronto: McClelland and Stewart Ltd.

1960 "Trade Habits and Economic Motivation among the Indians of North America." *Canadian Journal of Economics and Political Science* 26: 35-53.

Rich, Edwin E., ed.

1951 *Cumberland House Journals and Inland Journal, 1775-82.* Volume 1. London: The Hudson's Bay Record Society.

1957 *Hudson's Bay Copy Booke of Letters, Commissions, Instructions Outward, 1688-1696.* London: Hudson's Bay Record Society.

Richardson, John

1829 *Fauna Boreali-Americana; or the Zoology of the Northern Parts of North America.* London: John Murray.

1969 *Arctic Searching Expedition: A Journal of a Boat-Voyage through Rupert's Land and the Arctic Sea, in Search of the Discovery Ships under Command of Sir John Franklin,* 2 volumes. New York: Greenwood Press (originally published in 1851 by Harper and Brothers, New York).

Riddle, David K.

1981 "Archaeological Survey of the Albany River; Year 2: Triangular Lake to Washi Lake." In *Studies in West Patricia Archaeology No. 2: 1979-1980,* edited by C.S. Reid and W.A. Ross. Toronto: Ontario Ministry of Culture and Recreation, Historical Planning and Research Branch.

1982 "An Archaeological Survey of Attawapiskat Lake, Ontario." In *Studies in West Patricia Archaeology, No. 3, 1980-81,* edited by W.A. Ross. Toronto: Ontario Ministry of Citizenship and Culture.

Riley, J.L.

1982 "Hudson Bay Lowland Floristic Inventory, Wetlands Catalogue and Conservation Strategy." *Naturaliste Canadien* 109, 3: 543-555.

Robson, Joseph

1965 *An Account of Six Years Residence in Hudson's Bay, from 1733 to 1736 and 1744 to 1747.* Toronto: S.R. Publishers Ltd., Johnson Reprint Corporation (originally published in 1752 by T. Jefferys, London).

Rogers, Edward S.

1965 "Leadership Among the Indians of Eastern Subarctic Canada." *Anthropologica* 7, 3 (new series): 263-284.

1983 "Cultural Adaptations: The Northern Ojibwa of the Boreal Forest, 1670-1980." In *Boreal Forest Adaptations: The Northern Algonkians,* edited by A. Theodore Steegmann, Jr. New York: Plenum Press.

Rogers, Edward S., and Mary Black Rogers

1982 "Who Were the Cranes? Groups and Group Identity Names in Northern Ontario." In *Approaches to Algonquian Archaeology,* edited by Margaret Hanna and Brian Kooyman. Calgary: University of Calgary.

Rogers, Edward S., and J. Garth Taylor

1981 "Northern Ojibwa," In *Handbook of North American Indians.* Volume 6, *Subarctic,* edited by June Helm. Washington: Smithsonian Institution.

Ross, Alexander

1957 *The Red River Settlement: Its Rise, Progress, and Present State, with Some Account of the Native Races and its General History, to the Present Day.* Minneapolis: Ross and Haines, Inc. (originally published in 1856 by Smith, Elder and Co., London).

Rotstein, Abraham

1967 "Fur Trade and Empire: An Institutional Analysis." Unpublished PhD dissertation, University of Toronto.

Ruggles, Richard I.

1991 *A Country So Interesting: The Hudson's Bay Company and Two Centuries of Mapping, 1670-1870.* Montreal and Kingston: McGill-Queen's University Press.

Russell, Dale R.

1975 "The Effects of the Spring Goose Hunt on the Crees in the Vicinity of York Factory and Churchill River in the 1700's." In *Proceedings of the Second Congress, Canadian Ethnology Society.* Volume 2, edited by Jim Freeman and Jerome H. Barkow. Mercury Series, Canadian Ethnology Service Paper No. 28. Ottawa: National Museum of Man.

1991 *Eighteenth-Century Western Cree and Their Neighbours.* Anthropological Survey of Canada, Mercury Series Paper 143. Ottawa: Canadian Museum of Civilization.

Sauer, Carl O.

1969 *Land and Life: A Selection from the Writings of Carl Ortwin Sauer,* edited by John Leighly. Berkeley: University of California Press.

Scott, W.B., and E.J. Crossman

1979 *Freshwater Fishes of Canada.* Ottawa: Department of Fisheries and Oceans (first published in 1973).

Shrofel, S.M., and H.C. Wolfart

1977 "Aspects of Cree Interference in Island Lake Ojibwa." In *Papers of the Eighth Algonquian Conference,* edited by William Cowan. Ottawa: Carleton University.

Silvy, Antoine

1931 "Journal of Father Silvy from Belle Isle to Port Nelson." In *Documents Relating to the Early History of Hudson Bay,* edited by J.B. Tyrrell. Toronto: The Champlain Society (originally published in 1904).

Simpson, Thomas

1843 *Narrative of the Discoveries on the North Coast of America; Effected by the Officers of the Hudson's Bay Company During the Years 1836-39.* London: Richard Bentley.

Skinner, Alanson

1911 *Notes on the Eastern Cree and Northern Saulteaux.* Volume 9,1. New York: Anthropological Papers of the American Museum of Natural History.

Smith, James G.E.

1976 "On the Territorial Distribution of the Western Woods Cree." In *Papers of the Seventh Algonquian Conference,* edited by William Cowan. Ottawa: Carleton University.

1981 "Chipewyan," In *Handbook of North American Indians.* Volume 6, *Subarctic,* edited by June Helm. Washington: Smithsonian Institution.

1981 "Chipewyan, Cree and Inuit Relations West of Hudson Bay, 1714-1955." *Ethnohistory* 28, 2: 133-156.

Smith, Sheryl A.

1978 "On Population Fluctuations in Northern Ontario." *Arch Notes* (May/June): 8-12.

Stewart, James

1905 "Rupert's Land Indians in the Olden Time." In *Annual Archaeological Report for Ontario, 1904 (Appendix to the Report of the Minister of Education).* Toronto: L.K. Cameron.

Stobie, Margaret

1968 "Backgrounds of the Dialect Called Bungi." *Papers of the Historical and Scientific Society of Manitoba,* Series 3, 24: 65-75.

Swanton, J.R.

1952 *The Indian Tribes of North America.* Washington: Bureau of American Ethnology, Bulletin 145.

Thistle, Paul C.

1986 *Indian-European Trade Relations in the Lower Saskatchewan River Region to 1840.* Winnipeg: University of Manitoba Press.

Thompson, David

1916 *David Thompson's Narrative of His Explorations in Western America,* edited by J.B. Tyrrell. Toronto: The Champlain Society.

Thwaites, Reuben G.

1896-1901 *The Jesuit Relations and Allied Documents,* 73 volumes. Cleveland: Burrows Brothers.

Todd, Evelyn M.

1971 "A Grammar of the Ojibwa Language: The Severn Dialect." Unpublished PhD dissertation, University of North Carolina.

Tough, Frank

1990 "Indian Economic Behaviour, Exchange and Profits in Northern Manitoba during the Decline of Monopoly, 1870-1930." *Journal of Historical Geography* 16, 4: 385-401.

Townsend, Joan B.

1983 "Firearms Against Native Arms: A Study in Comparative Efficiencies with an Alaskan Example." *Arctic Anthropology* 20, 2: 1-32.

Trigger, Bruce G.

1985 *Natives and Newcomers: Canada's "Heroic Age" Reconsidered.* Montreal and Kingston: McGill-Queen's University Press.

Trott, Christopher G.

1978 "Report of the Constance Lake Historical Research Project, 1977." Unpublished manuscript, Ontario Ministry of Culture and Recreation.

Trudeau, Jean

1968 "The Cree Indians." In *Science, History and Hudson Bay.* Volume 1. Ottawa: Department of Energy, Mines and Resources.

Turner, David, and Paul Wertman

1977 *Shamattawa: The Structure of Social Relations in a Northern Algonkian Band.* Mercury Series, Canadian Ethnology Service Paper No. 36. Ottawa: National Museum of Man.

Tuttle, Charles R.

1885 *Our North Land: Being a Full Account of the Canadian North-West and Hudson's Bay Route, together with a Narrative of the Experiences of the Hudson's Bay Expedition of 1884.* Toronto: C. Blackett Robinson.

Tyrrell, J.B.

1913 "Hudson Bay Exploring Expedition, 1912." *Twenty-Second Annual Report of the Bureau of Mines (Ontario)* 12, 1: 161-209.

Tyrrell, J.B., ed.

1931 *Documents Relating to the Early History of Hudson Bay.* Toronto: The Champlain Society.

Umfreville, Edward

1954 *The Present State of Hudson's Bay: Containing a Full Description of that Settlement, and the Adjacent Country; and Likewise of the Fur Trade with Hints for its Improvement,* edited by W. Stewart Wallace. Toronto: The Ryerson Press (originally published in 1790).

Upham, Steadman

1986 "Smallpox and Climate in the American Southwest." *American Anthropologist* 88, 1: 115-128.

Van Kirk, Sylvia

1974 "Thanadelthur." *The Beaver* (Spring): 40-45.

1980 *"Many Tender Ties": Women in Fur Trade Society in Western Canada, 1670-1870.* Winnipeg: Watson and Dwyer.

Warren, William W.

1984 *History of the Ojibway People.* St. Paul: Minnesota Historical Society Press (first published in 1885 by the Minnesota Historical Society as Volume 5 of the *Collections of the Minnesota Historical Society*).

Wawatay

1992 "First Goose Guess." *Wawatay News* (May 7): 16.

Wesley, James

1993 *Stories from the James Bay Coast*. Cobalt, ON: The Highway Bookshop.

West, John

1967 *The Substance of a Journal During a Residence at the Red River Colony, British North America, in the Years 1820-23*. Vancouver: Alcuin Society.

Wheeler, Clinton J.

1977 "The Historic Assiniboine: A Territorial Dispute in the Ethnohistoric Literature." In *Actes du Huitieme Congres des Algonquinistes*, edited by William Cowan. Ottawa: Carleton University.

Williams, Glyndwr, ed.

1975 *Hudson's Bay Miscellany, 1670-1870*. London: The Hudson's Bay Record Society.

Williamson, Norman James

1979 "The Constance Lake Historical Project, Phase II, 1978." Unpublished manuscript, Ontario Ministry of Culture and Recreation.

Wilson, W.J.

1903 "Reconnaissance Surveys of Four Rivers South-West of James Bay." In *Geological Survey of Canada, Summary Report for 1902-03*. Volume 15.

Wissler, Clark

1917 *The American Indian: An Introduction to the Anthropology of the New World*. New York: Douglas C. McMurtrie.

Wolfart, H. Christoph

1973 "Boundary Maintenance in Algonquian: A Linguistic Study of Island Lake, Manitoba." *American Anthropologist* 75: 1305-1323.

Wright, J.F.

1927 "Island Lake Area, Manitoba." In *Summary Report of the Canadian Geological Survey*. Part B. Ottawa.

Wright, James V.

1968a "The Application of the Direct Historical Approach to the Iroquois and the Ojibwa." *Ethnohistory* 15: 96-111.

1968b "The Boreal Forest." In *Science, History and Hudson Bay*. Volume 1, edited by C.S. Beals. Ottawa: Department of Energy Mines and Resources.

1970 "The Shield Archaic in Manitoba—A Preliminary Statement." In *Ten Thousand Years: Archaeology in Manitoba*, edited by Walter M. Hlady. Altona: D.W. Friesen and Sons Ltd.

1971 *Cree Culture History in the Southern Indian Lake Region.* Bulletin 232, Contributions to Anthropology. Ottawa: National Museum of Man.

1981 "Prehistory of the Canadian Shield." In *Handbook of North American Indians.* Volume 6, *Subarctic,* edited by June Helm. Washington: Smithsonian Institution.

1987 "Cultural Sequences, AD 500—European Contact." In *Historical Atlas of Canada.* Volume 1, *From the Beginning to 1800,* edited by R. Cole Harris. Toronto: University of Toronto Press.

Young, T. Kue

1988 *Health Care and Cultural Change: The Indian Experience in the Central Subarctic.* Toronto: University of Toronto Press.

Index

2271669

LIBRARY

LIBRARY
THE UNIVERSITY OF TEXAS
AT BROWNSVILLE
Brownsville, Tx 78520-499